THE BRAIN DEVELOPMENT REVOLUTION

The science of human development informs our thinking about children and their development. *The Brain Development Revolution* asks how and why brain development has become the major lens for understanding child development, and its consequences. It describes the 1997 *I Am Your Child* campaign that engaged public attention through a sophisticated media communications effort, a White House conference, and other events. It explores the campaign's impact, including voter initiatives to fund early childhood programs and a national campaign for prekindergarten education, but also several missed opportunities. The study examines why brain development compels our attention, why we are – but shouldn't be – neurodeterminists, and the challenges of communicating developmental brain science. This book examines the framing of the brain development story, the selectivity of the messaging, and overpromising the results of early programs. Last, it discusses proposals for how science communication can be improved to better serve children and the public.

ROSS A. THOMPSON is Distinguished Professor of Psychology at University of California, Davis. He is an internationally recognized authority on the psychological development of young children and the applications of developmental science to public policy. His work integrates understanding of the developing brain with early experiences in both typical and at-risk children, and he consults extensively to legislative committees, public agencies, and private foundations.

THE BRAIN DEVELOPMENT REVOLUTION

REVOLUTION

Science, the Media, and Public Policy

ROSS A. THOMPSON

University of California, Davis

Shaftesbury Road, Cambridge CB2 8EA, United Kingdom

One Liberty Plaza, 20th Floor, New York, NY 10006, USA

477 Williamstown Road, Port Melbourne, VIC 3207, Australia

314–321, 3rd Floor, Plot 3, Splendor Forum, Jasola District Centre, New Delhi – 110025, India

103 Penang Road, #05-06/07, Visioncrest Commercial, Singapore 238467

Cambridge University Press is part of Cambridge University Press & Assessment, a department of the University of Cambridge.

We share the University's mission to contribute to society through the pursuit of education, learning and research at the highest international levels of excellence.

www.cambridge.org
Information on this title: www.cambridge.org/9781009304252

DOI: 10.1017/9781009304276

First published 2023

A catalogue record for this publication is available from the British Library.

Library of Congress Cataloging-in-Publication Data
NAMES: Thompson, Ross A., author.
TITLE: The brain development revolution : science, the media, and public policy / Ross A. Thompson.
DESCRIPTION: Cambridge ; New York, NY : Cambridge University Press, 2023. | Includes bibliographical references and index.
IDENTIFIERS: LCCN 2023012042 (print) | LCCN 2023012043 (ebook) | ISBN 9781009304252 (hardback) | ISBN 9781009304245 (paperback) | ISBN 9781009304276 (epub)
SUBJECTS: LCSH: Child development–Research–United States. | Brain–Growth–Research–United States. | Communication in science–United States. | Science and state–United States.
CLASSIFICATION: LCC HQ767.85 T46 2023 (print) | LCC HQ767.85 (ebook) | DDC 305.237072–DC23/eng/20230522
LC record available at https://lccn.loc.gov/2023012042
LC ebook record available at https://lccn.loc.gov/2023012043

ISBN 978-1-009-30425-2 Hardback
ISBN 978-1-009-30424-5 Paperback

Contents

Figures

Preface

When I begin teaching a class in human development, I ask my students to list the most important influences that have made them the kind of person they are today. I use their lists as a starting point for describing the range of processes that shape psychological development. The influences that my students identify are revealing of how they have come to understand themselves. Besides the typical nominations of heredity and family, some students identify influential peers, a teacher who made an enduring impression on them, or the culture in which they were born before coming to the United States. For many students, influences early in life are those they report having the most impact, such as care received from a loving grandparent, whereas for others, it is a traumatic experience that has left an enduring impact. Some students describe themselves as the "adult child" of a depressed or alcoholic parent.

The influences my students identify arise from how they reflect on their lives, of course, but there are also other sources of their understanding. Our society familiarizes us with the dynamic between nature and nurture that puts heredity and family close to the top of most students' lists. To those who have grown up in the United States, aphorisms like "as the twig is bent, so grows the tree" cause us to look at early life experiences as especially influential. Science has also affected how my students understand the unfolding of their lives. Current awareness of the physical and mental health consequences of adverse childhood experiences has raised their awareness of how stress and trauma might have affected their development. The students who describe themselves as adult children of some kind of dysfunctional parent are also reflecting the media's attention to studies of the enduring vulnerabilities of growing up in a troubled home. Science, along with culture and personal reflection, is important to how we construct the continuing narrative of our lives.

Science – and the communication of science – is important. On the first day of class, the science that has influenced my students' sense of their lives has been conveyed to them through the media and other sources. My goal as a professor is to disrupt and expand their understanding of what developmental science has to say about processes of psychological growth. My task is also to correct misconceptions, such as about the immutability of genetic influences on development, or the pervasive egocentrism of young children (or that people use only 10% of their brains, although I wish it were so). By the end of the course, I hope that students not only will have a richer understanding of the influences that have shaped their development but will also be able to apply this understanding to improving children's lives, and will be more thoughtful in their evaluations of what they hear from other sources.

My interest in the communication of science derives not only from teaching but also from my work in public policy. In addition to my research on children's development, I write and consult on issues requiring the thoughtful application of developmental science to inform policy. These include the impact on children of divorce and child custody policies, grandparent visitation rights, child abuse prevention, child mental health, and social-emotional learning in early childhood classrooms. I hope that by bridging knowledge about children's development with these policy areas, more thoughtful policy directions will result, such as encouraging custody arrangements that give children meaningful time with each parent, enabling judges to understand the impact on children of intergenerational conflict, and helping teachers know how to encourage emotional understanding and self-regulation in young children.

Ordinarily, science communication to the public occurs opportunistically when a science journalist learns of a new discovery and draws attention to it in an article, broadcast, blogpost or podcast. Sometimes researchers like me are contacted to provide perspective or analysis. Over time, these stories become part of the knowledge that people enlist when making sense of events, and occasionally the stories are noticed by policymakers (but more likely their staff) because of their relevance to a new policy initiative. This manner of science communication is decentralized, and the accuracy of the stories and issues they profile is entrusted to the science journalists who cover them.

In 1997, however, a national media campaign on early brain development appeared that broke all the rules, and it is the story of this book. The campaign bypassed entirely the ordinary routes of science journalism to present the public with a well-conceived multimedia portrayal of the importance of the early years to lifelong development. It featured celebrities, government officials, and an occasional developmental neuroscientist or two. The campaign provoked a scientific backlash, a White House conference, an authoritative study by the National Research Council, a voter initiative to fund early childhood programs in California, considerable commentary, the interest of children's toy manufacturers, and the attention of just about everybody. It was in all respects the opposite of what traditional science journalism does, instead resembling a political campaign, and it had immediate and enduring impact on how people thought about early childhood development.

When the campaign exploded into public awareness, I was writing a review of the research on early brain development for the Maternal, Infant, and Child Health Council of South Carolina. From this perch, I wondered about some of the decisions I was observing about the communication of developmental brain science and its applications compared with the scientific literature I was reviewing. Public communication needs to be selective, of course, but it is also strategic. Why focus narrowly on the first three years? Why the emphasis on nurturance rather than nutrition to support healthy brain growth? I also observed the power of brain development to captivate public attention, even though the field of neuroscience was still very young and many central questions were unanswered. Why was the story of early brain growth such a compelling one? In addition to questions about the messaging, I also became interested in the campaign's impact on public policy. From Mozart to prekindergarten to adult workforce productivity, what accounted for the far-reaching applications that were proposed for developmental brain science? In inquiring in these ways, I was fortunate that because of my work, I was invited to participate in many of the events following from the 1997 campaign and witnessed firsthand the continuing impact of what I am calling the brain development revolution.

This revolution in public understanding of early childhood development has had enduring impact on how people think about young children and brain development. It has also influenced many areas of public policy, especially early childhood education and children's health care, while failing to impact other areas equally relevant to the developing brain, such as child care quality and children in poverty. What accounts for these policy wins and losses is also part of my coverage in this book. Finally, as the business model of traditional journalism has eroded and new media have emerged in its place, the strategies of the 1997 campaign have foreshadowed elements of our current media landscape, particularly about how to make issues go viral. The brain development revolution is a story of science, the media, and public policy that is worth telling.

This account was written during the twenty-fifth anniversary of the 1997 campaign. The long gestation afforded the opportunity to observe the extended arc of the brain development revolution, the maturation of the science, and the eventual impact of the public policies it prompted (especially in light of the promises that were made when they began). In the end, I hope this book offers a useful new perspective on a unique and influential public communication effort and an opportunity to raise, and provisionally address, some broader questions about science communication, our understanding of children's development, and how we have come to be the kind of people we are today.

I benefited from the helpful guidance of many people in the preparation of this book. John Love, Patricia Calahan, Linda Jacobson, Rob Grunewald, Susan Bales, and Jack Shonkoff each read chapters and provided invaluable advice and correction – my thanks to each. Interviews with Michael Levine, Ellen Galinsky, Meg Bostrom, and Nina Sazer O'Donnell in the year following the 1997 *I Am Your Child* campaign provided essential information and perspective on the events documented in Chapter 4, as did conversations with Sharon Begley. Sara Watson, currently of Watson Strategies, added to my understanding of the campaign for prekindergarten education from her years as a Senior Officer at the Pew Charitable Trusts. David Michaelski and Adam Siegel of the University of California, Davis, library are wizard reference librarians who helped me locate material that I thought was inaccessible. The work on this book was supported by two sabbatical leaves from the University of California, Davis, that provided invaluable time to think and write. I am also grateful for funding support from the Amini Foundation for the Study of Affects.

As this project has spanned much of my career, I want to gratefully acknowledge some other debts. Michael Lamb, Emeritus Professor of Psychology at the University of Cambridge, whose research on the development of best practices for the forensic interviewing of children about child abuse, has been an inspiring example to me of scientific integrity in the service of children. The late Gary Melton, who directed the Center on Children, Families and the Law at the University of Nebraska when I was Associate Director, taught me much about building bridges between developmental science and public policy, especially when it is informed by an ethical commitment to children. Finally, Michael Wald, Professor of Law Emeritus at Stanford University, is an esteemed law faculty member who has also designed and conducted behavioral research on children and families. During my sabbatical leave at the Stanford Law School,

I benefited from his keen insights about psychology and law, especially the values incorporated into research and its interpretation.

Listed last but certainly first among them all is my gratitude to my wife, Janet, a gifted early childhood educator who has informed my own understanding of children and whose patience with a partner who was more preoccupied than usual while this book was being written is deeply appreciated.

This has been a difficult period for children around the world, who deserve much more from us. This book is dedicated to them, especially those who live in adversity in Ukraine, Afghanistan, Somalia, Sudan, Syria, and other troubled places in the world. Proceeds from the sale of this book are dedicated to their relief.

CHAPTER I

Science Does Not Speak for Itself

Parents in the 1990s had many things to think about besides making sure that the children were healthy, safe, and growing. "Is day care bad for babies?" had been a continuing question for more than a decade as researchers, opinion leaders, and, yes, politicians voiced their judgments. The V-chip was leading many parents to consider installing this device on their televisions to block programming containing violent, sexual, or "indecent" content. Worries about whether their young children would be socially ready for kindergarten, about whether their grade-schoolers would be popular with peers, and about preparing their sons and daughters for life in a world of changing gender roles joined Barney's theme song in parents' minds in the 1990s.

Fast-forward to the new millennium, we find that things have changed and things have stayed the same. The question of whether day care is bad for babies remains, but it has been supplemented by the question of whether early childhood education is necessary for school readiness because of the rapid pace of early brain development. In preparing children for a world of changing gender roles, parents today are informed by books like *Pink Brain, Blue Brain*[1] that gender roles are captured in differences in the brain's organization and functioning. Today parental concerns about kindergarten are focused not on social readiness but on whether their children have the cognitive and self-regulatory skills – that is, school readiness – to succeed. TV for children remains a concern, now because of its potential effects on the developing brain.[2] Parents today are still devoted to making sure that the children are healthy, safe, and growing, and dietary recommendations today inform parents how much children need carbohydrates, fatty acids, and antioxidants for brain growth. Infant formula companies like Nestlé advertise their baby formula as containing nutrients that are "essential for a healthy brain."[3]

Brain development occupies parents' thoughts today in other ways. Milestones in children's developing behavior or thinking are presented as indicators of brain growth. ("These 'social smiles' ... are heartwarming, but they're also a sign that the parts of your baby's brain that control eyesight and muscle movements are booting up."[4]) Parents cannot miss the advertisements urging them to talk, read, and sing to their infants to strengthen regions of the brain governing language, even before babies have uttered their first word. They also cannot miss the references to "toxic stress" deriving from trauma and adversity and its effects on the brain's emotion and coping capacities. And accounts from research on adolescent brain development tell parents what to expect from their teen's neurobiological capacities for impulse control and self-regulation (not much). When the seventh edition of Benjamin Spock's classic *Baby and Child Care* appeared in 1998, there were two pages devoted to the development of the brain. By the time the tenth edition was published in 2018, the index referenced more than thirty-five pages devoted to the brain, including topics such as anxiety disorders, gender, intelligence, and puberty. A similar evolution has occurred in popular magazines like *Parents*, reflecting the growing interest of its readers in the developing brain and how it is affected by experience at home. In the 1990s, few parents thought much about the developing brain. By 2017, a national survey with oversampling of parents of young children reported that 93% believed that brain development in babies and young children is important.[5] There has been a revolution in thinking about brain development.

The new way of understanding children deriving from the brain development revolution has affected not only parents but all of us – including, of course, children themselves. Building on public interest in brain development, for example, the Pew Charitable Trusts in 2001 inaugurated a national campaign for prekindergarten education, and helped create the Partnership for America's Economic Success to mobilize business leaders around the early education agenda.[6] This contributed to legislative activity in conservative states like Florida and in progressive states like Vermont to institute universal prekindergarten programs for four-year-olds, joining the majority of states that now provide public funding for prekindergarten.[7] The Biden administration in 2021 proposed universal pre-K as a cornerstone of the American Family Plan proposed to provide pandemic relief. Other states, such as California, Arizona, and Arkansas, passed voter initiatives to supplement early education programs with a rich variety of other services including health screening, prenatal care, and parent support programs. The preparation of professionals who work with children from infancy through adolescence has also changed to incorporate ideas from developmental neuroscience. For example, Zero to Three, a national nonprofit, developed *The Growing Brain,* a curriculum for child care providers, Head Start teachers, and other early childhood professionals to help them connect children's developing thinking and behavior to changes in brain development.[8] Commercial manufacturers have also caught the brain development message. They are marketing products for all ages advertised to train the brain, ranging from baby toys to online programs like Lumosity[9] to promote cognitive acuity, especially in older adults. These applications of the brain development message were first observed in the United States, which is the focus of this book, but similar policy, commercial, and advocacy efforts have appeared throughout much of the world.

And what have been the benefits of all this attention for children? A fuller accounting follows, but some consequences are unmistakable. For one, national attention to early learning, sharpened by the research on early brain development, has changed young children's experience in school. In one study, 2,500 kindergarten teachers responded to the Department of Education's Early Childhood Longitudinal Study survey in 1998 and in 2010.[10] Teachers were asked about their expectations for children's learning, their regular classroom practices, and their assessments of student outcomes. The survey showed that kindergarten teachers in 2010 held far higher academic expectations for children than in 1998. They also devoted more time to literacy and math skills, and to conducting outcome assessments such as standardized tests – and significantly less time to science topics, geography and cultures, art, music, and dramatic play. Moreover, kindergarten teachers in 2010 reported significantly more reliance on teacher instruction and worksheets over child-selected activities that follow young children's curiosity. One reason for these differences was teacher expectations for student achievement. On the question of whether most children should learn to read in kindergarten, for example, 31% of teachers agreed in 1998, but 80% did in 2010. The title of the article reporting these findings asked: "Is Kindergarten the New First Grade?" The researchers concluded that it is.

To be sure, it would be unfair to attribute these changes exclusively to new understanding of the developing brain. During the twelve years between 1998 and 2010, public education in the United States changed with the movement for standards-based education inaugurated by the No Child Left Behind Act of 2001 and the development of the Common Core standards that were adopted by most states. But with growing numbers of young children having experience in preschool and prekindergarten programs, owing in part to parents' concerns with stimulating early cognitive growth, research has shown that children's performance in kindergarten improved and increased teachers' expectations accordingly.[11] And the increase in early education[12] along with increased expectations for children's achievement are both connected by a new regard for early learning inspired by the scientific account of early brain development.

More broadly, more than twenty-five years of public interest in brain development has resulted in much greater attention to the influences that can help or harm the developing brain – stimulation, adversity, nurturance, stress, nutrition – by a far wider audience than has ever before been interested in children's development in the early years. And this has contributed to new ways of thinking about young children themselves, including a new appreciation of their sensitivity to the world around them. On the positive side, greater public funding for early childhood programs and greater public attention to the risks posed by early exposure to adverse childhood experiences (ACEs), trauma, and chronic stress at all ages reflect renewed concern for the opportunities and vulnerabilities of early childhood that the brain development framework has helped to highlight. There is no question that public awareness of the value and importance of early childhood education has grown, together with the availability of programs (of varying quality) to meet this increased demand. On the less positive side, the brain development message has provided a scientific justification for viewing "investments" in children's brain growth as a strategic investment in future prosperity[13] that has contributed, among the affluent, to greater high-intensity (also known as helicopter) parenting and, among the rest of us, to measuring the yield of early childhood programs in conventional indicators of cognitive achievement and school success rather than social competence and emotional well-being.

This book is an account of the brain development revolution and how it came to dominate public regard for childhood and development. Public attention was captured by the *I Am Your Child* campaign in 1997, and within a few short years its message changed how parents and other adults thought about children and their developmental potential. The campaign's watchword – "the first years last forever" – was not how most people thought about early childhood before 1997 when the school years, not early childhood, were viewed as developmentally formative. But the enduring legacy of early experience quickly became a truism that influenced how parents thought about their impact on the developing brain, helped propel a national movement for early education, mobilized concerns over the effects of stress and trauma on brain development, and encouraged businesses to advertise their products as beneficial for brain growth. The brain development revolution has also had extended influence, such as on Supreme Court decisions concerning adolescent responsibility and the design of brain-based programs for grade-schoolers to promote learning and achievement. It is a revolution in public understanding that has incorporated science, its dissemination in the media, and its implications for public policy.

The brain development revolution is important not only because it has contributed new scientific understanding of children's growth but also because it has provided new ideas, images, and metaphors that shape our thinking about what children are like. Throughout history, images and metaphors have been powerful avenues for articulating and changing central cultural beliefs about children and their characteristics. The images of children prevalent at a particular moment in time incorporate dominant cultural constructions of childhood, and the introduction of new images can highlight new needs, capabilities, or other characteristics of childhood that can be the foundation for changes in how children are regarded and treated. The brain development revolution is important not just for the knowledge it conveyed but also for new ways of thinking about children that it communicated.

What Is a Child?

> I would compare it to like a baby tree growing. If you give it a strong foundation to grow straight, it'll grow straight.. . . If you build a good foundation for them while they're at this age, like before five, I believe that you'll see it as they get older.
> —Angelo, the father of a young child in Chicago, interviewed in 2015[14]

What comes to mind when you think of a child? Do you imagine a plant poking up from the ground, cultivated by warm sun, the earth, and water? Or perhaps a building being constructed on a solid foundation? Does your image of a child look like a bubbling cauldron of impulses and emotions? Or perhaps a ball of clay awaiting the shaping of experience and nurturant care? And what do you think of when considering supporting a child's development? Is it like taming a wild animal? Cultivating a garden? Protecting an innocent? Building a strong structure? Training a loved pet? Making an investment in the future?

Our images and metaphors for childhood, like Angelo's, have always affected how adults think about children's characteristics and needs. They shape how parents view their responsibilities and orient their greatest concerns. They also influence how a society creates incentives and structures for institutions to guide children's development.[15] But different metaphors have prevailed at different times in history. Consider the following:

> [I]n children may be observed the traces and seeds of what will one day be settled psychological habits, though psychologically a child hardly differs for the time being from an animal. (Aristotle 350 BCE)[16]

> The little, and almost insensible impressions on our tender infancies, have very important and lasting consequences; and there 'tis, as in the fountains of some rivers where a gentle application of the hand turns the flexible waters into channels, that make them take quite contrary courses, and by this little direction given them at first in the source they receive different tendencies and arrive at last at very remote and distant places. (John Locke 1693)[17]

> Love childhood; encourage its sports, its pleasures, its lovable instincts. Who among us has not at times looked back with regret to the age when a smile was continually on our lips, when the soul was always at peace? (Jean-Jacques Rousseau 1762)[18]

> It being a part of Mrs. Pipchin's system not to encourage a child's mind to develop and expand itself like a young flower, but to open it by force like an oyster. (Charles Dickens 1848)[19]

> Children are completely egoistic; they feel their needs intensely and strive ruthlessly to satisfy them. (Sigmund Freud 1899)[20]

> Give me the baby and my world to bring it up in and I'll make it crawl and walk; I'll make it climb and use its hands in constructing buildings of stone or wood. I'll make it a thief, a gunman or a dope fiend. The possibilities of shaping in any direction are almost endless.... [M]en are built, not born. (John Watson 1928)[21]

Each of these statements, different as they are, reflects dominant beliefs about children that were prevalent during different periods in Western history. The Aristotelian view of children as animalistic was consistent with many ancient views that esteemed mature competencies and virtues and regarded children as sadly bereft of these. It is usually true, in fact, that when children's characteristics are measured against those of adults they are found lacking, but there are exceptions. Rousseau's celebration of childhood in its natural condition was a reaction, in part, to the decadent excesses of the French society in which he lived. He esteemed childhood because it reflected the quality of the natural person before the corrupting effects of the culture and, indeed, *Emile* is instructional for how children should be protected from these vices. An equally radical departure from traditional views of children is the Lockean portrayal of a child's natural tendencies being redirected by the guidance of parental instruction and education to chart the child's future course.

Both Lockean and Rousseauean views were departures from traditional views and had important cultural influence. The images of childhood innocence of Rousseau and the Romantics in the mid-eighteenth century softened prevalent beliefs about children's sinfulness from Christian theology. They also contributed, somewhat later, to sanctions on cruelty to children. The Lockean portrayal of a child as a *tabula rasa* (blank slate) awaiting the imprimatur of nurturance and education was equally contrary to traditional views of children's (largely negative) natural tendencies, and contributed to the movement for public education of the nineteenth century. The writing of social reformers like Charles Dickens and Victor Hugo in the nineteenth century, who dramatized the conflict between children's developmental needs and their harsh treatment in factories, mines and other institutions, led to the movement against child labor and for public education.[22] As images and metaphors for childhood have evolved, the social conditions that shape the experience of children have changed accordingly.

It is tempting to regard these images and metaphors of childhood as progressive advances toward the contemporary portrayal of children, such as the one by Angelo, that opens this section. But that would be mistaken. Rather, these views of children – as animalistic, shaped by education and experience, egoistic, innocents in a corrupt world – all continue to be influential long after their initial emergence because they justify practices and policies toward children, from punitive parenting to progressive education, that have contemporary resonance. They remain a continuing strand in the tapestry of current beliefs about children and their development. Aristotle might have found Freud's dictum in 1899 congenial to his own views (although Freud had much more to say that the ancient philosopher would have found incomprehensible), and the Lockean focus on education was embraced by the social reformers a century later and by contemporary early education advocates. These metaphors and images of childhood emerged from the historical times in which they were influential as they captured new public sentiments and beliefs, and they provoked new ways of treating children, but they remain part of our continuing social construction of childhood.

But something changed with the dawn of the twentieth century. Now the metaphors and images portraying children began to have their origins not in philosophy or literature, but in psychological science. The century began with a focus on the unconscious and ended with a focus on genetics and neuroscience.[23] And as the century proceeded, other images of the developing child also emerged, such as the little scientist expressed in Jean Piaget's theory,[24] the child as a sophisticated computational machine from cognitive science, and the image of a DNA blueprint capturing the view of the child as genetically predetermined. For more than a century, most of the dominant images and metaphors for child development have had their origins in psychology, human development, and related scientific fields.

And this has had consequences for how people think about children. For one, these twentieth-century images have required that experts explain their meaning and practical significance to parents, practitioners, and others informed by them. It was not (and may still not be) at all obvious, for example, how the unconscious is relevant to comprehending children's motives or feelings. But fortunately a corps of psychoanalytically oriented clinicians, academics, and popular writers provided guidance to an interested public as Freudian theory reached the shores of the United States with the arrival of European scholars in the years leading up to World War II. John Watson, an earlier founder of behaviorism (recall "men are built, not born"), wrote a best-selling guide for parents, *Psychological Care of Infant and Child*,[25] which eager parents read in order to benefit from the latest scientific understanding of children and how they should be raised. With the discovery of Piaget's theory in the United States in the early 1960s,[26] developmental psychologists and educators quickly applied his fourfold stages of cognitive development and his constructivist ideas to everything from language to numerical reasoning to moral judgment.

And as the meaning of these and other images of child development from psychological science gradually became better understood, they had a profound influence on children's lives in the twentieth century. Piaget's theory and the image of the child-as-scientist equipped parents and teachers with a new appreciation of how children construct their own understanding from everyday experience – not just tutelage – and this reformed classroom practice. Behavioral genetics gave parents an awareness of how much children's characteristics owe to their genetic endowment that balanced the dominant view of the 1980s that parents are responsible for the character and behavior of their offspring.

These images and metaphors became influential because they captured truths that were intuitively sensible and scientifically supported, and because they were interpreted by experts who were authoritative. They were, in other words, persuasive expressions of scientific understanding of how children grow and develop. And scientific claims are important because public attitudes toward science (and scientists) are very positive. According to national survey findings from December 2021 reported by the Pew Research Center, 77% of Americans report confidence in scientists to act in the public interest[27] – a proportion that has *risen* since 2016 – and a related poll showed that 63% say that the scientific method generally produces sound conclusions.[28] Confidence in the claims of science, and scientists, remains strong because of a shared conviction that its practitioners labor to be truth-tellers to the world.

This is especially true of the science of human development because this science is not only authoritative but also necessary.[29] Has anybody looked into face of a newborn baby as a newborn parent and not felt the mixture of delight, fascination, and utter terror presented by the daunting challenge of how to care for this young child? And although newborn parents turn most often to the wisdom of grandparents, friends, and social media as their primary sources of guidance, the discoveries of developmental science are not far from their thinking. Many professionals likewise draw on this science, whether they are educators, child care providers, pediatricians, family therapists, child welfare caseworkers, or family lawyers and judges. And quite often, it is not specific study findings or even a research literature that they enlist in their work, but the broader metaphors and images of the developing child that are expressions of the child's characteristics and needs, based in the science, that provide guidance to them. Once you have grasped the metaphor of the child as a scientist, you do not have to read the research to appreciate the importance of building on a young child's prior understanding to help them learn new skills. Once you have a sense of how the brain grows, you do not have to study developmental neuroscience to begin to understand the implications of the brain's rapid development in the early years. It is these images and metaphors, deriving from developmental science and explained by the scientists (and others), that provide the bridge between research and its necessary human applications.

People pay attention to the science of human development for another reason also. By understanding how children's lives take shape, we learn more about how each of us has become the person we are today. As "the child is father of the man," in Wordsworth's evocative line,[30] every adult gains insight into who they are by understanding the child they once were, and how that child gradually matured into an adult. Each new way of thinking about children and their needs thus leads reflectively to the continuing question of how each of us has come into being, and the influences that have made us who we are.

Why Brain Development?

The inquiry that led to this book began with a simple question: How and why did brain development so quickly become the dominant lens for public understanding of child development? As a developmental psychologist, I joined my colleagues in perceiving a peculiar irony in the sudden popularity of developmental brain science in the late 1990s. Hundreds of scientific studies on the growth of children's thinking, learning, reasoning, language, memory, and their developing feelings, social understanding, and emotion management, accumulated over decades of study, provided far greater insight into the growing brain than did the fuzzy neuroimages emerging from the first yield of developmental neuroscience. After all, these mental and behavioral achievements that we had long been studying obviously occur in the brain, so these well-known developments in behavior and thinking tell us much about the growing brain from which they emerge. Yet it very quickly became apparent that the images of areas of the brain "lighting up" in color on an fMRI scan of a child's brain compelled public interest and had far greater impact than even the most groundbreaking study of behavioral development. Why was this so, and why is it still true?

One answer is that the study of the brain is new, exciting, and compelling, as the following chapters illustrate. The rapid growth in the technological sophistication of brain imaging over the past decades means that we are regularly witness to unprecedented new insights into how the brain functions, its organization, and its development over time. The public's fascination with the new discoveries about the human brain is comparable to how earlier generations were captivated by the medical advances in the early twentieth century or the midcentury dawn of the silicon revolution. These exciting achievements make the familiar methods and findings of behavioral science seem ordinary and outdated by comparison.

Another answer is that neuroscience draws on enduring Western beliefs about the material substance underlying mental processes. The study of the brain identifies the neurobiological structures that are the basis for behavior, making tangible and "real" the physical mechanisms of thinking, feeling, and acting, based on research methods that seem more the province of medicine than of psychology. The advancing technologies of developmental brain science promise further revelations of how mental and psychological phenomena are really just reducible to the activity of neural structures that can be observed and measured, and possibly changed to promote human well-being. At the core is the hope or fear that ultimately psychology will become neuropsychology, and the study of mental events will become cognitive neuroscience.

Finally, a third answer is based not just on the science, but also on its communication. Public interest in developmental brain science derives also from the tremendous impact of a public engagement campaign that communicated the importance of understanding the brain's growth to realizing a child's developmental potential. Although there had been scientific and journalistic attention to early brain development before 1997, the *I Am Your Child* campaign was catalytic. By contrast with the traditional forms of science journalism by which research discoveries gradually find their way into public awareness, this campaign was something very different: a well-planned orchestration of celebrities, public officials, and communication specialists to collectively convey, during a concentrated period of media attention, a coherent and singular message concerning the importance of the first three years. The story of the brain development revolution begins, therefore, with a compelling scientific story coupled with a unique communication campaign to focus public interest on early childhood development and the lifelong significance of early experience and its impact on the developing brain.

The campaign also went beyond the brain science to explain its implications for how parents should raise their children, how child care providers should care for them, how early educators should teach them, and the support that policymakers should provide for them. It is necessary, therefore, to further inquire: Where did these messages come from, and what influences shaped how they built upon the science? These questions led me in several directions. For one, it was important to look at how scientists themselves sought to explain the meaning and significance of brain development, just as they had earlier explained the unconscious, the child-as-scientist, and other scientific images of human development. This led to the work of groups like the Committee on Integrating the Science of Early Childhood Development of the National Research Council, and the National Scientific Council on the Developing Child, a collection of researchers who introduced concepts such as "brain architecture" and "toxic stress" to public understanding of developmental brain science. The Council also wrote extensively about the public policy implications of the science, and therefore provided a window into how these messages about the broader implications of the brain development message took shape.

Another direction of inquiry led to public advocacy efforts with diverse sponsors from outside the scientific world that built on the 1997 campaign, such as the movement behind a voter initiative in California to tax cigarette products to fund early childhood programs. There was also the Pew Charitable Trust's ten-year campaign to institute prekindergarten education nationwide, the efforts of economists to connect early brain development to the growth of human capital and to promote brain development as an economic development strategy, and the efforts of business leaders to urge government support of early childhood initiatives. Like earlier images of the developing child, the image of the developing brain promoted through these and other efforts has, over the last twenty-five years, begun to change the social conditions that shape the experience of children at home, at school, and in their communities.

Thus the inquiry of this book led first to the events that kicked off the brain development revolution, and then to the people and agencies that harnessed the brain development message, framed it, and mobilized it to advance policy agendas in fields as diverse as early education, constitutional law, and economic development. Looking back on the origins of the brain development revolution twenty-five years ago provides an opportunity to consider how a scientific story of human development and its implications was shaped by actors and agencies within and beyond the lab. It provides an opportunity to consider its real successes and achievements, as well as its misadventures and missed opportunities.

This book also explores questions about science communication that are raised by the brain development campaign. If the major images and metaphors of childhood of the twentieth century come from science, and the meaning of these images must be explained to the public by scientists who are widely perceived to be working in the public interest, why were not scientists at the forefront of the public messaging of the brain development revolution? Why were celebrities, public officials, child advocates, communication specialists, and even business leaders chosen to convey this information? One answer is that scientists are usually not skilled public communicators. Indeed, their professional socialization works against the clarity and straightforward messaging required for a public engagement campaign, as illustrated by the jargon, obfuscation, and qualification characteristic of most research reports. Although scientists are trusted sources, therefore, they are not trusted communicators.

A different way of stating this is: science does not speak for itself. But if science does not speak for itself, who speaks for science? What happens when other voices become prominent in the messaging of science to the public? One of the inquiries of this book is what happens to scientific messaging when it is entrusted to those who are not scientists but have different goals, interests, and perspectives. Can the accuracy and integrity of scientific conclusions be productively harmonized with the requirements of a fascinating message and a compelling policy advocacy agenda? In short, who else should be shaping scientific messaging to the public, and what are the consequences of doing so?

Science Does Not Speak for Itself

"Science does not speak for itself" is the title of an article appearing in 2011 in one of the prominent research journals of developmental science, appropriately named *Child Development*.[31] The authors, Jack Shonkoff and Susan Bales, are widely recognized contributors to the communication of developmental science. Shonkoff is director of the Center on the Developing Child at Harvard University and chair of the National Scientific Council on the Developing Child, two interconnected academic groups that work at the bridge between developmental research and its public communication. Bales is the founder of the FrameWorks Institute, a Washington, DC, think tank devoted to helping nonprofits communicate better with the public. Their partnership in the work of the National Scientific Council is discussed further in Chapter 6 because of the innovative communications strategies they enlisted to influence public understanding of developmental brain science, which has been the primary mission of the Council.

Why does science not speak for itself? Shonkoff and Bales do not offer a detailed analysis, but they do lay the problem at the feet of scientists:

> The reluctance of scholars to engage in public communications has diverse drivers, including differences in opinion about when the science is ready for translation, challenges associated with conveying discrepant findings, concern over maintaining appropriate boundaries between scholarship and advocacy, and a desire to avoid charges from peers of publicity seeking.[32]

The problem is not just a matter of scientific caution when moving from the lab into the scrum of public communication, but also the habits of discourse that are baked into the professional socialization of scientists themselves. From the start of graduate school, novice scientists in all fields are cautioned against speculating beyond a solid foundation of empirical evidence, and this helps to account for why scientific communication can be so opaque, full of qualifiers, complex syntax, technical language, and jargon, a model of obscurantism. Policymakers request testimony from a "one-armed scientist" who will not constantly qualify their conclusions with "on the other hand"[33] (although, to be fair, they can also be critical of scientists who offer clear conclusions that conflict with their own views). Beyond the rhetoric of scientific discourse is the reward structure of the academy, which values peer-reviewed publications appearing in competitive research journals and named lectureships at prestigious universities, and which tends to regard nonacademic publications or talks as fluff. A young academic quickly realizes that developing a practice of effective nonacademic communication must compete for time and effort with the increasing demands of running a lab, securing grant funds, teaching, and other academic pursuits that are more consistent with that reward structure. No wonder that even if a scientist wished to be a more effective public communicator, they would have to work against a career of bad communication habits and the disincentives of their profession.

As an alternative, scientists can work with journalists who are more skilled communicators, and if the journalist has a science beat, might also have an interest in communicating their work. But here there can also be problems and pitfalls. Carol Weiss and Eleanor Singer,[34] in their classic study of how social science is reported in major newspapers, newsmagazines, and television networks, documented the "uneasy partnership" between social scientists and journalists.[35] Why is this partnership uneasy? The different cultures of the university and newsroom is one reason. While scientists strive to contribute to cumulative, enduring, generalizable knowledge that will stand the test of time and peer review, journalists are more interested in reporting information that is new, interesting, and unexpected, and which is relevant to the concerns of their audience. Their different approaches to knowledge contribute to uneven communication between them and can result in media representations of scientific advances that are criticized by researchers as misinterpreted and over-generalized. But, nevertheless, there are good reasons for them to work together. Journalists learn from their scientific contacts about significant advances in knowledge that deserve public attention, and scientists benefit from media accounts of their work and the public and professional attention it affords.

This "uneasy partnership" also extends to how science and the media relate to policymaking.[36] News media inform elected officials, executive agency heads, and their staffs of the direction of public interest and of new discoveries that may warrant their attention. Research findings can provide new information, draw attention to social problems, suggest potential solutions, and sometimes afford rhetorical ammunition to advocates.[37] News reports of scientific discoveries also serve, according to Weiss and Singer, as "the interdepartmental memoranda that notify policymakers of what other policymakers know and are doing"[38] and thus contribute to the coordination of policymaking initiatives. Journalists are therefore at the nexus of the connection between scientists and policy, and this is one of the ways that science becomes "usable knowledge"[39] beyond the laboratory.

The problem is that in translating scientific discoveries for a wider audience, including policymakers, journalists must necessarily simplify scientific complexities and create bridges to practical applications that scientists often view as moving too far and too fast from the lab. When experienced and knowledgeable science reporters, such as Sharon Begley (at the *Wall Street Journal, Newsweek*, and then Reuters before her death in 2021) and Gina Kolata (at the *New York Times*), are at the nexus of the partnership of science, the media, and policy, they have the expertise to evaluate when scientific findings merit public attention, to discuss (and sometimes resolve) discrepant findings, to place a broader context on this work, and to explain their collective significance. But experienced science reporters account for a small and diminishing proportion of news media coverage of scientific research, and many newsrooms simply cannot afford journalistic specialists like them. The result can be, and often is, the public communication of science that is decontextualized, uncritical, and sometimes misleading.

In their analysis of why science does not speak for itself, therefore, Shonkoff and Bales draw on a familiar story of scientists being unprepared for communicating effectively with nonacademic audiences and cautious, if not skeptical, about becoming involved in policymaking and advocacy. It is a story that fits many scientists today. If science does not speak for itself, then, who should speak for science? And what might be the advantages and disadvantages of nonscientific voices speaking for science?

In 2020, these questions presented themselves starkly to a public confronting the COVID-19 pandemic and seeking guidance concerning protection and treatment. Conflicting messages on such essential matters as whether masks could impede disease transmission, the conditions under which social gatherings should occur (with or without distancing, indoors or outdoors, with how many participants), the circumstances warranting the reopening (and potential reclosing again) of businesses and schools, how to treat people who were differentially susceptible to the virus, the prospects for the availability of a vaccine, and other important issues yielded confusion, anger, and, for some, dismissal of the science. There were many reasons for these mixed messages (including new discoveries about the virus itself), but certainly one cause for public confusion were the multiple voices claiming to speak for the science. These included political appointees at the Centers for Disease Control, the Department of Health and Human Services and other federal agencies, representatives of the World Health Organization, the varying interests of the scientists included on the President's White House Coronavirus Task Force, representatives from pharmaceutical agencies researching a vaccine, and experts with a range of pertinent and impertinent qualifications speaking within and outside the government.

In the end, the most trusted voice turned out also to be the most authoritative one. But what made Dr. Anthony Fauci so credible at the beginning were not his decades of service as head of the National Institute of Allergy and Infectious Diseases (the lead government agency for the diagnosis and treatment of infectious diseases) or his long career of research on human immune response, but rather his capacity to provide clear, useful information in direct, plain language and in a manner that was effortfully nonpartisan and gave due recognition to the limits of existing scientific knowledge. In other words, Fauci did not sound like a typical scientist, and in the beginning, his recommendations were more trusted by the public than those of the other spokespersons when the pandemic was at its height.[40] Unfortunately, even as the pandemic spread, the political environment leading up to the presidential election increased misinformation and confusion.

Fortunately, most scientific stories are not so contorted and confused with so much at stake. But the story of COVID-19 and public understanding underscores broader questions about who is speaking for science. What are the various interests that can influence different speakers for science, and how does this affect their messaging? How do speakers for science choose what is most important to communicate, and can they avoid overpromising scientific applications? And what is the responsibility of scientists, who know the evidence best, for monitoring and correcting those who speak for science? These kinds of questions form the framework of the inquiry of this volume into the public communication of developmental brain science.

In different ways, of course, these questions apply not only to communication about COVID-19 and developmental neuroscience but also to a wide range of other scientific problems relevant to the public and policymakers: climate change, environmental pesticides, nuclear power, smoking, mental health, corporal punishment, and child care quality, to name a few. Different scientific fields have different channels of communication that affect how new discoveries reach the public,[41] but they have in common the problem of providing new information that is accurate, balanced, and relevant to the problems that the research is believed to address.

One solution proposed by Shonkoff and Bales is that scientists should ally with communications researchers, not journalists, and together they should create simplified representations of developmental brain science to promote public understanding and specific policy recommendations. In this manner, public messages can be created that not only represent cutting-edge science but do so in a manner that advances broader goals for public understanding, such as to mobilize support for parental leave policies, early education, or eliminating environmental pesticides. This kind of messaging bypasses traditional media as a means of public communication in favor of other avenues, such as websites and social media, that enable more direct transmission of these messages without the mediation of journalists. Their proposal and the messages deriving from it are discussed in Chapter 6 where the work of the National Scientific Council on the Developing Child in collaboration with FrameWorks Institute is considered further.

But there are other proposals as well. Another is to improve the capacity of scientists themselves to communicate their work clearly and compellingly, together with the professional incentives to do so. Indeed, this may already be happening. Young scientists today are much more willing and motivated to communicate their work to nonacademic audiences as nontraditional (including social) media offer new ways of promoting their work in a manner that bypasses traditional academic and journalistic gatekeepers. To be sure, there are problems with these new forms of science communication, especially for how the brevity of these channels and the natural self-promotion of academics can undermine a balanced portrayal of these discoveries to the public. I return to these issues in the final chapter.

The twenty-five-year history of the public communication of developmental brain science beginning in 1997 is a story of remarkable change in public perceptions of children and their needs, significant advances in programs and policies to promote early learning and health, some missteps in the communication of developmental neuroscience, and a few failures to push the brain development message in directions where it might have proven most helpful. Much good was accomplished, but much could have been done better, and much good still remains to be done. Understanding the story of this revolution offers a perspective on the influence of science on the social construction of childhood, the communication of science through multiple messengers to the public, and the translation of science for parenting, programs, and public policy, all within a rapidly evolving media landscape.

Outline of This Book

In this volume, I profile the events, actors, and agencies that figured prominently in how the communication of developmental brain science was shaped and its impact on public thinking and public policy. I also acquaint the reader with the science itself, both what is now commonly known and what is uncommonly known, and some of the new advances emerging from research labs. While any account like this is necessarily selective, I focus on the most important influences, drawing on my perspective as a developmental psychologist who began as an interested observer and later as a participant in some of the stories I document. The following describes how the book unfolds.

In Chapter 2, I consider what makes developmental neuroscience so influential to our thinking about child behavior and development, illustrating these influences with a pair of Supreme Court decisions about adolescence. We share with the justices a Western culture that views neurobiology as the material basis for mental and psychological processes. This view that is nicely captured in the expression "the mind is what the brain does," and I explore why this expression is true but incomplete, and can thus lead to misleading conclusions. In the course of this discussion, I consider why we are – but shouldn't be – neurodeterminists, describe how the brain and mind are mutually influential in their development and how both are affected by experience, and consider the importance of context and culture on the development of brain and mind. Carefully examining the beliefs that people share about mind and brain helps us understand why the clear and accurate communication of the science is crucial to public understanding and responsible policy applications, such as in Supreme Court decisions.

This leads to Chapter 3, "Dispatches from the Laboratory," in which I describe the story of brain development. Actually, I tell two stories of brain development. The first story is told from the perspective of developmental neuroscience, surveying the core story of developing neurons, synapses, and the growth of the brain that has become familiar to the public during the past twenty-five years. The second story is told from the perspective of developmental science, summarizing some of the results of thousands of studies of children's mental and behavioral development to yield a fascinating, provocative, and sometimes surprising window into the developing brain. I then compare these two accounts. Developmental neuroscience and developmental science each concern children's development, so they *should* yield complementary conclusions, and they usually do. But sometimes it seems as if researchers in each field are speaking different languages because they approach children's development with different research methods, levels of analysis, vocabulary, and concepts. Integrating understanding of brain and mind is still a work in progress. Then I turn to some of the lesser-known or overlooked issues in the study of brain development, discoveries that you may (or may not) have heard about – such as the impact of poverty on brain development, or adolescence as a critical period for brain development, or the fetal programming of early brain development – that were not well incorporated into the public communication of brain development in 1997. This frames the question of why some of the insights of developmental neuroscience were highlighted when early brain development was introduced to the public and others were not, which is explored further in the chapters that follow.

Chapter 4 is an account of the *I Am Your Child* campaign and its consequences to explain how brain development so quickly became headline news. It was no accident. The campaign began with two years of planning involving representatives of the Clinton White House, media celebrities, and major foundation officials as well as child advocates and early childhood experts, and in consultation with the Ad Council. It was designed to compel public attention to the early brain development message in April 1997 through a prime-time special on ABC-TV, a White House conference on early childhood development, stories on programs like the *Today* show and *Good Morning America*, special issues of prominent newsmagazines, and a host of state and local events all focused on the importance of the early years to children's development. The campaign and its message were designed to provoke additional attention in the days and weeks that followed from news reporters, columnists, and other journalists and pundits, linking science and advocacy, and contributing to a continuing cascade of media coverage that enhanced the impact of the campaign. And because the *I Am Your Child* campaign bypassed traditional avenues of science journalism to carry a message directly to the public through the entertainment media, the creation of newsworthy political events, the release of digital media, and state and local events, its resemblance to a political campaign leads me to describe it as a model of "campaign journalism." Campaign journalism is important for foreshadowing the current environment of alternative media, social media, digital technologies, and other new strategies that diversity public communication and enable advocacy issues to go viral much more easily. The message of the campaign, the reaction to it from scientists and pundits, and the work of a blue-ribbon National Research Council committee appointed soon afterward to clarify and extend the story of brain development are also considered in this chapter.

Public information campaigns come and go; what contributes to enduring impact is follow-up. In Chapter 5, "'Follow the Science,'" I examine the initiatives that followed the *I Am Your Child* campaign to broaden the messaging about developmental brain science to new audiences in order to promote practices and policies to benefit young children. There were many such initiatives, including the proposal of the governor of Georgia to send the parent of every newborn a Mozart CD, congressional proposals to strengthen children's services, educators' efforts to understand the implications of the developing brain for teaching, the creation of an early childhood scholarship fund promoted by two officials of the Federal Reserve Bank of Minneapolis, and the advocacy initiatives of business leaders for increased government funding for early childhood programs. One of these was a voter initiative in California to approve a tobacco tax that yielded millions of dollars annually devoted to early childhood programs (a similar initiative followed in Arizona). Another was a national campaign of the Pew Charitable Trusts to support early learning through prekindergarten programs in every state. An important component of the Pew initiative was the development of a business campaign for early brain development and the creation of alliances with a wide variety of other professional organizations. Together, these and other efforts led to genuine wins for children and families, but they also fell short of achieving meaningful benefits for some children in greatest need.

Chapter 6 is titled "Framing Developmental Science." An important through line for the brain development revolution is how the message of children's brain development was *framed* to have the greatest impact on intended audiences. Understanding what this means leads to the work of the FrameWorks Institute, a national nonprofit that conducts *strategic frame analysis* to help advocacy organizations develop public communications that, by taking into account an audience's prior frame of reference, can lead the audience to a new understanding of the issue and its broader implications. Examining the collaboration of FrameWorks with the

National Scientific Council on the Developing Child provides an opportunity to consider how the public communication of developmental brain science was framed and for what purposes. This analysis probes the significance of some of the framing elements of this work, including metaphors such as *brain architecture* and *toxic stress*, that have entered public discourse and their association with some of the core assumptions people bring to their understanding of neuroscience. I also ask whether alternative approaches to messaging the story of brain development could incorporate different aspects of the scientific story and perhaps contribute to different applications of the science.

In the final chapter, Chapter 7, "Who Speaks for Developmental Science?," I return to some of the broader themes of this book with the perspective of the preceding analysis. I summarize what has been learned about how and why brain development so quickly emerged as a dominant lens through which we understand child development and the influences, both scientific and nonscientific, that contributed to this. I evaluate the impact of the brain development revolution for public understanding of developmental science and the policies and practices to support children's development. I also consider the problems that emerged in the messaging about early brain development, returning again to the questions of who speaks for science and what shapes the scientific messaging about children. The communication of developmental science, the evolving media environment in which that messaging takes place, and the translation of science into policy are all taken up in this final chapter, along with thoughts about how to improve the messaging of developmental science in the future.

The revolution in public understanding of the significance of developmental brain science is continuing. This book is for those who are interested in learning how our understanding of children and their needs has been shaped and, more broadly, about the processes by which the science of human development – the science of who we are – comes to us.

CHAPTER 2

The Supreme Court Considers Adolescence

I had been working late in my office, and it was finally time to go home. As I walked down the hallway, I saw light coming from the open doorway of a faculty colleague. He saw me and motioned me into his office. "Look at this," he said excitedly. He handed me a page with the fuzzy image of a brain with different colored spots lighting up areas of the cortex. He explained that a junior researcher had conducted neuroimaging on a student who was doing an experimental procedure that my colleague had developed. He was excited to find that the brain had reacted to it. "But what did you expect?" I responded. "You've been using this procedure for years – didn't you think the brain was responding?" "Yes, of course," he replied. "But this makes it *real.*"

Why does the image of the brain make it real – even to a seasoned psychologist – when our behavior does not? What do we think we learn from neuroimaging, and does it really tell us all that we think it does? When we consider children and youth, what does the developing brain tell us that careful observation of their behavior does not? And do the answers to these questions tell us why developmental neuroscience has become such a compelling influence on our thinking about children and youth?

To consider these questions, I turn first to an unusual place: the United States Supreme Court. I do so because two cases considered by the Court, both concerning adolescent responsibility, illustrate the intersection of developmental neuroscience, its communication and interpretation, and its influence on public policy, which are themes of this book. Then I pause in the story of these cases to consider the reasons that the Justices of the Supreme Court may have found arguments from neuroscience so persuasive in their consideration of adolescent responsibility, and evaluate some of the reasons why we should be careful in our interpretation of neuroimaging studies. Finally, I return to the Supreme Court and, with these considerations in mind, discuss whether the neuroscience of the adolescent brain contributed constructively or misleadingly to the Court's judgment.

Adolescent Brain Development and Adolescent Responsibility

Christopher Simmons said he wanted to murder someone, and over the course of several days in 1993 he developed a plan to do so with two friends. The plan was to break in and burglarize a home, tie up a victim, and throw the victim off a bridge. This was not an impulsive offense in the heat of the moment. Simmons assured his friends that they could "get away with it" because they were minors. Simmons was seventeen, a junior in high school, and his two friends were ages fifteen and sixteen. Early one morning, they carried out their plan. They broke into the home of Shirley Crook, a forty-six-year-old woman whom Simmons had earlier encountered during a minor traffic accident, and bound and gagged her. The youths were careful in committing the murder, reinforcing her bonds and wrapping her face in duct tape before throwing her into the river. Crook drowned, and Simmons was arrested for murder shortly after bragging about the killing to other friends.

The trial court quickly convicted Simmons, and at the penalty phase the jury accepted the prosecution's recommendation of the death penalty. These judgments were affirmed in state and federal appellate proceedings. But a 2002 US Supreme Court decision[1] prohibiting the execution of mentally disabled individuals provoked a new appeal by Simmons's attorneys. They argued that the same constitutional considerations prohibiting the execution of a mentally disabled person should also forbid the execution of juveniles under age eighteen because of their diminished mental capacity. On this basis, the Missouri Supreme Court set aside Simmons's death sentence, and the subsequent appeal landed the case on the docket of the US Supreme Court.

Roper v. Simmons

After hearing oral arguments in 2004, a majority of the Court affirmed the judgment of the Missouri Supreme Court in *Roper v. Simmons*, concluding that the constitution does not permit the execution of minors.[2] In doing so, the Court overturned its own precedent that permitted the execution of minors over age fifteen who were guilty of capital crime.[3] Writing for the majority, Justice Anthony Kennedy pointed to three characteristics of adolescents: (1) their underdeveloped sense of responsibility and greater impulsivity, (2) their greater susceptibility to negative influences (including peer pressure), and (3) their underdeveloped character. Taken together, he argued, these characteristics diminish adolescents' judgment and consequently their criminal culpability, and exclude adolescents as a group from consideration as being among the "worst offenders" for whom the death penalty is reserved. In Justice Kennedy's words, "[t]he differences between juvenile and adult offenders are too marked and well understood to risk allowing a youthful person to receive the death penalty despite insufficient culpability."[4]

The Court was assisted in reaching this conclusion by the arguments of an amicus curiae (friend of the court) brief from the American Psychological Association (APA).[5] In conclusions that anticipated the Court's own findings, the APA amicus brief argued:

> At ages 16 and 17, adolescents, as a group, are not yet mature in ways that affect their decision-making. Behavioral studies show that late adolescents are less likely to consider alternative courses of action, understand the perspectives of others, and restrain impulses.... The unformed nature of adolescent character makes execution of 16- and 17-year-olds fall short of the purposes the Court has articulated for capital punishment.... On average, adolescents are risk takers to a far greater degree than adults. Behavioral studies indicate that adolescents often undervalue the true consequences of their actions. Instead, adolescents, as a group, often value impulsivity, fun-seeking, and peer approval more than adults do. (pp. 2, 7)

The brief further argued that individualized determinations of criminal culpability are not feasible because adolescents are "'moving targets' for assessments of character and future dangerousness, which are two important considerations in the penalty phase of capital trials" (p. 3). In other words, their development proceeds so rapidly and in such a manner that a teenager's capability and responsibility at sentencing might be much different from what it was when the crime was committed. Consequently, the brief concluded that a blanket prohibition on capital punishment for all youth under eighteen was warranted.

An important element of the APA brief was the argument that neuroscience supports this portrayal of adolescent immaturity:

> Why do adolescents show differences from adults with respect to risk-taking, planning, inhibiting impulses, and generating alternatives? Recent research suggests a biological dimension to adolescent behavioral immaturity: the human brain does not settle into its mature, adult form until after the adolescent years have passed and a person has entered young adulthood. (p. 9)

Following this conclusion were several pages summarizing the results of neuroimaging studies of adolescents, with a focus on changes in the structural and functional characteristics of the frontal lobes that "play a critical role in the executive or 'CEO' functions of the brain" (p. 9). Although the brief was weak in denoting the specific connections between neurodevelopment in adolescence and the behavioral characteristics at issue (such as differences from adults in "risk-taking, planning, inhibiting impulses, and generating alternatives"), the brief made a compelling argument that at the same time in their development that adolescents show poor judgment and self-control, the brain areas known to be related to these capacities have not yet fully matured.

This is likely to have been new news to the Court. By contrast with the behavioral studies that showed (in Justice Kennedy's words) what "any parent knows" about adolescents' poor judgment and decision-making, the evidence from studies of adolescent neurodevelopment was important for confirming this view and also providing a scientific *explanation* for why all adolescents are cognitively and emotionally limited in these ways. Stated differently, rather than immature judgment deriving from deficiencies in character, deficient rearing, or inexperience, the brief argued that it derives instead from age-related limitations owing to brain maturation, for which youth are not really responsible.

In oral arguments before the Court, Seth Waxman, the attorney arguing for the prohibition of the juvenile death penalty, devoted most of his time to the arguments raised in the APA brief. Just in case the evidence from neuroscience would be overlooked, he commented in response to a question from Justice Stephen Breyer about "the very fact that science . . . and I'm not just talking about social science here, but the important neurobiological science that has now shown that these adolescents are – their character is not hard-wired. It's why, for example – here's a – here's an interesting and relevant scientific fact."[6] However the evidence of behavioral studies might be disputed, he seemed to argue, the conclusions of developmental neuroscience were new, important, foundational "scientific facts" supporting the familiar portrayal of diminished adolescent responsibility.

But What about Hodgson v. Minnesota?

These arguments also fell under scrutiny in the dissents to the majority opinion to *Roper v. Simmons*, particularly the one written by Justice Antonin Scalia, who found the majority opinion deficient on several grounds. Scalia pointed out that the APA brief argued for a view of adolescent capability that was exactly *opposite* of what it had previously argued in an amicus brief submitted for a 1990 case. The 1990 case, *Hodgson v. Minnesota*,[7] tested the constitutionality of a Minnesota statute that required both parents to consent to the decision of a minor daughter to have an abortion. The statute included a judicial bypass provision, however, that enabled the youth to obtain an abortion without parental consent if a court deemed it to be in the minor's best interest and determined that the minor was "mature and capable of giving informed consent." The Minnesota statute, which was similar to legislation in other states, was based on the view that minors who could demonstrate their mature judgment and responsibility should be allowed to make their own decision in such an important matter without parental consultation that might, in some circumstances, be coercive or punitive. The "mature minor" rule was challenged in lower courts but affirmed by the Supreme Court in *Hodgson* in an opinion written by Justice John Paul Stevens.

In the *Hodgson* majority opinion an amicus brief by the APA[8] again proved influential, this time in the Court's determination that some minors could exercise sufficiently mature judgment for making a responsible abortion decision on their own. Indeed, the APA brief went beyond the Minnesota statute by arguing not just that *some* adolescents are capable of mature judgment, but that *all* adolescents are at an age when their reasoning and judgment are sufficiently mature. The APA brief offered strong evidence that by mid-adolescence, youth have developed conceptual skills that

> include the capacity to reason abstractly about hypothetical situations; the capacity to reason about multiple alternatives and consequences; the capacity to consider more variables and combine variables in more complex ways; and the capacity for systematic, exhaustive use of information ... In fact, by middle adolescence (age 14–15), young people develop abilities similar to adults in reasoning about moral dilemmas, understanding social rules and laws, reasoning about interpersonal relationships and interpersonal problems. (pp. 18–19)

After reviewing relevant behavioral studies, the brief concluded that "by age 14 most adolescents have developed adult-like intellectual and social capacities including specific abilities outlined in the law as necessary for understanding treatment alternatives, considering risks and benefits, and giving legally competent consent" (p. 20).

During oral arguments for *Roper v. Simmons*, even Justice Kennedy couldn't resist commenting on the discrepancies between the two APA briefs in their portrayal of adolescent competence. He caustically noted that the American Psychological Association "completely flip-flop in this case," and asked Mr. Waxman helpfully, "Is that just because of this modern evidence?" Justice Kennedy seemed to be referring to the neuroscience.

Comparing Roper *and* Hodgson

Reflecting on these two cases, we have to ask: Are the two APA briefs as discordant in their portrayal of adolescent responsibility as Justices Kennedy and Scalia believed? In response to Kennedy's question, Waxman replied that there is a difference between the cognitive competencies relevant to abortion decision-making and the emotional and social competencies underlying responsibility for capital crime. In other words, these portrayals of adolescent competence are apples and oranges.

A similar argument was also offered later by one of the primary contributors to APA's *Roper* brief, Dr. Laurence Steinberg, a professor at Temple University who is an authority on adolescent development. Steinberg claimed that it is unreasonable to expect developmental researchers to identify a single age by which mature responsibility has developed across such dissimilar domains of competence: "By age 16, adolescents' general cognitive abilities are essentially indistinguishable from those of adults, but adolescents' psychosocial functioning, even at the age of 18, is significantly less mature than that of individuals in their mid-20s."[9] From this perspective, therefore, the two views presented in the briefs accurately reflect different timetables for the development of cognitive and socioemotional skills during the teenage years. It is a perspective that might be shared by many parents of adolescents.

But however accurately this argument represents developmental science, its application to these two cases is misguided. A teenage woman contemplating terminating an unwanted pregnancy exercises not just abstract reasoning skills but also the self-possession and emotion management required for coping with a painful and unexpected decision involving a medical intervention. Christopher Simmons's responsibility for capital murder is based not only on assumptions about his impulsivity and inclination to risk-taking but also on the careful planning over several days that preceded the break-in. Each situation reflects *both* the cognitive capabilities and psychosocial capacities that are discussed in the two briefs, which indeed is true in most of the situations in which adolescents have to make important and responsible decisions. The reason the APA briefs in 1990 and 2005 are so conflicting is that each portrays adolescent competence too narrowly and too comprehensively at the same time. In other words, each provides only a partial view of the complex competencies of adolescents that is generalized to all adolescents all the time.

Of course, other considerations entered into the *Roper* and *Hodgson* opinions besides portrayals of adolescent responsibility. The consequences of the Court's decisions in each case were very different – whether an adolescent is required to tell her parents about her pregnancy versus the execution of a minor – and this required balancing different rights and responsibilities. This could have contributed to the different decisions that ensued. In addition, other Supreme Court precedents were trending in the same directions that each case was decided, toward increased recognition of the "mature minor" exception in 1990, and toward greater restrictions on the capital punishment of minors in 2005. These changes in the Court's thinking over these years were consistent with the changing politics of abortion and the death penalty in the United States.

Each decision may also have been influenced by changing cultural views of adolescence. Historians have long noted that public attitudes toward adolescence evolve over time in response to changing national concerns (e.g., wartime mobilization, juvenile crime statistics) and how the media cover youth culture.[10] In 1990, the view that youth can – and should – speak for themselves was prominent after years in which young people had contributed to the end of an unpopular war and were at the vanguard of a growing environmental movement, the push toward racial equity, and other social change. The rights of youth were broadening. Adolescence in 2005 was viewed, by contrast, in the context of substance abuse, mental health problems, violence, suicidality, and other serious problems that caused many people to believe that youth needed to be protected from their own poor judgment.[11]

These considerations notwithstanding, the *Roper* opinion was widely read as a landmark decision about adolescent responsibility that was noteworthy because it was influenced by developmental neuroscience. Indeed, subsequent Supreme Court decisions even more explicitly extended the Court's applications of developmental neuroscience to the culpability of minors for capital offenses.[12] The *Roper* decision also had implications for other areas of the law. Shortly after *Roper*, I received a call from an attorney asking to consult on how to address a growing number of state legislative efforts to eliminate "mature minor" provisions in abortion statutes in light of the *Roper* decision, and I was not alone in being asked to consult about the capabilities of youth.[13] The question of whether adolescents are responsible in relation to driving (and the conditions under which youth could get behind the wheel), drinking (and the circumstances in which youth could drink), voting, marriage, freedom of speech, decisions to continue or discontinue education, and many other issues hinges, to an important degree, on how legislatures and courts understand the capabilities of youth to exercise mature judgment on these matters. Standards in these and other areas have moved in more conservative directions in recent years.

Developmental science is relevant to these concerns. Even though they offered contradictory portrayals of adolescent responsibility, the APA briefs for *Hodgson* and *Roper* enlisted state-of-the-art research at the time they were written. But one important difference between the two briefs is the prominent place of developmental neuroscience in *Roper*, providing a new and compelling *explanation* for the behavioral evidence of adolescent impulsivity and poor self-control. The record of the oral arguments and the majority and minority opinions suggests that neuroscience had the attention of the Justices and was an important part of their thinking about the case. Before turning to the question of whether developmental neuroscience was appropriately influential in the Court's thinking in 2004, however, we must first consider why neuroscience would be so persuasive to the Justices, and to the rest of us.

Why We Are Neurodeterminists

An answer can be found in a 1998 cartoon by Mark Parisi (Figure 2.1), one of many parodying the era's preoccupation with brain science as an explanation for all kinds of human behavior.

There were similar parodies appearing at this time of the "anatomy" of male and female brains and the teenager's brain, each purporting to explain the elusive qualities of its target. These depictions included brain centers for sex, music lyrics, an "I told you so" reflex, the ball sports node, the "cool" gauge, and the "all the answers" center (you can decide to which brains these belong). In each case, the cartoons capture what we hope neuroscience will reveal about human behavior: explanations for the characteristics of different types of people, their foibles (such as the enormous cortical space devoted to toddler tantrums in the figure), their limitations (such as the pea-shaped "ability to share"), their vulnerabilities ("spill reflex"), and strengths ("involuntary 'why?' reflex"). They are parodies: I have often used the Parisi cartoon to disarm audience expectations when I talk about the developing brain. But they are nevertheless revealing

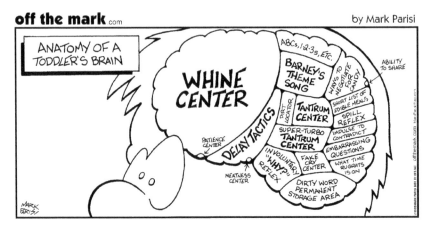

Figure 2.1   Mark Parisi, "Anatomy of a Toddler's Brain."
© Mark Parisi, permission granted for use, www.offthemark.com.

about why we find neuroscience such a compelling view of human behavior. They show why we tend to be neurodeterminists.

Neurorealism

One reason we find neuroscience compelling is its clarity: neuroimaging provides "visual proof" of the brain's influence on psychological processes. Human feelings, thoughts, motives, intentions, and other psychological phenomena are complex, multidetermined, sometimes ambiguous, often puzzling, and difficult to see and measure. By contrast, although the technology of neuroimaging is complex and difficult to grasp, the public quickly learned that something important was happening whenever areas in the brain lit up in color, and this commended realism and substance to the brain's role in the phenomenon being studied.

In addition, the technology of neuroimaging is impressively complex and sophisticated. Functional magnetic resonance imaging (fMRI) is a brain imaging procedure conducted in a sophisticated medical or research center using very expensive, state-of-the-art machinery to map blood-oxygen flow in the brain. It more closely resembles research in the biomedical and other "hard" sciences than the questionnaires and simple experiments of the "soft" behavioral sciences. This is one reason for my colleague's enthusiasm for the fMRI of his experimental procedure: it made the phenomenon more real as visual proof in the brain of what he had long been studying behaviorally. Neurorealism was also persuasive to the Supreme Court Justices deciding *Roper*. Determining adolescent responsibility or culpability for capital crime involves complex judgments of competency and understanding. Far clearer and more straightforward is learning that the "executive or 'CEO' functions of the brain" are lacking because the adolescent brain is biologically immature.

Neuroimaging also commands attention because a researcher's interpretation of the meaning of those illuminated, colored areas, and their relevance to psychological and behavioral processes, is authoritative. Most of us cannot really understand the significance of these imaging depictions without the help of a trusted expert in neuroscience. In this respect, neuroscience differs from behavioral science because people are more comfortable questioning the findings derived from observations, questionnaires, experiments, and other behavioral methods (and they should be) – but not the meaning of the colored areas on the brain scan. Consequently, it is not only the "visual proof" offered by neuroimaging but also our acceptance of the expert's interpretation of its meaning that makes it such convincing evidence of the connection between brain and mind. If we can trust the neuroimaging expert, and especially if different experts agree in their judgments about the brain, neuroimaging seems to offer solid and compelling evidence about brain functioning.

The term that has been applied to this is *neurorealism*,[14] and it means that neuroimaging can make the brain's influence appear uncritically real, objective, and persuasive. Neurorealism makes neuroimaging "uncritically real" because the depictions it provides of the brain are technically sophisticated and the visual evidence seems unassailable. Experts' interpretation of the meaning of these images is authoritative and persuasive because most people have limited understanding of the technical complexities and interpretive challenges of neuroscience research, so they are not capable of questioning the expert's interpretation even if they were inclined to do so.

In 2008, psychologists David McCabe and Alan Castel[15] asked undergraduate students to read brief articles summarizing real or fictitious reports of neuroimaging research, some of which included incorrect conclusions from the data. Some reports were accompanied by a brain image, others by a bar graph or another visual representation of the brain, and others by no illustration at all. Across three experiments, the researchers reported that student ratings of the quality of the writing and the reasoning in the article were significantly higher when the article was accompanied by brain imaging. These findings have since been replicated,[16] although there have also been failures to replicate,[17] leading to a general conclusion that there may be a small but important effect on peoples' judgments of the veracity of research when it includes neuroimaging illustrations.

But whether presented as visual images or other documentation, it seems clear that people endow neuroscience with uncritical and persuasive influence when it is incorporated into discussions of human behavior and thought. In the words of the Temple University psychologist Laurence Steinberg, who contributed to the APA *Roper* brief,

> In science, familiarity often breeds skepticism, and the lack of familiarity that most laypersons have with the workings of the brain, much less the nuances of neuroscientific methods, leads non-scientists to accept findings from brain science uncritically. I admit that I have exploited this naiveté shamelessly in my efforts to persuade judges and lawmakers that adolescents are fundamentally different from adults in ways that need to be taken into account in the formulation of legal and social policy.[18]

Neuroscience is endowed by neurorealism for another, related reason: it provides evidence of the material substance of psychological processes, the place in the brain where these processes actually occur. And why wouldn't physical evidence like this be persuasive? Most scientists are *materialists*: they believe that physical matter is the fundamental substance of all things, including mental events. Many of us in the general public are also materialists. From the time of the Enlightenment, materialism has accompanied rationality as the foundation of a serious, scientific understanding of natural phenomena. And over an even longer reach of human history, people have sought to find physical, material causes of the invisible psychological processes that are so significant in human affairs. From the ancients' explanations of mental illness as the movement of internal humors in the body to the localization of reason, soul, and other psychological functions in the spine, heart, or brain to the emergence of phrenology in the nineteenth century that identified mental abilities and dispositions in the contours of the skull, people have sought to find the physical, material locations of mental and emotional processes. Neuroscientific approaches are the legacy of this history of human inquiry. Identifying psychological processes with underlying neurobiological functions provides material, visual evidence of the elusive psychological world.

Neuroessentialism

A second reason we are neurodeterminists is even more important: neuroscience is believed to provide *causal explanations* for psychological phenomena. *The mind is what the brain does*[19] expresses this belief in the causal primacy of the brain. To most people, this also makes a lot of sense (after all, psychological processes do not emerge from the spleen) and is consistent with how we intuitively think about the origins of our thoughts, feelings, and actions. These processes all arise from the activity of the brain, and the brain's causal mechanisms are confirmed in the technology and language of neuroscience. When researchers speak of the "wiring" of neural "connections" and "networks" of brain areas that become "activated" in experience to create the "architecture" of the brain, psychological processes seem to be grounded in predictable causal mechanisms like those from engineering. The *mechanism* in the language of neuroscience may be one reason, in fact, why the brain development revolution attracted new audiences to an interest in early development. The growth of children attracted attention when the mechanistic language of developmental neuroscience seemed to promise predictable, causal, scientific explanations for the mysteries of how children grow and develop. In a similar manner, neuroessentialistic thinking helped make an account of the immaturity of the adolescent brain – its incomplete wiring of neural architecture – sufficient to explain the impulsivity and irresponsibility of adolescent behavior to Supreme Court Justices.

The term that has been applied here is *neuroessentialism*, which means that brain processes are the fundamental reality of psychological phenomena.[20] It is not just that behavior and mental events are biologically initiated in the brain, but also that the functioning of brain processes is the basis for psychological functioning: cognitive processes, personality, emotions, biases and disposition, and social capacities are all founded in mechanistic brain processes. Neuroessentialism promises that ultimately we can trace psychological processes to their neurobiological substrates.

Three Illustrations of Neuroessentialism

There are abundant illustrations of neuroessentialist thinking in studies of human psychological functioning. I offer three examples.

The first enlists a neuroessentialist explanation of political polarization (and other attitudes and dispositions). Why is our social and political discourse so unceasingly polarized? It could derive from the fact that the brains of conservatives and liberals process information differently, a phenomenon that one research team labeled "neural polarization."[21] This team of scientists from UC Berkeley, Stanford, and Johns Hopkins University examined brain activity using fMRI in people who had been identified through questionnaires as endorsing politically liberal or conservative attitudes toward immigration. Each group watched twenty-four videos profiling immigration policies while their brain activity was monitored. The researchers reported that brain activation was significantly different in the two groups, particularly in an area of the prefrontal cortex (the dorsomedial prefrontal cortex [DMPFC]) that, according to the research team, is associated with the interpretation of narrative content. These brain activation differences were especially evident during episodes in the videos that included threat-related and moral-emotion language. The more a respondent's brain activity matched that of other participants in their political group, furthermore, the more the respondent reported that after watching the video, their attitudes had changed to better match those of other group members. The researchers concluded that "these results shed light on the psychological and neural underpinnings of how identical information is interpreted differently by conservatives and liberals"[22] through their biased interpretations of the narrative content.

Neuroimaging has been enlisted in a similar manner in other studies to explain differences in optimism,[23] proneness to conformity,[24] and a variety of personality factors.[25] In each case, how the brain functions is the reason we have these biases, attitudes, dispositions, and personalities, a common illustration of neuroessentialist explanations for mental processes.

A second example of neuroessentialism answers the question, What connects us emotionally to others? Mirror neurons in the brain are nerve cells that are active during the execution of an action *and also* during the observation of the same action in another. Mirror neurons neurobiologically match "my action" and "your action," and are thus believed to contribute to understanding another's behavior and goals by referencing them to one's own. The discovery of mirror neurons first in monkeys and later in humans in the 1990s led to an explosion of research investigating the functions of mirror neurons for basic capacities such as action understanding, speech perception imitation and also complex social behavior, perspective-taking ability, and empathy.[26] The general idea underlying these diverse inquiries is the possibility that there exists in higher primates an evolved, neurobiological capacity to connect one's personal behavior, feelings, and experience with that of another.[27]

A third example of neuroessentialist thinking concerns social development. How do children and youth become socially competent? One research group has focused on the development of a collection of brain structures that together they call the "social brain."[28] This brain network[29] is particularly active in situations involving social understanding or "mentalizing" (the ability to reflect on mental states in oneself and/or others).[30] The social brain develops significantly, both structurally and functionally, in late childhood and adolescence, at the same time that capacities for social understanding are also rapidly developing.

In light of this, does the pace of development of the social brain network explain the development of social competence in adolescence? To answer this question, 300 adolescents were studied on three occasions, each testing occasion separated by two years.[31] Neuroimaging of the social brain was conducted on each occasion, at ages fourteen, sixteen, and eighteen, and the youth responded to measures of the quality of their friendships at ages fourteen and eighteen. The research team reported that higher levels of maturity in two of the structures of the social brain predicted stronger improvements in friendship quality by the age of eighteen. Adolescents who showed more advanced brain maturation in these areas also reported improved friendships over this time. This work is representative of a large and expanding research literature on the neurodevelopmental changes in childhood and adolescence that can predict the development of social skills – but also the growth of emotional disorders, such as depression and anxiety disorders. In each case, changes in social and emotional functioning are attributed, from a neuroessentialist perspective, to underlying changes in the brain's development.

The discoveries of these and other studies of the developing brain and mind are consistent with the neuroessentialist claim that brain processes are the fundamental reality of psychological phenomena. To understand political polarization, emotional connectedness, developing social competence, and so many other human characteristics, we must look to the brain's development and functioning. Research like the three studies summarized here is impressive work, and it is easy to see how the past twenty-five years of research in the neurosciences have inspired public interest in the developmental connections between brain and mind. It is also possible to see how findings like these contribute to a broader neuroessentialist belief that in the (not too distant) future, all psychological phenomena will eventually be reduced to their material, neurobiological mechanisms; psychology will have become neuropsychology; and cognitive science will have become cognitive neuroscience.

Why We Should Not Be Neurodeterminists

But before proceeding too far down a neurodeterminist pathway, it is important to recognize several cautions in how we interpret the findings of neuroscience. Many of these cautions come from neuroscientists themselves as they have sought to curb the public's overinterpretation of brain-based research. In general, these interpretive cautions derive from the fact that neuroscience is still a very young science, and developmental neuroscience especially so. The remarkable advances in understanding yielded by recent decades of research are dwarfed by how far the science must further advance to yield the kind of comprehensive brain-based explanation of psychological phenomena that many believe is in the future. In this sense, we should not confuse the promissory note of neuroessentialism with its present actuality.

In this section, I discuss five reasons we should not be neurodeterminists.

- First, researchers are only beginning to understand the daunting complexity of the neural networks, and their interaction with neurohormonal and neurotransmitter systems, that together contribute to complex psychological functioning. Our understanding of the association of these brain systems with psychological processes will evolve significantly in the future, and will likely alter our neuroessentialist assumptions about this association.
- Second, neuroscientists sometimes disagree about the particular functions of specific brain structures. Without an overall theory to guide understanding of the association of brain and mind, the "visual proof" of psychological processes provided by different studies can be divergent and confusing. Proof of what?
- Third, one reason that there is disagreement about the specific functions of brain structures is that many brain structures have multiple functions and mental states are multidetermined. This makes it difficult to enlist earlier research findings to interpret associations between brain processes and mental states, a problem called "reverse inference."
- Fourth, brain and mind are mutually influential, and both are affected by experience as they develop. If *the mind is what the brain does* at any moment in time, then over time it is also true that *the brain is what the mind does* because of how brain development incorporates experience and its processing by the mind.
- Fifth, despite our neuroessentialist tendency to perceive brain and mind as distinct (called "mind-body dualism"), with brain as the fundamental reality, we must recognize that human behavior and development are conjointly influenced by both. The divide between brain and mind as causal agents may ultimately be less important than understanding how they continuously interact.

Finally, in the last section, several of these cautions are drawn together in a discussion of neuroessentialism, culture, and adolescence in China. After this, we return to the Supreme Court.

All Together Now!

One caution in interpreting neurobiological research is that brain regions – whether we are considering the dorsomedial prefrontal cortex, mirror neurons, the social brain network, or other areas – do not function in isolation from other brain regions, but work together with them. As we shall see in more detail in Chapter 3, the multiple brain structures underlying memory, language, and other capacities can be widely distributed throughout the brain. The Supreme Court Justices were told of the immaturity of the frontal lobes in accounting for adolescent irresponsibility, but subsequent research has shown that a broader network of brain areas is involved in the development of self-regulation. But even this is incomplete. Brain regions also interact with other neurobiological systems, such as the neurotransmitter system (e.g., dopamine, serotonin) and the neurohormonal system (e.g., oxytocin, cortisol) that also mature significantly in childhood and adolescence, and are relevant to responsible conduct. Neuroscientists are beginning to understand the complex interactions among the biological systems of the brain and body that collectively influence psychological functioning. This interaction is likely to be particularly complex when sophisticated psychological processes, like adolescent responsibility, are studied. As researchers understand these linked networks, however, this knowledge can transform understanding of brain and mind and their connection.

This transformation is currently happening in the study of emotion. For years, conventional scientific understanding was that specific emotional states are generated by delegated brain structures that underlie universal human emotional experience. The amygdala, for example, is often described as the locus of fear responding in humans. But research findings have challenged this "locationist" account in several ways. First, neuroimaging studies have shown that these emotion-related brain structures are also associated with other psychological functions besides emotion (the amygdala, for example, has an important role in memory). Second, neuroimaging shows that emotional responses are based on the simultaneous activation of multiple regions of the brain.[32] Emotion involves brain processes associated with sensory evaluation, cognitive appraisal, short- and long-term memory, self-regulation, and other functions that are not specific to different emotions, and that collectively contribute to emotional experience. Emotional reactions can also involve activation of the hypothalamic-pituitary-adrenocortical axis and other neurohormonal systems. The brain's response to an emotional event like a scary animal is thus astonishingly complex, integrating widely distributed neurobiological areas, not just activation of a core emotion structure such as the amygdala.

These discoveries have led, in turn, to the reconsideration of some central facets of psychological emotions theory. Emotions researchers are increasingly questioning the existence of distinct, universal emotional states in favor of the view that emotions are psychologically constructed experiences based on culture, early development, language, gender, and other influences.[33] This newer view is consistent with studies showing that the kinds of emotions experienced by people in different parts of the world can be very different, and these differences are reflected in the language that encodes emotional experience, the social rules for how emotions are felt and expressed, gendered expectations for feelings, and many other processes. The emotional world of a Parisian man is, for these reasons, very different from that of a Hindu woman.[34] These cultural differences make sense if emotions are psychologically constructed responses that involve the intersection of many brain regions; they make less sense from a locationist view of universal human emotions based on delegated brain areas. Because neuroscientists are discovering evidence for the complex integration of multiple brain regions in emotional responding, behavioral researchers are recognizing that emotions are psychologically complex and vary by culture and place.

Discoveries such as these have important consequences for understanding brain and mind because they are at the heart of defining what we mean by "mind" (what is an emotion? what is adolescent responsibility?) and "brain" (which neurobiological systems play a role, and what do they do?). The answers to questions like these await greater future understanding of the neural networks and their interaction with neurohormonal and neurotransmitter systems that contribute to complex psychological functioning. That understanding may also lead to reconceptualizing the psychological processes under study. Current conclusions about brain-mind connections based on simple associations between one or a few brain regions and psychological phenomena almost certainly simplify a much more complex picture. The mirror neuron system may play a role in empathy, for example, but certainly other brain regions involved in emotion and social understanding also play a part (including, quite likely, structures of the social brain). The neuroessentialist view that brain processes are the fundamental reality of mental states awaits greater clarity about what those brain processes are and how they interact with each other in their association with mental and behavioral states.

There Is Nothing as Practical as a Good Theory

Another challenge in connecting brain and mind concerns theory – or the lack of it. Behavioral science has been a theory-driven, top-down inquiry throughout most of its history. Psychological theories provide a conceptual road map for researchers: they contribute to generating hypotheses, provide ways of explaining behavior, direct attention to important topics, and help fill in the gaps in understanding yielded by research findings. Although the risk of theoretical blinders is always present, it is more often true that, in Kurt Lewin's famous maxim, "there is nothing as practical as a good theory."[35]

But neuroscience is not theory-driven. Instead, it is a basically atheoretical,[36] bottom-up inquiry in which researchers empirically construct understanding of the brain through the progressive accumulation and integration of specific research findings about different areas of the brain.[37] This inductive approach has the benefit of being data-driven, so that knowledge of the functions of brain regions or neural networks is guided by the evidence, not by prior theoretical expectations. But since data have to be interpreted – that is, what do those illuminated areas on an fMRI scan mean in relation to behavior and thought? – researchers do so on the basis of how they understand the findings of specific studies without a guiding theoretical perspective.

The problem of atheoreticality is that when neuroimaging shows that a brain region is activated in response to a particular task, the interpretation of its functioning depends on the nature of the task. When the same brain region is activated in different studies using different tasks, however, the interpretations of its functions can be very different. How should one make sense of these differences when trying to understand the function of that part of the brain?

Consider, for example, the medial prefrontal cortex, one of the structures of the social brain discovered to predict adolescent social competence.[38] A survey of the research literature shows that in other studies the medial prefrontal cortex is described as an "action-outcome predictor,"[39] a component of working memory and memory retrieval,[40] a contributor to decision-making,[41] with consequence for aging and dementia.[42] So what does the medial prefrontal cortex do, and how could this be relevant to a "social brain" in adolescence? This problem is more typical than exceptional in the neuroscience literature, especially because brain regions (like the amygdala) are often associated with different, apparently unrelated, functions. The cerebellum was long identified as the brain structure devoted to motor control and coordination, but studies in the last two decades have documented its role in attentional processes, emotion regulation, decision-making, and language processing. What, therefore, is the cerebellum for? And how do we understand its influence on behavior and thought?[43]

As earlier noted, confidence in the interpretation of neuroimaging is based on the experienced judgment of a neuroscientist, since most of us are unprepared to interpret neuroimaging results. But when neuroscientists disagree in their interpretations, as they sometimes do, it raises the question of what is the "visual proof" that neuroimaging promises and neurorealism expects. Visual proof of what? It would be helpful to have a theory to guide thinking about the organization of brain functioning, but the data-driven orientation of contemporary neuroscience (and the fact that it is such a young science) means that a generally accepted theory like this does not exist. It is possible that in the future, a widely accepted general model of the brain's functioning will provide the conceptual road map that researchers need, but for now, this means that different studies often yield different understandings of particular brain structures.

In addressing this problem, researchers typically integrate their findings with the insights of previous studies of the same brain region to derive a more accurate interpretation of that region's functioning. This makes sense, right? But as we shall see, this can also be tricky.

Reasoning Forward, Not in Reverse

One way to interpret the functioning of the brain areas that have been activated by an experimental procedure is to think about which other procedures have caused the same activation in other studies. Perhaps the same process is happening here? But deriving conclusions on this basis can be problematic, and the following is an example of why.

Recall the study of "neural polarization" described above. The dorsomedial prefrontal cortex (DMPFC) is the brain region showing increased activation during polarized responses to immigration videos in this research. To explain this, the researchers cited earlier studies showing that the DMPFC is also activated in procedures involving the interpretation of narrative content, such as when trying to figure out the meaning of a story or a video. They concluded, therefore, that perhaps neural polarization derives from how conservatives and liberals interpret the same narrative content differently. This seems sensible. But as the authors acknowledged (and this should be a familiar story by now), the DMPFC has been found in other studies to be associated with a variety of other cognitive functions, including memory retrieval, impression formation, and reasoning about other people's mental states (aka mentalization); it is also involved in emotion regulation and decision-making. It is therefore difficult to know with certainty whether the group differences in DMPFC activation owe to the differential processing of narrative content, as the researchers concluded, or instead to reflections on the thoughts and intentions of the actors in the video (mentalization), the retrieval of relevant information from memory, managing the emotions evoked by the video, or other processes associated with the DMPFC. The absence of control procedures (such as watching videos with no immigration content) makes clear conclusions especially difficult.

When neuroscientists experimentally alter a specific mental state and denote the change in brain activity, they derive conclusions using forward inference, and this approach is the basis for a large and substantive research literature. Forward inference occurs when a change in mental state A activates brain activity X (see Figure 2.2).

Reverse inference (Figure 2.3), however, is when a change in mental state B also activates brain activity X, and, without specifically measuring A, researchers conclude that A must be one reason X was activated.[44] For example, mental state B (watching immigration videos) activates brain activity X (DMPFC), and researchers infer that mental state A (interpretation of narrative content) is a reason why, based on previous research findings.

Reverse inference can lead to misleading conclusions, however, because it makes an unverified assumption about the role of an unmeasured mental state in brain activity. Reverse inference is particularly risky when the brain area of interest is associated with many different mental states, which we have seen can be true (recall the earlier discussion of the medial prefrontal cortex and its role in memory, decision-making, and adolescent social

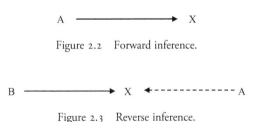

A ⟶ X

Figure 2.2 Forward inference.

B ⟶ X ⟵- - - - - - - - - - A

Figure 2.3 Reverse inference.

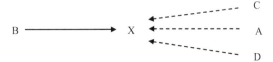

Figure 2.4   Complications in reverse inference: a brain area is associated with
multiple mental states.

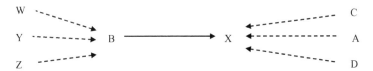

Figure 2.5   Complications in reverse inference: eliciting conditions are
psychologically complex.

competence) (see Figure 2.4). How can we know which of these is relevant
to the mental state activating X in response to B?

Reverse inference is also risky when the brain area activated by a research
procedure is not well defined (such as watching immigration videos); that
is, it could be affected by several different mental states, such as emotion
(W), recall of relevant past events (Y), or evaluating the characters in the
video (Z) (see Figure 2.5).

Identifying a causal association between a mental state and brain activation
is more difficult when the functioning of either is multidetermined, and this is
more likely to occur when the psychological and neurobiological processes are
complex. This can occur, for example, when a sophisticated brain region (such
as the frontal lobes) is causally linked to a complex psychological phenomenon
(adolescent responsibility). One way of managing the problem of reverse
inference is by enlisting appropriate control groups in follow-up studies, but
this makes the research task more difficult and expensive.[45] The neuroessentialist belief that brain processes are the fundamental reality of mental states is
more challenging to comprehend when brain processes have multiple functions and mental states are multidetermined. The expectation of a one-to-one
association between brain and mind is likely to be a frustrated expectation.

*Brain and Mind Are Mutually Influential, and Both Are Affected by
Experience as They Develop*

Neuroessentialism begins with the brain, and proceeds to explain how the
brain causes mental and psychological responses. But how does the brain

develop? As I describe in more detail in Chapter 3, brain development is a fascinatingly complex intersection of genetic guidance, self-organizing processes within the brain, and the influence of experience. Developmental scientists have been especially interested in the role of experience because it reveals how the daily events of ordinary life have, over time, an influence on the brain's developing capacities. Researchers call this the *biological embedding of experience*, and it reflects how experience "gets under the skin" to shape the brain and other biological systems.[46]

Experience is important because it not only affects the brain's development but also shapes how people think and act – it influences patterns of behavior and cognitive responses as experience is mentally processed. Therefore, over time, experience is a shared influence in the development of brain and mind. Repeated experiences over time have been shown, in many research investigations, to be associated with changes in behavior and thinking and simultaneously with changes in the structure and functioning of brain systems. Sadly, some of the clearest evidence of this comes from studies of children in chronic adversity, such as children experiencing neglect, poverty, or physical abuse, in which maltreatment is associated with impairments in the growth and functioning of critical brain areas and also impaired cognitive and social capacities.[47] There is also abundant evidence for the impact of experience on brain and mind in typical circumstances throughout life.[48]

The association between brain and mind, therefore, reflects the impact of experience on each as they develop. Furthermore, as repeated experiences over time reinforce and refine habits of thought, styles of emotional responding, and other mental and behavioral tendencies shaped by everyday experience, this *psychological embedding of experience* also influences the brain's functioning. As I describe in Chapter 3, the mental processing of experience strengthens some neurobiological networks and refashions others in a manner consistent with the familiar "use it or lose it" principle of brain development. Thus *the mind is what the brain does* – but also over time *the brain is what the mind does*.

Recall the study of neural polarization described earlier and how conservatives and liberals responded differently to immigration videos. When interpreting their results, the research team acknowledged that the group difference in brain processing could arise from the biases that developed in the two groups over time as they responded to preferred media sources, engaged with different social networks, conversed about politics with different people, and had a variety of other experiences contributing to liberal or conservative attitudes. Viewed in this light, "neural polarization" and responses to immigration videos had a common foundation in the tribalism of contemporary politics, and group differences in the brain's activation probably developed as a consequence of the growth of polarized attitudes, not as a cause of them.

When we consider the association of brain and mind not just at a single point in time (when brain activation is the precipitant of psychological processes) but in their development, the mutual influences between brain development and behavioral and mental growth become more apparent. Viewed developmentally, it also becomes apparent that both are influenced by experience over time. This offers a different perspective on some of the associations between brain and mind that are often attributed to intrinsic brain differences, such as differences between men and women[49] and between individuals with different personality profiles.[50] In each case, differences in behavior and differences in brain networks can simultaneously be shaped by years of experience. Neuroessentialism claims that the brain is the fundamental reality of the mind, but closer to the evidence is that experience influences the development of both, and brain and mind have continuous mutual influences as they develop over the life course.

Dualism and Naive Dualism

One of the practical consequences of neuroessentialism is that it reinforces people's tendency to view neurobiological (and generally, biological) processes as fundamentally different from mental and psychological processes. Because brain processes are basic to how people act and think, for example, they are viewed as more fundamental influences, mechanistically determinative, less susceptible to rational or voluntary control, and exerting influence outside awareness. Because mental events are perceived as more derivative from biological processes than determinative, they tend to be viewed as more voluntary, flexible, and conscious. This view of two domains of human functioning – brain (biological) and mind (psychological) – is called mind-body dualism, the belief that fundamentally different processes govern biological and mental events. We do not intuitively expect the biological activity of our bodies to function according to the same principles as our mental activity does: hunger and sleeping operate according to different principles than do consciousness and hope. Dualism is a common and longstanding feature of Western thinking about the causes of behavior that has a long history in philosophy and psychology.[51] It is fundamental to the influence of neurorealism and neuroessentialism in our thinking about the origins of human behavior and thought because it emphasizes the basic differences between brain and mind rather than their interaction.

Dualism is also practically consequential because it can influence judgments of personal and legal responsibility, and the Supreme Court's *Roper* case that opened this chapter had elements of dualism in the majority opinion. In contrast to previous decisions concerning minors convicted of capital offenses, in which criminal conduct was attributed to poor judgment, the introduction of neuroscience in *Roper* led the Justices to perceive adolescent conduct as biologically determined, with diminished judgment deriving from the brain's developmental immaturity. This causes adolescents to be regarded as less responsible and less culpable because their conduct was not in their control, by contrast with attributing their conduct to poor judgment or bad character. And this has implications for punishment, deterrence, and even rehabilitation.

To illustrate how this occurs, a research team invited college students and suburban residents to evaluate different situations involving people who had acted in a harmful manner, and then to judge the person's culpability, blameworthiness, the reasons for their actions, and how sympathetic they were as people.[52] The stories concerned events ranging from a violent killing to failing to follow through on important plans. Embedded in the stories was information related to the cause of their harmful conduct, which derived from either the influence of past experiences (e.g., severe abuse as a child) or biological processes (e.g., an imbalance in brain chemicals). The researchers found that respondents consistently viewed individuals whose behavior was biologically caused to be less culpable than someone who acted the same way based on past experiences, and to view behavior in the biological case as more "automatic" than in the past experience case, and less susceptible to deterrence or treatment. Although adverse past experiences elicited greater sympathy, they also resulted in judgments of greater blame and responsibility when they led to harmful conduct. These findings are consistent with the practical concerns of legal scholars about the influence of neuroscience in court cases, especially its potentially mitigating influence on jury decision-making concerning criminal culpability or punishment.[53]

The researchers designed their study to illustrate the influence of dualism in judgments of personal responsibility, but they concluded that the responses of their participants better illustrated "naive dualism" because of the either/or quality of their judgments.[54] In naive dualism, behavior has *either* neurobiological causes (and therefore you're not responsible) *or* psychological causes (and therefore you are responsible). In real life, of course, *both* brain and mind are involved because behavior is influenced by the brain and mind simultaneously. Nevertheless, everyday examples of naive dualism are frequent. Outside the courtroom, most of us have encountered people who excused their conduct because it was biologically caused: because they were high, for example, or had too much to drink, or because of their temperamental traits, age, or the immaturity of their brain. This way of thinking has also appeared in the psychotherapeutic field as it has led some in treatment to conclude that "it's my brain that is has OCD, not me" when they learn of the effects of obsessive-compulsive disorder on brain functioning[55] or to conclude that addiction had "hijacked" their brain.

The problem with naive dualism is that behavior is not solely a result of brain or mind. Addiction is not just a "brain disease" but a disease in which neurobiological and psychological dysfunction have become mutually locked in a downward spiral, and in which pharmacological and behavioral therapy together can prove helpful.[56] Of course, there are some situations in which biological causes have a more prominent role in certain behavior, such as with autism or brain disease, just as there are some situations in which psychological causes are more preeminent. The researchers of this study argued, however, that rather than asking whether behavior is either biologically or psychologically caused, as naive dualists do, it is better to ask how strong the association is between behavior and an alleged (biological or psychological) cause. If the association is weak (a small proportion of people experiencing an "imbalance in brain chemicals" commit murder), then there is less justification in judging them not responsible than if the association is strong (a high proportion of people with the chemical imbalance commit murder). The same evaluation can apply to the psychological causes of behavior, such as child abuse. In most instances, of course, neither "an imbalance in brain chemicals" nor child abuse provide by themselves strong associations with bad behavior, because many people with chemical imbalances in the brain or a history of child abuse do not act badly. Instead, we best understand their actions in the interaction of biological and psychological influences.

If this approach is an appropriate response to naive dualism, it also offers a perspective on neuroessentialism. For all of the reasons discussed in this section, the important question is not whether the brain assumes a role in behavior and thought (of course it does), but rather how brain and mental influences intersect over the course of development. Viewed in this light, then, the divide between brain and mind as causal agents is less important than their interaction.

Neuroessentialism and Developmental Cultural Neuroscience

The neuroessentialist claim that the brain is the fundamental reality of psychological phenomena compels attention to neuroscience for the insights it provides about how people function mentally and psychologically. It is the reason that brain-based explanations of behavior and mental processes, whether of adolescent impulsivity, the challenges of cognitive aging, the origins of psychological disorders, or the different predilections of men and women, are so compelling. Because they are so compelling, however, these explanations must be carefully examined because they provide not just explanations but also expectations for how we function. Older adults who believe that cognitive slowing is an inevitable consequence of neurobiological aging, for example, may begin to withdraw from intellectually taxing experiences and, in doing so, fail to engage in the cognitive challenges that can keep aging brains active. Adolescents who believe that their brains cause them to be more impulsive and less self-regulated than adults may act consistently with these expectations, even when they are capable of greater responsibility and planfulness. The messaging of neuroscience is important, therefore, for telling us how our brains guide our conduct and, in some instances, creating self-fulfilling prophecies.

A series of studies about the influence of adolescent stereotypes on the behavior of youth in China and the United States illustrates how such expectations can shape youth behavior. They also show how those expectations influence not just behavior, but also the developing brain itself.

In the United States, stereotypes of adolescence emphasize characteristics like their disengagement from parents, peer orientation, emotional instability, and irresponsibility. By contrast, the teenage years are viewed more positively in China as a period of increasing maturity, duty to family and society, and skill development in preparation for a place in the competitive adult world.[57] There is, however, diversity in Chinese stereotypes of adolescence. Cultural beliefs about adolescence are more similar to those of the United States in the larger urban areas of Hong Kong, Beijing, and Shanghai than in more rural, inland areas because of the influence of Western values and culture in large cities.

These stereotypical expectations influence youth behavior. In a study with several hundred sixth- and seventh-graders and their mothers in the United States, middle-schoolers' expectations that certain negative stereotypes would describe them in adolescence predicted their actual behaviors a year later.[58] Youth who expected that they would feel alienated reported less parent-adolescent closeness, more parent-adolescent conflict, and higher susceptibility to peer influence a year later. Youth expectations that they would exhibit risk-taking or rebellious behaviors predicted actual reports of greater behavior problems a year later. Expectations of mothers for their adolescents were also significantly associated with the adolescents' later behavior.

The same associations are also true in China. In one longitudinal study, researchers recruited Chinese seventh-graders living in Hong Kong and Chongqing (an inland city).[59] Measures of the teenagers' endorsement of adolescent stereotypes (i.e., independence from parents, obligation to family, school disengagement, peer orientation) and their problem behavior (e.g., self-reported drinking, petty theft) were obtained, and then these measures were obtained a second time six months later. The researchers found that youth in Hong Kong saw disengagement from school, along with independence from parents and an orientation toward peers, as more characteristic of the teenage years than youth from Chongqing. Hong Kong youth endorsed family obligation less often compared with the youth from Chongqing. The endorsement of negative adolescent stereotypes in Hong Kong was thus similar to the reports of youth in the United States.

Stereotype endorsement and problem behavior were mutually influential across time for each youth group in China. Youth who supported the school disengagement stereotype reported greater problem behavior six months later. Early problem behavior was, in turn, associated with greater endorsement of the school disengagement stereotype six months later. The same mutual associations over time were evident for the endorsement of positive adolescent stereotypes. Youth who endorsed traditional family obligations showed less problem behavior six months later, but the reverse was also true. In short, for youth in both Hong Kong and Chongqing, stereotype endorsement and problem behavior became consistently linked over time, with more negative adolescent stereotypes associated with greater problem behavior. Hong Kong youth, who tended to endorse more negative stereotypes of adolescence, also showed an increase in problem behavior over time, and by the end of the study, rates of problem behavior were significantly higher than for the youth from Chongqing.

Adolescents' beliefs about what society expects of them can thus influence their behavior, potentially creating a self-fulfilling prophecy (you expect bad behavior, so you'll get it). But what are the implications for brain development? In a follow-up study with seventh-graders in the United States, teenagers' endorsement of stereotypes involving family obligation were again obtained.[60] In follow-up assessments one and two years later, their problem behavior was also assessed, but in addition, fMRI scans were conducted on the teenagers as they completed several cognitive tasks, with a focus on structures in the prefrontal cortex (PFC, specifically the ventrolateral prefrontal cortex) and other areas associated with impulse control and self-regulation. The researchers reported that the more that seventh-graders perceived adolescence as a period of disinterest in family obligations, the more their problem behavior increased by eighth and ninth grades (consistent with the earlier study). But neurobiologically, the more that seventh-graders viewed adolescents as disinterested in fulfilling family obligations, the greater the activation required of the prefrontal brain region to exert cognitive control in follow-up assessments. Furthermore, youth who showed the poorest functioning in this prefrontal region in eighth and ninth grades also showed the greatest increases in problem behavior over the same period. In short, negative stereotype endorsement by adolescents was associated with increased problem behavior and diminished neurobiological self-regulation in the two years following, and these dual outcomes seemed to be associated with each other.

Here is how the researchers interpreted their findings:

> Youth who see the teen years as a time of irresponsibility may not exert the cognitive control involved in acting responsibly – for example, disregarding family obligations may mean that they do not refrain from risky behavior that may be rewarding, but violates parents' expectations. Youth's infrequent exertion of cognitive control may lead to increases in PFC activation in the context of such control over time, as they need to recruit more PFC activation to regulate their impulsive behavior. Such altered neural development of cognitive control may make subsequent responsible behavior ... difficult.[61]

The conclusion that cultural beliefs, behavior, and brain develop hand-in-hand in adolescence is supported by other research as well. In one study, a research team showed that Latin American adolescents who endorsed cultural values of positive family obligations showed different patterns of brain activation to risk-taking and cognitive control tasks compared with those who rejected those values.[62] Those who endorsed these values showed decreased activation of brain regions sensitive to reward during the risk-taking probe, and greater activation of PFC brain regions governing self-regulation in the cognitive control task. Moreover, they also reported less risk-taking in their everyday behavior and greater care in decision-making. Consistent with the familiar portrayal of the developing brain being shaped by experience ("use it or lose it"), therefore, stereotype-conforming conduct may constitute, over time, some of the experiences that support or undermine brain areas relevant to impulsivity and self-control.

The focus of these studies on cultural values and stereotypes is important because these are some of the most important sources of social guidance affecting adolescent behavior, along with the messages of peers. These findings are drawing new attention to the influence of cultural values on the developing brain, and are contributing to the new integrative field of developmental cultural neuroscience.[63] The *contexts* in which the brain develops are important in shaping how the brain functions.

It is no accident, of course, that studies of adolescent neurodevelopment focus on areas of the brain related to reward motivation, self-regulation, and impulse control, since these behaviors have been the focus of negative stereotypes of adolescence in the United States. These behaviors have also been the concern of public policies affecting youth. As media reports of the developing brain increasingly portray many of these problematic behaviors as based in adolescent brain development, they send a message to youth: this is because of your brain, there's nothing you can do about it (you're not responsible). As these expectations are internalized by young people, they may contribute to self-fulfilling prophecies by influencing behavior and, indirectly, the developing brain. As these expectations are internalized by adults, furthermore, they affect how youth are treated in communities and in the justice system, including how youth are viewed by Supreme Court justices.

In this section of the chapter, I have explored some of the interpretive cautions that must be kept in mind when considering how brain and mind are associated. These cautions concern the complexity of neurobiological processes and our early stage of current understanding, the difficulties of establishing brain-mind connections when processes of each are multi-determined, and that brain and mind both incorporate experience and interact continuously in their development. With these considerations in mind, therefore, let's return to the Supreme Court.

Reconsidering Adolescent Responsibility

In the amicus curiae brief submitted by the American Psychological Association in *Roper v. Simmons*, the Justices learned of neuroscientific studies documenting that the adolescent brain has not yet fully matured and that, in particular, the frontal lobes ("'CEO' functions of the brain") have an especially prolonged maturation. This view of adolescent brain development was current at the time the brief was written, and still remains fundamentally correct. But it has been elaborated considerably in the years following to become what is now known as the "dual systems" model of the developing brain in adolescence.

The dual systems model argues that early- to mid-adolescence constitutes a particularly vulnerable period for irresponsible conduct because of the juxtaposition of the maturation of two neurobiological systems.[64] One is called the socioemotional system, consisting of a network of structures located in the limbic and paralimbic areas of the brain, particularly the ventral striatum and nucleus accumbens, whose development is closely tied to puberty and which rapidly matures in early adolescence. This system accounts for an increase in risk-taking and other kinds of sensation- and reward-seeking behaviors during this period, especially when youth are in the company of peers, because of an increase in neurotransmitter activity (specifically, dopamine) that mediates reward. The other system is called the cognitive control system, and this neural network includes structures located in the prefrontal cortex and associated regions (particularly the lateral prefrontal cortex) that account for increasing self-regulation and impulse control. As indicated in the APA brief, this system is much slower to mature, typically showing gradual improvements in functioning throughout adolescence and early adulthood. Consequently, according to this model, there is a period of vulnerability in mid-adolescence during which the socioemotional system has reached a high level of activity before the cognitive control system has matured sufficiently to regulate it.

In the more than ten years since the dual systems model was developed, there has emerged an expanding research literature supporting major elements of the model.[65] The research consists of developmental neuro-imaging studies (using simulations of risk-taking) and behavioral studies, including adolescent self-reports and experimental assessments of sensation seeking, risk-taking, and impulse control. Together, this literature documents increased self-reported sensation seeking and greater reward sensitivity in adolescents compared with adults, and the greater proneness of youth to engage in risky behavior and to be sensitive to rewards especially in emotionally arousing circumstances (such as the presence of peers). This research literature also documents the more limited impulse control of adolescents compared with adults in challenging (but not ordinary) circumstances. Neuroimaging evidence is generally consistent with the expected developmental maturation of these two systems, although, to my knowledge, the interaction of the dual systems with other neurobiological systems has not been examined. The research is also weaker in establishing causal connections between neurobiological changes in adolescence and concurrent behavioral developments, and in showing that these associations generalize beyond the laboratory.[66] Concerning the latter, according to one recent research review, "[B]ecause of differences in opportunity to engage in risky behavior outside the laboratory environment, the effects of maturation of the socioemotional system and cognitive control system on real-world risk-taking are likely to be modest and difficult to detect."[67]

This observation underscores an important and often overlooked feature of the dual-process model: its emphasis on the context in which adolescents exercise judgment. Although the maturational status of the adolescent brain is believed to constitute a risk factor for impulsivity and risk-taking, whether that risk is realized depends substantially on the opportunities afforded in the environment to behave irresponsibly (such as the negative incentives of peers) and the buffers that exist to constrain dangerous conduct (such as parental guidance, peer support, or legal regulations). Consequently, whether any particular young person will behave irresponsibly depends significantly on the environment in which they live. This helps explain why individual differences in adolescent conduct are so considerable, and why cultural differences in adolescent behavior are so great. As one might expect from the preceding section, for example, several studies have documented that Chinese adolescents are less prone to delinquent behavior than are youth in the United States, and, not coincidentally, they also experience greater protections against bad conduct, including supportive cultural values and stereotypes, family practices, and peer encouragement of self-regulated conduct.[68] Notably, virtually all of the studies testing the dual process model have been conducted with youth living in the United States or Western Europe where negative cultural stereotypes of adolescent impulsive risk-taking are prevalent, by contrast with the more positive stereotypes of China and other Asian countries.[69] One wonders if different results might ensue from research conducted in Asia.

In most discussions of adolescent impulsivity and risky conduct, including the *Roper* brief, the neurobiological changes in these two systems are described as accounting for genuinely distressing demographic trends concerning reckless behavior in adolescence. These include increases in unsafe sexual activity (including sexually transmitted diseases), drug abuse, dangerous driving, suicides, homicides, criminality (including violent criminal conduct), delinquency and conduct problems, and a general increase in mortality for preventable causes.[70] The authors of the *Roper* brief summarize: "Adolescents, as a group, are overrepresented in virtually every category of reckless behavior."[71] The relevance of this portrayal to Christopher Simmons and other adolescent defendants in capital punishment cases is self-evident. But this portrayal of dangerous behavior in adolescents extends beyond these specific defendants because it is presented as documentation of the implications of brain development for the behavior of *all* adolescents. How representative of the typical adolescent are these statistics of reckless conduct?

Consistently, research indicates that only a small proportion of deeply troubled adolescents account for a large proportion of serious, chronic forms of reckless behavior.[72] Statistics concerning drug abuse, criminality and delinquency, and other dangerous conduct do not describe the large majority of adolescents, but rather a small group of genuinely troubled youth with multiple problems. For this small minority, serious problems are often rooted in the contexts of their lives, such as enduring family difficulties, child abuse, affective psychopathology, and peer deviancy. The environmental context in which they are living is, in short, full of difficulty, and there is evidence that these youth are also neurobiologically atypical.[73] Quite often, their reckless behavior begins much earlier in childhood, well before imbalanced adolescent brain maturation has occurred. They are further distinguished by the longstanding childhood foundations of their chronic problems as well as the greater severity and persistence of their recklessness. Indeed, the serious, early emerging and enduring difficulties of these multi-problem youth are distinguished even from others who begin showing behavioral problems during adolescence, and who subsequently remit in early adulthood.[74] Taken together, the behavioral profile that characterizes chronic, serious reckless behavior in adolescence fits Christopher Simmons, but it is not a good profile of most youth. As summarized by an authority on adolescent development:

> We should not gloss over the fact that many healthy adolescents at one time or another experience self-doubt, family squabbles, academic setbacks, or broken hearts. But it is important to keep in mind as we look at psychosocial problems during adolescence that there is an important distinction between the normative, and usually transitory, difficulties encountered by many young people and the serious psychosocial problems experienced by a minority of youth.... [P]roblem behavior during adolescence is virtually never a direct consequence of the normative changes of adolescence itself.[75]

Adolescence is not an easy stage of development. Even if they do not engage in serious forms of delinquency, most young people experience stressors of various kinds, and the risk of depression increases during the teenage years.[76] But we may not require an account of neurobiological immaturity to explain why. Adolescence is novice adulthood, and youth's inexperience with many new aspects of life that will eventually become part of the ordinary tapestry of adulthood almost ensures that mistakes and errors in judgment will occur, whether in learning to drive, relationships with romantic partners, or gaining experience with independent decision-making. Added to this are the compounding changes that occur over a relatively short time in physical growth, sexual maturation, cognitive skills, self-awareness, and social expectations, multiple and overlapping transitions that any adult would find difficult to manage.[77] And adolescents are novice decision makers before they have acquired experience with risk estimation and the prediction of unknown consequences that, in later years, will help to make their adult judgments more balanced (and cautious).[78] These are the reasons why growing up in an environment that confers guidance and support is important, along with experience in making independent decisions. These considerations also help to account for the wide range of individual differences in adolescent competence and responsibility.

If the ability of youth to navigate adolescence successfully relies so significantly on the social support they receive (or has been denied them), then why is an account of the brain maturation of *all* adolescents necessary to account for the extreme deviancy of a small minority of teenagers? Should we not focus instead on the contexts that render some adolescents more vulnerable to irresponsible risk-taking than most? I asked these questions of Laurence Steinberg, the authority quoted above (from his best-selling *Adolescence* textbook) and one of the authors of APA's *Roper* amicus brief. I had invited him to present his work at a departmental colloquium at my university, and as we walked to dinner afterward, I asked him about the dual systems model and the behavior of typical adolescents. He replied that most teenagers engage in minor misbehavior as they are growing up; the examples he offered were incidental shoplifting and drinking from the parents' liquor cabinet. He acknowledged that these and other kinds of risky conduct rarely escalate to the level of serious problems. Drinking alcohol occasionally at home does not typically become a drinking problem that impairs schooling and relationships, and stealing small items at a store rarely escalates into serious criminality. But they reflect, he said, the same neurobiological vulnerability to sensation seeking with poor regulation by cognitive controls that also accounts for the more serious and chronic criminality of a Christopher Simmons. In his view, the maturational brain-based account generalizes well to the typical teenager, as it does to Simmons and other criminal defendants.

When I looked again at the research on the dual systems model, I realized that Steinberg was correct. At least partially. Recall that these studies usually include behavioral measures of impulsivity and sensation seeking to document the behavioral characteristics associated with adolescent neurodevelopment. Although they are called measures of sensation seeking and impulsivity, however, the behavioral measures used in these studies more closely resemble the benign offenses of the typical adolescent than they do the extremities of risk-taking to which this research is often generalized. In these studies, for example, sensation seeking and impulsivity are often assessed through self-report. For instance, when youth endorse items such as "I'll try anything once" and "I tend to begin a new project without much planning on how I will do it," they are deemed high on sensation seeking and impulsivity. Researchers also use simulated game-type scenarios involving imaginary driving and gambling situations with no tangible benefits or costs for the adolescent player.[79] For ethical reasons, of course, laboratory studies must use rather benign simulations of risk-taking, especially in studies with minors. But because of this, the generalizability of these results to more extreme adolescent criminality and deviancy is certainly open to question. Based on this research, in other words, the dual-systems model denotes an association between adolescent brain maturation and the ordinary, somewhat benign hallmarks of adolescent immaturity, not the dangerous, reckless conduct of the delinquent. A brain-based explanation of adolescent responsibility falls short when the terms "risk-taking" and "impulsivity" cover such a broad range of ordinary and serious behaviors (and the discussion of reverse inference shows how this leads to misleading conclusions).

Stated differently, if the only thing in common between Christopher Simmons and a typical teenager in the United States (or China) is an adolescent brain, then this might not be the right place to look in determining the foundations of criminal conduct or determining culpability for wrongdoing. That certainly follows from the discussion of naive dualism: if an alleged cause (brain maturation in mid-adolescence) is only weakly associated with behavior (in this case, criminal conduct) in adolescence, it is probably not very responsible for the behavior. Instead, why not look at the *contexts* that distinguish a typical teenager from a defendant for capital murder? In the case of Christopher Simmons, this included long-standing family adversity, parental dysfunction, child abuse, and affective psychopathology.[80] This is the context that, according to the dual systems model, can elevate the relatively benign risks of neurobiological immaturity to the level of capital crime.

Although the APA brief argued that individualized determinations of criminal culpability are impossible because adolescents are "moving targets" for such assessments – a view subsequently adopted by the majority opinion – this is clearly mistaken. Courts are very familiar with conducting individualized determinations in cases ranging from criminal culpability (including those in juvenile justice) to mental health competency to child custody determinations. In these evaluations, they take into account the characteristics of the individual, how they have changed over time, and the contexts in which they live and have grown up. The individualized conditions that shaped Christopher Simmons are a far more compelling explanation of his criminal conduct, and culpability, than characteristics of his developing brain.

In the end, it is difficult to escape the conclusion that the account of adolescent neurobiological maturational vulnerability is oversold – to the Supreme Court as well as to the public – when it is framed by risk statistics documenting criminality, drug abuse, suicides, and other serious problems that occur for only a small proportion of adolescents. The misdemeanors of youthful immaturity that this account explains are comparable to those of adults for which we neither seek nor need a brain-based explanation. In adults, these include taking office supplies home from work, driving after having had several drinks at a party, underreporting income to the IRS, driving over the speed limit – the list could go on.

Worse, perpetuating cultural stereotypes of adolescent dysfunction and danger through this interpretation of neuroscience can do great harm. This is because one reason the dual systems account is so readily understood and accepted by Justices and other audiences is the same reason that irresponsibility, impulsivity, and reckless behavior are viewed as typical characteristics of adolescence: each accords well with prevalent negative adolescent stereotypes in the United States. The view that these characteristics derive from incomplete brain maturation also accords with a history of biologically based explanations for negative adolescent behavior, whether attributed to the upsurge of sexual and aggressive drives, the hormonal effects of puberty, adjustment to rapid physical growth, or other causes. But as the research with adolescents in China shows, these negative stereotypes of teenagers are not universal, and negative stereotypes can have their own powerful effects on the behavior of teenagers, providing justification for them to act consistently with behavior they believe is expected or allowed – or even unavoidable – given what they are told about their developing brains. And as I have reported, several studies show that negative adolescent stereotypes can potentially influence neurobiological development as they shape the conduct that can affect brain development.

The enduring influence of these stereotypes on public perceptions of teenagers as well as the views of psychologists, neurobiologists, and Supreme Court Justices are problematic because the stereotypes are mostly wrong: the risk-taking of a typical adolescent (like a typical adult) is far more benign than stereotypically portrayed. Furthermore, many, perhaps most teenagers (in the United States as in China) are unfairly portrayed by these stereotypes because they are striving to do as well as they can in school and life, balancing academics with sports, work, or other activities, and planning for the future. This is why teenagers themselves object to how their behavior is characterized by these neurobiological portrayals of diminished self-regulation. They believe that these portrayals fail to account for all the ways that they are constructively managing their lives and activities to support their current and future goals.[81] The inaccuracy of these negative stereotypes might also explain why the parents of adolescent sons and daughters have more positive regard for their own children than for adolescents in general, because parents are applying to "those teenagers" in the broader world the negative stereotypes that they know do not fit their own sons or daughters.[82] But these stereotypes, as misleading as they are, can become self-fulfilling prophecies if they are believed by youth – who may conform to these expectations and in so doing influence their own neurobiological maturation – and as they are believed by school administrators, juvenile authorities, public policymakers, and Supreme Court Justices.

The American Psychological Association's arguments in *Roper*, and before that in *Hodgson*, described the characteristics of adolescents as a group rather than focusing on the individual context relevant to teenage behavior. The decision to treat adolescents as a class rather than as individuals in context may have derived from an effort to develop arguments that would maximally benefit youth in each case, either through empowerment (in *Hodgson*) or through protection (in *Roper*). It is not difficult to understand, and even sympathize, with the desire to protect youthful offenders with a broad-brush account that attributes their conduct not to their bad choices, but to their developing brain. Recall the research study described earlier in which participants read short stories describing a person's harmful conduct that was attributable either to biological causes in the brain or to early experiences (such as child abuse).[83] Biological causes led to judgments that the person was less culpable and their behavior was more "automatic" than did causes owing to background experiences.[84] Portraying adolescent misconduct as attributable to brain immaturity is a surer course to judgments of diminished culpability and responsibility than blaming misconduct on early experiences or a bad environment (such as poor parenting). Isn't that a good thing?

Not really. The problem in doing so is that public policy is a double-edged sword: attributing misconduct to a fixed cause like brain development also reduces confidence in deterring or preventing bad behavior and increases reliance on social control. A view of adolescent decision-making that is used to support policies to protect them from the consequences of bad choices can also justify restrictively paternalistic practices that leave them inexperienced and poorly prepared to make good choices on their own when they reach adulthood.[85] This view of adolescence also justifies coercive practices to restrict their decision-making in health care, juvenile justice, privacy, freedom of expression, voting, and other areas. When neuroscience research becomes enlisted into broad policies of this kind, the downstream consequences of such policies are seldom anticipated, and are often not good.

The *Roper* opinion was wrongly decided because it was based on a limited portrayal of adolescent brain and behavioral development erroneously applied to all adolescents, while it ignored the powerful role of context in brain and behavioral growth. It illustrates the challenges in communicating developmental science to the public and policymakers in an accurate and balanced manner that acknowledges what science has established and also what is unknown, that takes into account prevalent frames of understanding (such as stereotypes) that can influence how people interpret the science, and that resists infiltrating policy preferences into the scientific messaging. Communicating developmental science also requires recognizing the powerful role of neuroessentialist thinking in how people understand the developing brain and its influence on the mind and behavior, sometimes in misleading ways. These are themes that constitute a continuing through line for this book.

The *Roper* decision has had extended implications. Five years after Roper, the Supreme Court ruled in *Graham v. Florida*[86] that minors could not be sentenced to a life term without the possibility of parole for crimes short of murder, with some in the majority reasoning on the basis of the diminished culpability of juvenile defendants owing to brain immaturity. Two years later, in *Miller v. Alabama*,[87] it extended the prohibition on life without parole to capital crimes, reasoning again that minors are constitutionally different in these ways from adults for sentencing purposes. In 2016, the Court ruled in *Montgomery v. Louisiana*[88] that the prohibition on juvenile incarceration without the possibility of parole extended retroactively (a decision partially reversed in *Jones v. Mississippi*[89]). There has also been state legislative activity, including revised sentencing guidelines in capital crimes and sexual assault cases (including retroactive sentencing for individuals convicted of crimes committed while they were minors), revised definitions of juvenile competency, "graduated licensing" laws for driving privileges, and other provisions designed to restrict the decision-making autonomy of adolescents.[90] There are good reasons for establishing age thresholds for driving, drinking, voting, and other privileges of adulthood, just as there are good reasons for creating age cutoffs for sentencing options. But the reasons for these thresholds and cutoffs are important because of the social messages they convey, and developmental neuroscience is not currently capable of providing useful guidance on these issues.

Ironically, these extensions of the legal model of adolescent irresponsibility and impulsivity have occurred at the same time that psychological models of adolescent development are evolving in a more positive direction. The Positive Youth Development (PYD) model portrays adolescence as a period of growth and opportunity that most youth navigate successfully to achieve important developmental milestones and build mental health, competence, and character.[91] From this strengths-based perspective, although risks to healthy development exist and a minority of youth experience serious and chronic psychosocial problems, the large majority of adolescents make their way successfully through this developmental stage as they achieve the skills necessary to move into adulthood, and the orientation of research in this field is to identify the supports (in relationships and institutions) that make this happen. The literature on PYD does not draw on the developmental neuroscience of adolescence in a manner comparable to approaches emphasizing risk-oriented models of youth development, even though expanding research on adolescent brain development and the experience-based plasticity of the brain during this period provides scientific support for the PYD approach (a point that I explore further in Chapter 3). It perhaps goes without saying that the PYD model is also contrary to prevalent adolescent stereotypes, at least in the United States.

Developing Brains and Minds

The theme of this chapter is the connection between brain and mind.[92] This connection helps to account for why developmental neuroscience is such a compelling influence on our thinking about children because of the "visual proof" of the brain's influence as it is revealed in neuroimaging. The neuroessentialist belief that behavior and development are founded on the developing brain contributes to the perceived power of neuroscience as a way of understanding children's growth. But a deeper examination of neuroscience research shows how challenging it is to establish causal connections between specific brain networks and mental processes, illustrated by an inquiry into a series of Supreme Court decisions highlighting the potential for misleading connections between brain and behavior when the research is not carefully interpreted and understood. One of the lessons of this journey into Supreme Court jurisprudence is that the story of brain development does not begin and end with neuroimaging. Without thoughtful applications to behavior, due consideration of the multiple influences on behavior, and examination of the context in which brain and behavior both develop, mistaken applications of developmental brain science are almost inevitable. It is thus essential for those who are paying attention to the story of brain development, and those who are communicating that story, to be careful in how they interpret it.

Even so, when we reflect on the achievements of developmental neuroscience during the past two decades, there is every reason for confidence in its future applications to children's behavior and mental processes. Even though the hopeful, but naive, expectations of neuroessentialism are not well supported by current work, the story of the next several decades will continue to change our expectations for how brain processes are associated with the mind, enhance our appreciation for how experience influences each simultaneously, and provoke greater respect for the reciprocal relations between brain, mind, and context.

This chapter also illustrates the intersection of developmental neuroscience, how it is communicated and interpreted, and public policy – and the challenging connections between them. As the Supreme Court case and its wider implications illustrate, even when developmental neuroscience is applicable to public policy concerns, the way it is interpreted and applied can contribute to misleading policies. As we have seen, there are many influences that affect how developmental brain science is construed, some of them deeply connected to cultural values (including values about brain functioning as determinant of the mind, about mind-body dualism, and about adolescence) that make it difficult to approach neuroscience in a balanced manner.[93] I consider these themes further in the chapters that follow.

In Chapter 3, I explore further the connections between brain and mind by telling two stories of brain development: one from the perspective of neurons, synapses, and neural networks, and the other from the perspective of concepts and reasoning skills. Both accounts offer a viewpoint on how the brain develops, so it is not surprising to find that they are highly complementary, as we should expect. In comparing them, however, I also show how they offer somewhat different perspectives on development because of differences in levels of analysis, research methods, vocabulary, and concepts. Finally, I turn to some of the lesser-known or overlooked aspects of the brain development story to begin considering why the public messaging of early brain development included certain scientific stories but left others out.

CHAPTER 3

Dispatches from the Laboratory

What is the story of brain development?

Since the brain development revolution, public attention has been focused on the exciting discoveries of developmental neuroscience. This is the story of multiplying neurons and neural connections, the complex "wiring" of the brain that underlies sophisticated thought and action, and the "use it or lose it" influence of early experience. It is also the story of the technology underlying these discoveries that permits detailed and time-sensitive imaging of the brain's activity as it occurs. It is a provocative and compelling account.

But if the mind is what the brain does – and the brain is what the mind does over time – then there is another story of brain development that should complement this one. This is the story of developing concepts, language, memory, self-regulation, and social understanding that reveal the mind's growing capacities with increasing age. All of this takes place in the brain. It is also the story of the startling findings that emerge from the clever experiments designed by researchers to uncover what infants and young children know and think. These are the exciting discoveries of developmental science that predate the brain development revolution and continue to this day. This is also a provocative and compelling account. And it offers insight into the developing brain not just because the brain is where these psychological accomplishments occur, but also because these accomplishments influence – and are influenced by – the changes occurring in neural networks. Together, the integrated development of mind and brain help to explain why, by the time children are ready for kindergarten, they more closely resemble the adults they are to become than the newborns they were such a short time ago.

In this chapter, I briefly outline these two stories of brain development because each tells the brain development story. Then I compare them. Not surprisingly, the findings of developmental neuroscience and developmental science are strikingly complementary and mutually informative, sometimes in really interesting ways (do you wonder why babies are so distractable? Keep reading). This complementarity is exactly what we should expect, and it underscores how much confidence we can have in this developmental story when it is revealed in both brain and behavior. But comparing these two stories also reveals some of the differences in the accounts of the developing brain and mind that arise from differences in levels of analysis, assumptions about how development occurs, and even the kinds of questions that scientists ask. For these reasons, the task of integrating brain and mind is more complex than we often expect. In a final section, I outline less well-known discoveries of developmental brain science to show that the story of brain development is incomplete and continuously changing. This can present challenges to the communication of this story to an interested public.

The Brain Development Story: Neurons, Networks, and Experience

Let me tell you the story of brain development.[1]

The brain is the most complex biological system of the human body, by far. It consists of billions of nerve cells of different cell types that are interlinked by trillions of connections, organized into distinct neural circuits and located in regions that differ structurally and functionally. Consequently, brain development is a prolonged process, beginning in the first two to three weeks after conception and lasting through the life course. This extended maturation derives from the complexity of neurobiological growth, of course, but also from its continuous incorporation of experience. The brain's development is shaped throughout life both by genetic guidance and by experience – the classic nature-nurture dynamic. The brain also develops rapidly, especially early in life. Whereas a newborn's brain is already 26% of its adult weight, by age five, the brain has reached 88% of its adult weight.[2] The latter figure helps to account for the well-known claim that the brain is 90% developed by the age of five.

Brain weight is not a very informative index of its maturation (after all, men's brains are 10% heavier than women's). More important is what is going on *within* the brain. These processes are summarized in Figure 3.1 (a much better depiction than the one in the preceding chapter).

The neural architecture of the brain develops early and rapidly. Early in prenatal development, new neurons (nerve cells) and other supportive cells are generated at an astonishing rate – by some estimates, several hundred thousand *each minute*[3] – and then migrate to their eventual destinations in the fetal brain. Throughout this process, neurons develop further through

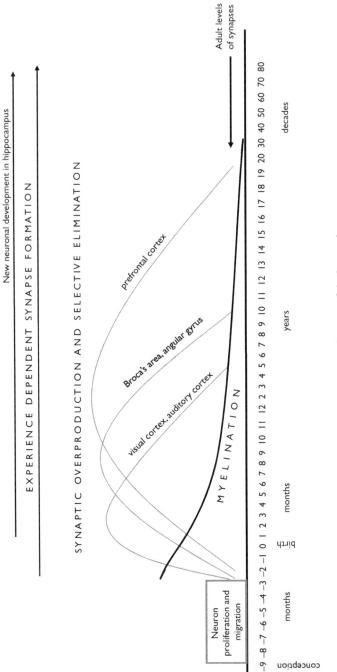

Figure 3.1   Developmental course of the human brain.

gene expression within the cell and the influence of adjacent neurons. By the twenty-third week of gestation, synapses (junctions between neurons permitting the transmission of activation, or neural communication) begin to proliferate as the structural organization of the brain begins to form. Before birth, the vast majority of neurons that populate the brain have been created.

At the beginning of the brain development revolution, there was scientific consensus that *all* of the neurons that populate the brain develop prenatally. None are added after birth, and neurons that were lost (such as through disease or damage) could not be replaced. But as this brain development account was becoming well known, researchers in Sweden and California discovered that new neurons also develop later in life, including in adulthood.[4] Furthermore, one of the locations where adult neurons develop – the hippocampus – is significant for new learning and memory.[5] Subsequent discoveries have shown that the formation of new neurons in the hippocampus in adulthood is enhanced by physical exercise[6] but impaired when individuals are chronically stressed,[7] indicating how important experience is to neurobiological growth not only early but also later in life. These findings constitute a major advance in understanding brain development because of their implications for adult cognitive function and other capacities (including disease management).[8] It also illustrates that the story of brain development is being continuously updated through new discoveries that alter our appreciation of the importance of early and later experiences.

An important characteristic of early brain development is the overproduction of synapses and their selective elimination (or "pruning") based, among other things, on how frequently they are activated over time. This process is fundamental to brain development and to the refinement of the brain based on individual experience. Neurons exuberantly and excessively create connections with other neurons early in brain development, and it is estimated that up to 40% more synapses are produced early in life than will be retained in the mature brain.[9] This exuberant proliferation of synapses is primarily under genetic control. Consequently, the young brain is a more active and densely packed organ than it will be at maturity.[10] Overproduction of synapses is a good thing because it affords considerable potential for growth as these synapses can become enlisted into the neural architecture of skill development, such as learning multiple languages. But overproduction has liabilities, including a poorer signal-to-noise ratio in neural transmission (i.e., lots of incoming transmissions reaching neurons when only a subset may be functional), and some forms of mental disability are associated with an atypical proliferation of synaptic connections.[11] Therefore, an important step in brain development is the selective reduction and elimination of synapses, partly through the influence of experience, to increase the efficiency of neural processing.

The following is one way of thinking about this process. On the first day of summer camp (or freshman orientation), some kids quickly make contact with lot of other kids – they are a whirlwind of sociability. They don't expect to develop close relationships with all of them, but the potential is there for these connections to deepen with some people in the days that follow. These kids eventually have a pretty good social network before long. They are usually more successful than the kid who slowly develops relationships, one at a time, as opportunity allows. The brain has the strategy of the socializer: it becomes a whirlwind of neural connectivity in order for the child to develop essential capabilities as rapidly as possible. It is one reason the young brain develops new knowledge and skills so quickly.

Experience influences this process by strengthening neural connections that have formed when they are activated. When the brain responds to stimulation (such as overhearing spoken French at home), it activates synaptic networks, and those networks become strengthened in the process. By contrast, synapses that are never or only rarely activated wither and eventually disappear. Thus early experiences are a significant influence on the retention of synapses in the developing brain, and this is the basis for the well-known maxim "use it or lose it."[12] The result is a brain that is adapted to the world in which the child is developing: becoming a French speaker in Paris, for example, even though the potential for learning Russian becomes lost because the child never overhears spoken Russian. This also illustrates the profound adaptability, or *plasticity*, of the developing brain, which we consider further below.

There are at least two less understood elements to the "use it or lose it" maxim. The first is that retaining lots of synapses by enhancing the range of early experience is not helpful and may be harmful, especially if the young child becomes overstimulated by the effort. Rather, strengthening the synapses that are most functional to the child's everyday experience is important. There is not much value in ensuring that a baby is exposed to the sounds of as many languages as possible to preserve the potential to learn these languages if they will not be acquired later. Rather, frequent opportunities to hear French in the context of social interaction with

Parisian parents best promotes language growth. The second is that the brain is nondiscriminating in the kinds of experiences contributing to the refinement of neural connections. Experiences of abuse or threat can be as influential as language exposure in shaping the neural connections that are retained, and each kind of experience can become biologically embedded in the developing brain. Likewise, deprivation of important stimulants (such as nurturant care) can also significantly influence the developing brain through the loss of experiences that would otherwise strengthen important neural networks.

Because the overproduction and subsequent pruning of synapses is one of the major avenues by which brain development occurs, it is significant that the timing and pace of this process vary for different brain regions, which has consequences for the developing brain and behavior (look again at Figure 3.1 that opens this section).[13] Synapse production is fairly rapid prenatally, for example, in the primary auditory cortex and in the visual cortex of the brain during the first three to four postnatal months. The rapid pace of early synaptic production is followed by the selective elimination of synapses in these regions in early childhood. By contrast, synaptic production continues longer in brain regions related to language (e.g., Broca's area, angular gyrus), reaching a peak later in the first year before progressively declining and reaching adult levels in later childhood. By contrast, the peak of synaptic production is between three and four years of age for brain regions related to self-regulation (e.g., prefrontal cortex), which do not reach adult levels until early adulthood. These timetables roughly accord with changes in behavior: children develop early acuity in vision and hearing, while language development has its most rapid growth after the end of the first year (just before the "vocabulary explosion" of toddlerhood). Self-regulation, however, is a slower and more extended achievement for children and adolescents, despite the fervent hopes of their parents.

This timeline for synaptic connections is paralleled by advances in another major aspect of brain development: myelination. Myelin is a fatty protein sheath covering neurons that provides insulation and speeds the conduction of neural activation (in some areas of the brain, over 100-fold).[14] Whereas synaptic overproduction and pruning refine the brain's neural networks, myelination contributes speed and efficiency to them. Myelination of neurons occurs sparsely before birth but increases significantly postnatally, and the timetable for myelination is similar to the one described for synapse development, with earlier advances in sensory regions and much later development in brain regions governing complex information processing and self-regulation. Although neural transmission can occur in unmyelinated neurons, the efficiency of myelinated neural networks is significantly greater.

This description of these advances in early brain development refers to "sensory regions" and "brain regions governing self-regulation." It is important to recognize, however, that from the beginning each region is networked to other neural systems, often widely distributed throughout the brain, that also contribute to these capacities. This was noted in the preceding chapter, and the example of emotion is instructive. As we saw in that chapter, although it is common to describe brain regions like the amygdala as the locus of fear responding, each emotional response enlists and integrates brain processes associated with a variety of emotion-related functions, including sensory evaluation, cognitive appraisal, short- and long-term memory, self-regulation, and other processes. This networked integration of widely distributed neural areas relevant to emotion is typical rather than unusual in describing the brain's processing. This helps explain why locationist accounts of the brain's functioning (e.g., the amygdala is where fear responding occurs; the hippocampus is where memory occurs) have become supplanted by accounts describing more complex, extended neural networks for these functions.

Neural networks are especially necessary when trying to model brain processes associated with complex psychological functions (such as self-regulation), although neural networks also characterize simpler and more basic behavior (such as emotion). These networks develop initially through synaptic connections between neurons in anatomically nearby regions, but eventually extend to neurons in more distant brain regions, based on factors such as the codevelopmental timing of these neural areas, coactivation in response to experience, and genetic and chemical guidance.[15] (As the adage goes, "neurons that fire together, wire together.") In this respect, in addition to the roles of genetics and experience, brain development is also self-organizing. Over time, as neurons assume increasingly specialized functions within the regions to which they have migrated and in the networks to which they are connected, their specialized functions become increasingly fine-tuned and consolidated as the mature brain takes shape. In other words, neurons and neural networks become increasingly *committed* to certain specialized processes. This is one of the reasons why the flexibility, or *plasticity*, of the brain slowly diminishes with time. For mature neural networks as for old dogs, it becomes more difficult to learn new tricks.

Brain Plasticity – And Maturational Constraints

Even so, one of the remarkable discoveries of developmental brain science is how long plasticity endures, and its significance for development and behavior. Early plasticity has been demonstrated in experimental studies showing that transplanted brain tissue can assume over time the functions of the region to which it was transplanted, rather than its origin. Plasticity has also been demonstrated therapeutically when clinicians "retrain" brain areas contributing to behavioral problems, such as squinting in the case of strabismus amblyopia (or "lazy eye"). This condition causes very young children to prefer looking through one eye rather than using both. It can lead to impaired or permanent vision loss by weakening the neural pathways leading from the nonpreferred eye. A widely used therapeutic approach is to temporarily patch the preferred (nonsquinting) eye, forcing the child to look through the nonpreferred eye, and in that manner retraining and strengthening the relevant neural pathways between that eye and the visual cortex.

Brain plasticity is most profoundly apparent, however, in the everyday impact of environmental experience on brain development. It is the brain's plasticity, in other words, that enables the developing brain to flexibly learn and adapt to the environment into which children have been born and in which they live (remember "use it or lose it"?). Developmental neuroscientists have been particularly interested in two kinds of environmental influence.

The first, *experience-expectant development*, is when normal brain development depends on exposure to specific environmental events at particular times in order to organize neurobiological pathways. Without these exposures, the brain will not develop normally. Experience-expectant development is necessary because our genetic "blueprint" cannot possibly specify the trillions of synaptic connections that must develop in the mature brain, and consequently the genetic program incorporates ("expects") these experiences in the developmental process by which these connections form. Experience-expectant development displays the brain's plasticity as the brain's growth depends on specific environmental stimulants.

These expected experiences are ubiquitous early in development (indeed, throughout life) and include exposure to patterned light, gravity, the sound of human voices and language, touch on skin surfaces, and social contact.[16] Although these are universal experiences in everyday life (indeed, an environment without these experiences wouldn't really be considered a human environment), these exposures must occur when relevant neurobiological systems are maturing. Their failure to occur, or to occur at the right time, can result in the substantial or permanent loss of relevant brain capacities. Consequently, experience-expectant development is often viewed in terms of critical periods (or sensitive periods, known informally as "windows of opportunity") of environmental exposure. In short, experiences for which brain development is expectant are exposures that are essential for certain neural connections to occur, without which brain development will not proceed normally.

Some of the most compelling evidence for experience-expectant development comes, sadly, from studies of early deprivation. When the thirteen-year-old girl named Genie[17] was rescued by the Los Angeles County child welfare authorities in 1970, the psychologists assisting in her care realized that her extraordinary deprivation and neglect had, among other harms, deprived her of exposure to language.[18] To what extent, they asked, would she be able to catch up in language ability, having missed the ordinary developmental period during which language emerges for typical children? In the years of therapeutic care that followed, Genie's vocabulary growth surpassed the researchers' expectations, but she never acquired mastery of basic grammar and language pragmatics. This is consistent with other studies pointing to a critical period for language acquisition that begins in early childhood but closes by the end of the first decade, well before Genie's rescue. In her case, language deprivation was made worse by her profound cognitive and social neglect: she had been deprived not only of language but also of any opportunity for social interaction and communication.

The second kind of experience affecting brain development is called *experience-dependent development.* This consists of environmental events of any kind that have an influence on the brain's growth. These experiences are often unique to the individual (rather than universal); their influence can occur at any age (not just during an early sensitive period); and they contribute to the development of new synapses or modify existing synaptic connections in the brain. Any kind of new learning or skill acquisition constitutes experience-dependent development. Experience-dependent development is shown in the effects on the brain of living in an enriching environment or in an impoverished one, or of regular experiences of nurturant care or of stress. Experience-expectant development constitutes lifelong brain plasticity and helps to account for the increasingly individualized character of brain growth as the years proceed.

Experience-expectant development and experience-dependent development illustrate the complex and diverse effects of experience on lifelong brain development. They also show how the impact of experience depends on the relative maturation of the brain and characteristics of the individual that determine how they respond. The same event, whether it consists of seeing a text, hearing a warm greeting, or seeing birds fly across the sky, is experienced differently by the brain based on its prior experiences and its stage of development.

Most important, experience-expectant development and experience-dependent development show how the lifelong growth of the brain reflects a dynamic tension between its changing plasticity and its growing constraints. As we have seen, early brain growth is oriented to incorporating experience into its neural networks – experience consequently becomes biologically embedded – as it adapts to the opportunities and requirements of the world into which the child has been born. This profound developmental plasticity is one reason the brain is such a powerful learning organ, and it helps to account for the astonishingly early and rapid mental advances that are described in the next section. Over time, however, as neurons assume increasingly fine-tuned functions within maturing networks and specialized regions, they become increasingly committed to modes of functioning that have developed as the result of accumulated experience, genetic guidance, and the changing capacities of the brain itself. Simply stated, brain maturity constrains its plasticity. This helps to explain why it takes longer, and requires greater effort, to "rewire" a mature brain with new skills or changed habits. As the adage goes, you can't teach an old dog new tricks – but, as it turns out, this isn't really true. Despite the constraints of maturity, the adult brain retains some of its plasticity, helping to account for its continued adaptability and modifiability (and the ability to learn new tricks). A new language can be learned in adulthood, although not with the ease that the first was acquired, and it will always be spoken with an accent. A new job inspires the growth of new skills for an older person, although it might take longer to achieve mastery compared with younger workers. The ability of individuals to adapt to the changing requirements of life, and to do so with flexibility and the lessons of experience, reflects the continuing dynamic between the constraints that arise from maturing neural networks and the plasticity that endures. It is how we learn new tricks, even as adults.

Memory, Language, Self-Regulation

Extending this developmental story, researchers have learned a great deal about neurobiological growth underlying developmental achievements in particular domains. Their discoveries take us closer to bridging brain and behavioral development, and illustrate some of the features of developmental neuroscience discussed here. This is an exciting and expansive research literature, far exceeding my capacity to document it here.[19] Instead, three brief examples of these discoveries follow:

- As is true of many domains of developmental neuroscience, research on the development of memory in children is built on research on the neuroscience of adult memory. Because it is difficult to do neuroimaging of young children, this is a good place to start, but not necessarily an infallible one: early competencies in memory may have a different neurobiological basis than do mature competencies, and young children (and their brains) may interpret memory tasks differently from adults. What is clear in both developmental and adult cognitive neuroscience, however, is that the task of remembering is not a singular ability, but rather a variety of skills with different neurobiological foundations, often integrating higher (and evolutionarily newer) with lower (evolutionarily older) regions that are widely dispersed throughout the brain.

To illustrate, one-month-old infants show recognition memory: they discriminate between an object they have previously seen and a novel one, and they prefer looking at novelty. Based on studies with adults and with young rhesus monkeys, researchers think that this reflects functioning of the hippocampus, an important contributor to memory formation, as well as lower brain structures in the subcortex. Later in the first year, however, infants exhibit dramatic improvements in recognition memory, including the ability to sustain memory over longer periods. This suggests that the neurobiological network for recognition memory has expanded, likely integrating developmental growth in the hippocampus with higher brain structures in the cerebral cortex, especially the prefrontal cortex, that are also involved in adult forms of recognition memory.[20] Later maturation of other cortical brain regions and their interconnections contribute to subsequent improvements in recognition memory and other forms of *explicit* (i.e., consciously experienced) memory, such as autobiographical memory and recall of general knowledge.

By contrast with these forms of conscious memory, *implicit* (i.e., nonconscious) memory is also apparent in the early months, such as when infants respond in ways that have been rewarded in the past or anticipate sequences of familiar events.[21] Implicit memory is the kind of memory that people access without having to try, such as an experienced bicyclist knowing nonconsciously how to ride a bike. Researchers believe that implicit memory is based on a different network of lower brain structures (such as the cerebellum), and there is little evidence that this kind of learning develops appreciably in the years that follow or that its neurobiology changes significantly. In short, the development of memory is based on several different neurobiological systems with different maturational timetables manifested in the emergence of distinct kinds of memory capacities with increasing age. In some cases, development occurs hierarchically (integrating lower with higher brain structures), resulting in cumulative advances in memory function. We have a single concept ("memory") but it encompasses diverse neurobiological processes.

- A newborn's brain is already prepared to learn language, as revealed by studies showing relatively greater activation to the sound of speech in the left hemisphere (where language processing occurs in adults) than the right. By age two to three months the neurobiological response has matured, with the left temporal lobe and other specific language-related regions showing increased activation to speech in a manner similar to adult speech processing. But experience is also influential in the development of this network. One research group found, for example, that seven-month-olds showed activation when hearing speech sounds from both the language they heard at home and a foreign language. But between seven and eleven months there was an increase in response to the home language only, and by eleven months infants showed neural activation only to sounds of the home language.[22] In other words, the brain had become neurobiologically more committed to speech processing in the language the child was overhearing at home, and was beginning to learn.

This perceptual narrowing reflects the reorganization of language-related brain networks in the first year. This reorganization sets the stage for the monumental expansion of language ability in the months that follow, including the "vocabulary explosion" beginning at eighteen months, when toddlers acquire several new words daily (and parents must be careful what they say in the child's presence). The rapid growth of vocabulary, in turn, has further effects of fine-tuning neurobiological networks specialized for language.[23] Language development, in short, combines a newborn brain that is biologically prepared for human language with the powerful influence of experience-expectant learning to yield very rapid language acquisition in the early years.

- The brain is self-regulating, and the neurobiological development of self-regulation is important because it is relevant to many cognitive and social skills. Self-regulation is also complex and involves many components: planning and carrying out actions, maintaining information in mind in order to act on it, inhibiting responses that may not be useful, focusing attention, and other capacities.[24] The prefrontal cortex (PFC), which accounts for almost one third of the total cortical surface in the human brain, has a major role in the development of self-regulation. But different early-maturing areas of the prefrontal cortex underlie different aspects of behavioral self-regulation.

Early maturation of the dorsolateral PFC, for example, supports a one-year-old's ability to accurately retrieve, after a short delay, an object they had watched being hidden, even if the object's location is different from where it was previously retrieved.[25] This is not just a memory task, because the information held in mind must also guide successful retrieval after the delay, and neuroimaging studies with older children and adults implicate the dorsolateral PFC in self-regulated behavior of this kind. Successful performance also requires a second self-regulatory skill: the infant's ability to inhibit the impulse to search at the previous, and incorrect, location. An early-maturing region of the PFC, the ventral PFC, has been shown in neuroimaging studies with children aged seven to twelve and adults to be active during response inhibition.[26] These and other tasks also involve self-regulation from a third PFC region, the anterior cingulate, which is involved in attentional control and focus.[27] Like memory, therefore, self-regulation is not a singular ability, and different behavioral components of self-regulation draw on the coactivity of different regions of the PFC beginning in infancy.

The prefrontal cortex has a more extended maturation than most other brain regions, with myelination of neural networks lasting through adolescence (remember Figure 3.1 that opened this section). Its prolonged development has been one explanation for the impulsive conduct of youth, as discussed in the previous chapter. But as this chapter indicates, the prefrontal cortex influences behavioral regulation beginning in infancy, with continuing and growing influence throughout childhood. Stated differently, self-regulation is not an all-or-none capability but rather a developmentally graded skill, and the PFC is influential throughout the extended maturation of self-regulatory ability. Equally important, neuroimaging studies indicate that different PFC areas are not independent of each other but coactive in guiding self-regulation, and function in concert with other brain regions to influence planning and behavior. Because developing self-regulation is so important to many developing cognitive and social competencies, therefore, it should not be surprising that its neurobiological foundations are diverse and coordinated, develop early, and have an extensive maturation. We call it "self-regulation," but the brain has many forms and functions to accomplish it.

How Do We Know These Things?

These three brief profiles of the developmental neuroscience of memory, language, and self-regulation illustrate some of the processes of brain development discussed in this chapter. Neural networks rather than specific brain structures best characterize how the brain influences behavior. The catalysts of experience are central to how the brain organizes developmentally. Specific developmental domains (e.g., memory, language, self-regulation) are founded in multiple neural networks with complex maturational timetables. There is no one-to-one correspondence between psychological development and neurobiological growth. Our concepts of behavior are often mapped onto complex neurobiological functions.

These profiles also illustrate some of the methods by which the science of early brain development proceeds. The technology required to conduct neuroimaging of infants and young children has only recently been developed, so researchers have been required over the years to integrate multiple alternative sources of insight on the developing brain: neuroimaging studies of older children and adults (to map the maturational course in humans) and monkeys (to model these neurodevelopmental processes when more invasive procedures are required); research with rats and other mammals (for experimental studies when the brains of sacrificed animals can be examined); studies of children and adults with neurodevelopmental disorders, brain damage (through accident or disease), or informative therapeutic interventions (such as hemispherectomies to treat severe epilepsy); and research on human cadavers that permits removal and study of normal brains at different developmental stages. Each of these research approaches has advantages but also liabilities for advancing developmental neuroscience, and consequently some innovative research combines multiple approaches. For example, comparative studies of young children with older children and adults using comparable "marker tasks" to assess specific cognitive functions can help with modeling the developmental process. Sometimes neuroimaging studies of monkeys responding to tasks that are similar to those presented to young human children can also yield valuable insights.

Developmental neuroscientists can directly study the brain in older children and adults through a broadening array of research technologies. These include neuroimaging through electrophysiological procedures (electroencephalogram [EEG], event-related potential [ERP]), radioactive imaging (positron emission tomography [PET], with primarily clinical rather than research applications), imaging of oxygenated blood flow (magnetic resonance imaging [MRI], functional magnetic resonance imaging [fMRI], or diffusion tensor imaging [DTI], which enlists the diffusion properties of molecules in tissue), and new procedures that are noninvasive and have greater potential for younger research participants (such as functional near infrared spectroscopy [fNIRS], which also images oxygenated blood flow, and magnetic encephalography [MEG], which uses the magnetic field to image the flow of bioelectric signals). One of the reasons for major advances in developmental neuroscience in recent years has been the growing range of technological options for neuroimaging, their increasing affordability for researchers, and their astute implementation by scientists to address research questions for which they are well suited.

Beyond these research approaches, one of the most valuable resources for developmental neuroscience has been decades of research on children's behavioral development. This is especially so in light of an observation from the preceding chapter: developmental neuroscience is primarily atheoretical, and advances in understanding the developing brain occur inductively through the progressive accumulation of research findings. Without a theoretical road map, therefore, how do developmental neuroscientists know where to begin when seeking to understand the neurobiological bases for human behavior? They go, among other places, to the study of human behavior for clues.

The Brain Development Story: Concepts, Memory, and Relationships

Let me tell you another story of brain development.[28]

The growth of the mind is evident in everything a child says and does. But it is not always transparent. An eight-year-old can be a model of focused concentration. With head bent over a notebook and lips pursed, it is easy to see the wheels turning within the mind as text is read or problems solved. Not so an eight-month-old, whose casual playfulness seems to betray little of the mind's growth. The short attention span and erratic moods of a baby can cause even the most careful observer to be doubtful about the activity of the mind. The early twentieth-century psychologist William James characterized the infant's world as a "blooming, buzzing confusion," and even the great developmental psychologist Jean Piaget described the infant's intelligence as only "sensorimotor" in quality, bound up in sensory experience and movement but lacking any of the rich conceptual capabilities of the older thinker. While it is logical, therefore, that the story of developmental neuroscience begins at conception, with prenatal neural proliferation and neural migration to create the building blocks of mature neural networks, the study of the mind's development traditionally began with middle childhood This is when the building blocks of mature cognition become apparent in the school-age child's dawning capacities for logical thinking, scientific reasoning, and causal analysis.

It was not until the 1970s that developmental scientists began taking a closer look at the mind of a baby.[29] And because their expectations were so low, they were truly astonished by what they found, and researchers today continue to be surprised. They discovered that early learning occurs rapidly because infants are hungry for novel visual stimulation. Beginning from birth, infants vigorously scan the world, seeking out new and interesting sights, looking away from things that are familiar (and thus less interesting), staring at events that are unusual or unexpected, and reasoning about what they perceive. To illustrate, mothers in one study helped their one-month-olds mouth a small object that was either rigid (a plastic cylinder) or flexible (a wet sponge) without the newborn being able to see it. Then infants watched as both objects were displayed and manipulated by a pair of black-gloved hands. One-month-olds looked significantly longer at the object that was different from the one they had earlier mouthed.[30] At one month of age, they had integrated their sense of touch and sight to determine which object was familiar – and preferred looking at the new one.

Exploiting the same visual novelty preference, other research groups have shown that by three to four months, infants have learned much about the properties of physical objects: they know that objects are solid (other objects cannot move through them), that they have integrity (parts of the object do not move independently), that they can move through unobstructed space (they do not pass through solid barriers), that they can act on other objects when they contact them (such as in a collision), and that they continue to exist unchanged even when they are hidden from view.[31] Researchers know this because infants look longer when shown objects that seem to move through solid barriers, or when parts of the object move independently, as if recognizing that this should not be expected. Yet amazingly, infants have learned all this despite their poor physical coordination for manipulating objects at this age. Five-month-olds are also sensitive to differences in number and can do simple addition or subtraction of small quantities.[32] During the second half of the first year, infants begin to make predictions about object motion that take into account gravity, inertia, and other physical forces.[33] By ten months of age, they are beginning to understand cause and effect: they act like they expect one object that has hit another to propel it forward.[34]

How do developmental scientists account for so much early understanding of the world? There have been at least two views. One is that even though they are physically not very capable of object manipulation, infants are astute observers of the world around them, and from these observations, they deduce some of the central properties of objects. Their hunger for novel visual stimulation combined with their strong interest in what they observe (because so much of the world is new to them) leads to astonishingly rapid early learning. An alternative view is that such knowledge is far more sophisticated than what even an astute infant observer could deduce. Instead, the human mind is endowed with innate modules of core knowledge of the world that help infants quickly make accurate inferences about the properties of objects.[35] According to this view, there are at least four (maybe five) core knowledge systems: one concerning inanimate objects and their interactions, another concerning animate agents and their actions, a third concerning the numerical relationships among objects, and a fourth concerning objects in the spatial world and their associations (there may also be a fifth core knowledge system concerning the behavior of social partners). These core knowledge systems, functioning as mental modules, bootstrap early knowledge development with critical assumptions about how the world operates that enable young infants to quickly make accurate inferences about the world. These inferences are important for enabling young infants to learn more quickly how to interact with objects and people in a complex world. These mental modules are believed to be information processing units that are specialized for stimulation coming from particular kinds of experiences or events.

Another kind of mental module that is long believed to contribute to early learning is for language. Since the work of Noam Chomsky,[36] the view that an innate mental module (he called it a "language acquisition device") facilitates language development has been one way of comprehending the astonishingly rapid pace of early language learning. Research on early language acquisition has documented how quickly infants and young children acquire the rudiments of language. Studies of their early perception of phonemes (i.e., the basic units of spoken speech) show that during the first six months, babies can discriminate the phonemes found in languages all over the world, including phonemes that their parents cannot differentiate. A Japanese infant can discriminate, for example, between the sounds /l/ and /r/, even though her parents cannot readily do so. For this reason, young infants are sometimes called "citizens of the world." But by ten to eleven months, speech perception has become more narrowly channeled to the sounds of the home language(s), and infants can no longer discriminate foreign speech sounds.[37] They have become, over the first year, perceptually fine-tuned to the language system(s) that they are overhearing and preparing to learn. A similar phenomenon has been observed with respect to the child's own sounds: by ten months, infants have incorporated the sounds of the home language into their babbling.[38]

Equally remarkably, during this period infants begin to segment the streams of speech they overhear into meaningful words in that language system. This is, of course, crucial to beginning to learn vocabulary, as any novice in learning a new language can attest. The manner in which they do so seems to involve detecting regularities in the frequency with which certain phonemes occur together in the speech they overhear. For example, when the baby is greeted by an English speaker, the phonemes "he-lō-bá-bee" heard in sequence are more likely to be parsed as "he-lō" and "bá-bee" because the combination of "lō-bá" occurs infrequently in English, so it is unlikely to constitute a unit of speech. And because they are likely to hear "bá-bee" frequently in everyday speech, these phonemes become discriminated as a connected unit – in other words, a word. As they are overhearing spoken language, in other words, infants are detecting the regularities in phoneme sequences that help them differentiate words and, eventually, associate those words with objects and events in the world. Quite appropriately, developmental scientists call this an example of early "statistical learning."[39]

And that's not all. During the first three years, infants also engage in "fast mapping" of the meanings of new words based on the contexts in which they are encountered.[40] In their initial hearing of a new word, young children develop a provisional idea of its meaning, often a broad, overgeneralized meaning, that becomes progressively refined on subsequent hearings in different contexts (this later refinement is called "extended mapping"). Initially "doggy" is used for any four-legged animal, but with further experience, "doggy" becomes more specific and differentiated from cats, horses, and other four-legged animals. Taken together, these processes help to account for the explosion of vocabulary growth beginning at around eighteen months, when toddlers are learning eight to ten new words daily. But the same processes also help to explain why word learning is an extended development as the specific meanings of these words become better refined and understood. These processes also put a spotlight on the social processes by which word learning occurs and the importance of language in adult-child interaction (more on that later).

Concept development is related to children's language development: early language draws from an infant's earliest concepts, but language also influences concept development. The earliest concepts are prelinguistic, of course, when infants as young as four months old can group together objects of similar appearance, such as different kinds of animals, based on their perceptual features. Objects that are similar in shape, texture, density, and other properties also become clustered in the mind of a baby. Later in the first year, however, their concepts become more, well, conceptual: not necessarily wedded to perceptual features and other tangible properties, and sometimes ignoring those properties entirely, these categories are based on underlying (sometimes invisible) features, such as classifying birds as animals and airplanes as vehicles even though birds and airplanes both have wings and fly. Concepts also become constructed multidimensionally. By nine months, for example, infants distinguish between animate and inanimate objects on the basis of motion cues (animate objects move voluntarily, but inanimate object are moved),[41] and in subsequent years they elaborate their animate/inanimate distinction with additional differences in the capacity to grow, biological inheritance, emotions, reciprocated actions, and other distinctions.[42] In the second year and following, young children's concepts become more refined as they evolve from global, overinclusive conceptions based on physical features to categories that are more specific, discrete, and based in nonvisible qualities.

One manner in which young children refine their concepts is by seeking to understand the qualities that make certain objects alike and distinguish them from others. It is easy to see why this would be valuable. If you can identify the fundamental characteristics of different kinds of animals, plants, inanimate objects, natural phenomena, even manufactured items, you can readily identify the group to which a new object belongs, associate it with other members of the same group, and confidently attribute to it the other characteristics of that group. *Essentialism* is the belief that things have basic (essential) characteristics that make them what they are, and these characteristics are ingrained, unchanging, established early, and help to distinguish one thing from another.[43] Beginning at age three, young children become committed to understanding what are these essential qualities, and this is a significant advance in their concept development.[44] In response to the clever stories created by developmental scientists, for example, preschool-age children understand that a dog barks, wags its tail, and gives birth to puppies, regardless of what kind of dog it is. They also understand that a dog will remain a dog even if it is wearing a disguise as a cat, even if a doctor performs an operation to make it look like a cat, and even if it is raised from birth in a family of cats.[45] A dog, in other words, will always be essentially a dog no matter what. By appreciating the internal, essential qualities that distinguish different things in the world, young children's conceptual distinctions become far more sophisticated, abstract, and multidimensional.

But essentialism can, at times, be misleading. It can cause children (and adults) to underestimate the amount of variability that exists within a concept (e.g., carnivorous plants such as the Venus flytrap) and that categories of objects can change over time (in fifteen years your phone morphed into a pocket computer). Essentialism can, in other words, create conceptual rigidity. Perhaps the most important inflexibility of essentialism is that children are also essentialist in their understanding of many social categories, such as gender, race, and social class.[46] They consider these social categories to be like natural categories: as unchanging, established early, and conferring on members of these groups certain essential characteristics that all of its members share (e.g., boys like playing with trucks). Equally importantly, as young children begin identifying the social categories to which they belong, their intuitive essentialism causes them to conform to the essential qualities that they perceive as belonging to members of their group. If I am a boy, and this is what boys like and do, then I should be like them and do the same things. It takes considerably further conceptual development before older children can recognize that greater flexibility exists between and within social categories, and that many social categories (such as team membership) can be temporary or arbitrary. Despite this, essentialism remains influential in how even adults think about the characteristics of individuals in ways that can contribute to racism, sexism, heterosexism, classism, or other forms of discrimination.[47] I will say more about this later.

As noted earlier, children's concept development is infused with the language they overhear and are learning.[48] As adults lexicalize the child's experience through conversation, they provide infants and young children with words that confer ready-made categories with which to understand their experiences. Language is further influential through adults' explanations to children of conceptual differences ("well, that looks like a horse, but it's called a donkey"). In their efforts to build understanding, furthermore, most adults use generic language ("bats live in caves"), and the generic attributes of things are also inherent in the questions they pose to young children ("and what does a cow say?"). In doing so, adults reinforce an essentialist mindset in the child: all bats live in caves, and all cows go "moo." Early language in social conversation feeds young children's intrinsic interest in discovering what are the essential characteristics of different objects, animals, and people.

It is easy to overlook how much these early achievements in understanding the properties of physical objects, animals, plants, and people are predicated on rapidly developing memory skills.[49] Developing memory is, of course, enlisted into many aspects of early mental activity. Infants' early explicit memory is aptly demonstrated in their visual novelty preferences, which motivate them to look longer at unfamiliar than familiar objects, and to stare at events that violate their expectations and to learn from them. After six months, explicit memory improves considerably: infants can retain memories of events over longer delays, they can remember multistep sequences more accurately (such as remembering to attach a ramp to a base before running a toy car down the ramp, after having watched an adult perform the same actions), and their memory for events is more robust (more resistant, for example, to interference). These early achievements in memory are only the beginning. During the preschool years, young children become increasingly proficient at remembering specific events (such as yesterday's trip to McDonald's) and also generalized event memories, such as the script for eating at a fast food restaurant. Autobiographical memories that document and integrate recollections of the personal past begin to develop during this period, such as your birthday party at McDonald's when you turned five. With increasing age, memory becomes more acute as older children develop skills associated with *metamemory* (knowledge of one's own memory processes): they become more capable of source monitoring (such as distinguishing what they personally experienced from what they were told), evaluating the certainty of their recollections, using mnemonic devices to facilitate remembering and recall (such as bringing to mind the context in which a past event happened), and other capabilities. The important achievements in the development of memory are not increases in the size of memory capacity, but the enlistment of increasingly sophisticated cognitive processes for encoding, organizing, and retrieving memories.

How Do They Do This?

Let's pause this tour through the developing mind for a simple reflection.

This section has highlighted that young children construct new understanding rapidly and in a variety of areas, and also the reasoning processes by which they do so. Those reasoning skills are important because they are key to fueling further understanding. For example, eight-month-olds demonstrate statistical learning not only in parsing speech sounds but also in other quantitative judgments, such as estimating the relative volumes of containers or developing expectations for what adults will do in certain situations.[50] In one study, eight-month-olds observed an adult draw red or white balls from a bin that the infants learned was full of balls primarily of one color. Infants looked longer, as if it was not what they expected, when the adult's sampling (several white balls) was inconsistent with the pool from which it was drawn (primarily red balls).[51]

Their developing reasoning skills also enable infants and young children to experiment in order to learn further. One research group presented elelven-month-olds with toys that acted in a way that violated their expectations about physical causality.[52] In one case, a toy truck appeared to move down an incline and through a solid physical barrier to its destination. In another, a toy truck was pushed over a ledge and, instead of falling, it unexpectedly hovered in midair. Afterward, the toy trucks were presented to the infants. Those who had seen the truck moving through a physical barrier banged the truck on the high chair tray, as if to determine whether it was truly as solid as it appeared (or perhaps it was a hologram?). Those who had seen the truck remaining in midair without support instead dropped the truck over the edge of their high chair, as if to determine whether it would hover again. The researchers documented that infants paid greater attention to and learned more from the events that were unexpected than from those that were consistent with their expectations. This is how we all learn, right?

Another way of appreciating the reasoning skills fueling mental growth is how early young children can enlist the executive functions that are the basis for self-regulated thought. Executive functions are cognitive capacities that enable self-control of thinking and behavior, and they include working memory (to keep in mind relevant information), inhibition of irrelevant or interfering impulses, and mental flexibility. Throughout these pages, there have been abundant examples of these executive functions facilitating young children's thinking, whether in remembering the steps of a complex task or inhibiting the impulse to search in an earlier location after seeing a toy hidden elsewhere. Over the course of their first years, young children make great strides in thinking adaptively and creatively rather than perseverating with familiar approaches, acting planfully rather than reactively, and responding strategically rather than requiring external guidance.[53] Despite their early emergence, however, executive functions have a long developmental course, and this helps to explain many of the improvements in children's thinking and reasoning in subsequent years that cause them to become more capable, systematic, self-regulated thinkers.[54]

How do we explain the rapid growth of understanding in the early years? As earlier noted, innate mental modules are one explanation. Another is that infants and young children are astute observers of the world around them. A third explanation, however, is that in addition to the growth of knowledge, young children are also acquiring reasoning skills that enable the expansion of understanding, skills like experimentation, statistical learning, and self-regulated thinking. In this respect, Piaget was correct in describing the child as a scientist, and he was probably also correct in his explanation why. From early in life, children do not await explanations from others around them. Their minds are oriented toward deriving their own explanations from their experiences and their actions on the world. Their experiences over the early years equip them with foundational knowledge and also with foundational strategies for acquiring more knowledge.

Understanding People

Infants and young children also learn and reason about the people with whom they live. Indeed, they are motivated to understand people even more than other things because of the importance of their daily interactions with adults, and also siblings and peers. Beginning as early as three or four months of age, infants begin differentiating among people according to their characteristics, including a person's race, gender, spoken language, and even language accent.[55] In doing so, infants use readily perceptible attributes for their initial social categories (just as they do for other categories) such as skin color, vocal timbre, and language. Furthermore, they orient toward people who have the same characteristics that they do: they are more likely to look at, approach, imitate, and interact with people who are similar racially[56] and who speak the same language(s) or with the same accent the child is overhearing daily at home.[57] Familiarity appears to be one major reason for these social category distinctions: infants affiliate with those who are familiar.

Infants are attentive to social categories for the same reason that adults are. Category membership is an important way that people are similar and different, and infants expect people in the same category to interact with each other and to be alike in other ways, such as the food they prefer.[58] With increasing age, young children begin to include themselves in these categories, and, in doing so, they identify with others who share the same group membership. By early childhood, they also expect that members of their group have special obligations to each other, such as to provide assistance and to follow the same expectations, that are not extended to nongroup members.[59] This is one of the ways that young children develop their gender, racial, and other forms of social identity. But as noted earlier, their essentialist thinking can cause them to be unduly rigid in their beliefs about the characteristics of members of their group, and this heightens their motivation to conform to those expectations for the group with which they identify.

Another way that infants develop understanding of the social world is in their growing awareness of why people act as they do. Once again, researchers have found that these achievements begin early as infants not only comprehend the regularities of people's behavior but also begin to grasp some of the mental processes that account for their behavior. Contrary to the traditional view that young children are egocentric and thus prone to generalizing their own subjective perspective to others, it now appears that early in the first year, infants become aware that others have distinct subjective viewpoints that are different from the child's own. This motivates children's efforts to figure out what goes on in others' minds and how it affects their actions.[60]

One of the earliest insights to develop concerns people's visual regard. By the first birthday, infants appreciate that whatever has someone's attention is in their mind, so to speak – people respond to what they are looking at. This motivates infants to try to establish joint attention with other people, such as following an adult's gaze to see what they are looking at, or pointing to get someone to look at what interests them. Joint attention involves altering one person's attention to align with another's so that they are oriented to the same thing – in an important sense, this creates a meeting of minds.

At about the same time, infants also begin regarding people as intentional agents, acting according to their mental intentions and goals. Observing an adult's trips to the refrigerator is now animated by an awareness that the trips are *in order to* get something (what will it be?). Gesturing toward a cookie not only shifts the adult's attention toward the treat but also (the child hopes) changes the adult's intentions to give the cookie to the infant. Interestingly, the emergence of this insight about the goal-directedness of other people's actions occurs at the same time that infants are themselves becoming more goal-directed, facilitated by their ability to crawl or walk wherever their interests and intentions lead them.

With increasing age, infants add further to their understanding of the contents of people's minds. In the second and third years, for example, toddlers supplement their understanding of emotion with the awareness that people are also motivated by their desires: they act in order to get what they want. Desires are linked to emotion, of course. Toddlers can begin to deduce what people desire by reading their emotions, since people look happy when they get what they want, but sad when they do not (or when they get what they do not want). Deriving inferences like these can lead to some sophisticated (and nonegocentric) judgments. In a well-known experiment,[61] eighteen-month-old toddlers gave broccoli rather than gold-fish crackers to a research assistant for a snack after the adult had previously shown a preference for eating broccoli (smiling while doing so), even though the toddler preferred the crackers.[62]

Later, during the fourth year, young children add to their toolkit of mental concepts. They begin to comprehend the influence of thoughts and beliefs, such as observing another child looking toward the door because the child *thinks* their parent is due to arrive. Further, children of this age are capable of making surprisingly astute judgments about the influence of *mistaken* beliefs on behavior (such as believing the parent is due to arrive at the wrong time).

In these advances, young children seem to be functioning as theorists of the mind, developing increasingly complex ways of understanding and explaining the behavior of other people. This is why research on these developing abilities is called *theory of mind*,[63] and it presents developmental scientists with the familiar problem of explaining the rapid pace of these early conceptual achievements. An innate mental module consisting of core knowledge of human behavior is one possible explanation – recall the module concerning animate agents and their actions described earlier. Other researchers focus on the astute observations and sophisticated reasoning skills earlier discussed as better explanations for developing theory of mind, extending Piaget's description of the child as a scientist to the idea of the child as a scientific theorist of the mind.

The Significance of Social Experience

There is, however, another explanation for the rapid development of theory of mind. Everyday interactions with other people are full of clues to their mental processes.[64] Beginning early, the human back-and-forth of social interaction is infused with insights into other people's mental states. There are many examples, such as in joint attention to an event (especially an event that also involves shared emotions, actions, or words), when shared attention can create a shared motivational or emotional state that the infant can witness in the other person. Quite often an adult's verbal references to feelings, desires, intentions, or thoughts of another person provides insight into another's mental states.[65] Young children also participate in the playacting of mental states during pretend play with peers, and debates about preferences, interests, and negotiation of conflict with siblings. Young children can also observe people playing tricks, lying, or socially manipulating others, and they also experience the nonverbal cues of social bias conveyed by adults.[66] People who interact daily with infants and young children inhabit a world enlivened by their awareness of others as psychological beings, so it would be surprising if this understanding was not incorporated into what they say and do with young children, and convey this understanding to children in their interactions with them.

Beyond specific shared experiences, a significant element of sensitive responding to a young child is treating the child as a psychologically animated person, an attribute called *mind-mindedness*.[67] Adults who are sensitive in this way to a child's feelings, intentions, desires, and thoughts are likely to make explicit reference to them, and they may imitate or mirror these mental states to show they understand. They may also show respect for these mental states by accommodating them such as providing substitutes for what the child desires (offering a cracker instead of the cookie the child gestured toward), and act in other ways to recognize the psychological experience of the child. Just as concepts of physical causality are built on everyday experiences of interacting with objects, therefore, interactions with people fuel young children's developing understanding of what people's minds are like.

This leads to a broader question of how much are the *other* mental achievements in the early years also built on interactions with other people. How important is social interaction, in other words, to the growth of the mind?

Human infancy evolved in the context of small cohabiting groups in which a range of adults were present and many contributed to infant care. Consequently, it would be surprising if the early development of the human mind did not incorporate some of the influences deriving from everyday experiences with other people. In fact, we know this to be true: exposure to human voices and language is one of the most important experience-expectant contributions to the development of the brain and mind. Just hearing language is not enough: social *interaction* is key to language development. In one study, English-speaking nine-month-olds were exposed to Mandarin Chinese over twelve twenty-five-minute sessions. Some of the infants interacted with a native Mandarin speaker as she sang songs, read books, and played with them. Others watched a TV recording of the same sessions, and a third group listened to audio recordings of these sessions. The same amount of language was heard by infants in each group. On follow-up measures of phonetic discrimination, however, only the infants who had interacted with the Mandarin speaker showed increased proficiency, while infants in the other two groups showed no learning.[68] In other words, language was learned only in the context of social interaction. This conclusion is consistent with other studies. In one large longitudinal study, the quality of parents' social interaction with their two-year-olds, such as simple conversations, storybook reading, and language during play and familiar routines, was a better predictor of children's language a year later than the number of words that children heard in these interactions.[69]

There are many other ways that everyday social interactions fuel mental growth in the early years. Young children learn about physical causality while imitating another's actions on objects.[70] Joint attention facilitates their word learning and memory for an event.[71] Adult language promotes early concept development (and essentialist thinking) in young children.[72] The growth of executive functions benefits from supportive parenting and is impaired by negative control practices by parents.[73] According to a prominent theory of cultural learning, in fact, these everyday social interactions are so influential because they are colored by the child's growing knowledge of the other person's intentions, goals, and other mental states.[74] In this sense, the influence of what another person *does* is enhanced by the young child's understanding of *why* they are doing it. For this reason, eighteen-month-olds imitate the intentions underlying an adult's behavior rather than the specific actions they observe;[75] preschoolers interpret adult instruction about objects or people as generically true;[76] and young children learn more when interacting collaboratively with peers, especially those who have different viewpoints than they do, compared with learning by themselves.[77] Early social interactions are more than learning about the social world: they are learning about the world in general.

A foundation for these social influences is the *relationships* that young children share with others. In the small cohabiting groups in which human infancy evolved, infants developed emotional attachments to their care-givers around whom their emotional security was organized. These attach-ments (and other close relationships) are important for providing safety and nurturant care, emboldening infants and young children to explore their worlds, buffering stressful experiences and supporting self-regulation, and promoting the development of social skills and understanding and many culture-specific capabilities.[78] Early relationships are, in this sense, more than the sum of their parts: intimate interaction with another person over time has compounding and cumulative influences on children's developing understanding, sense of self, emotional well-being, and other core developmental achievements.[79] As such, they provide a crucial rela-tional context for the growth of the mind and brain.

Brain and Mind

I have related two stories about brain development: one told from the perspective of synapses and neural networks, and the other from the perspective of concepts and reasoning skills. Both concern the developing brain, but from very different perspectives and research methods. Comparing the two affords at least three observations about the codeve-lopment of brain and mind.

The Stories of the Developing Brain and Mind Are Complementary

First, and most obviously, is the complementarity of these stories – which is exactly what we should expect if mind and brain are mutually influen-tial.[80] Consider:

- Newborns are hungry for novel stimulation, which is exactly what we would expect knowing that new experiences are driving how their brains are creating and refining neural connections at an astonishing rate. Stated differently, novelty fuels synaptic proliferation and pruning, and infants seek it. Their hunger for novelty causes infants to devote more focused attention to new events than adults do (especially because they are not mentally multitasking, preoccupied with their cellphones, worried about the future, or regretting the past), and consequently they are deeply receptive to opportunities for new learning.[81] A preference for visual novelty also has other consequences, such as making young infants highly distractable (whenever something new is seen or heard) and, because this activity is mentally taxing, prone to fussiness if denied regular naps.

- Advances in the development of sensory acuity, language, self-regulation, and many other processes follow a predictable sequence that parallels the timetable for synaptic proliferation and pruning, and myelination, in each of the relevant brain regions where these functions are believed to be organized (as summarized in the opening Figure 3.1 of this chapter). Since these developmental achievements are causally linked, this is just as we should expect.
- Changes during the first year in how infants respond to speech sounds parallel changes in brain activation to speech: there is an initial period of responsiveness to familiar and unfamiliar language sounds followed by the progressive narrowing of responding to the home language alone – that is, the language(s) that infants are beginning to learn. This perceptual narrowing of responsiveness to familiar speech sounds, observed in both behavior and brain, sets the stage for further advances in language development. The documentation of concurrent changes in behavior and brain contributes to a deeper understanding of early language development.
- Growth in episodic memory occurs during the first two years at the same time that the neurobiological connections governing this form of memory expand to incorporate higher cortical regions, consistent with the growing sophistication of memory retention over this period.
- Prefrontal regions underlying self-regulation begin to mature very early, consistent with the infant's behavioral transition from an erratic, somewhat disorganized newborn to a toddler capable of planful action. But these regions also have an extended maturational course, consistent with continuing growth in executive functions and behavioral self-regulation witnessed throughout middle childhood and adolescence to early adulthood.

The list could go on (perhaps you noted additional correspondences between brain and mental development in the preceding pages). The consistency of these developmental processes confirms expectations for how the growth of mind and brain are deeply related, and strengthens confidence in our understanding of these achievements because they are manifested consistently in brain and behavioral growth.[82]

Integrating the Stories of Brain and Mind Is a Work in Progress

A second observation, however, is that some of the mental advances documented by developmental scientists do *not* (yet) find parallel support in developmental neurobiology, and thus they constitute provocative directions for further study. In the preceding chapter, we looked at one of these areas: the development of the "social brain" associated with social understanding, mentalizing, and theory of mind. Many researchers are studying the brain areas associated with these achievements in social understanding, but because different research groups have identified different candidate brain regions, and others disagree about how theory of mind develops and what mentalizing is, a consensus has not been achieved and much more work remains.[83] Stay tuned.

Another example of an emergent area of mind-brain association concerns statistical reasoning, which researchers have found to be a contributor to language development and other skills in early childhood. Research on the developmental neuroscience of statistical reasoning is still very new, however, because researchers are modeling the brain processes associated with statistical reasoning in adults before extending their conclusions to young children, who are also much more difficult to study.[84] As they do so, the concept of statistical reasoning is becoming further refined. Again, stay tuned.

A third area of emerging research concerns the brain regions associated with the development of metamemory, a collection of skills related to the awareness of one's own memory processes, such as knowing how to use strategies for memory retrieval, or being able to evaluate whether a particular memory is the result of personal experience or being told by another. Adult studies have identified a number of candidate brain regions associated with different metamemory skills, and researchers are currently engaged in the hard work of confirming their association with developing metamemory in children.[85] This is a particularly interesting area of inquiry because of how the development of metamemory integrates basic brain structures associated with memory formation and retrieval, such as the hippocampus, with higher (including prefrontal) regions associated with self-regulation and strategic functioning. At the same time, researchers are recognizing that the brain areas relevant to different forms of metamemory are distinct, contributing to a better appreciation of the diversity of the developmental processes incorporated into this concept.

These examples illustrate how developmental neuroscience is continually changing as researchers extend their understanding to new areas of psychological development, guided by the findings of researchers who are studying children's thinking and reasoning. As they do so, researchers identify and study candidate areas of the brain that are implicated in these psychological processes, and the results of their research may confirm their influence, perhaps identifying additional influential brain areas, or may provoke a revision of current understanding of the brain's role in these processes. The mental and psychological processes that these studies are seeking to model neurobiologically may also be reexamined, such as when concepts like mentalization are refined or even redefined based on evidence from neuroscience. This research is quite exciting as it illustrates how the cross-talk between study of the developing brain and the mind benefits thinking in each field. This process also illustrates, however, how premature it is to accord priority to either mind or brain in studying their codevelopment as understanding of concepts and processes in each field is evolving, and their interaction is only beginning to be understood. Taken together, this work confirms the need for studying the development of brain and mind in an integrated fashion, connecting findings from each field related to common developmental achievements in order to benefit from the insights afforded by each.

The Stories of Brain and Mind Have Somewhat Different Perspectives on Development

A third observation from the foregoing stories of brain development is that there are also differences in these accounts of the developing brain and mind. These differences are not simply hypotheses requiring further exploration, but different perspectives on development that make the tasks of connecting mind and brain more challenging.

There are concepts in developmental science, for example, that have proven difficult to bring into developmental neuroscience. Mental modules for core knowledge were described earlier in this chapter as potential explanations for early achievements in developing language and understanding physical causality, basic numerical awareness, social perception, and other aspects of early thinking. The concept of mental modules has long been influential in cognitive science, linguistics, and evolutionary theory as well as developmental science.[86] But although mental modules are believed to exist in delegated brain areas, the concept has thus far not provided neuroscience researchers with much guidance about how to identify their neurobiological foundations. Furthermore, the realization that complex mental processes involve widely distributed neural networks that incorporate brain structures with multiple functions argues against finding evidence for localized mental modules in the brains of young children or adults.[87] This is a problem in connecting mind and brain that arises perhaps because mental modules simply don't exist (or not as they are currently conceptualized), because developmental neuroscience lacks the capacities for identifying and measuring them, or for other reasons.

Mental modules are an illustration of a number of concepts in developmental science that are challenging to translate into neurodevelopment. Essentialism is another concept relevant to many aspects of early conceptual growth that is likewise difficult to submit to neuroscientific inquiry because of its broadly inclusive quality. The same is true of other familiar concepts in developmental science, such as intelligence and personality (or temperament). These concepts are important to developmental science because they provide holistic, integrative understanding of central aspects of psychological development, but their breadth and abstraction make them unlikely candidates for guiding developmental brain imaging. It is possible that, like other complex psychological processes, researchers will deconstruct concepts like these into more discrete components that can guide inquiry in developmental neuroscience (this is already happening with theory of mind). But doing so risks robbing them of the integrative quality and conceptual breadth that makes them useful to the study of psychological development. On the other hand, it is possible that narrowly defined concepts with links to developing neurobiology will better serve developmental science as well as developmental neuroscience.

Beyond specific concepts, the approaches to understanding development taken by developmental neuroscience and developmental science also diverge. As noted in the previous chapter, neuroscience adopts an atheoretical, empirical orientation to understanding development as involving the progressive construction of neural networks and specialized brain regions based on the interconnections between neurons through the influence of genetics and experience. Developmental scientists concur with this approach, but they have more to add drawn from the influences of systems biology, comparative psychology, and other approaches to the study of human development. As one example, this leads them to an interest in how developmental processes are not only mechanistically constructed but also emergent and self-organizing, often involving the reintegration of developing skills for new purposes.[88] They regard language development, for example, not just as the maturation and interconnection of language regions in the brain, but also as the recruitment and reorganization of a range of general cognitive abilities to create language-specific competencies.[89] Similar (re)organizational views have been applied to the development of working memory,[90] theory of mind,[91] and other cognitive abilities. Viewed in this manner, the whole of mental development may be greater than the sum of its parts.[92]

Developmental scientists also regard the developing child as having an active role in psychological development. They recognize, for example, that how children represent and interpret their experiences is an important influence on conceptual growth. Earlier this was illustrated in the study showing eleven-month-olds experimenting with and learning from their encounters with toy trucks that violated their expectations by appearing to hover in midair or pass through barriers. Piaget described these experiences as creating mental disequilibrium from which new cognitive schemas emerge, which is why the infants experimented on the trucks as they did to figure out why they acted so unexpectedly. Developmental neuroscientists recognize, of course, that brain development is shaped by the brain's activity (this is what "use it or lose it" describes), and that young children assume an important role in the brain's activity in their play and exploration. But the view that growth emerges from how the brain acts on itself (e.g., to resolve discrepancies in understanding) is more difficult to conceptualize and model neurobiologically in real time.[93] The role of children as catalysts of their own development is thus viewed somewhat differently in each field.

Developmental scientists thus tend to ask different questions and enlist broader and more integrative concepts into their study of mental development than do developmental neuroscientists in the study of the brain. They are also more theoretically guided, which provides them with a top-down approach that complements but extends the bottom-up orientation of developmental neuroscience. Taken together, it is important to wed understanding of the developing brain to knowledge of mental and behavioral development to ensure that conclusions about mind and brain are well founded. This wedding of two sciences of human development devoted to understanding common phenomena is also essential to understanding the complex mutual influences that occur between brain and mind. But the task of cross-talking mind and brain is more complex than we may expect owing to differences in vocabulary and concepts, methods, levels of analysis, and even understanding of how development occurs by researchers who study mind and brain.

Lesser-Known Brain Development Stories

In the next chapters I discuss the emergence of a story of brain development that combines elements of the two stories profiled here. That story is centered on the early years, the formative influences of early experience, the rapid pace of brain and mental development, and the importance of nurturant care. This is the story that, beginning twenty-five years ago, has become familiar to the public, and remains iconic in public understanding to this day.

But even in 1997, the field of developmental neuroscience extended well beyond this well-publicized account, and a number of research areas that were part of the scientific story at that time were not included in the public messaging. They constitute additional, somewhat lesser-known or overlooked stories of brain development that did not become as familiar to the public in 1997, but might have made a difference to public understanding if they had. One of the questions orienting the inquiry of the next chapters is understanding the influences that guided what was included in the public messaging about the developing brain, and what was left out. In order to put this inquiry into perspective, I profile some of these research areas that constitute lesser-known brain development stories at that time.

Poverty

What is the most important early predictor of a child's future? Included on the list of candidates must be poverty in childhood. Adults who experience at least one year of poverty during childhood are more than ten times as likely to be poor at age thirty-five than those whose families were never poor.[94] The impact is particularly large for early childhood. Family poverty during the first five years was found, in one large study, to be associated with large and significant decrements in earnings and hours worked and greater probability of receiving food stamps in adulthood, even with poverty later in childhood controlled.[95] This is important because the younger the child in the United States, the more likely is the child to be living in poverty. In 2020, nearly 18% of the children under age five lived in families with incomes below the poverty level, which is the highest proportion of any age group. Another 20% of children in this age group lived in families below 200% of the poverty level, deemed "poor" by any standard. [96] Thus nearly 40% of infants and preschool-age children in the United States are living in families in economic distress.

Developmental scientists have long known that poor children are at greater risk of experiencing a variety of negative outcomes, such as lower cognitive and educational achievement, poorer physical health, and higher rates of mental illness.[97] One reason is that poverty is a multisystemic stressor for children. It is associated with family stress, such as parents who are depressed and anxious and who are consequently less sensitive to and invested in their offspring.[98] Poverty is accompanied by resource deprivation, including nutritional inadequacy, housing instability, and inadequate medical and dental care. Poverty is also associated with neighborhoods that are drained of resources for families and are sometimes dangerous, as well as having poor child care, and poor and failing schools.[99] All of these stressors contribute to the profound and enduring effects of poverty on young children.

An additional explanation for the multifaceted and enduring consequences of poverty for children is its effects on the developing brain. Childhood poverty is associated with decrements in both the structure and functioning of brain regions related to memory, cognition, language, and emotional processing, including the hippocampus, prefrontal cortex, and amygdala.[100] These neurobiological problems are associated with some of the mental and emotional difficulties of children in poverty, such as their poorer academic achievement.[101] Furthermore, consistent with the multiple stresses associated with family poverty early in life, additional research shows that children in poverty show significant difficulties in neurobiological systems governing stress regulation, consistent with their behavioral problems of emotion management.[102] The effects of poverty on brain and behavior have been shown to begin during the first year after birth.[103]

These studies underscore, therefore, another way of understanding brain-mind interconnections – that is, with respect to the effects of early adversity on their codevelopment.[104] The consistent association of early childhood poverty with behavioral problems and with deficits in the neurobiological systems relevant to those behaviors is what we would expect to find if mind and brain are codeveloping in the context of adversity. These findings also provide a foundation for the design of early interventions for children in economic difficulty.[105] As one illustration, an innovative experimental program provided large, unconditional monthly payments for several years to a sample of mothers in low income, beginning shortly after they gave birth. Unconditional cash transfers of this kind have been shown in previous research to be an effective means of reducing poverty and some of the effects of poverty on children's development. Preliminary findings from this study in 2022 indicated that, compared with a control sample that received only nominal monthly payments, infants of mothers receiving the larger payments showed, at one year of age, changes in brain activity consistent with stronger early cognitive development.[106] These are the first experimental findings of the impact of income supplements on the brain development of young children, and complement a more extensive research literature on the cognitive and behavioral gains for children yielded by similar kinds of early interventions.

Because poverty is a multisystemic stressor for children, it is important for future research to conceptually unpack poverty to better understand its specific effects on brain and mental development. Among the multiple (and overlapping) stressors associated with poverty are the effects of nutritional deficiency and exposure to harmful substances.

Nutritional deficiency associated with poverty is important because the developing brain consumes up to 60% of the total metabolic rate early in development.[107] And because the neurobiological effects of food inadequacy can even be observed prenatally, it poses a significant hazard to the developing brain. More specifically, malnutrition constitutes a serious threat to structural brain development, including risk of decreased numbers of neurons and synapses, impaired myelination, and thinning of the cerebral cortex. In addition, because malnutrition is accompanied by diminished attention and responsiveness to environmental stimuli,[108] it has behavioral consequences that pose indirect threats to brain and cognitive growth. Young children in families experiencing economic adversity may fall behind cognitively because of its effects on their ability to devote full attention to learning opportunities. These threats are especially acute the earlier they occur in brain development, and they justify concern for the early detection of nutritional deficits because of the possibility of reversing harms with interventions that can restore nutritional adequacy.

Concerning hazardous exposures, a wide range of harmful substances also pose potential threats to early brain development beginning prenatally, including lead exposure (encountered by the families in Flint, Michigan, who were exposed to sustained high levels of lead from their water system in 2014–2019) and other environmental chemicals (such as mercury from fish and organophosphates used in pesticides), controlled substances, and chemicals found in consumer products. These and other harmful substances (such as maternal alcohol use) are hazards to brain development prenatally as well as following birth.[109]

The serious consequences for early brain development of nutritional deficiencies and hazardous exposures underscore a general rule about development: the younger the organism, the greater the pace of growth but also the greater the vulnerability. Our astonishment over the rapid pace of early development of the brain and mind should be coupled with concern for the many risk factors that can undermine healthy development, along with a commitment to reducing and eliminating these hazards as much as possible. Fortunately, the young brain's plasticity is also a protective factor because it holds the promise of recovery from early harms if hazardous conditions can be remediated. This is one reason for an emphasis on early detection and intervention – an emphasis that research on the developing brain and mind supports.

Fetal Brain "Programming"

When in development is brain growth most rapid? Not during the first three years of life. Rather, it is the nine months of prenatal development. Prenatal development is not only the period of the most profound growth of brain and body, but it is also a period of heightened vulnerability to nutritional deficiencies, hazardous exposures, and other harms to the developing child. As noted in the preceding paragraphs, vulnerability to these harms is especially acute during the prenatal months because of the rapid development of fetal body and brain, and most of these hazards are mediated by the mother's condition during pregnancy.

Prenatal development is also when preparation begins for life after birth. In addition to growing rapidly, the fetus also adjusts to signals from the mother's body concerning the conditions of life outside the womb. These signals consist, for example, of the mother's caloric intake and other indicators of nutritional status (reflecting food (in)sufficiency in the environment), stress hormones like cortisol in the mother's bloodstream (reflecting threat in the environment), and other aspects of the mother's physiological condition. Prenatal growth is altered by these signals in a manner that suggests the preparation of the body and brain for the same environmental conditions after birth. Some of the most compelling evidence for this, which began causing researchers to think about the biological programming of prenatal development in new ways, is research on the Dutch Hunger Winter, as described below.

During World War II, the German military occupying the Netherlands imposed a blockade of food transports in reprisal for a strike on the Dutch railways in support of the Allied invasion. As a result, official rations for the adult population fell abruptly to 400–800 calories daily from December 1944 to April 1945, when the Allied liberation of the Netherlands began to succeed and food transport was quickly restored. These circumstances, tragic as they were, created a unique opportunity for researchers to subsequently examine the effects of a time-limited period of maternal malnutrition and subsequent nutritional adequacy on the immediate and long-term development of offspring. The children born to the women who were pregnant in the Dutch Hunger Winter have now been followed into late adulthood. Studies have shown that many of the immediate effects of maternal malnutrition on newborns (such as lower birth weight) did not, surprisingly, foreshadow poorer developmental outcomes in later years. But there were other enduring consequences based on the effects of malnutrition on organ system and brain development, especially for those whose mothers were malnourished early in their pregnancy. Their children were at significantly greater risk as adults for a variety of health and mental health problems, including adult obesity, heart disease, high blood pressure, and schizophrenic disorders, compared with children of different gestational age or same-sex sibling controls who did not experience the same prenatal malnutrition early in gestation.[110]

Why did these outcomes occur? One explanation is that fetal malnutrition had caused changes to energy metabolism and growth rate that made newborns more capable of living after birth in conditions of food scarcity, which was an environmental challenge signaled by the mother's malnutrition. By adapting biologically in these ways, the infants born to malnourished mothers were more likely to survive after birth. In this manner, the fetus is biologically prepared for conditions early in life. But the survivors of the Dutch famine did not grow up in deprivation but grew up instead in conditions of plenty, and they were biologically unprepared for this. This dyssynchrony between their fetal programming and the conditions after birth likely contributed to their later health and mental health problems. Biological and neurobiological systems developed for limited food intake, appetite regulation, and small physical size, for example, did not function well in postnatal settings of generous food supply.[111] Added to these were the effects of chronic maternal stress during the winter months, which undermined developing fetal stress reactivity and regulation. These and related findings contribute to the view that the conditions of prenatal development allow early detection of characteristics of the environment to which the developing fetus biologically adapts in preparation for life after birth.[112]

Guided by this view, researchers have been especially concerned with the effects of chronic maternal stress on the developing fetus, especially given that 15–20% of pregnant women experience depression or anxiety symptoms, and these rates increase in the context of other stresses of pregnancy, such as difficult employment conditions, strain in close relationships, and low income.[113] Chronic maternal stress has direct effects on the fetal brain: it increases cortisol levels in the brain and contributes to the development of heightened stress reactivity in newborns.[114] By six months, the infants of mothers who were prenatally depressed showed weaker connections between the amygdala and the prefrontal cortex,[115] which suggests compromised emotion regulation beginning early in infancy. The behavioral effects of fetal exposure to maternal stress can be enduring, and include heightened emotional reactivity and enhanced risk for depression or anxiety as late as adolescence.[116] In one study, for example, the offspring of nearly 8,000 mothers who had been screened for symptoms of depression and anxiety during pregnancy were followed through early adolescence. Children of mothers who showed higher levels of anxiety and/or depression scored higher on an inventory of emotional and behavioral problems from age four through age thirteen, and had twice the risk that they would later be diagnosed with an emotional or mental disorder.[117]

If maternal stress provides biological signals of a world that is aversive, then the behavioral and brain development observed in the offspring of these mothers should reflect preparation for postnatal life in a challenging environment. Although we do not ordinarily consider emotionally reactive and dysregulated responding to be adaptive, these behaviors may prepare a developing child to respond quickly and strongly to threats that arise, and so promote survival in an aversive environment.[118] These and related behaviors may be adaptations to a threatening world, although when the environment is not dangerous – such as in a school classroom – the same dysregulated behaviors may prove to be dysfunctional. Young children who respond quickly and strongly to perceived threat are likely to overreact to ordinary peer provocations, for example, compared with children whose prenatal growth has been less stressed.

For this reason, research on fetal programming, especially in the context of maternal stress during pregnancy, has been coupled with intervention efforts to reduce sources of stress for expectant mothers. The research on fetal programming also suggests other preventive avenues owing to the different ways that developing brains and behavior are influenced by the intrauterine conditions of rapid physical growth. In particular, broadening access to prenatal care for pregnant women, especially those in economic difficulty, is important to preventing potential harms to the developing fetus deriving from maternal health practices, chemical exposures, nutritional inadequacy, drug dependency, and other problems. More broadly, this work raises questions about the extent to which early intervention programs for infants and young children growing up in adversity should begin prenatally to address the developmental consequences of these conditions. There is some evidence that programs with a prenatal component show greater benefits for the children of families in adversity compared with programs that begin after birth.[119]

Adolescence and the "Resculpting" of the Developing Brain

Chapter 2 profiled adolescent brain development within the framework of psycholegal debates about adolescent culpability and responsibility. In that discussion, the emphasis was on the immaturity of critical brain areas (particularly in the prefrontal cortex) governing self-regulation. But the immaturity of the adolescent brain is not the most important story of adolescent brain development to have emerged in the last twenty-five years of research, although it may be the most well known. Rather, it is the discovery that as the result of multiple neurobiological changes over a few short years, adolescence may be "a critical period for experience-dependent neural plasticity,"[120] especially for the development of higher cognitive skills and social understanding.

Developmental neuroscientists have long known that adolescence witnesses significant growth in brain structure and function as the neurodevelopmental processes earlier discussed continue to be influential throughout the teenage years. During adolescence, for example, there is continued synaptic proliferation followed by pruning based on experience. In addition, myelination continues apace, and there is also continued growth in neural networks in different brain regions.

What is new during adolescence is, of course, puberty.[121] Puberty consists of two biological processes: adrenarche (maturation of the adrenal glands, beginning in middle childhood and continuing throughout adolescence) and gonadarche (maturation of the gonadal glands, beginning in early adolescence and continuing throughout adolescence). Although the latter has been studied more extensively, there is evidence that many of the neurobiological changes associated with puberty actually begin earlier with adrenarche.[122] Together, the upsurge in pubertal hormones is associated with the growth of prefrontal function and expanded neural connections between higher (cortical) and lower (subcortical) brain regions, greater activity in brain areas associated with reward processing, and the emergence of sex differences in the hippocampus, amygdala, and other brain areas.[123] There are also changes in a suite of brain networks underlying social responding, such as those implicated in the "social brain" and the capacity for mentalizing (described in the preceding chapter), as well as growth in social-emotional processing (e.g., the analysis of emotion in faces) and heightened sensitivity to peer evaluation.[124]

These neurobiological advances are consistent with some of the distinguishing features of adolescent development: significant advances in reasoning and abstract thinking, greater competence with and orientation toward peers, and growing sex differences in behavior and thinking. Although much work remains in connecting these behavioral changes in adolescence to growth in specific brain areas,[125] there is general agreement among researchers that these multifaceted neurobiological changes create new plasticity in the brain's development, perhaps in preparation for managing the challenges of the adult world.

If this is true, what does it mean for how we should think about adolescent development? Some argue that this period of heightened brain plasticity in adolescence creates a "window of opportunity" for the promotion of positive brain and behavioral growth.[126] Strategies for doing so build on emergent abilities enabled by these neurodevelopmental changes, such as youth participation in STEM activities that enlist higher cognitive skills, or peer counseling activities that enlist growing social sensitivity. Other strategies seek to mitigate some of the developmental vulnerabilities of this period, such as promoting the early detection of mental health or substance abuse problems, and improved management or regulation of social media. In many respects, these proposals are similar to those of the Positive Youth Development movement profiled at the conclusion of Chapter 2. As noted then, it is ironic that as selected elements of the developmental neuroscience of adolescence are enlisted in public messaging to reinforce cultural stereotypes of troubled youth, a much more substantive neuroscience literature documents the significant growth and experience-based plasticity of the developing brain that could inspire more positive cultural portrayals of adolescence as well as less coercive and more supportive public policy.

More broadly, the developmental neuroscience of adolescence calls into question an exclusive focus on early childhood as the only formative period of brain development. This narrow focus on early childhood is wrong on two counts: it begins too late (prenatal development witnesses faster and more vulnerable brain growth) and ends too soon (adolescence is a second period of significant neurobiological growth and plasticity). Furthermore, if adolescence is a time of experience-based "resculpting" of the developing brain, it is possible that programs to support healthy brain development can be oriented toward the emergent capacities and vulnerabilities of youth, and may provide unique opportunities compared with early childhood for strengthening those and other developmental competencies.

Emergent Issues in Developmental Neuroscience

The topics discussed in this section – poverty, fetal brain programming, and adolescence – are important to understanding the developing brain and the experiences and influences that shape its growth. Each topic was the focus of considerable research at the time that public messaging about the developing brain began to take shape in the late 1990s, but they are described as "lesser-known" in this chapter because they were not included in the public campaign. Discussing them here raises the question of why not – and sets the stage for the next chapters, in which I discuss the orientation of the media campaign that introduced the public to early brain development, along with the subsequent framing of this message for multiple audiences and different purposes. In the chapters that follow, I consider how and why the prevailing story of early brain development was created and shaped, some of the public messaging priorities it reflected, and why some aspects of the brain development story were included, and others were not.

The topics discussed in this section also illustrate how much the story of brain development is continuously changing as the result of new scientific discoveries. This can be a source of confusion or consternation to public audiences who do not expect that current scientific understanding – whether concerning dietary recommendations or preventing COVID-19 infection – should evolve so quickly. But if the science seems to be a moving target, it reflects the fact that science is not static. As this chapter was being written, for example, interesting new research was emerging on the influence of the immune system on brain development,[127] the interactions between the gut microbiome and the developing brain,[128] and the influence of sleep on brain functioning in childhood and adolescence,[129] as well as other topics. These and other current issues will continue to reshape the science of the developing brain in the years to come and, depending on how it is communicated, change public understanding as well.

The theme of this chapter concerns the story of brain development – or rather, the stories of brain development told via developmental neuroscience and developmental science. Although highly consistent, the divergences between these two accounts underscore the different frameworks, levels of analysis, and concepts used by scientists in each field that yield different perspectives on the developing child. In the next chapter, I show how these divergent approaches proved to be problematic to creating an integrated, consistent account of early development for public communication.

In Chapter 4, I begin exploring how the story of brain development that became familiar to the public was created, and the goals and interests that guided its messaging. We turn now to the events leading up to the *I Am Your Child* campaign that began in April 1997, and its continuing legacy.

CHAPTER 4

I Am Your Child

While enjoying their breakfast cereal and coffee, television viewers on the Monday morning of April 14, 1997, found Katie Couric talking about early brain development on the *Today* show. They would find her doing the same on Tuesday through Friday of that week, discussing research discoveries and their implications with leading researchers. On Wednesday, the White House Conference on Early Childhood Development and Learning was broadcast across the country, where Bill and Hillary Clinton listened to scientific experts discuss the importance of the early years. During the week following, *Good Morning America* (*Today*'s rival on ABC) broadcast its own five-day series on parenting and brain development. ABC also presented a one-hour primetime special, *I Am Your Child*, on the following Monday, April 28, featuring Tom Hanks, Robin Williams, General Colin Powell, Oprah, Charlton Heston, the President and First Lady, and many others talking about the developing brain. Viewers learned how to send for a booklet, video, and CD-ROM and access a website explaining the science and its implications in more detail. At the newsstand, a special issue of *Newsweek* magazine (one of the two major weekly newsmagazines) was released on April 25 devoted to early brain development (*Time* magazine, the other major newsweekly, had published its own special coverage earlier in the year). Depending on where you lived, there may have been other state and local events devoted to the importance of early experience on brain growth. The message about the significance of early brain development in the initial years of life would have been difficult to miss.

The events of April 1997 were the beginning of a three-year campaign called *I Am Your Child* to increase public awareness of the influence of early experience on brain development. It was the result of more than two years of planning that involved the contributions of media celebrities, major foundation officials, developmental scientists and neuroscientists, specialists in advertising and communications, and the Clinton administration. Planning for the April events also included the development of public service announcements (PSAs) to be broadcast on different media channels, outreach to national and community organizations advocating for young children to encourage coordinated efforts of their own, preparation of campaign materials in Spanish and other languages and their targeted distribution, the release of national polling data on the beliefs and needs of parents of young children, publication of a major study by the RAND Corporation on the economic benefits of public investment in early childhood programs, outreach to the military and the business community, and planning for follow-up broadcasts and testimony before Congress.

For many people, encountering one or more of these events was their first serious exposure to brain development research and its implications for parents and society. The *I Am Your Child* campaign is important for at least two additional reasons. The first is that it is one of the earliest and most ambitious examples of what I have called "campaign journalism."[1] Campaign journalism is the effort to create public engagement in an issue through a large-scale communications strategy that weds science and advocacy and is designed to generate continuing attention to the issue in the media. It derives its name from its resemblance to the strategies and goals of a political campaign, and its purpose, like a political campaign, is to generate and mobilize public attention and support for its ideas. Traditional forms of science journalism rely, as I noted in Chapter 1, on the relatively piecemeal reporting of new discoveries by science journalists who can apply a critical perspective to their reporting by comparing new discoveries with earlier knowledge and soliciting other viewpoints. Campaign journalism bypasses this model entirely by bringing a large body of science and its applications directly to the public through TV, media events, videos and CDs (now online forums) and, by combining the messaging with other newsworthy events, creates a cascade of continuing coverage that enhances its impact: media momentum. Campaign journalism thus combines an uncritical message with wide dissemination. Other examples of campaign journalism over the years can be observed in advocacy efforts to engage public concern about smoking, teenage pregnancy prevention, youth substance abuse, divorce (and the "deinstitutionalization of marriage"), and the politicized public debates for or against abortion. The *I Am Your Child* campaign emerged just as the economic model of traditional journalism was breaking down along with the emergence of a broadening variety of alternative media sources as well as nontraditional and social media. Campaign journalism is manifested today when advocates work to make issues go viral on social media in a manner that combines a comparably uncritical message and an action agenda with its wide dissemination. The approach of campaign journalism of *I Am Your Child* is a model, therefore, for how science becomes public knowledge to influence policy and practice that is increasingly relevant to the current era, but was unusual at the time in its scale and impact.

The second reason this campaign is important is because it created enduring themes for public understanding of early brain development and its implications. It did so because it was the first large-scale communication of developmental brain science that incorporated strategies for continued messaging, and thus most other subsequent coverage of the developing brain was built on the central ideas of the 1997 campaign. Consequently, the core messages of *I Am Your Child* – that early experiences are crucial in shaping the developing brain; that key experiences must occur during early "windows of opportunity," especially during the first three years; and that among the most important of these experiences is nurturant, warm parental care – have helped to shape enduring elements of public understanding about the developing brain. How did these core messages come about? Why these messages and not others? What influences, in short, shaped the campaign? Understanding the answers to these questions can help explain some of the important influences on public understanding of developmental science, both in 1997 and today, with implications for how to improve the public communication of science in the future.

Preparing the Way

The brain development revolution began in 1997. But revolutions never begin as suddenly as they appear. Both the scientific world and the public was prepared for the 1997 campaign by events of the preceding decade.

One was the explosion of new technologies for imaging brains. Throughout most of the twentieth century, clinical and research progress in neuroscience was limited by the technologies available for examining the brain's structure and functioning. In the 1980s, however, the development of magnetic resonance imaging (MRI), followed quickly by functional MRI (fMRI), significantly extended earlier technologies by offering much greater specificity and temporal resolution of the data they provided. They also presented compelling visual images of the brain that could be appreciated, in a general manner, even by nonspecialists. The result was an explosion of neuroscience research and medical applications in the 1980s that has continued to this day. The designation of the 1990s as the Decade of the Brain by President George H. W. Bush foreshadowed significantly enhanced public investment and public interest in neuroscience research and clinical applications not only in the United States but also in the United Kingdom and other countries.[2]

Developmental neuroscience broke into public awareness not because of its clinical applications, but as a means of reconsidering longstanding questions about child development. One example is a series of articles by Ronald Kotulak published in the *Chicago Tribune* in 1993 that were stimulated by an editor's question: "Why do some children turn out bad?"[3] Kotulak's series devoted considerable attention to brain development as one reason, describing the influence of early experience on the brain's neural connections, the importance of critical periods of formative influence, the influence of neurohormones, and the impact of impoverished and stressful early environments. Although the scope of his inquiry (for which Kotulak won the Pulitzer Prize in 1994) was much broader,[4] his attention to brain development for understanding "why children turn out bad" appeared to confirm the relevance of neuroscience to important questions about children's development. By seamlessly integrating insights from developmental science with those of developmental neuroscience, Kotulak offered a compelling account, although it was a story that exaggerated the explanatory power of the neuroscience as it existed in the early 1990s.

Shortly after Kotulak's series appeared, the Carnegie Corporation of New York released *Starting Points: Meeting the Needs of Our Youngest Children.*[5] By "youngest children," the task force of developmental scholars and public figures writing the report focused on birth to age three, a period of development generally overlooked in public policy. Perhaps for this reason, the 132-page report described a "quiet crisis" among families with young children, citing the high poverty rates of families with young children, high infant mortality, and deficiencies in children's school readiness. The report devoted only about twenty pages to analyzing this crisis, however, and only three pages discussed early brain development. The conclusions offered by the task force in these three pages, however, are similar to those of Kotulak: the developing brain is vulnerable to early environmental influences and these effects can be long lasting; experiences affect how the brain becomes "wired"; and early stress has a negative impact.

At the report's release, extensive media coverage focused on the news about brain development – building perhaps on the impact of the Kotulak series – and not on the policy proposals, which were fairly pedestrian recommendations to "promote responsible parenting," "ensure good health and protection," and "guarantee quality child care choices." An article titled "Children in Peril" by *Washington Post* columnist Judy Mann is representative of these media accounts:

> The Carnegie report is particularly startling because it is grounded in scientific research about what happens to the brain. It is adamant on this point: The single most important way to avoid psychosocial problems later on is for infants and toddlers to enjoy loving, caring relationships with their parents.[6]

In fact, the section on the developing brain said nothing about the importance of nurturant care, although this was discussed extensively elsewhere in the report. But the commentariat, taking their cue from the report, moved smoothly from discoveries in developmental neuroscience to research conclusions in developmental science and, in doing so, gave the impression that the neuroimaging research was more substantive and pointed about the importance of nurturant care than it actually was.

Perhaps this is one of the reasons why *Starting Points* received the attention it did. Another reason is that it aligned very well with the policy priorities of the Clinton administration and its liberal constituencies. After the failure of health care reform in 1994, the administration turned to other domestic initiatives, including a guaranteed twelve weeks of family and medical leave, a children's health insurance program, the enactment of the Goals 2000 Education Standards (including the goal that "all children will start school ready to learn"), a child tax credit, Head Start reform and expansion, and increased funding for child care and child care subsidies. Each of these initiatives found support in the *Starting Points* report recommendations, so it was not surprising that the report was released at a press conference attended by major cabinet officers and the First Lady, and that members of the task force were already working with Congress to advance administration initiatives. Legislation to create a new Early Head Start program for one- to three-year-olds, for example, was passed by Congress a week after the release of the *Starting Points* report.

One of the readers of *Starting Points* was Rob Reiner, Hollywood producer and cofounder of Castle Rock Entertainment, but probably best known at that time as Archie Bunker's beleaguered son-in-law Meathead in the popular 1970s sitcom *All in the Family*. Since then, Reiner had established himself as one of the most prominent producers and directors in the field, directing well-known movies such as *When Harry Met Sally* and *The Princess Bride*. But he had also endured a painful divorce that propelled him into Kleinian therapy[7] for nine years and a new look at his own childhood and its effects on his life. By 1994, he had a new wife, Michele Singer Reiner, two young children, and another on the way. The *Starting Points* report crystallized his concern that although the first three years are crucially important to human development, they are largely ignored by the public and politicians alike. He set out to change that.

I Am Your Child

Reiner did what anybody would do: he placed a cold call to Tipper Gore, wife of Vice President Al Gore.[8] For a longstanding Democratic party contributor with public visibility and access, it was a natural starting place because of Gore's high-profile work in mental health and children's issues. Tipper Gore encouraged Reiner to promote the "0–3 field," so he contacted Michael Levine, the senior program officer at the Carnegie Corporation who had helped direct the *Starting Points* report, to ask him to prepare a briefing for Reiner and his associates to dig deeper into the issues discussed in the report.

The briefing took place in December 1994 at Reiner's home in the exclusive Brentwood section of Los Angeles. Levine had invited Barry Zuckerman, a pediatrician at Boston University who was part of the task force that wrote *Starting Points*, and Ellen Galinsky, who was president and cofounder of the Families and Work Institute (FWI), a nonprofit devoted to work-family issues, and who had consulted on *Starting Points*, to help lead the briefing. Galinsky was an important choice because of her long track record of bridging science and family policy. She was also important because of the extensive state-level advocacy networks of the FWI: after the 1994 midterm elections had given Republicans unified control of Congress, it was clear to Levine that state-level initiatives would be important to advancing the goals of the report. Several members of the Vice President's staff were also present, along with representatives of Carnegie and several other child development experts. Reiner and his wife invited actor Warren Beatty and his wife, actor Annette Benning; director Steven Spielberg and his wife, actor Kate Capshaw; Los Angeles mayor Richard Riordan; and other friends and colleagues to the gathering.

After the briefing concluded, the focus of the group's discussion was on what to do next. After several ideas were proposed and rejected, Warren Beatty suggested that they should do what Hollywood knows best: sell these ideas to the public. The public relations approach took hold, and

Reiner began talking about doing a TV special and other high visibility events. Galinsky mentioned that FWI had received funding from AT&T to create a public awareness campaign on parent involvement in children's education, and suggested coordinating this effort with Reiner's public engagement campaign. Carnegie would also be involved in several ways as a follow-up to the *Starting Points* report.

The project then proceeded on several tracks. Reiner began working on the media side of the campaign, assisted by his wife and by Ellen Gilbert of International Creative Management, a talent agency. By early 1995, Reiner had secured a commitment from ABC-TV for a primetime special on early childhood development that his production team would develop. During the week of the special, local ABC affiliates would join the ABC-TV morning news program *Good Morning America* to present their own daily reports about the local implications of the new science of early development. *Newsweek* magazine also committed to a special issue on the developing brain that would appear concurrently with the television special, and which would follow another cover story entitled "Your Child's Brain" by Sharon Begley that was to appear in the February 19, 1996, issue. The special issue would be solely sponsored by Johnson & Johnson, which had emerged as one of the major corporate funders of the campaign. Other corporate sponsors included AT&T (which supported the FWI work as well as the creation of PSAs), IBM (which funded the development of a CD-ROM for parents), Kaiser Permanente (which sponsored a conference for business leaders), and the Heinz Foundation. Greer, Margolis, Mitchell, and Burns, a political communications firm, was enlisted to promote the campaign and to assist in creating the state and local coalitions that would help to advance its agenda. The Ad Council was commissioned to create PSAs to promote the campaign's message and worked with Public Agenda, a public opinion analysis group, to refine the messaging of the campaign.

The goal was to create a series of media events that would compel public attention to early developmental issues and create continuing coverage of these issues. It was already clear from the response to *Starting Points* that focusing on the developing brain was a powerful tool for eliciting public attention, which could then be used to educate and inform audiences about broader developmental concerns. But by contrast with the *Starting Points* report, in which brain development received fairly minimal coverage, this campaign would foreground discoveries about the developing brain because of strong response that neuroscience messaging was evoking. The campaign would be called "I Am Your Child" to personalize the message and establish its relevance to every family,[9] and the tagline "the first years last forever" succinctly summarized its primary message. At a preparatory meeting subsequently hosted by Carnegie of public communication specialists who had worked on large national public awareness campaigns on smoking, drug abuse, child abuse, and other concerns, representatives from the Ad Council noted that crisis-oriented messages (e.g., "the kids aren't ready for school") were ineffective because of a tendency of viewers to blame "bad parents" and overlook any constructive recommendations. Instead, the campaign would emphasize a positive, can-do orientation: parenting is difficult, we all need support, we want to give kids a good start.

In the meantime, Galinsky and Levine worked on developing the scientific messaging. With funding from Carnegie and several other philanthropies,[10] they convened a two-day conference in June 1996 at the University of Chicago with more than 150 neuroscientists, developmental scientists, clinical child psychologists, program administrators, and experts in early education, as well as business leaders, philanthropists, policymakers, and reporters. The goal of the conference was to discuss recent advances in developmental neuroscience and to consider how it can be communicated to the public – or as Galinsky put it, "what is the story to tell." A report of the conference was subsequently written by Rima Shore, a faculty member at Bank Street College of Education in New York and a contributor to *Starting Points*, entitled *Rethinking the Brain: New Insights into Early Development.*[11]

By contrast with *Starting Points*, brain development was center stage at the June conference and the *Rethinking* report, which was released to coincide with the White House conference in April 1997. The report was elegantly written and produced, and managed to convey both what was known and, to its credit, the significant gaps in understanding the developing brain that existed in the late 1990s. Concerning what was known, the report described "five key lessons" learned from neuroscience that were presented very broadly: development is an interplay between nature and nurture; the human brain has a remarkable capacity to change, but timing is crucial; early care and nurture have a decisive impact; there are times when negative experiences or the absence of appropriate stimulation can have serious and sustained effects. Another lesson, one indicating the "wisdom and efficacy of early intervention," required generous extrapolations from the limited neuroscientific evidence of therapeutic efficacy and relied instead on research on behavioral interventions. The report underscored the importance of early care for "how people develop, their ability to learn, and their capacity to regulate their own emotions" by drawing on significant research literatures in developmental science, including attachment theory. The report recognized, however, that the unanswered questions far exceeded existing knowledge, and among the "tough questions" it posed (without providing answers) were those concerning whether new mothers (apparently not fathers) should stay home with their young children, how rigid is the timing of critical periods, and the relative importance of nurture in relation to the influence of genes.

In its effort to recognize the tension between exciting discoveries and daunting unknowns, the report reflects tensions that were already emerging among the organizers of the *I Am Your Child* campaign. In particular, there were disagreements between Reiner and Galinsky concerning the scientific messaging, particularly the strong emphasis on development from birth to age three, which Reiner believed was the most critical period of life, but Galinsky and Levine argued that such a claim about such a narrow early developmental window is not supported by the evidence. Reiner earned the respect of his collaborators for his commitment to working within the science, but he also understood the compelling impact of a dramatic message: at a National Governors Association winter meeting in February 1997, Reiner commented that "by age 10, your brain is cooked and there's nothing much you can do."[12] As Levine noted to me, "we had concerns, and we expressed those concerns, and they were considered and more or less rejected."

As the planning proceeded, the political world was preparing for a national election. Late in 1996, Reiner and his wife requested an opportunity to discuss their public engagement campaign with the President, who was in the midst of his reelection campaign. To their surprise, they were given fifteen minutes with the President and one of his aides (it helps to be a major party donor). When Clinton asked at the end of their presentation what they wanted him to do, the Reiners were prepared. They proposed a White House conference devoted to the topic of early brain development and placing a priority on early childhood development for his next term. They also asked Clinton to mention these issues in his next State of the Union address, which he later did. Referring to the "startling new findings" to be presented at the promised White House conference, Clinton said in his address to Congress that "scientists are now discovering how young children develop emotionally and intellectually from their very first days, and how important it is for parents to begin immediately talking, singing, even reading to their infants."

This set the stage for the White House conference in April. For most of the twentieth century, White House conferences on children were a regular decennial event. The first White House Conference on Children was inaugurated by Theodore Roosevelt in 1909, and subsequent conferences were organized regularly until 1980, when it morphed into a White House Conference on Families and then was never heard from again. In their heyday, these conferences led to significant policy reform on behalf of children and their families, including promoting initiatives for the support of dependent children, improvement of health care, and the creation of federal agencies to monitor and support children's development. The Clinton administration sponsored several White House conferences (including a subsequent conference on child care), but the White House Conference on Early Childhood Development and Learning was central to Hillary Clinton's longstanding interest in children's issues. She had written about the discoveries of early brain development a year earlier in her book *It Takes a Village.*[13] The subtitle of the conference, "What the Newest Research on the Brain Tells Us about Our Youngest Children," helps to explain why the conference was known among White House staffers during its planning as the "White House Conference on the Brain."[14]

The First Lady opened the conference by summarizing the themes of the day (and, incidentally, of the *I Am Your Child* campaign):

> And as we now know, for the first three years of their life, so much is happening in the baby's brain. They will learn to soothe themselves when they're upset, to empathize, to get along. These experiences can determine whether children will grow up to be peaceful or violent citizens, focused or undisciplined workers, attentive or detached parents themselves.[15]

Even though she cautioned that brain development is not over at age three but continues (at least for emotions, she said, "until a child reaches 15"), the focus on early brain development in the opening years was described as most important for establishing a foundation for what follows. But after the conclusion of her remarks, only one neuroscientist spoke at the conference. The rest of the speakers discussed research or clinical work on children's attachments, language, emotional growth, and other topics, or profiled interventions that enlist this work.[16] Consequently, participants and viewers learned a great deal about research on early development and learning, but relatively little about the developing brain. However, the attentive presence of the President and First Lady throughout the morning session, its broad dissemination (broadcast by satellite to nearly a hundred hospitals, universities, and schools in thirty-seven states) and extensive news coverage made the conference a highly visible kickoff to the campaign.

The other media events of April 1997 continued the same theme. On the *Today* show, Katie Couric interviewed experts throughout the week on a wide range of themes, including child care quality, early language, music and brain development, and even the growth of character and values, but always with reference to the developing brain. Likewise for Joan Lunden and her series on *Good Morning America* the following week. Rob Reiner appeared throughout the month on talk shows (including *The Oprah Winfrey Show, The Tonight Show,* and *Larry King Live*) to further promote the campaign's messaging. The ABC special on April 28[17] was a combination of information (with Tom Hanks, the host, speaking directly to the camera), humor, entertaining skits, profiles of programs to assist parents, and many first-person interviews with parents of young children, but the messages were unmistakable and were consistent with the themes of the White House conference.[18] Bill and Hillary Clinton closed the show with a living-room conversation about whether they had provided enough hugs to Chelsea in her infancy, and Colin Powell was filmed reading *Goodnight, Moon* to his grandson.

The campaign provided information to parents and practitioners in other ways, including videocassettes, booklets, a CD-ROM that could be purchased, and a well-designed website. In most of these materials, the messages of the campaign were summarized in a set of ten "tips for parents and caregivers" that included "be warm, loving, and responsive," "talk, sing, and read to your child," "encourage exploration and play," "make television watching selective," "use discipline as an opportunity to teach," and "choose quality child care and stay involved." The website included further information about the developing brain, advice from experts in early development and clinical medicine, responses to frequently asked questions, and a description of major developmental accomplishments through age three. The I Am Your Child Foundation was created to administer these materials as well as promote further messaging, and Levine moved from his position at Carnegie to become executive director of the foundation in 2000. In addition, the Families and Work Institute enlisted and expanded its network of state and community organizations to create local coalitions and initiatives that could build on the national rollout of *I Am Your Child.*

Excitement and Anxiety

All of this messaging informed parents, but it was less clear whether they were helped or reassured. On the first episode of the *Today* series, a parent said, "it's kind of like a catch-22 – the more you know, the scarier it is," and Couric asked at the close, "Parents should trust their instincts, right?"

But maybe not. With all the emphasis on the importance of early experiences *but also* the documentation of wide variability in language, learning, and even brain size by age three, parents had reason to be made anxious by these broadcasts. Suppose they didn't provide what their young child's brain required? In the results of a national survey of more than 1,000 parents conducted during the previous month released at the time of the White House Conference, the national nonprofit Zero to Three reported that most parents of children under age three did not feel that they could identify the signs of healthy intellectual, social, or emotional development in their young child. Furthermore, one in four did not know what they could do to stimulate their child's intellectual growth, and 87% believed that the more stimulation a baby received, the better off the child would be.[19] It was unclear whether these statistics would have changed if the poll was conducted again after the campaign. Matthew Melmed, executive director of Zero to Three, indicated that the campaign created "almost a sense of frenzy" among parents for further information about what to do.[20] Benjamin Spock's well-known advice to parents was to "trust your own common sense," but one effect of the brain development messaging was to convince parents that maybe they did not know enough to do the job right.

The media coverage of the campaign likewise reflected both the excitement of new discoveries in developmental brain science and new anxieties for parents. Frank Newman, president of the Education Commission of the States, was quoted in the *St. Louis Post-Dispatch* in August 1997 as saying, "I don't think there is any question that these revelations have a major impact on education policy and child rearing" but offering few specific suggestions about what those revelations were.[21] Not so pediatrician Bruce Epstein, quoted in the *Tampa Bay Times* in July as recommending: "Children need to feel confident about what to expect from their environment. A child needs discipline. A child needs a balanced experience of freedom and limits,"[22] but reporter Susan Duerksen's story in the *San Diego Union-Tribune* was headlined "Researchers Unsure about Links between Music and IQ."[23] Syndicated columnists offered their own views, from the *Chicago Tribune*'s Joan Beck ("Our goal must be to provide all children with ample opportunities to learn well starting at birth")[24] to the *Orlando Sentinel*'s Kathleen Parker:

> But if the President and Mrs. Clinton really want to do something good for the country, they should encourage parents to stay home the first three years. Staying home might mean postponing some things – material items, job advances, even other kids. But that's what our nation's children really need, and in our hearts, we know it.[25]

Whether mothers should stay home was, of course, one of the "tough questions" unanswered in *Rethinking the Brain*, but Parker was not alone. *Time* magazine's feature story on early brain development (subtitled "And What It Means for Child Care and Welfare Reform")[26] was followed immediately in the same issue by an article on the "day-care dilemma." Furthermore, *Newsweek*'s initial story in 1996 about the developing brain cited worries that the reason Head Start had "fallen short" was because it provided educational assistance too late (beginning at age three) to benefit young children's developing brains.[27] In short order, advocates of early childhood education, parent training programs, prenatal care, and educational television – and critics of commercial TV, maternal employment, and welfare reform – each cited the emerging brain development science as support for their causes. Commercial manufacturers, meanwhile, began marketing products featuring classical music to improve early learning and academic performance. The brain development revolution was underway.

Scientists Respond

Like many researchers who study child development, my ambivalence about the unfolding campaign was mirrored in the messages I was reading on academic listservs. One prominent neuroscientist with whom I was acquainted fired off a note criticizing the misrepresentation of basic developmental neuroscience in the campaign's messaging, only to follow it the next day with another note applauding the unique opportunity the campaign presented to advance children's interests. The mixed feelings were understandable. Many scientists embark on their research careers hoping that their discoveries will make a difference, and this is especially true of those who study children's development. Yet by contrast with many other scientific fields (think biomedical research, information technology, or, more recently, environmental science), research on childhood development rarely makes front-page news. The *I Am Your Child* campaign created, for the first time, a national focus on issues we had been studying throughout our careers, featuring our colleagues on national television and a White House conference presenting their ideas to the world. With a few exceptions, moreover, the take-home messages of the campaign seemed well founded, whether concerning early childhood as a period of rapid and formative growth of the mind, the positive parenting practices that promote children's healthy development, or the importance of the public policies that support young children and their families. It was not so much that these messages derived directly from the brain science but rather that they were consistent with much of what was known about children and broader values about children and their development that were widely shared among academics and child advocates.

Even so, many researchers felt uncomfortable with the campaign's representation of developmental neuroscience, particularly its exaggerated and sometimes misleading conclusions about brain development. Central to their concerns were some of the key themes of the *I Am Your Child* campaign that also happened to be some of Reiner's core beliefs about the early years. These included the focus on the first three years and the view that their influence "lasts forever," the emphasis on critical periods of brain development, and the recommendation that parents enrich early experiences to promote greater brain connections. Some elements of these messages were well founded, but they were coupled with misleading exaggerations. William Greenough, a neuroscientist whose work was foundational to much of the research on which the campaign was based, wrote a commentary entitled "We Can't Focus Just on Ages 0 to 3" in the newsletter of the American Psychological Association in late 1997, urging that the years following age three also receive attention.[28] Charles Nelson, a prominent developmental neuroscientist, and I wrote a critique somewhat later in *American Psychologist*, the flagship journal of the American Psychological Association, in which we pointed out that critical periods are exceptional, not typical, in the early growth of the brain; that human brain development is lifelong; and that the specific experiences that are essential to early brain development remain to be understood.[29]

The strongest critique came from John Bruer, president of the James S. McDonnell Foundation, which is a major funder of research in neuroscience, first in a 1997 article[30] and then in his 1999 book, *The Myth of the First Three Years*.[31] As the title implies, Bruer took issue with the emphasis on infant determinism that he found in media coverage of the developing brain, arguing that this view is not based on neuroscience. Contrary to the campaign, furthermore, he claimed that developmental neuroscience actually had very little to contribute to understanding young children's developing thinking and emotions because it was such a young science with many unanswered questions.

Bruer's critique focused on three aspects of the "myth." First, he argued that contrary to "the first years last forever," there is very little evidence (certainly none from developmental neuroscience) that early experiences and influences have that kind of enduring impact. Instead, drawing on attachment theory and other research literatures, Bruer concluded that early influences are provisional and must be continued over time if they are to have impact on a child's development. He argued further that the view that early enrichment ("talk, read, and sing to your baby") promotes synapse formation that contributes to brain development is mistaken, noting that the neuroscience instead shows that it is synaptic *elimination* rather than proliferation (the "pruning" rather than the "blooming" of neural connections) that strengthens cognitive skills, and that this process extends well beyond the first three years. More synapses are not better, and early experience is at least as important for the selective pruning of synapses as for their creation. Second, Bruer argued that while some critical periods exist in brain development, they are few, often long lasting, and that the experience-expectant stimulation they require is present in ordinary human experience. Special stimulation during early time-limited "windows of opportunity" is unnecessary. Third, Bruer pointed out that enriched early experiences are not necessarily a guarantee of lifelong cognitive gains in light of all the subsequent experiences influencing the development of mind and brain. The benefits of cognitively stimulating experiences and the experience-dependent learning they promote can occur throughout all of life, not just the first three years.

Bruer's critique elicited a powerful response from the commentariat. Syndicated columnist David Boldt wrote, "Remember all that stuff you've been told about how the first three years of life are the most important period for brain development? Well, forget it."[32] Mona Charen's column was simply titled, "Child's First Three Years Not as Critical."[33] Amid the concern of developmental scientists and child advocates that reactions like these would provoke an exodus of interest in the early years as rapidly as interest had earlier grown, there was the recognition that some corrections to the campaign's messages were in order. The first three years are not the only important period for brain development (as Hillary Clinton noted at the White House Conference, "the early years are not the only years,"[34] observing that the brain is a work in progress). Critical periods are not an appropriate general model for thinking about the impact of experience on the developing brain, especially in light of the brain's continuing plasticity. Enriching early experiences should be, as every early childhood educator knows, developmentally appropriate lest young children become overstimulated or overwhelmed. These correctives reflected some of the reservations about the *I Am Your Child* campaign voiced early by people like Levine and Galinsky, and they became quickly incorporated into subsequent messaging about the developing brain, such as in the *From Neurons to Neighborhoods* report discussed below that appeared a few years later.

By focusing his critique on the low-hanging fruit in the campaign's mismessaging, however, Bruer overlooked some important ways that the messaging advanced rather than misled public understanding of developmental neuroscience. If most people did not think very much about brain development at all, much less during the years before formal schooling, there are some ways that the campaign helped move public understanding significantly forward. By contrast with the view that brain development is not important until children develop capacities for rational (and nonegocentric) reasoning in middle childhood, for example, the message of the campaign was that the brain develops very rapidly and significantly in the early years, and provides a foundation for later cognitive growth. By contrast with the view that the brain's structure and functioning are genetically fixed, the message of the campaign was that the developing brain is far more susceptible to environmental influences, and earlier in life, than many people realized. By contrast with the view that brain development is relevant primarily to children's cognitive growth, the message of the campaign was that brain development is relevant also to developing self-regulation, emotion, and social interaction. By contrast with the view that impairments to brain development are fixed and unchanging, the message of the campaign was that the growing brain retains considerable plasticity that sometimes enables recovery. By contrast with the view that early stress is transient, the message of the campaign was that there are important effects of stress on the developing brain that make young children's chronic stress a serious concern. Each of these is a valuable advance in public understanding of early brain development.

An unfortunate feature of Bruer's critique is that he was so focused on how the neuroscience was mischaracterized that he overlooked other evidence from outside developmental neuroscience that supported the central claims of the campaign. This is unfortunate because developmental science can (as I argued in Chapter 3) offer a window into influences on the developing brain even when direct neuroscience evidence is lacking. For example, while developmental neuroscience did not have direct evidence for the benefits of nurturant parental care on brain growth, there was plenty of evidence in developmental science, particularly attachment theory[35] and research in developmental psychobiology,[36] for these benefits. While Bruer was critical of the campaign's emphasis on the benefits of early enrichment, the other side of this story – the harms from early environmental impoverishment or deprivation – he ignored completely, even though there was considerable evidence for these losses from developmental science and preliminary evidence from developmental neuroscience. Indeed, the campaign's jarring neuroimages comparing the brains of typically developing young children with the brains of children liberated from Romanian orphanages attested to the significant neurodevelopmental impacts deriving from early environmental deprivation that sadly complemented distressing behavioral evidence of children's impaired functioning. While the campaign's organizers should be faulted for exaggerating the extent of the knowledge provided specifically by developmental neuroscience, there were more substantial contributions from other fields that pointed to important influences on brain development identified by the campaign.

At the same time that Bruer's critique drew attention to the limitations of developmental neuroscience, another publication from 1999 offered a more exciting, integrated portrayal of the developing mind and brain. *The Scientist in the Crib: Minds, Brains, and How Children Learn*,[37] by Alison Gopnik, Andrew Meltzoff, and Patricia Kuhl, extended and deepened the picture of early childhood from the brain development campaign. As the title implies, the authors – each accomplished developmental scientists (Kuhl presented her work at the White House Conference) – embraced Piaget's portrayal of the child as scientist and enlivened it with vivid descriptions of the findings of behavioral studies that unfold how children think. In their discussion of cleverly designed experiments that present young children with problems to solve, they showed how infants and preschoolers develop intuitive theories of the world around them, interpret evidence in relation to those theories, and revise them to make new, better theories in the face of disconfirming evidence. Young children do so in light of their close observations of the results of their own experiments performed on objects and other people in the everyday settings, whether dropping objects over the edge of a high chair to see how they fall or purposely violating parental rules to see how they react. Their account will be familiar to readers of the preceding chapter.

Appearing at the same time as *The Myth of the First Three Years* and shortly after the *I Am Your Child* campaign, *The Scientist in the Crib* indirectly offered its own critique both of Bruer and of the campaign. Concerning Bruer, the authors' evocative account highlighted how limited is any effort to characterize children's development on the basis of neuroscience alone while ignoring the remarkable behavioral achievements by which the developing brain is manifested.[38] Bruer was looking at only half the story, and missing a lot. Concerning the campaign, the account underscored how much infants and young children are active participants –

indeed, instigators – in their own brain development, by contrast with the campaign's emphasis on parents providing the right early experiences at the right time to stimulate the developing brain. The active agent in early brain development is not parents, the authors argued, but young children themselves.[39] *The Scientist in the Crib* also illustrated the insights to be derived from a wedding of the ideas of developmental science with those of developmental neuroscience in understanding early childhood. As another reflection of scientists' responses to the *I Am Your Child* campaign, Gopnik and colleagues embraced public interest in early childhood and showed why it was well founded.

From Neurons to Neighborhoods

At the same time that the story of early brain development was breaking, other issues related to young children were also occupying public and scientific attention in the late 1990s. These issues provide an important context for how the brain development campaign was being perceived and interpreted.

It would have been difficult for parents to hear the messages about the importance of early enriched experiences, especially within specific "windows of opportunity," without thinking about child care and its quality. As earlier noted, this was one of the "tough questions" posed but not answered in the *Rethinking the Brain* report, but for the Clinton administration child care was a domestic policy priority because of its importance to many families. Unfortunately, the Clinton administration complicated the issue in 1996 by passing the Personal Responsibility and Work Opportunity Act – welfare reform – that included new work requirements, capped lifetime eligibility, and shifted responsibility for the program to the states. Welfare reform was, in Clinton's words, "the end of welfare as we know it," in part by requiring the recipients of public assistance to seek employment, even if they cared for young children, and to find their own child care arrangements. Despite the increased availability of child care subsidies, there was little attention in this legislation to the quality of care for the children of adults facing new work requirements, or to its affordability, and the state regulations governing child care where one lived made it easier in some states but more difficult in most to find affordable, good-quality child care. Consequently, the messages of the *I Am Your Child* campaign raised new concerns about the effects of child care on children in relation to the enrichment needs of the developing young brain, especially for young children in lower-income families.

Even though *Rethinking the Brain* feared to tread into this thicket, others were more daring. As noted, columnist Kathleen Parker concluded that the campaign's messages meant that parents should stay home with their children during the first three years, even if this meant sacrificing job promotions and other conveniences, although it is doubtful that the costs of staying home to care for young children could have been so readily borne by lower-income parents, especially those on public assistance. Taking the opposite tack, Deborah Phillips, who was executive director of the Board on Children, Youth, and Families of the National Research Council in Washington, DC, spoke at the morning session of the White House Conference on the need for high-quality and affordable child care. She contrasted that standard of quality with the quality typically found in child care programs in the United States, which she characterized as "barely adequate," especially for the youngest children. But she proposed no strategy for improving the typical care of young children while main-taining its affordability, and nobody else had come up with politically feasible solutions to this problem either.

Early in her remarks, Phillips commented that "we now know . . . that placing a baby in child care does not interfere with the development of the mother-infant attachment relationship or the father-infant attachment relationship,"[40] but this conclusion was not yet conclusive. As the result of extensive public debate in the 1980s about the developmental effects of child care experience on infant-parent attachment, especially when out-of-home care is for extended hours when children are very young, the National Institute of Child Health and Human Development inaugurated a large longitudinal study in 1991 of more than 1,000 infants living with their families at ten sites throughout the United States who, based on their parents' choices, entered child care of various types and quality at different ages. The goal of this large study was to follow the infants over time to determine what were the later consequences for them of the child care choices their parents had made. The results of the study were only just beginning to emerge at the time of the White House Conference, and although they offered some reassurance that infants in child care did not immediately develop insecure attachments to their parents as the result of child care experience, there were also some preliminary indications of vulnerabilities for young children arising from child care, especially if the quality of care was poor.[41]

Taken together, parents of young children had cause for concern. Against the backdrop of their own child care choices was an ongoing public debate about whether mothers (always mothers) of babies should instead stay home to care for them, activated by the conflicting goals and priorities of the women's movement, conservative religious groups, and both political parties. The debate had motivated the federal government to invest substantial funding in a major study to investigate the effects of early care experience,[42] whose results were only just beginning to appear. On top of this, parents now heard about the science of early brain development and its emphasis on enriching early experiences, time-limited critical periods of essential stimulation, and the importance of warm, nurturant parental care. Because higher-quality child care – the kind that might provide this kind of stimulation – is also significantly more expensive, parents felt caught in a bind. How could they afford the quality of care that the brain development messages were urging them to seek, and if they could not, decide instead for one parent to remain at home while the family lived on only one income?

At least everyone could agree that parental nurturance is important. But not so fast. In the fall of 1998, parents learned that their nurturance may not make much difference after all: it's all in the child's genes. In a best-selling book titled *The Nurture Assumption: Why Children Turn Out the Way They Do*,[43] Judith Rich Harris enlisted the science of developmental behavioral genetics to argue that children "turn out the way they do" because of their genetic endowment. Parenting is all about providing a sufficiently adequate environment to support the unfolding expression of those inherited characteristics. Parents do not create their children's characteristics except for the genes they contributed at conception, and the reason that family resemblance exists is not because of parental practices, but rather the genes shared by parents and offspring. The most unexpected aspect of Harris's argument, again borrowing from behavioral genetics research, is that peers and the neighborhood environment are the most significant contributors to children's distinctive individual characteristics. If you want to shape your children, in other words, choose the right friends for them in the right community.

Developmental scientists had long been debating these claims, but when Harris's book erupted into public awareness – with parallel headlines in *Newsweek*,[44] the *New Yorker*,[45] and other media asking, "Do Parents Matter?" – they were faced with a dilemma. If anything should be a settled matter in developmental science it is the importance of parenting, and if there was genuine scientific disagreement over the significance of parents, what can developmental science claim to know at all about children's development? Harris's conclusions were exaggerated and misleading, but explaining why Harris was wrong to nonscientists required explaining the methodology of twin studies, the proper interpretation of their results, and the use of analysis of variance in twin research that defied easy understanding. As for parents, Harris's book added to their confusion and uncertainty. Is what I do important to my child's development? And if it's all in the child's genes, what does this mean for the experiences that supposedly are essential to early brain development?

Committee on Integrating the Science of Early Childhood Development

As a consequence of these gathering streams of confusion, and motivated by the White House Conference, the Institute of Medicine and the National Research Council empaneled an eighteen-member study group, the Committee on Integrating the Science of Early Childhood Development, to create a report summarizing the important conclusions about the development of children from birth to age five. These federal agencies have a long tradition of commissioning blue-ribbon scientific committees to write authoritative reports about important public issues, although typically their reports have one day of publicity and then gather dust on the shelf. But this report was more visible than most because the committee began its work in the context of these conflicting debates about fundamental questions concerning young children.

As a reflection of the scientific stakes in this task, the committee[46] was surprised at its inaugural meeting with funders in the fall of 1998 to hear Steven Hyman, director of the National Institute of Mental Health (one of the major federal funders of research in developmental science, and a major funder of this study), describe developmental psychology as a "noncumulative science." The idea that a scientific field does not progress but is instead "noncumulative" warrants serious concerns about the quality of the science, and this is a special worry when this criticism is voiced by the director of a major federal funding agency. When I asked him during a break to explain this unexpected comment, he asked in return whether developmental science created cumulative knowledge if it could not even agree about the importance of parenting. Hyman was frustrated with these conflicting scientific voices working in their own silos and not finding consensus about these fundamental issues, and he was issuing a challenge to the committee: tell us what we know about young children's development and its practical value.[47]

The committee was chaired by Jack Shonkoff, a pediatrician who was dean of the Heller School for Social Policy and Management at Brandeis University. It met six times over the next year and a half and produced a volume in early 2000 titled *From Neurons to Neighborhoods: The Science of*

Early Childhood Development.[48] Early brain development was not the only issue occupying the committee's attention: early childhood poverty, families and culture, the genetics of human development, early intervention, and, of course, child care were among the important topics. But early brain development was central. In its final report, the committee offered a number of conclusions that directly addressed the public concerns that had emerged in recent years. They included:[49]

- "Early experiences clearly affect the development of the brain. Yet the recent focus on 'zero to three' as a critical or particularly sensitive period is highly problematic . . . because the disproportionate attention to the period from birth to 3 years begins too late and ends too soon."
- "The long-standing debate about the importance of nature *versus* nurture, considered as independent influences, is overly simplistic and scientifically obsolete . . . genetic and environmental influences work together in dynamic ways over the course of development."
- "Parents and other regular caregivers in children's lives are 'active ingredients' of environmental influence during the early childhood period.. . . Children's early development depends on the health and well-being of their parents."
- "During infancy, there is a pressing need to strike a better balance between options that support parents to care for their infants at home and those that provide affordable, quality child care that enables them to work or go to school."
- "Developmental neuroscience research says a great deal about the conditions that pose dangers to the developing brain and from which young children need to be protected. It says virtually nothing about what to do to create enhanced or accelerated brain development."[50]

In light of its focus on the first five years, the committee's report was surprisingly balanced in its portrayal of the importance of early experiences and the potential of later experiences to strengthen, redirect, undermine, or otherwise change the impact of those early experiences. Even so, in its wider view of the early years the committee occasionally offered conclusions reminiscent of "the first years last forever" thinking, such as:

> Although there have been long-standing debates about how much the early years really matter in the larger scheme of lifelong development, our conclusion is unequivocal: What happens during the first months and years of life matters a lot, not because this period of development provides an indelible blueprint for adult well-being, but because it sets either a sturdy or fragile stage for what follows.[51]

A "sturdy or fragile" stage on which later development is built is a powerful image of the importance of early childhood, anticipating the metaphor of brain architecture that would appear a few years later in scientific and public discourse about early childhood development. The sturdy or fragile foundation is also a strong basis for a range of public policy recommendations offered by the Committee, which I discuss in Chapter 5. These recommendations, including new investments to address children's mental health needs, expansion of family and medical leave policies, and substantial investments in early care and education programs, are based on creating a sturdy stage for later development in the early years. But in these recommendations, the committee may have risked exaggerating how much these investments alone can accomplish without comparably substantial investments in programs that continue to support children's healthy development in later years. Building a sturdy foundation is important. Maintaining that foundation is important also.

There were other conclusions and recommendations included in the report. Unfortunately, the report's release on October 3, 2000, coincided with the first of the presidential debates of the 2000 election between Al Gore and George Bush, so even the one day of publicity normally accorded blue-ribbon committee reports was eclipsed by the presidential election. Nevertheless, the report achieved wide dissemination and, at a ten-year anniversary celebration of the report in 2010, a gathering of federal policymakers, academics, child advocates, and funders praised the report's impact on the federal policy environment, research priorities, and program innovation – although much less was said about the influence of the report on those who care for young children.[52] Perhaps that is as it should be. After all, most people would not be expected to slog through a densely written report of more than 600 pages. In the end, the impact of *From Neurons to Neighborhoods* would be better measured by its influence over time on the thinking of people who were in a position to have the greatest impact on young children and their families: parent educators, child care providers, home visitors, early educators, and others who support and guide parents, as well as the public officials, program managers, and business leaders who shape the conditions in which they do so.

This seems to have been Shonkoff's view also. At the same time that he chaired the committee, he was also a member of the MacArthur Research Network on Early Experience and Brain Development, a small panel of scientists funded in the aftermath of the *I Am Your Child* campaign to study further how the developing brain is altered by experience. Before the release of the *From Neurons to Neighborhoods* report, Shonkoff had already sought funding from the MacArthur Research Network to create a Working Group on Public Dissemination and Social Policy composed of selected members of the MacArthur Network, the Committee on Integrating the Science of Early Childhood Development, and specialists in public communication. It had its first meeting in 2001 to brainstorm how to better convey the message of the science of early brain development to the public and correct some of the mistaken representations of the science that had already begun to emerge and which were a source of growing frustration to developmental scientists. The Working Group met on several occasions and, with a grant from the MacArthur Foundation, became the National Scientific Council on the Developing Child in 2003. The National Scientific Council, which was briefly profiled in Chapter 1 and which I discuss more extensively in Chapter 6, has been a major contributor to advancing and developing public messaging about developmental brain science since 1997, furthering the impact of the *I Am Your Child* campaign and the *From Neurons to Neighborhoods* report.

Taking Perspective

Michael Levine, the Carnegie Foundation senior program officer who helped shepherd the *I Am Your Child* campaign and eventually became executive director of the I Am Your Child Foundation, reflected in a conversation with me that the campaign found the right formula for achieving public attention and advancing public policy. The formula was right, the execution was strong, but he thought there might have been more development and refinement of the messaging. His opinion was shared by several others involved in the campaign's development with whom I talked. As campaign journalism – using a multifaceted, large-scale communication strategy to create public engagement and generate continuing media momentum – the campaign was exceptionally effective in making early brain development go viral in public awareness. In the hands of a committed and intelligent celebrity with connections and resources who could mobilize public officials, researchers, advocates, and philanthropists, creating such an impactful campaign to change public awareness was the easy part. Getting the messaging right was the hard part, for several reasons.

What Communicates Well Is Not Necessarily Most Important or Accurate

The first is that what communicates well is not necessarily what is most important or even most accurate. The lead to a broadcast story or news article is likely to be the most surprising, upsetting, or distressing element of the account, which, examined further, sometimes proves to be exaggerated or somewhat misleading. Nevertheless, the lead is what engages a person in the story to begin with, which was the goal of the communicator.

The *I Am Your Child* campaign's organizers were schooled by the response to the *Starting Points* report that a brain development lead would uniquely compel public interest in early childhood development. Focusing on the brain had this effect for all of the reasons considered in Chapter 2: neuroimaging provides "visual proof" of the brain's activity in thinking and development; neuroscience offers compelling mechanistic and material causes for developmental processes because the brain is where these occur; brain development research is impressively sophisticated; and (perhaps for these reasons) brain development draws the interest of many who would not otherwise be as interested in child development. The *I Am Your Child* campaign confirmed the lesson of *Starting Points*: foregrounding brain development creates a compelling message.

The problem is that in 1997, and even today, developmental neuroscience alone could not tell people what they wanted to know about early childhood once you had their attention. Early brain development is important, yes, but the neuroscience could not answer questions about the influence of parents and of parenting quality, the kinds of experiences that support early development (and whether those influential experiences change with the growth of the brain), how to help children learn and grow mentally, and how to think about discipline, child care, television watching, and other practical issues. Developmental neuroscience, in other words, could not speak to the everyday concerns of the audiences whose interest has been captured by the brain development lead and who were convinced of the importance of the early years. Consequently, the messaging of the campaign had to pivot quickly to the much richer research findings of developmental science to provide those audiences with this usable knowledge.[53] But as Bruer and other critics pointed out, it was never very clear which "tips for parents and caregivers" derived from neuroscience, and which from other sources, and sometimes the confusion was misleading.

Why was it misleading? Because part of the appeal of developmental neuroscience is the perceived determinism linking early influences with brain development and, through the developing brain, later behavior and development. But psychological development is much more complex and multicausal, incorporating context, culture, and other influences, and it is not so easy to predict future outcomes. This distinction, however, was obscured by the campaign's messaging. Thus in 1997, when audiences were presented with compelling neuroanatomical evidence of permanent vision loss in kittens deprived of visual stimulation during an early critical period of brain growth, they were justified in their anxiety that variations in parental warmth or talking to the baby comparably determined significant developmental outcomes in children. But parents had no need to fear harming their child's brain development – by talking insufficiently or singing infrequently or allowing too much television watching – because the influences contributing to healthy language and cognitive growth are ubiquitous in typical family experience.[54] The biological model of critical experiences during critical periods does not generalize well to the multicausal, probabilistic character of psychological development. Indeed, it is misleading. And even in 1997, it was apparent that the strong perceived determinism of developmental neuroscience required a second look. Shortly after the original studies of visual deprivation of kittens appeared, for example, subsequent research[55] showed that kittens deprived in this manner showed some recovery of sight after all.[56] Early experiences did not last a lifetime.

Getting the messaging right was hard, therefore, because while developmental neuroscience was a compelling communication, it did not carry the practical knowledge that audiences wanted. Developmental science could address those practical questions, but it did not comparably compel attention, and the outcomes it promised were uncertain and multidetermined. It makes sense to integrate messages from each field, as I argued in Chapter 3, especially when they offer convergent accounts of the growth of brain and mind. But the campaign should have been much clearer about the nature of the science that was being explained so that audiences could better understand the basis for its messages. In particular, it would have been helpful to explain how early psychological health depends on a cascade of influences within and outside the child that together over time shape the course of development, rather than depending on a small set of crucial early determinants that may be absent from early experience. It would have been especially helpful to reassure parents about how the essential catalysts to healthy brain development are ubiquitous in most family environments. And it would have been very helpful for scientists to acknowledge the limitations of existing knowledge. The campaign's messaging instead left audiences with worries about the determinism of early experience but limited understanding of what this meant for supporting their child's healthy growth.

Cultural Frameworks Shape Understanding Child Development

There is a second reason that getting the messaging right was hard. It concerns the specific challenges of communicating about children's development. As those who do so regularly are aware, nobody is objective about children. Many people are parents, grandparents, or other kinds of caregivers. Many people have plenty of experience with children in formal and informal contexts. Everybody has been a child once with memories of their own development from which they have drawn the lessons of experience. And everybody lives in a culture with values and beliefs concerning children and their development. By contrast with a public engagement campaign focused on chlorofluorocarbons or climate change, therefore, increasing public awareness about children must occur in a context of substantial prior knowledge and audience beliefs about the topic. And those beliefs can have a powerful influence on how new messages about children are interpreted and remembered. They can cause people to question or reject ideas that are inconsistent with the lessons of their own experience. They can also cause people to unquestioningly accept ideas that are harmonious with broader cultural beliefs about children, even if they are not well supported by the research. Getting the messaging about early brain development was hard because the messaging was heard by an audience with a wealth of prior ideas about the development of young children.

What kinds of beliefs underlie Americans' thinking about young children and their development? One is the belief that early influences have enduring consequences for human growth: "as the twig is bent, so grows the tree" goes the American adage.[57] This is what the late Harvard developmental psychologist Jerome Kagan called "the allure of infant determinism," one of three "seductive ideas" he profiled in a 1998 book.[58] Belief in the enduring effects of early experiences arose historically in Western Europe and America during the eighteenth century when a combination of improved economic conditions and a gradual decline in child mortality enabled parents (primarily mothers) to invest emotionally and reallocate other resources to the nurturance of young children. Early influences were seen as important when parents could devote much greater attention to children's development and could see its benefits unfold. By the dawn of the twentieth century, this belief was so normative in the Western world that it became incorporated into mainstream theories of psychological development, such as those of Freud and Erikson, as well as attachment theory.

Another belief is that experience, more than inheritance, shapes lifelong capability. This belief is an American creation, reflecting the convictions of a society that self-consciously divorced itself from the constraints of European lineage and embarked in a professedly more egalitarian direction. It is also consistent with American individualism. The short passage from John Watson's behaviorist volume quoted in Chapter 1 ("Give me the baby and my world to bring it up in and I'll make it . . . ") reflects the optimistic, can-do American confidence that it is experience, not inheritance, that makes the man (and woman). This belief is one reason that Judith Rich Harris's claim in 1998 that it is genes, not parenting, that cause children to "turn out the way they do" was so disconcerting to parents.

A third belief underlying Americans' thinking about children is that parents are crucial to optimizing or blunting a child's potential. It is one reason that parents are perceived as the linchpin to children's development more than genes, more than social class, and more than family heritage, which have been preferred alternative explanations in other cultures and historical times. The emphasis on parents helps to account for both the parental blaming that occurs when children and youth go awry and the esteem accorded parents whose children succeed and exceed.

Another belief is that there is untapped potential in the human brain. The charming belief that emerged in the earliest days of neuroscience still endures: we use only about 20% of the brain's capacity, with the remaining 80% untapped and currently inaccessible reserve potential. My students are dismayed to learn that this is not true, and that we use all of the brain's capacity. Despite its inaccuracy, the persistence of this belief reflects optimism that our brains are capable of great(er) things if we only understood how to enlist our native neuropotential. The hope that this might be accomplished technologically or neurosurgically is a current version of this enduring belief.

Related to this is the belief that science can contribute to optimizing or accelerating the developmental accomplishments of young children. Piaget called this "the American question": What can we do to accelerate cognitive growth? It reflects the quintessential American interest in doing things better, faster, and bigger, and the classic American optimism in the improvability of human life. The belief that science contributes to these accelerated achievements helps to explain the effort to apply the insights of brain development research to improve education; create toys that enhance language, math, or reading skills; or incorporate practices into early care environments that stimulate brain development, which are some of the

applications of the brain development messaging that are explored further
in the next chapter.

Finally, if the first years last forever, this might be true for early
deprivation and damage as much as it is true for early enrichment and
nurturance. There is thus another belief that the effects of early deprivation
or damage may not be easily remedied later. It is thus essential that early
problems be identified and remedied as quickly as possible lest they endure
and become consolidated.

What is important about these cultural beliefs about young children and
their development is not whether they are true. Some are clearly false,
others are probably valid. But what is important is that they are core
assumptions, or frames, that people intuitively incorporate into their
understanding of children's development and which condition their acceptance of new ideas and information.[59] I will consider further the influence
of the framing of ideas about the developing brain in Chapter 6. Ideas that
are consistent with these frames tend to be easily and unquestionably
accepted; those that are inconsistent are greeted skeptically, whether one
is an interested member of the public, a journalist, policymaker, or even a
developmental scientist.[60] The fact that these framing beliefs are shared
among cultural members can obscure the realization that these beliefs are
not necessarily universal truths about children. We can trace the historical
origins of most of these beliefs, and many are not shared by citizens of
other (particularly non-Western) cultures that have different presuppositions about children, their nature, and their development. This helps to
explain why influential theories of development emerging in different
cultures have different ways of explaining children's development. The
sociocultural construction of childhood development of Vygotskian theory
originating in the Soviet Union, for example, is very different from the
stimulus-response orientation of contemporaneous behavioral theories in
the United States, and each had distinct culturohistorical applications.

Because many of the core messages of the *I Am Your Child* campaign
converged with these American cultural beliefs about children – and
indeed, these beliefs likely shaped the campaign's messaging – they contributed to the perception that these enduring beliefs were now confirmed
by brain science. In this light, the brain development story became an
attractive, and perhaps overoptimistic, account of human possibility. Early
experiences are essential for achieving the brain's potential by provoking
the neural connections that shape lifelong capability. There is great intrinsic capacity to the developing brain, and by starting early and providing the
right experiences, parents can enhance the potential of their children by

helping to build bigger, better brains. The effects of early deprivation or damage may not be easily undone, which is why parents must be vigilant to provide every opportunity to stimulate and support early brain development. The first years last forever. It is easy to see how quickly the messaging of early brain development overpromised the possibilities of developmental neuroscience for improving human welfare because it enlisted these longstanding, optimistic American cultural beliefs. By messaging in this way, the campaign failed to tap the brakes on inordinate expectations deriving from the brain science, and indeed may have accelerated those expectations.

Selecting the Right Message Is Important but Hard

This leads to the third reason that messaging about early brain development was hard. Science communication is selective. It must be so in order to provide a comprehensible message of what is known. How, therefore, to decide what to include? The answers depend on science communication being not only selective, but also strategic. One answer is to lead with what elicits attention and interest, which in this case meant leading with the neuroscience of brain development. As observed by others, the brain development message communicates well. Another answer is to draw on the cultural beliefs about children and development that find resonance with the neuroscience and behavioral research, and let this be the intuitively appealing frame through which the brain development story is told.

But while the messaging based on neuroscience and cultural beliefs spotlights important influences on children's development, it also overlooks other influences that are also important. By foregrounding the role of parents and experience in the early years, for example, the messaging overlooks the influence of prenatal experience or the effects of economic deprivation or biological (e.g., medical, nutritional, ecological) hazards to healthy brain development. This may be a necessary result of the selectivity of science communication, but the problem is that what is omitted may be important to a clear and accurate understanding of brain development.

There were at least three areas of research in developmental neuroscience whose omission from the messaging was problematic. The first concerns how the brain continues to develop after early childhood. Adolescent brain development was, in 1997, an important area of research (and still is) because, as described in Chapter 3, it reveals another period of experience-based "resculpting" of the developing brain. Through the influence of pubertal hormones, there are important changes in the growth, functioning, and interconnectivity of brain areas significant for higher cognitive reasoning skills, social interaction, and reward processing. But even though this was an important body of research at the time of the *I Am Your Child* campaign, its findings did not advance the campaign's emphasis on the first years and early critical periods for the developing brain. Adolescent brain development was not incorporated into the public messaging, even though including it would have helped to broaden appreciation of the extended duration of formative influences on the developing brain.[61]

A second overlooked body of research concerns prenatal development, even though (as noted in Chapter 3) it is the most formative period of brain development. It is also the period of greatest vulnerability to nutritional deficiencies, hazardous exposures, and other potential harms. Devoting greater attention to prenatal development would have significantly broadened awareness of how parents influence the developing brain by incorporating consideration of the effects of maternal prenatal stress, nutritional quality, and other aspects of prenatal care on the development of the brain. But this would have departed from the campaign's focus on parental warmth and nurturance in infancy. Another problem with attention to fetal brain development, moreover, is that this could have become entangled with the politics of abortion, with studies of the developing brain potentially being enlisted to highlight fetal responsiveness to the external environment, capacity for pain, recognition of the mother's voice, and other indicators of emergent personhood. Prenatal brain development was not incorporated into the public communication of the developing brain, even though including it would have sensitized audiences that newborns' brains are already different from each other at birth. In other words, it is not only a matter of what happens after birth; the developing brain is also affected by what happens before birth.

Finally, the consequences of childhood poverty for the developing brain were a third omission from the early brain development messaging. In the late 1990s (and today), the study of the effects of poverty was a vigorous field of developmental brain science because of emerging evidence of the impact of poverty on brain structure and functioning, as documented in Chapter 3. Even though the reports leading up to the *I Am Your Child* campaign (i.e., *Starting Points*, *Rethinking the Brain*) and following it (*From Neurons to Neighborhoods*) devoted attention to poverty, none discussed poverty and the developing brain despite considerable available research evidence, and childhood poverty was not a theme of the campaign. One reason may have been the campaign's effort to create a positive narrative about brain development that would personalize the message ("I am your child") and establish its relevance to the viewing audience and its children, few of whom are likely to have been living in economic distress. In addition, the guidance of the Ad Council was that crisis-oriented messages, such as about families in economic difficulty, would alienate the intended audience and contribute to "bad parents" attributions of blame.[62] The othering of children in poverty would be consistent with the campaign's focus on *your* child.

But by narrowing the campaign's messaging to the influence of parents in the family, the campaign's organizers may have done public understanding a disservice by separating the growth of brain and mind from the broader socioeconomic contexts that are so influential on children's healthy development. As brain development later became linked to the development of human capital, especially with the involvement of economists like James Heckman (whose contributions are described in Chapter 5), it was especially unfortunate that brain development was never considered in the context of the economic, social, and even cultural capital that connects the developing brain to problems of inequality and deprivation.[63] Doing so, however, would have required acknowledging that for many children, healthy brain development is less a consequence of parental nurturance or talking and singing and more of the presence of neurotoxins in drinking water, environmental pollutants in the air or ground, food insufficiency, or inadequate early health care. The opportunity was lost to enlist developmental neuroscience into a critique of the tolerance of childhood poverty that might have been heard by audiences with the capacity to make a difference, and this opportunity has never been recovered. This is especially disappointing because many of the hazards of poverty to developing brains are preventable through public health interventions and other remediation efforts.

Campaign messaging on the impact of poverty on early brain development would have significantly broadened its public policy impact in additional ways. Enhanced public information about the significance of prenatal care, early nutrition, regular health screens, and immunizations would have urged attention to ensuring these safeguards for all children. Messages about scheduling vision and hearing tests in light of the importance of early sensory experience to neurobiological growth would have helped to reduce other risk factors for developmental problems. Beyond these, attention to poverty and brain development could also have internationalized the campaign's messaging, recognizing that risks to the developing brain of malnutrition, chronic stress, homelessness, and other adverse conditions exist outside the United States as well as within. In light of all this, the campaign's tagline "the first years last forever" seems even more relevant, but sadly the recommendations for parents to nurture and talk to their young infants, as important as these are, seem inadequate compared with the multifaceted ways that parents and others can promote healthy early brain growth.

Getting the messaging right about brain development was hard, therefore, because the selectivity necessary to the clear and coherent reporting of the science required careful judgment of the immediate and longer-term impact of different facets of the science, both for the success of the messaging and for the benefit of children. Each choice about the science to include and the science to exclude was both a messaging problem and a problem for representing science and its potential benefits to children's well-being. By excluding serious consideration of adolescence, prenatal growth, and poverty, the campaign ignored the extended period of formative influences on the brain, the realization that infants are born with different brains owing to different prenatal influences, and that socioeconomic inequities can profoundly affect childhood brain growth.

These considerations raise important questions. How can a campaign balance the effort to package an appealing message with a necessary one, to draw a large audience but also to include crisis-oriented messages that are important to promoting children's well-being, and messages that may complicate the campaign's theme (the early years are important, but then there is adolescence) because of the need to present the science accurately? How much can a campaign risk the inattention of a disinterested or alienated public by the presentation of disturbing but necessary messages? How much can it risk misrepresenting the science of children's development by the effort to create an appealing and impactful public message? The manner in which these values and priorities are strategically balanced is likely to differ according to the purposes of the messaging, the organizers of the messaging effort, and those who communicate the brain development story. This is one reason why the question of who speaks for science is so important.

These questions are taken up in the following chapters, especially Chapters 6 and 7. But for now the story of the brain development campaign is not complete. After its launch, the campaign expanded in scope to engage more audiences with new messages about the importance of the early years. In addition, many others took up the story of early brain development and applied it to their own concerns, whether to increase funding for early childhood programs or to create a national campaign for prekindergarten education or to promote community development. In turning to the impact of the campaign on public policy, in Chapter 5 I raise further questions about the choices and decisions involved in shaping the story of early brain development in ways that would intentionally guide policies and practices that affect children's development, but also impact the continuing evolution of public understanding of early brain development.

CHAPTER 5

"Follow the Science"

> And while I'm on children, I want to tell you about another initiative
> I'm proposing and am very excited about. We know that a baby's
> brain continues to form after birth, not just growing bigger as toes
> and fingers do, but developing microscopic connections responsible
> for learning and remembering....
>
> Why am I telling you all this in a speech that is already far too
> long? Because I want to propose something extraordinary that I don't
> think any other state does. And it is this. Research shows that reading
> to an infant, talking with an infant and especially having that infant
> listen to soothing music helps those trillions of brain connections to
> develop, especially the ones related to math....
>
> So I propose that the parents of every baby born in Georgia – over
> a 100,000 a year – be given a cassette or CD of music to be played
> often in the baby's presence. It's not a big-ticket item in the budget –
> only $105,000 – but I believe it can help Georgia children to excel.
>
> I have asked Yoel Levi, the world-famous conductor of the Atlanta
> Symphony, to help me with the musical selections for the tape,
> although I already have some ideas. For instance, here's one that a
> Georgia baby might hear....
>
> That, of course, is Beethoven's "Ode to Joy." Now don't you feel
> smarter already? Smart enough to vote for this budget item, I hope.
>
> —Governor Zell Miller of Georgia[1]

By all accounts, Governor Zell Miller of Georgia had a longstanding
interest in education that predated the events of April 1997. He cam-
paigned in 1990 for the creation of the Georgia Lottery for Education,
which was approved by voters in 1992, and which led to the development
of a universal, voluntary prekindergarten program and a college scholarship
program, both funded entirely from lottery revenue. The combination is
still unique for the country. Although Miller's proposal for a Mozart
mailing[2] to the parents of each newborn was not included in the state
budget, Miller secured private funding sufficient to provide a copy of "The
Little Engine That Could" to accompany the classical music CD given to

the parents of each newborn in Georgia in 1998. The program lasted only a year, but similar initiatives appeared at the same time in Tennessee and other states. A Florida statute mandated that classical music should be played in child care programs to stimulate brain development.[3]

Miller's proposal was not the only immediate response of the policy world to the events of the *I Am Your Child* campaign. Others included:

- In the US Senate, the bipartisan Early Childhood Development Act of 1997, cosponsored by Senators John Kerrey (D-MA) and Christopher Bond (R-MO), was introduced to provide enhanced funding for Early Head Start programs, child care referral services, and a variety of other initiatives to support the healthy development of children under age six. It died in committee.

- The RAND Corporation released a report in April 1997 on the costs and benefits of early childhood interventions for disadvantaged children.[4] It concluded that some of these programs have documented benefits for children and generated savings to the government that exceeded program costs, although the report's scope did not include typical child care or preschool programs.

- As a follow-up to *Starting Points*, the Carnegie Corporation created the Starting Points Initiative in 1996 to foster statewide and local efforts to implement the report's recommendations.[5] Ten states and six cities received two-year grants to stimulate local investment in projects to implement one or more of the four goals articulated in the *Starting Points* report, such as promoting high-quality child care or responsible parenthood. A subset of these recipients subsequently received additional two-year grants. The typical hope for such short-term seed grants is that the projects they inaugurate would be maintained and strengthened with local public or private funding as the community supports the program. But sometimes instead the projects flourish for a time and then disappear, underscoring the challenge of sustainability without continued funding. Both outcomes seem to be true of the initiatives supported by the Starting Points Initiative, although the enduring impact of some of them, such as West Virginia's Starting Points family and child resource centers, has been impressive.[6]

- In his testimony at a congressional hearing on public-private partnerships in early childhood interventions, Rob Reiner urged House members to invest in programs like these, claiming, "[w]e now clearly know that if we want to make a real impact on crime, teen pregnancy, drug abuse, child abuse, welfare dependency, and homelessness, we must make a real investment in a child's earliest years."[7]

These proposals show how much the brain development revolution was early perceived as a public policy campaign as well as messaging for parents. To be sure, the focus of the *I Am Your Child* campaign was primarily to inform parents of their essential contributions to early brain development through their nurturance, reading, and care. Yet every one of the public communications surrounding the events of April 1997 had strong recommendations for public policy. The *Starting Points* report urged policymakers to confront the "quiet crisis" of families with young children through initiatives to promote responsible parenthood, guarantee quality child care choices, ensure good health and protection, and mobilize communities to support young children and their families. These recommendations were subsequently reiterated in *Rethinking the Brain* and the messaging of the *I Am Your Child* campaign. Other recommendations were to ensure comprehensive prenatal care, improve parental leave benefits, provide needed health care services for infants and toddlers, move toward family-centered communities, and a plea to "reinvent government." The White House Conference on Early Childhood Development and Learning included recommendations (presented to President Clinton and the First Lady in attendance) to strengthen prenatal and pediatric health care, improve family leave, and increase support for child care – all priorities of the Clinton administration. The ABC-TV special, which was primarily focused on messaging parents, included episodes on abuse prevention and community support.

The *Neurons to Neighborhoods* report, which was explicitly tasked with examining the implications of the developmental science for policy and practice, had the most expansive recommendations of all. They included:

- substantial new investments and enhanced professional training to address young children's mental health needs
- expansion of the Family and Medical Leave Act to all working parents and extending the exemption period before states require parents of infants to return to work under welfare reform provisions
- Presidential establishment of a joint federal-state-local task force charged with reviewing "the entire portfolio of public investments in child care and early education" with the goal of promoting high quality programs that are "safe, stimulating, and compatible with the values and priorities of their families"

- a national effort devoted to environmental protection, reproductive health services, and early intervention efforts to reduce exposure to prenatal and early postnatal neurotoxic exposures harmful to brain development, "comparable to the attention and resources that have been dedicated to crime prevention, smoking cessation, and the reduction of teen pregnancy" in earlier years
- a dedicated portion of major funding sources for child care and early education programs set aside to improve the qualifications and increase the compensation and benefits of children's nonparental caregivers.

These policy recommendations derived from the committee's view that there are two complementary agendas presented by the research on early brain development. One concerns how to use this knowledge to ensure the health and well-being of young children. The other is much broader:

> [It is] rooted in contemporary concerns about promoting human capital development in a highly competitive and rapidly changing world. It asks: How can society use knowledge about early child development to maximize the nation's human capital and ensure the ongoing vitality of its democratic institutions?[8]

To many child advocates, these policy recommendations flowed naturally from the science, mandated by the importance of addressing the needs of young children and their families and a shared progressive view of the importance of enlisting public resources to meeting those needs. Although most of these policy proposals predated the brain development revolution, the findings of developmental neuroscience were perceived as adding weight and urgency to issues that had been longstanding elements of the children's cause. To many child advocates, the *I Am Your Child* campaign would constitute the final push needed to align public concern with their longstanding goals.

From the perspective of twenty-five years later, how have these proposals fared? There have certainly been some real achievements: health care access and affordability have improved with the Affordable Care Act, and there has been national growth in attention to early childhood education. On other central goals, however, the picture remains disappointing. We are still awaiting significant, sustained new public investments in child care access and improvements in its quality; paid parental leave remains on the wish list of child and family advocates; there has been no national effort devoted to reducing environmental neurotoxins; and early childhood mental health services are still in short supply, despite increased need of them.

What accounts for the mixed picture? In some cases, such as the ideas emanating from the Mozart effect, the science was simply too limited or insufficiently compelling to justify new programs.[9] In other cases, such as incorporating brain development science into educational practice and policy, the connection between the science and its applications was, in Bruer's evocative phrase, "a bridge too far"[10] to make a clear, compelling argument for educational policy reform (except in one key area, early childhood education, which I will further explore later in the chapter). In some other cases, such as child care policy, the need for improved access and quality was clear but there was less consensus about how to accomplish these aims (government mandates? market incentives? private investments?); there were doubts (especially from conservatives) about the capacity of public policy to achieve them; and there remained controversy over whether child care was a private or public concern. Sometimes cost projections stymied progress on other public initiatives (such as for expanded paid parental leave) and raised questions about whether this was a government or business responsibility. Some claims – such as the direct connection between early childhood investments and crime, teen pregnancy, drug abuse, child abuse, welfare dependency, and homelessness – were insufficiently documented by research evidence to support policy initiatives, and it was unclear what those initiatives would be. Some recommendations, such as mobilizing communities or reforming government, simply bore little meaningful relation to developmental brain science at all. And finally, there are the usual obstacles of the policymaking process: conflicting values and priorities (not all people share progressive values), the legislative/executive calendar, and the changing winds of public interest. This is perhaps why one of the longstanding goals of the brain development campaign – improving early health care access and affordability – derived from a broader health care initiative requiring more than a year of congressional negotiation.

During the quarter century since the brain development revolution began, the path to significant policy benefits for young children and their families has been more fraught and uncertain than expected. This was surprising to many child advocates because these policy proposals seemed to derive naturally from the brain development message that had received such public acceptance. If parental nurturance is important to young infants, for example, why require mothers and fathers to return to work so soon after birth? The uncertain path to policy wins is surprising also because the design of the *I Am Your Child* campaign might have been expected to smooth the route to public support of these policy proposals.

Campaign journalism bypasses traditional, incremental science reporting in the conventional press in favor of highlighting the campaign's central themes on TV, media events, videos and CDs, and other nonjournalistic forums. In 1997, campaign journalism succeeded in generating media momentum through the dissemination of a straightforward scientific message, and this message aligned well with prevalent optimistic American beliefs about children and their development. So campaign journalism might also have been expected to generate a groundswell of public support for its policy recommendations, which were also consistent with American confidence in the ability to improve human capability by providing the right early developmental experiences. Why did these proposals fail to receive an immediate, enthusiastic response from the public and, in turn, from public officials?

One reason is that traditional science journalism has certain advantages over campaign journalism for building public trust and policymakers' support for new, potentially controversial policy proposals.[11] The gradual (albeit piecemeal) reporting of new discoveries helps to educate the public – including legislators and their staff, executive agency officials, and lawyers and judges – about emergent ideas in science that might be relevant to their interests. Over time, these ideas gradually begin to constitute the background knowledge that people draw on when considering future proposals. This "knowledge creep"[12] prepares the groundwork for new policy ideas, and even the critical reporting of science journalists helps persuade policymakers of the credibility of the science and its potential usefulness to current issues.[13] By instead uncritically presenting a collection of public policy proposals as the obvious implications of the developmental brain science, the *I Am Your Child* campaign did not build into its messaging a more persuasive policy argument that considered the value choices, financial considerations, implementation complexities, downstream consequences, and other policy dimensions of these proposals. The argument was simply that these were what babies and young children need. Such an argument can be persuasive to child advocates but not necessarily to policymakers, and simple appeals like this can be particularly problematic when policy issues are complex or controversial. It is one thing to message with clarity: "this is your brain on drugs" or "just say no" in a campaign to reduce youth substance abuse. It is something else to tackle the complex issues surrounding public support for child care or paid parental leave in the context of campaign journalism. Campaign journalism created media momentum for developmental brain science, but that was insufficient to generate enthusiasm for policy proposals, especially for issues that were knotty and controversial.

Despite this strategic weakness, however, the brain development revolution eventually resulted in some real policy wins for young children and their families. In this chapter, I describe several of the initiatives that illustrate both the achievements that have made a difference for many young children and the shortcomings of some of the policy directions following the campaign. These initiatives also illustrate the continued evolution of the messaging of early brain development as it was adapted to new audiences and different goals. In some cases, they also illustrate the continuing debate among developmental scientists who were sensitive to the accurate communication of their science and were interested in seeing their work publicized and used to advance children's interests through responsible policy reform. Finally, these initiatives illustrate the intersection of science with values – progressive, neoliberal, even conservative – in the determination of child and family policy, underscoring that science can indicate what is empirically true, but values enter into deciding what to do as a consequence. These have continued to be some of the dilemmas of developmental science and child and family policy in the years since.

California's Proposition 10

In the aftermath of the *I Am Your Child* campaign, its organizers sought to build on the campaign to further advance public understanding and public policy. The I Am Your Child Foundation was created, led by Michael Levine of Carnegie, to promote further messaging through the sale and distribution of informational materials in pamphlets, CDs, videocassettes, and the maintenance of a well-designed website. Ellen Galinsky of the Families and Work Institute, concerned that public interest in early brain development would not be sustained, sought to create other media events through collaboration with the Corporation for Public Broadcasting. Together they developed proposals for the creation of new materials on the developing brain involving well-established children's programs like *Mr. Rogers' Neighborhood*, *Reading Rainbow*, and *Sesame Street* and PBS news programs such as the *MacNeil-Lehrer NewsHour*.[14]

Rob Reiner went in a different direction. As the *I Am Your Child* campaign was unfolding in the spring of 1997, Reiner was already making plans to introduce a voter initiative to fund early childhood programs in California. The idea had been suggested to him by Mike Roos, a former California assemblyperson who heard Reiner speak at the annual winter meeting of the National Governors Association in February.[15] Funding new early childhood programs was consistent with Reiner's longstanding grievance that programs for the youngest children were chronically under-funded, and doing so through a California voter initiative was also a good idea. The California initiative process was enacted in 1911 as a form of direct democracy, and it has been used more frequently than in almost any other state to pass far-reaching ballot propositions, such as limiting property taxes, mandating a minimum percentage of the state budget for K-14 education, and establishing an independent legislative redistricting commission. The required number of petition signatures in California makes it easier than in many other states for a new initiative to qualify for the ballot. In recent years initiatives have become a major means for corporations, advocacy groups, and other interests to bypass the legislature to create new laws by funding the initiative process, leading from the propositions they have drafted to campaigns they have funded to, quite often, voter approval.

In the case of the proposal that Reiner and Roos contemplated, further-more, an initiative was probably necessary because of the unusual nature of their proposal. It would fund a wide range of (unspecified) programs for children from birth to age five through the work of California's fifty-eight country commissions, with funding derived from a tax on tobacco prod-ucts, including an increase in the state cigarette tax of fifty cents per pack. The ballot language did not specify which programs would be supported because that would be the decision of each county commission in relation to local needs. Within the proposition's broad language of supporting healthy development and early learning, these block grants could poten-tially support early literacy curricula, parenting classes, child care pro-grams, early health promotion efforts, abuse prevention initiatives, dental care, developmental screenings, and many other kinds of programs. There was also an expectation that some programs would also qualify for federal matching funds. Not surprisingly, a major criticism of the initiative as the campaign ensued was the decentralized decision-making concerning which programs would be funded, together with fears that there would be little or no accountability for the spending, and this helps to explain why the initiative processes was a better bet for Reiner and Roos than the levels of review and evaluation involved in legislative politics. Perhaps to justify the tobacco tax, the proposition also mandated spending on smoking cessation programs. A total of 80% of the funding would be allocated to the fifty-eight county commissions, with the amount for each based on local birth rates, and the remaining 20% used by a statewide commission for public education and outreach, research and technical assistance to the counties, anti-tobacco advertising, and administration.

The initiative quickly qualified for the November 1998 ballot as Proposition 10, the California Children and Families Initiative, and early polling predicted high levels of public support. As with the *I Am Your Child* campaign, Reiner recruited a bevy of Hollywood celebrities in support, including Charlton Heston (recently elected president of the National Rifle Association), Pat Boone, Robin Williams, Dustin Hoffman, Nicole Kidman, Tom Cruise, and Michael Douglas, and politicians, including former Vice President Al Gore, California Senator Barbara Boxer, San Francisco Mayor Willie Brown, and Surgeon General C. Everett Koop. Despite their efforts, vigorous opposition funded by the tobacco industry led to gradually eroding polling numbers in the face of arguments that parents, not Reiner, should be making these kinds of choices for California's children. By the time of the election there was genuine anxiety among its supporters that the proposition would not succeed. Proposition 10 was approved in November with only 50.5% of the vote. The initiative went into effect at the beginning of 1999.

Creating First 5 California

A seven-member statewide commission, named the Children and Families First Commission and later First 5 California, was appointed in the spring, with Reiner as the inaugural chairperson. But much more time was required for the county commissions to become organized, enabling legislation and bylaws to be passed, volunteer members appointed, executive directors hired, and strategic plans developed, all overseen by each county's board of supervisors, before proposals could be solicited and considered for funding. As a consequence, it was a year or longer after the initiative went into effect before funds began to be committed in most counties, provoking marked criticism by some in the commentariat and spearheading a new initiative drive for a ballot proposition to rescind Proposition 10. The initiative drive succeeded and the proposition qualified for the ballot, but Proposition 28 was rejected in 2000 by 72% of the voters, who perhaps felt that the public had already decided this issue. The county commissions could now proceed with their work in earnest.

Here is a thought experiment. If you were to consider distributing several million dollars annually to promote healthy development and early learning of young children in your county, how would you do so? Would you analyze existing services for gaps that could be filled through new targeted funding, or seek to build upon existing program strengths? Would you seek to prioritize the needs of the most disadvantaged children and families, or instead support services with the widest impact possible? Would you strive to support programs and services that are provided by few others, or instead coordinate with local service delivery systems to deepen and expand their outreach? Should project proposals be evaluated by their history of demonstrated success ("evidence-based," in current parlance), or should promising experimental programs receive support if they address worthwhile goals? Or both? How important is it to use funds to subsidize and expand choice, such as to extend paid maternity and family leave, or to supplement the low salaries typically earned by child care providers, or even to make it possible for a parent to stay home with a newborn child for a more extended period? Should a county commission invest funding in as many valuable proposals as possible, or instead seek to provide extensive support for only a few? Should each initiative receive support for a year, for multiple years, or should this decision be left to evaluations of program impact? Should evaluations of impact be required or left to the discretion of programs, recognizing that evaluation studies are also expensive?

Child advocates tend not to want to make such choices. And they have a point because of the significant need and chronic underfunding of services for young children and their families. Everything is needed. But funding choices between worthwhile programs have to be made, and this helps explain why the county commissions took so long before making their initial funding decisions. If done well, these decisions are based on data (such as a needs assessment, information about local resources, and detailed data about the population) and the values shared by those making the decisions.[16] Values can be especially important in prioritizing alternative goals for the commission's allocations (such as broadening access, strengthening quality, or addressing unmet needs) and the relative importance of alternative benefits to be achieved (such as strengthening school readiness, improving health care, or reducing child abuse).[17] Across California's counties, moreover, prevalent political values ranged from highly progressive to deeply conservative, and within most counties there was a range of values guiding thinking about solutions to the needs of children and families. It can take time, therefore, to gather the relevant data and arrive at a consensual values framework, so it is unsurprising that county commissions required longer than the public expected to begin funding program proposals.

And as a consequence, different county commissions settled on different priorities for their funding allocations.[18] With the largest inaugural annual budget of more than $150 million, for example, the Los Angeles County commission (First 5 LA) embarked on a ten-year plan to provide free, full-day preschool for all three- and four-year-old children.[19] The commissioners in Alameda County, by contrast, devoted a major portion of their inaugural budget of $21 million to collaborate with the local public health department to implement a home visitation program for the parents of the nearly 20,000 infants born annually in the county.[20] The First 5 Santa Cruz commission, learning about the county's high rate of child maltreatment in its strategic planning process, targeted at-risk families by implementing an evidence-based parenting program (Triple P) as well as in-home services.[21] A Mobile Early Childhood Program was initiated by the First 5 commission in rural San Benito County with a bilingual early childhood teacher and a nurse traveling to remote areas to provide developmental screening, immunizations, parent education, and early childhood education.[22] In Santa Clara County, the First 5 commission launched the first Children's Health Initiative featuring a Healthy Kids program to expand insurance coverage to children in low-income families, while in Santa Barbara the commission facilitated the creation of a county Office of Early Care and Education as a coordinative infrastructure for early childhood programs in the county.[23]

What Were the Results?

In the twenty-plus years since county commissions were formed, the goals and programs they initially supported have evolved in response to changing conditions and changing funding levels. In those years, the challenges faced by children from immigrant and refugee families, the state's implementation of a transitional kindergarten program, the national movement toward the development of Quality Rating and Improvement Systems (QRIS) for evaluating early childhood programs, growing concern with adverse childhood experiences (ACEs) and their mental health effects on young children, growing numbers of dual language learners in the classroom, and the COVID pandemic have each reordered program priorities and goals in the state and at local levels. The programs supported by each First 5 county commission thus look different today compared with how they began.

At the same time, First 5 has been victimized by its own success in reducing tobacco use by half through an expensive tax, and as proceeds from the tobacco tax have declined from around $675 million in 1999 to $334 million in 2021, state and county commissions have had to cut back.[24] Many First 5 commissions strengthened partnerships with other community agencies to develop services, based on a shared vision of children's needs, that have enabled the funding to continue as tobacco funds declined. In other circumstances, First 5 commissions were able to end services that could be picked up by other agencies, such as fluoride treatments for young children provided by First 5 Amador County that were adopted by physicians in the county during their well-child visits.[25] All of these adaptations to a declining funding picture have further changed the profile of programs supported by each county commission.

One of the significant strengths of the First 5 approach has been the local control of programs and services to ensure their responsiveness to local needs. This has also enabled each commission to learn from the others.[26] In addition, First 5 has benefited from a comprehensive view of how school readiness is supported in young children that includes more than just fostering literacy and numeracy skills and extends to physical and dental health care, family well-being, and early childhood mental health. Both of these desirable characteristics of First 5 – local control and a broadened view of school readiness – are unfortunate obstacles, however, to an inclusive, comprehensive evaluation of the impact of Proposition 10. If each county commission supports a different and changing portfolio of programs over time, with different goals and intended benefits for children and families, on what basis can the overall impact of First 5 be evaluated? How can the public know whether the significant multiyear investment of tobacco tax revenue in state and county First 5 initiatives has improved children's lives in California?

The problem of documenting progress on key indicators of young children's well-being was pointed out by the critics of Proposition 10 and was early acknowledged by state and county First 5 organizations. There were some efforts early in the implementation of First 5 to address the problem of documenting statewide outcomes for a major decentralized initiative. Shortly after the county commissions began their work, for example, the UCLA Center for Healthier Children, Families and Communities commissioned a paper by Mark Friedman, founder of the Fiscal Policy Studies Institute, on "results accountability for Proposition 10 commissions."[27] The paper is basically a Program Evaluation 101 tutorial for the county commissions, describing the steps of establishing well-defined goals for programs supported by First 5 county commissions, identifying measurable indicators of progress on those goals, creating a logic model denoting the causes of children's current standing on those indicators and the specific ways that the program would alter those causes to improve outcomes, and the importance of monitoring progress through systematic measurement along the way.

Unfortunately, it appears that none of these steps was taken by any of the county commissions. In some respects, who would be surprised at this? There was already considerable public pressure in 1999 to get money out the door to fund children's programs, and county commissioners were certainly more concerned with doing local needs assessments and strategic planning than they were with creating a logic model for how local programs would improve specific outcomes for young children.[28] It is a common tendency of program planners to devote considerably more effort to the design and implementation of programs than to their evaluation, motivated by time and funding constraints but perhaps also by some anxiety over having program outcomes evaluated early in the program's development and the risk that the results might threaten continued funding.[29] But this means that twenty-five years later, there still is no careful, systematic appraisal of the benefits to California children derived from a quarter century of programs funded by the tobacco tax.

Instead, First 5 proponents point to specific successes at the local level. Santa Clara's Healthy Kids program, for example, was adopted by other First 5 commissions around the state to provide health insurance coverage to children from immigrant families or those who did not otherwise qualify for the state's Medicaid program. Later, implementation of the federal Affordable Care Act and the state's expansion of coverage to undocumented children boosted health care coverage to 98% of California's children, one of the highest rates in the nation, in part attributable to the early efforts of First 5 Santa Clara.[30] The First 5 San Joaquin commission enlisted an external evaluator to appraise the effects of its early childhood school readiness and preschool programs.[31] The evaluation indicated that preschool program attendees had lower absenteeism, lower grade retention, and better language arts and math performance (according to teacher ratings) in the early primary grades compared with children who had not participated.[32]

These reports and others like them are unlikely to be satisfactory to critics whose early concerns about lack of accountability of the tobacco tax revenues seem to have been confirmed in these piecemeal outcome reports. Critics may instead point to some of the broad promises made by Proposition 10's supporters during the campaign for the ballot proposition. Typical of these promises is this from Rob Reiner: "I think you're not going to really know for 10 or 15 years, when you see lower teen pregnancy rates, lower crime rates and lower remedial educational costs."[33] Recall that in his congressional testimony, Reiner made similar claims concerning long-term changes in drug abuse, child abuse, welfare dependency, and homelessness.

Twenty-five years later, then, how do these predictions hold up? Can we see changes in these indicators in California, and can they be attributed to First 5 influence?

With respect to teen birthrate, the story is positive. The birthrate of California teenagers decreased by 74% between 2000 and 2018. This decline was also observed throughout the United States (a decrease of 64%) but it was greater in California. The conventional explanations are that more youth today are using reliable contraceptive methods, delaying sexual intercourse, and/or having less sexual activity. No reports that I have found attribute this change to the effects of Proposition 10, although it is possible that there are hidden long-term benefits of early childhood interventions on the development of characteristics like responsibility, future time perspective, and even self-image that could affect reproductive behavior in adolescence. Here are where carefully designed evaluations might have helped to document these influences, but even so the news is positive.

A marginally positive picture also emerges with respect to crime. From 2000 to 2018, violent crime decreased by 28% in California, and property crime decreased by 24%, For the United States there were similar trends: violent crime decreased by 25%, and property crime decreased by 39%.[34] The decline in California was roughly comparable to the decrease in the country as a whole, and both experienced a slight uptick in crime, especially homicides, in the years immediately following 2018. The decline in crime statistics over this period has been conventionally attributed to changes in policing and broader social forces, such as declining unemployment, growth in income, changes in alcohol consumption, and an aging population. I found no reports attributing this change to the effects of Proposition 10 in California.

What about educational achievement? Here the story is more negative. On the National Assessment of Educational Progress, California fourth-graders trailed the national average on reading and math in 2019, just as they did in 2002. The same is true of eighth-grade reading and math achievement.[35] Although the gaps between California and US children in reading and math narrowed from 2002 to 2019, California children continue to lag behind the rest of the country. There is evidence, furthermore, that young children in California still begin school poorly prepared. Although California has no statewide school readiness assessment, more than half the First 5 county commissions used their own school readiness measures to assess the preparation of young children when they began school.[36] Their findings suggest that during the past five years, fewer than half the children were ready for school based on assessments of cognitive skills, social-emotional responding, and self-regulation.[37] There has been some improvement, but little evidence for major gains in school readiness and academic achievement in the years since Proposition 10 was implemented.

Taken together, it is difficult to conclude that teen birthrates, crime rates, and even educational achievement have been significantly improved in California because of First 5, especially when the same trends were observed elsewhere in the country. To be sure, holding First 5 accountable for these long-term outcomes may be an unfair expectation because many county programs had other goals. County First 5 programs have provided improved health insurance coverage, home visitation programs, the development and implementation of QRIS systems, support for a statewide transitional kindergarten program, as well as improved child care quality, to name a few achievements. First 5 California has also been a model for similar initiatives in other states. In 2006, for example, Arizona voters approved an increase on tobacco products of eighty cents per pack to fund early childhood programs to create First Things First for Arizona. In the same year, Nebraska voters amended the state constitution to permit the redirection of revenue from the Permanent School Fund to early childhood programs, creating the Nebraska Early Childhood Education Endowment Fund Sixpence Program. Other initiatives similar to First 5 have emerged elsewhere.[38]

But on some of the broadest outcome metrics so often promised in the campaign for Proposition 10, even enhancing school readiness and academic achievement, there is little evidence that the needle has moved significantly. Deborah Stipek, former dean of the Graduate School of Education at Stanford and a widely respected authority on early childhood education, commented that First 5 is a "very positive force, but it's like throwing a pebble into the ocean. We can't expect First 5 to make everything right for the state."[39]

But Stipek's balanced conclusion is also a critique of the overpromising that accompanied the Proposition 10 campaign and the early days of First 5. It is difficult to make firm predictions of developmental outcomes from early interventions, and the difficulty compounds the greater the amount of time following the intervention because of the variety of influences on children's development in the interim. Voters deserved a more thoughtful estimation of the benefits that could reasonably be expected from these diverse and decentralized programs, and a logic model that was more sophisticated than "the first years last forever." Such a logic model would have taken into consideration how the benefits that children might derive from different First 5 programs related to the complex problems contributing to poor school achievement (and other outcomes). It would have taken into account the diversity of programs and their ability to collectively improve early learning and school readiness. It would have also considered how enduring these benefits would be after age five, especially without follow-up programs to maintain and strengthen them in subsequent years. Perhaps most important, a responsible logic model would have moved beyond the general goal of "shifting the odds" for improved youth and adult outcomes to considering *how much* early interventions alone can make a difference.

In the context of such a logic model, proponents of the California Children and Families First initiative might have chosen to focus on predicting narrower, short-term benefits that would more reliably derive from the programs to be funded, such as safer and more supportive family relationships, strengthened self-regulation in young children, greater cognitive and noncognitive skills at school entry, and children's greater physical health and well-being. Promises such as these would probably not have resulted in a more compelling campaign than the one for Proposition 10, just a more realistic one. This is where greater modesty by those speaking for the science would have been desirable.

There are, however, other considerations. Recognizing that many worthwhile programs were funded by Proposition 10, what was the harm of promising exaggerated benefits in order to achieve the funding necessary to produce these good outcomes? After all, there are certainly also many other unmeasured benefits from county First 5 programs that are not even discussed here. On balance, is it fair to criticize the strong claims of child advocates for Proposition 10 when the initiative resulted in substantial funding for many worthwhile programs for young children and their families – especially when overpromising is a staple of political advocacy?

There are, however, at least two problems to overpromising relevant to the themes of this book. The first is that *predicting* such significant, long-term outcomes misrepresents the strength of the science on which these promises are based. It contributes to the view that the science of brain development enables researchers to identify the specific causal influences necessary early in life to predestine greater school achievement and other desirable long-term outcomes. This is more than developmental science and neuroscience are currently capable of delivering. Overpromising also contributes to the view that early experience (more than later experience, inheritance, economic conditions, or luck) determines long-term developmental outcomes, and that we can improve human well-being through these early interventions alone. Stated differently, the overpromising enlisted and strengthened some of the more misleading elements of the public messaging of developmental neuroscience.

The second problem of overpromising is equally important. Developing public trust in science is hard and incremental, but it is a valuable resource to public understanding. Violating that trust is a serious problem because trust can be difficult to win back.[40] Ambitious campaigns to influence public policy based on science can be particularly threatening to the integrity of science because overpromising seems justified by the worthwhile policy initiatives it can advance. But if voters later conclude that they were sold a false bill of goods, the harm to science can be enduring and ultimately more damaging over time.

The campaign for California's Proposition 10 and its implementation illustrates how the messaging of developmental brain science continued to evolve after the *I Am Your Child* campaign as the message was adapted to different purposes and new audiences. Whereas the effort of April 1997 was to present the science of early brain development in a compelling manner to parents and practitioners in order to improve the care of young children, the subsequent effort to pass a voter initiative in California broadened the brain development message to mobilize voter enthusiasm for supporting a wide range of programs with a number of different purposes. Now the goal was not just emotionally secure children but children who would excel in school; avoid delinquency, crime, and teenage pregnancy; and become productive members of the workforce. As we shall see in other examples that follow, overpromising has become characteristic of the efforts to translate developmental neuroscience into public policy, with important implications for public understanding of the science.

Enter the Economists

Developmental scientists and economists usually don't have much to say to each other. They speak different languages: economists speak of income shocks and externalities, while developmental scientists think about family finances and relationships. Economists work with large national datasets, while developmental scientists more often use small experimental studies (and developmental neuroscientists neuroimage the brain). But developmental scientists and economists frequently study issues in common, such as the means by which employment skills are acquired and the effects on children of family economic insufficiency. This is why child advocates love economists, because when economists speak to these child-related concerns, policymakers are more likely to listen because of their longstanding attention to economics data.

As public understanding of the importance of the early years for brain development grew after 1997, several economists offered complementary analyses of their own about the significance of the early years. This was unusual, because childhood – especially early childhood – had not previously been of much interest to economists. The most prominent of these was James Heckman of the University of Chicago, who shared the 2000 Nobel Prize in Economics with Daniel McFadden for his work in the 1990s on selection bias and self-selection in econometrics. Besides his research in econometrics, Heckman was interested in the origins of human capital. "Human capital" consists of the personal attributes of individuals that contribute to economic productivity – it is, so to speak, the psychological parallel to the financial capital that is more often the concern of economics. Human capital is necessary, along with financial capital, to make systems run productively. Human capital consists, for example, of the workplace knowledge and job skills that are the focus of professional preparation or on-the-job training. Human capital also consists of individual qualities that are not job-specific, such as knowledge and cognitive skills, motivation, conscientiousness, persistence, and self-control. Educational attainment is important to the human capital that individuals acquire and that economies depend on.

In a 2000 paper, Heckman criticized current thinking about workplace skill formation and proposed several new ideas about the development of human capital.[41] First, by contrast with the emphasis on cognitive skills that guides thinking about the importance of education and job training, Heckman argued that a variety of "noncognitive" skills are equally or even more important to success in the job and in life. These noncognitive skills[42] include social skills and self-discipline, along with perseverance, motivation, self-esteem, and risk aversion.[43]

Second, by contrast with the view that individual differences in basic abilities are fixed from an early age (a belief derived, in part, from hereditarian thinking about the origins of differences in intelligence), Heckman argued that basic abilities can be altered and, indeed, typically grow and develop substantially. Furthermore, this claim led him to the view that "dynamic complementarity" characterizes ability formation by which more capable individuals can acquire more skills over time than those who are less capable (stated differently, "to those who have, more shall be given"). The intellectual and self-regulatory abilities an individual acquires, for example, provide the tools for further developing cognitive capabilities and other skills over time. Thus a reasonable emphasis of public policies that are intended to promote human capital should be on promoting the early competencies by which developing abilities can be compounded over time.

Third, Heckman argued that by contrast with an emphasis on formal education as the fundamental avenue promoting skill development, the important role of families in promoting basic abilities has been overlooked. This view follows from the foregoing because when noncognitive skills are considered important to work productivity, families rise in importance because it is in the home that many of these noncognitive skills are shaped. It is in families that children begin to develop self-esteem, social skills, and habits of perseverance. When combined with his idea of the dynamic complementarity of skill development, Heckman was led to focus on early childhood in his 2000 analysis:

> Learning starts in infancy long before formal education begins and con-
> tinues throughout life. Recent research in psychology and cognition dem-
> onstrates the vital importance of skill formation of the early pre-school years
> when human ability and motivation are shaped by families and non-
> institutional environments. Success or failure at this stage feeds into success
> or failure in school which in turn leads to success or failure in post-school
> learning. Early learning begets later learning and early success breeds later
> success just as early failure breeds later failure.[44]

This led, in turn, to Heckman's view that it is important to invest in learning during the early years and also to support efforts to identify early deficits because the later in life that deficits are allowed to endure, the more costly their remediation becomes. Furthermore, Heckman recognized, in a way that child advocates have sometimes been slow to acknowledge, that early investments in skill development are not enough. It is also essential that these early investments are followed by later investments that main-tain, support, and build on the gains achieved earlier, consistent with the principle of dynamic complementarity. Heckman has had much less to say, unfortunately, about the nature and importance of these follow-on programs compared with the attention he has devoted to early childhood interventions.

It is worthwhile pausing here to consider what a debt Heckman owes to the research in developmental science. Most of these ideas – school success based on motivation and self-regulation as well as basic intelligence, the rapid development of cognitive and noncognitive skills in childhood, the family as a central influence on children's growth – are noncontroversial to developmental scientists, who have been studying these processes for many years. In subsequent papers, Heckman dipped further into the well of developmental science, incorporating research in developmental neuroscience and studies of the effects of stress and adverse childhood experiences into his basic arguments.[45] Although his understanding of the research on children's development was not always on target (such as his repeated claim that basic academic skills are set by age fourteen[46]), Heckman in most respects has been an attentive consumer of developmental science. By incorporating these research literatures (with which he may have become more familiar because of the 1997 campaign) into sophisticated economic analyses of workplace skill formation, Heckman exposed large numbers of scholars in economics, public policy, and other fields to the ideas of developmental science and neuroscience. He also commanded their attention to the importance of early childhood development for workplace success and, indirectly, the economic prosperity of a community. He has had, in fact, a significant impact on the field of labor economics, which has been challenged by his work to rethink its traditional neglect of the early years in the development of human capital.

In a sense, these ideas enabled Heckman to construct a broad foundation in developmental science for his arguments concerning the early origins of human capital. These conclusions were also essential to Heckman's critique of conventional approaches to improving skill formation at later ages to promote human capital. The conventional approaches Heckman criticized, familiar to economists concerned with promoting workforce development, included reducing class size and raising per-pupil spending in K-12 schools (Heckman: "The evidence . . . indicates that the U.S. may be spending too much on students"[47]), adolescent mentoring programs, providing tuition subsidies to encourage college attendance (Heckman: "The disincentive effects of college tuition on college attendance are dramatically weakened when ability is entered into the analysis of college attendance"[48]), job skills training programs, and even tax policies to promote adult education and skills enhancement. All of these approaches were found to be inadequate, especially, by comparison with the benefits of investments in early childhood education. Heckman's conclusion from his analysis comes close to portraying the difference in investment returns as a conflict in generational interests:

> The returns to human capital investments are greatest for the young for two reasons: (1) younger persons have a longer horizon over which to recoup the fruits of their investments; and (2) skill begets skill.... A reallocation of funds from investment in the old and unskilled to the young and more

trainable, for whom a human capital strategy is more effective, is likely to produce more favourable outcomes in the long run.[49]

The Heckman Curve

These conclusions are summarized in a figure developed two years later that has become iconic among early childhood advocates, and is now called the "Heckman curve" (Figure 5.1).[50]

The figure summarizes Heckman's comparison of the return on investment – especially the immediate and long-term benefits of skill development programs – from his review of the evidence of specific programs at each age. Return on investment (ROI) is, in economics terms, the profitability of investment in a program, and it is calculated as the benefits from the program minus its costs. The Heckman curve shows a progressive decline in return on investment from its prenatal and early childhood peak, continuing through the effects of K-12 education, with the least return on investment from adult programs such as job training initiatives. The curve involves comparisons of ROI at different ages, although it is important to remember that what is being compared are dissimilar programs promoting different skills at different ages, ranging from letter and number skills in preschoolers to work-related skills in adults. This apples-and-oranges comparison of dissimilar programs means that the age differences in ROI

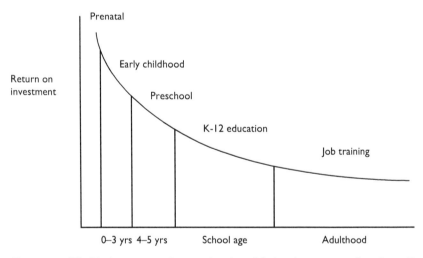

Figure 5.1   The Heckman curve. Reprinted and modified with permission from https://heckmanequation.org/resource/the-heckman-curve/ (retrieved June 16, 2022).

could occur for many reasons, such as the structure, setting, and duration of programs, the kinds of skills developed, and how investment return was estimated. In presenting this analysis, moreover, Heckman has done what economists often do, which is to smooth the curve to summarize the overall pattern of results. The Heckman curve should therefore be viewed as a conceptual summary, not as a quantitative study of changes in ROI across development.[51]

It is easy to see, however, why early childhood advocates would be enthusiastic about the Heckman curve.[52] Never before has a Nobel laureate – in economics! – devoted such concerted attention to early childhood development in a manner that confirmed the importance of the early years. The conclusions about comparative return on investment for programs at different ages suggested that public and private funding for early childhood programs has greater benefit than comparable investments at later ages. There is now a website based on his work (https://heckmanequation.org) that includes further information about early childhood interventions, additional resources for presenting evidence about early childhood programs to interested audiences, and Heckman's responses to his critics. Included are resources entitled "Make Your Case on Social Media: Sample Content," a video entitled "Early Childhood Education Has a High Rate of Return," a "Heckman Equation Flyer," a PowerPoint-style "Research Presentation for Birth-to-Three Advocates," and "How to Use Professor Heckman's Work." Having drawn deeply from the science of early childhood development and developmental neuroscience to deepen his arguments about the early origins of workplace skills, Heckman has repaid the field with a full commitment to the children's cause in his writings and resources.

There is something else that Heckman has bequeathed to early childhood advocates besides a prestigious ally and advocacy resources. It is a view of *why* people should be interested in early childhood. Rob Reiner believed that the early years are crucially important because of the foundation of security and well-being evoked by nurturant relationships. This foundation, he believed, would constitute the psychological context for improved school achievement, reduced criminality, diminished teenage birthrates, and other benefits to children in later years. Many of the public policy dimensions of this messaging – advocating for increased child care quality, strengthened parental leave programs, improved prenatal and pediatric health care, family-centered communities – were to strengthen this early childhood foundation of relational security and support. His focus was on benefits to the individual child.

But with the language of benefit-cost ratio and return on investment, Heckman portrayed early childhood in more transactional terms. Investments in young children contribute to their skill development and educational success and, in so doing, contribute more broadly to the aggregate human capital on which businesses, communities, and societies rely for their economic growth and prosperity. As communities invest more in early childhood programs, primarily through early education, they should witness over time the growth of a more skilled workforce capable of contributing to economic productivity in new ways that yield greater tax returns and fewer social costs owing to delinquency, criminality, or dependence on public assistance. The workers who have developed in this manner are also consumers who can purchase the goods and services provided by local businesses and power regional and national economies. Because of this, compared with other investments in human capital development, investments in young children have a greater payoff – for children, families, *and communities* – that enable their benefits to more than pay for the costs of the investment. Promoting early childhood development is thus a good economic development strategy.

Viewed in this light, Heckman's arguments concerning early childhood investments are as consistent with late twentieth-century neoliberalism[53] as is Reiner's regard for young children rooted in early twentieth-century Kleinian psychotherapy.

Economic Analysis and Child Advocacy

The view of early childhood programs as economic investments had resonance throughout the policy world. For example, a 2011 report prepared by Labour MP Graham Allen in Great Britain summarized the brain development research related to the impact of early interventions on children's development, and the cover of his report, *Early Intervention: Smart Investment, Massive Savings*,[54] tells the story, as shown in Figure 5.2.

The cover evocatively illustrates the economic costs to the government and society of the young children who experience early neglect and the cost savings of supporting healthy brain development. To ensure that the message is not missed, the gold bars symbolizing costs to the taxpayer are accompanied by two pictures: one representing a healthy, typical three-year-old brain and another of a shrunken brain (labeled "extreme neglect") to represent three-year-olds with very different early experiences.

For child advocates, Heckman's ideas elevated a new way of making the case for supporting early development. They could argue for improved

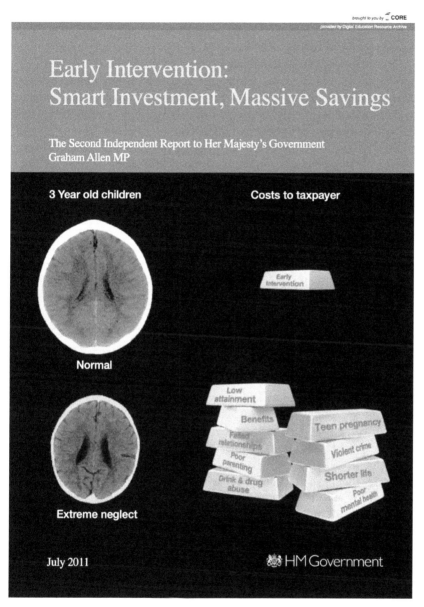

Figure 5.2   Cover of the report by MP Graham Allen.
Reprinted with permission.

early education programs and other initiatives not just because of their benefits to young children, but as investments in skill development with future returns to society that would more than pay for their costs.[55]

Heckman and other child advocates had evidence to support this argument. One of the most frequently cited model early childhood programs, the Perry Preschool Project, provided three-year-olds with two years of daily preschool and other services during the early 1960s. Long-term follow-up studies of child participants and controls through mid-adulthood (age forty) showed a return of greater than $16 for every dollar invested[56] and a benefit-cost ratio of more than eight to one.[57] Closer examination of these studies reveals that most of this return on investment was to the public in averted costs for remedial education, welfare, and crime, and increased tax revenues that more than repaid program costs, although most of these returns were over a very extended period of time. By contrast, direct benefits to program participants, such as increased education and earnings, accounted for about 20% of program benefits. Thus the economic benefits of this program to the public were considerable compared to the direct benefits to participants, which were more modest.

The Perry Preschool Project is not the only one showing such impressive long-term outcomes. The Abecedarian Project and the Chicago Parent-Child Centers are two of several other well-known long-term follow-up studies of children who were provided early education and other benefits and who continued to show positive adult outcomes compared with control children, yielding significant returns on investment.[58] It is not surprising that the results of benefit-cost evaluations like these were frequently presented to policymakers as a compelling justification for investing in programs for young children. The programs would help children; they would contribute to the economic development of the community; and they would pay for themselves over time.

The problem for child advocates, however, was that as time progressed and a larger number of evaluations of early education programs accumulated, the results of benefit-cost analyses proved to be lower and considerably more variable. These studies showed positive benefit-cost ratios in the range of $2 to $4 (rather than $16) for every dollar invested, and some programs showed no positive return on investment at all.[59] It turned out that the benefits of these programs were contingent on many things, such as the quality and duration of the program, the sociodemographic conditions (and languages) of the families of program participants, whether control children participated in alternative programs or none at all, whether program and control children entered schools of good or poor quality, the implementation of follow-up programs, the nature of the outcome measure(s), child gender, and many other factors. Strong early education programs will yield different long-term benefits depending, for example, on whether the schools that children enter are also strong.

Even when the focus was on the most immediate educational benefits to children, such as increased school readiness or early academic achievement, studies showed some significant benefits but also wide variability in the developmental impact of these programs.[60] As summarized in a review by two economists:

> Many early childhood education programs appear to boost cognitive ability and early school achievement in the short run. However, most of them show smaller impacts than those generated by the best-known programs, and their cognitive impacts largely disappear within a few years. Despite this fade-out, long-run follow-ups from a handful of well-known programs show lasting positive effects on such outcomes as greater educational attainment, higher earnings, and lower rates of crime. Since findings regarding short- and longer-run impacts on "noncognitive" outcomes are mixed, it is uncertain what skills, behaviors, or developmental processes are particularly important in predicting these longer-run impacts.[61]

Like many interventions, the impact of early education programs is greatest immediately after the program occurs, and outcomes tend to weaken over time. Predicting reliable long-term benefits to these programs is hazardous. Researchers have increasingly good evidence of what constitutes high-quality early education that is most likely to yield near-term benefits for children, but high-quality programs are also typically more expensive. As more evaluation studies document lower and more variable returns on investment over the long term than initially reported, it has become increasingly apparent that there is no guarantee that new programs will necessarily produce impressive long-term outcomes, such as those reported by some of the well-known programs like Perry Preschool. In fact, very few have done so. Furthermore, keeping in mind that the most significant economic benefits of the best-known early childhood programs were realized years after young children were in preschool – such as through increased tax revenues from adult earnings and reduced criminality – legislators and the public must also be prepared to be patient for the rewards to come from their investments, and those rewards are contingent on a changing world.

Taken together, although there are other reasons to support high-quality early education programs, such as for their immediate benefits to children (particularly those at risk of underachievement), the long-term benefits they can potentially provide to communities and their economic development remain uncertain and contingent.[62] It is equally uncertain whether they can pay for themselves, even over several decades. This is one of the reasons why policymakers have tended to discount their consideration of long-term program benefits of all kinds because long-term benefits are simply less predictable than are immediate returns. This unfortunately diminishes enthusiasm for funding early childhood programs, benefit-cost estimates notwithstanding.

The arguments of Heckman and his colleagues thus changed the landscape of thinking about the value of supporting early childhood development, and changed the calculus of benefits to be expected. They made it possible to perceive the needs of young children as consistent with the economic interests of the community, and to mobilize support for early education for this reason. These arguments were widely influential in the early years of the twenty-first century as neoliberal arguments about the importance of investing in worker productivity to promote economic development gained prominence.

It may be important, however, to question the value of regarding young children as future avenues of economic productivity. By casting the value of early childhood investments within a framework of capital appreciation (or "dynamic complementarity"), these approaches decontextualize how skills and dispositions actually develop by portraying human capital as an intrinsic characteristic of the developing child ("skill begets skill") in whom parents, schools, and societies invest. But the lived experience of children is shaped by many things, including the cultural values of their family and community, the influence of social and racial inequities, the broader economic and socioeconomic conditions in which they live, the quality of schools and neighborhoods, and the examples and incentives of peer relationships, to name just a few. The development of workplace productivity is a function of all of these influences (and more), and even an exemplary early childhood program cannot alone be expected to set the child on a determinate path toward workplace or lifetime success. To argue that the economic prosperity of communities builds significantly from early childhood investments is to impose undue responsibility for prosperity on developing individuals to the exclusion of the broader economic, social, and structural conditions that magnify or constrain the growth of human capital in children.

More broadly, is it right to think of our investments in young children in transactional terms? For centuries, parents (especially in low- and middle-income countries) have hedged their bets on the future by nurturing offspring who can provide for them in old age. It is from this longstanding and universal tradition that we speak of children as "our future" in families and communities. When children grow up, they are expected in these contexts to provide for those who earlier cared for them. But when societies rather than families are concerned, this trans- actional approach does not work. It gives way to a more deontic, humanistic orientation that regards children's well-being as an end in itself, not as an avenue for maximizing the benefits that can accrue to society. We "invest" in people because that is what we owe them as fellow human beings – the social contract of a human community – whether they are children, the disabled and elderly (who have fewer opportunities to provide a return on investment, as Heckman recognized), or citizens of any age or status. During the past century, this approach to human well-being has motivated the emergence of social safety net programs like Social Security, Medicare, public assistance, and affordable health care without any serious expectation that these investments would yield a satisfactory economic return to the public. These programs and others like them have been motivated instead by the view that people of any age and station in life deserve support. And this is especially true of children, who are reliant on the care and solicitude of adults, particularly parents but also communities, who are motivated out of love and devotion to their well-being, not their potential to contribute to future economic prosperity.

What about children in greatest need? In an important and widely cited 2006 paper, Heckman argued that investing in disadvantaged young children promotes social justice, and he is certainly correct.[63] Early, substantial, and continuing investments in well-designed early education and health programs can meaningfully improve the lives of disadvantaged young children, and the evidence shows that children who are most delayed benefit the most from early education programs.[64] But it does not necessarily follow that investing in marginalized young children pro- motes productivity in the economy and society in light of the large hurdles that these children encounter throughout their lives. Developmental sci- ence and developmental neuroscience both point to the important effects on developing brains and minds of adversity, food insufficiency, and stress. Enlisting this science to argue that early interventions focused on early childhood will yield lifetime benefits misses the importance of this con- tinuing context unless the context itself is addressed substantively in efforts to strengthen human capital.

Consequently, the economic productivity argument of early childhood investments, for all the benefits it offers in public perceptions of the importance of the early years, also risks misleading public expectations concerning what early interventions can accomplish and the reliability of the outcomes to be expected. This is unfortunate, because creating economic estimates of the benefits of early education programs offers a powerful argument for public and private support when these estimates are more conservatively calculated. Indeed, as the work of other economists described below shows, these arguments are often much more powerful than those supporting competing investments (such as public support for office parks and entertainment centers). As Heckman pointed out on his 2006 paper, it is not difficult to demonstrate that society's investment in improving the developmental capacities of young children growing up in disadvantage is one of most rewarding possible – even if these investments do not yield benefits to the economy.

Creating Economically Informed Early Childhood Initiatives

Meanwhile, other economists were advancing thinking about early childhood investments in ways that complemented Heckman's arguments but pushed in somewhat different directions.

In 2003, Art Rolnick, senior vice president and director of research at the Federal Reserve Bank of Minneapolis, and Rob Grunewald, a regional economic analyst at the Fed, coauthored an economic argument for enhanced public investments in early childhood programs. The article was straightforwardly titled "Early Childhood Development: Economic Development with a High Public Return."[65]

The authors began their paper with a critique of the conventional avenues by which state and local governments try to spur economic growth. Governments often try to generate growth through tax and investment incentives to private businesses, building sports stadiums and entertainment centers, developing office parks, and other strategies. Rolnick and Grunewald concluded that these approaches are rarely successful, instead promoting job relocation rather than job creation and supporting business development that would have occurred anyway, as well as stimulating regional and national bidding wars to attract new businesses. They argued, however, that while publicly subsidized K-12 education is a longstanding government investment with substantial economic benefit to communities, early childhood development could potentially yield compatible benefits but has suffered from chronic underinvestment. This should change, they argued, because of new under-standing of the foundations of brain development established in the early years and its significance for the growth of cognitive and social skills. Drawing on findings from the Perry Preschool Project in a manner similar to Heckman's analysis, the authors argued that the rate of return from public investment in early childhood programs is substantially greater than for other kinds of public economic development strategies.

Rolnick and Grunewald further proposed the creation of a public/private Minnesota Foundation for Early Childhood Development to fund high-quality early childhood education programs through scholarships for all three- and four-year-old children living in poverty in Minnesota. Using figures from the Perry Preschool Project, they calculated a cost estimate of the funding needed (beyond existing publicly supported preschool pro-grams, such as Head Start) to provide these services to approximately 20,000 disadvantaged young children. Based on this estimate, they pro-posed the establishment of a $1.5 billion endowment gathered from government and private sources over a five-year period. The fund would provide more than $1 million annually for scholarships as well as start-up funding to establish new early childhood programs and improve existing ones. Parent mentoring programs for the same population were also envisioned, although this aspect of their proposal was developed in less detail.[66]

There are several noteworthy aspects of this proposal. First, the empha-sis on children in poverty targets the children most likely to benefit from early education in families least capable of paying for a high-quality program. Perry Preschool and other early childhood programs that have provided a strong return on investment were likewise focused on young children from families in economic need. Second, a public endowment is a clever alternative to annual legislative appropriations to ensure more reliable funding as the program scales up. Too often, legislative appropri-ations are accompanied by oversight mechanisms that can lead to the withdrawal of funding before programs have become sufficiently estab-lished to demonstrate their benefits. A public endowment bypasses this risk. Third, making scholarships the subsidy avenue (rather than provider-based subsidies) gives funding portability that enables families to transition to better-quality or more convenient programs, as long as the program satisfies quality requirements. Fourth, including a parent mentoring com-ponent is, at least in design, a desirable way of increasing the benefits to children from program participation. Finally, the expectation of a high public rate of return from this initiative still depends on cost savings realized over many years through averted costs in public assistance and criminality and increased tax revenue from program participants. The success of the endowment would depend, therefore, on the patience of Minnesota voters and public officials in realizing the benefits of the program.

The Rolnick-Grunewald proposal generated broad interest, but the $1.5 billion endowment was not appropriated by the Minnesota state legislature. In the years following the Rolnick and Grunewald paper, however, other smaller-scale initiatives adopted elements of their plan. For example, the Minnesota Early Learning Foundation was created in 2005 with private funding, and in 2008 it piloted an Early Childhood Scholarship Program for residents of St. Paul. In this program, 348 three-year-olds received two-year scholarships to attend high-quality preschool programs, and mentoring services were provided for their parents.[67] An evaluation study later showed significant improvements for program children on measures of language, math, and social competence, but fewer differences with comparison children, many of whom had also improved in other early childhood education programs elsewhere.[68] The Minnesota legislature declined to provide continuing support for the St. Paul pilot, but in 2013 it approved nearly $25 million in annual funding for an Early Learning Scholarship program of need-based scholarships for three- and four-year-olds. This was because in 2013, the legislature and Governor Mark Dayton were trying to alleviate a chronic educational achievement gap, and the funding for preschool scholarships was part of a package of initiatives that included funding for full-day kindergarten. After 2013, the legislature and governor maintained the scholarship program and gradually increased its funding. At the time of this writing, the Early Learning Scholarships are annually capped at $8,500 per child, far below the cost of a high-quality early childhood program, although higher scholarship support is provided for children in families with special needs. The legislative appropriation funds approximately 10,000 scholarships annually, far below the level of need.[69] But this is a creative response to a serious educational problem, and it is unlikely that a program of this scope and design would have appeared without the catalyst of the 2003 paper from the Fed Bank in Minneapolis.

At the same time, another economist was studying the effects of preschool education and the essential ingredients contributing to its benefits for young children.

In 2001, Steven Barnett, a professor of economics and policy at Rutgers University, established the Center for Early Education Research (renamed in 2002 the National Institute for Early Education Research [NIEER]) with funding from the PEW Charitable Trusts. Later in this chapter, I discuss PEW's ten-year effort to advance prekindergarten programs in the United States. The establishment of NIEER was part of Pew's campaign, which invested more than $33.4 million in NIEER over the ten-year period. One of Barnett's first research publications was a benefit-cost analysis of the Perry Preschool Program, and his subsequent work on the economics of early childhood education and early intervention programs prepared him well to lead NIEER and the research arm of Pew's advocacy efforts.

During the period of Pew funding, Barnett published influential papers on early childhood program design and economic returns, crystallizing knowledge of the program factors contributing to improving children's developmental outcomes. His concerted advocacy of public investment in early childhood programs in the United States and abroad established him as one of the leading child advocates of this period. Under his direction, the NIEER group conducted and disseminated original research on early childhood development, regularly published newsletters and briefs for practitioners, and assisted states in the evaluation of their early childhood programs. This work continued after the end of Pew support in 2011, and NIEER has continued to be a leading source of research and analysis of early childhood programs and their developmental impact. NIEER has had continuing support from a range of federal and state agencies and private foundations since 2011.

One of the more important contributions of NIEER has been the publication of an annual *State of Preschool Yearbook* in which state-by-state enrollment and funding data and quality ratings of all fifty state preschool programs are reported together with summary information about changes in the "state of preschool" in the United States.[70] The focus of the report is on state preschool programs – defined as public programs, usually serving three- and four-year-olds, with an educational focus – and therefore does not include private preschools and child care programs, which are typically more numerous and are differently regulated and resourced. The *Yearbook* is designed to provide a comparative index of how well each state is serving young children, and indeed it resembles the report card it is intended to be with scorecards and boxes checked.

A central feature of this comparative evaluation is a list of how many of ten "quality standards" are met by each state preschool program. These benchmarks, which have evolved since the first *Yearbook* appeared in 2002, capture some of the aspirational standards recognized by researchers of early childhood program quality. The benchmarks include metrics related to teacher preparation (lead teachers have a BA degree and assistant teachers a Child Development Associate degree), state expectations (state Early Learning and Development Standards aligned with the National Education Goals Panel and with child learning assessments), a state-approved curriculum (including assistance with classroom implementation), maximum class size (twenty) and staff-child ratio (1:10), and a state-level Continuous Quality Improvement System requiring the systematic collection of data on classroom quality.[71] Not surprisingly, states vary significantly in how many of the quality standards are satisfied by their programs, and the report cautions that "no state's prekindergarten policies should be considered fully satisfactory unless all 10 benchmarks are met."[72]

Taken together, economists like Heckman, Rolnick, Grunewald, and Barnett extended the brain development revolution by making a more systematic, quantitative argument for the long-term benefits to children of early educational interventions than child advocates had previously offered. Their work provided more precise estimates of the costs of these programs and their expected benefits, incorporating judgments about the nature and duration of these benefits that were drawn from the results of a few early model programs, particularly the Perry Preschool Project. In subsequent years, as the results of other preschool evaluations have yielded more disappointing reports, it has become apparent that relying on these early programs for generalizable conclusions concerning return on public investment risked obscuring how contingent these benefits might be, as well as that many of these benefits accrue many years after children have left preschool. Even so, the economists – especially Rolnick and Grunewald – also challenged policymakers with carefully designed proposals for early education programs that included innovative elements drawn from their economic background, and these proposals have had an impact on public policy. Together, they provided child advocates with strong arguments for early childhood investments promising impressive public returns (better than the stock market!) but leaving less clear how contingent and long-awaited these benefits might be.

Education and Brain Development

Educational applications of developmental neuroscience had already appeared before the 1997 *I Am Your Child* campaign and colored public perceptions of its implications for policy and practice. As discussed earlier in this chapter, the "Mozart effect" alleged that the rhythms and structure of music stimulate logical processing and spatial-temporal reasoning. It led to recommendations that young children should be provided musical experiences at an early age and that music education should continue throughout childhood and adolescence. Despite the lack of substantive evidence for these effects,[73] proposals for early classical music training reached the floor of the Georgia legislature in 1998, and Disney marketed a product line called "Baby Einstein" based, in part, on the Mozart effect.[74]

Likewise, evidence that phonological areas of readers' brains are active when they read led to arguments that reading should be taught using phonics rather than whole-language methods, enlisting developmental neuroscience unnecessarily into a controversial area of reading education.[75] In many cases, these early recommendations resulted from premature applications of neuroscience to complex learning processes, and sometimes also from the effort to enlist the persuasive appeal of brain development to support preexisting educational views. Sadly, these wayward applications emerged alongside some of the more informative early applications of developmental neuroscience to education. One such recommendation was moving foreign language instruction to younger ages when brains are neurobiologically primed for language learning. Researchers were also developing new therapeutic interventions based on neuroscience for treating speech and language problems like dyslexia.[76] Taken together, these confused and constructive proposals reflected debates among scientists and educators about the clarity and relevance of the science to education, and led to more searching inquiry.

One response appeared in the book *The Learning Brain: Lessons for Education* (2005) by British psychologists Sarah-Jayne Blakemore and Uta Frith.[77] Written for educators, the book is both a prospective look at how developmental neuroscience can potentially inform educational practice and a cautionary tale about neuromyths to be avoided. Many of their lessons for educators will be familiar to readers of Chapter 3. The brain is shaped by experience, which can include formal and informal learning. The brain's plasticity is a lifelong resource for learning and adaptation to experience. Early experiences are important but not determinative for the developing brain: they build on sensitive periods (such as for vision and hearing) that provide a foundation for later learning and development, but later experiences are also important. There is no reason to try to accelerate early learning or to provide enhanced early experiences to promote better brain development. Adolescence is a period of significant brain development and cognitive advances, accompanied by the slow growth of self-regulation combined with susceptibility to reward incentives. Use it or lose it. These are sensible lessons from developmental neuroscience, but if an educator read these recommendations it is doubtful that they would find anything here that provided unusual or unexpected applications to contemporary educational practice. How informative was the brain development research after all?

Several years later, a working group commissioned by the Royal Society in Great Britain released their own report in 2011, *Neuroscience: Implications for Education and Lifelong Learning*.[78] Their central conclusions were similar. Both nature and nurture affect the learning brain. The brain is plastic. The brain's response is influenced by expectations and uncertainty. The brain has mechanisms for self-regulation. Education is a powerful form of cognitive enhancement. There are individual differences in learning ability with a basis in the brain. Neuroscience informs adaptive learning technology. Again, these are sensible ideas, but most of these conclusions could be reframed as characteristics of human thinking rather than of the brain ("A person's response is influenced by expectations and uncertainty," and "Individuals have mechanisms for self-regulation"). It is difficult, in other words, to identify these claims as unique derivatives of neuroscience or as a significant advance on what educators already knew about children's learning.[79] It was not apparent from these reports that the brain development revolution had been revolutionary for education.

It is possible that these educational applications were limited by the state of the science that existed years ago. Consequently, one might look at current thinking about the relevance of developmental neuroscience to education to see whether advances in science have yielded more consequential recommendations. An article that appeared in 2022 in *Scientific American* caught my attention because of its title: "U.S. Kids are Falling behind Global Competition, but Brain Science Shows How to Catch Up."[80] The recommendations, based on brain science: support nurturing interactions with caregivers and protect children from stress. This can be accomplished, the authors argued, by public policies supportive of paid parental leave, child allowances and tax credits, and access to quality child care. These are very familiar recommendations and policy implications.

It appears, therefore, that after an early flurry of recommendations for specific educational practices based on developmental neuroscience, some of them clearly misguided, researchers began instead to identify more general lessons that align better with developmental science and educational practice. Although these lessons do not offer especially novel or innovative implications for practice, they are consistent with the view that the most useful applications of developmental neuroscience to education are those in harmony with what is already known of how the mind learns.[81] This may be one reason many cognitive and developmental scientists have long been doubtful of the revolutionary impact expected of developmental brain science on education, beginnning with Bruer's claim in 1997 that it is simply "a bridge too far."[82]

This theme was renewed in the Santiago Declaration published ten years later.[83] Written by a prominent international group of developmental scientists and educators meeting at the University of Chile, the declaration offered its own guidance concerning children's learning. Their conclusions included the following: "Children are active, not passive, learners who acquire knowledge by examining and exploring their environment," and "Young children learn most effectively when information is embedded in meaningful contexts rather than in artificial contexts that foster rote learning." These are good points, but the writers of the declaration emphasized that these principles were based on social and behavioral research findings, not brain research. Concerning neuroscience, the signatories wrote, "Neuroscientific research, at this stage in its development, does not offer scientific guidelines for policy, practice, or parenting."

This may or may not have been a justified conclusion even in 2007, as I noted in my discussion of Bruer's critique of the *I Am Your Child* campaign in Chapter 4. Many claims arising from the brain development messaging are important to education, including the recognition that learning in the primary grades builds on a foundation of brain and mind established in earlier years, that emotions and motivation are important to learning and develop neurobiologically at a rapid rate in childhood, and (from the intervention literature) that developing brains can be retrained when necessary to support learning.

The educational commentators also overlooked another connection between developmental neuroscience and learning: the importance of the context of learning. By contrast with the general, decontextualized recommendations about the brain and education summarized above, the conclusions of multiple studies of children's educational achievement during the last thirty-five years[84] have consistently emphasized the importance of school and instructional quality, socioeconomic stressors, nutritional inadequacy, conditions at home, and many other features of the environments in which children learn. Although developmental neuroscience does not directly address all of these contextual influences, there are extensive neurobiological studies of the effects of poverty, chronic stress, and the quality of nutrition on brain development (summarized in Chapter 3) that constitute important lessons for educators. In the spirit of the reports earlier described, these lessons might read:

- Brains have trouble paying attention and learning when stressed.[85]
- Adequate, nutritious meals are necessary to fuel the brain's thinking and reasoning.[86]
- Socioeconomic adversity goes under the skin to impair language learning and self-regulation. But teachers can adapt their instruction to help these students learn better.[87]
- Children living in poverty have trouble achieving the emotional well-being needed for achieving in the classroom.[88]

These lessons recognize that the contexts in which learning occurs is important biologically as well as behaviorally, and they broaden the educational focus from the individual to the child in context.

Let us pause to ask: Why have so many of the policy and practice applications of developmental brain science discussed in this chapter neglected (with a few exceptions) attention to the broader social and economic context of brain development? This has been true of not only the many educational applications of developmental brain science (including the Pew campaign for prekindergarten discussed next) but also the work of prominent economists concerned with early childhood development as well as the promises of the Proposition 10 campaign. This omission could simply be a byproduct of the focus on brain development, which centers attention on the individual child. But the substantial neurobiological research discussed earlier on the effects of adverse environments, stress, and deprivation on the developing brain shows how important is context to developmental brain science, and this has been true for a long time.[89] It is also possible that because these issues received relatively little attention in the 1997 campaign,[90] they were also overlooked in its subsequent policy applications.

A different explanation is that inattention to context may have derived from broader currents of public thought at the time the brain development revolution was emerging. Rose and Rose[91] have argued that prevalent applications of neuroscience to public policy tend to be in line with the neoliberal belief in competitive individualism and the exploitation of human resources (including the brain) to maximize economic productivity. The neoliberal view, which flourished during the Reagan and Thatcher administrations of the 1980s, may have oriented many of the policy applications of developmental neuroscience discussed in this chapter.

From this perspective, it follows that starting early to promote the development of human capital is important to supporting individual achievement in school and work and to undergird business development and the prosperity of communities in a competitive world. Communities must begin early so that the benefits of investing in children have more time to accrue and, as children build skill upon skill, local governments receive a return to the public from their investment contributions. The neoliberal concept of competitive individualism is consistent with the view that the decontextualized individual's effort and skill, especially as they are developed by education, determines success independently of the challenges or support of the socioeconomic context, language, race, culture, and other influences.

Perhaps without realizing it, therefore, educators, economists, and even child advocates focused naturally on how to promote brain development as an engine of individual productivity and prosperity. The influence of social and economic conditions, which does not enter into the neoliberal view in a major way, was simply neglected.

The Pew Campaign for Prekindergarten Education

In some respects, the most important consequence of the brain development revolution for education was not a matter of *what* is taught or *how* education is conducted, but *when* it begins. Although the field of early childhood education has a rich and generative history that long predates the events of 1997, public interest in early education grew significantly as people learned of the importance of early experience to the developing brain. After 1997, early education became viewed not just as a benefit for the small minority of young children whose parents could afford half-day nursery school or preschool, or as an ancillary of high-quality child care when parents worked, but as a public good meriting public investment. An important catalyst to this growing public interest that also guided its direction is the ten-year campaign for prekindergarten education funded by the Pew Charitable Trusts.

In 2001, after a sustained period of funding K-12 educational initiatives, the Pew board approved a recommendation from program officers for a shift in strategy to prekindergarten.[92] There were several reasons motivating the change.[93] First, the research on early brain development and growing public awareness of this research combined to create a new opportunity to focus on early learning. Many program officers had concluded that efforts to close the achievement gap through improvements in K-12 education alone were insufficient because of the large gaps in learning

and cognitive skills that were apparent at school entry, and greater attention to the years just before kindergarten seemed necessary.[94] Second,
many four- and five-year-olds were already in some kind of out-of-home
care, and polling data indicated that the public accepted that children of
these ages received care and education services outside the home, which
would ease acceptance of a campaign for prekindergarten education.
Finally, the world of prekindergarten was not encumbered by the
entrenched advocacy interests and bureaucracy that impeded reform in
K-12 education, and even though prekindergarten programs were sometimes affiliated with local public schools, there was greater opportunity for
new ideas and initiatives in programs for younger children. Pew began
grant making in 2001 with a projected investment of $10 million annually
for seven to ten years. By the time the campaign concluded in 2011, Pew
had committed more than $104 million to this effort.

The Pew initiative was unique in child advocacy for its strategy, comprehensive scope, and funding. Unlike other efforts focused on improving
child care access or parental leave, the Pew strategy focused on the states
rather than the federal government because this is where educational policy
is shaped. Furthermore, with several states – including Georgia, New York,
and Oklahoma – having already passed legislation for universal preschool
education, there were good models of successful advocacy efforts. Pew also
created or enlisted many partner organizations to further important elements of the campaign, including creating a research and dissemination
agency (NIEER), an advocacy agency that would provide guidance and
technical assistance to local allies in targeted states (PreK Now), an agency
to enlist business leaders in the advocacy work (Partnership for America's
Economic Success), as well as providing funding for two media organizations to heighten public attention to preschool education in a manner that
would advance the campaign (the Hechinger Institute and the Education
Writers Association), and supporting a range of other organizations with
potential interest in early childhood education, including those in law
enforcement (Fight Crime), K-12 education (Council of Chief State
School Officers), child advocacy (Voices for America's Children), and
other fields. The effectiveness of this web of allied organizations is reflected
not only in the initiative and leadership of each partner agency but also in
their close coordination. In her excellent analysis of Pew's strategy, Brenda
Bushouse summarized it this way:

> Pew chose to fund a network of actors that would advocate for a specific
> policy alternative: universal preschool for all three and four year olds. What

emerged was a complex network of Pew-funded actors attempting to frame the "problem" of school readiness so that the policy solution was investment in universal preschool.[95]

As one of the largest philanthropic foundations in the United States, moreover, the generous funding Pew made available to these initiatives was a significant contribution to the campaign's achievements.

It is noteworthy, however, that omitted among the partner organizations were leaders in early childhood education, such as the National Association for the Education of Young Children (NAEYC) and the National Child Care Association (NCCA). As Bushouse has noted, this is because of Pew's effort to align prekindergarten with K-12 education rather than with child care in order to define prekindergarten as an educational aim worthy of public investment and to avoid the political controversies that still existed concerning child care.[96] This alignment with K-12 education was consistent with defining the goal of prekindergarten as closing the achievement gap and enabling more children to enter school ready to learn. Midway into the campaign, Pew expanded its argument to frame prekindergarten as a contribution to the nation's fiscal health – drawing on the arguments of Heckman, Rolnick, and Grunewald – and in this way the promise of economic productivity became further identified with prekindergarten, not with child care (not even high-quality child care). As Sara Watson, who directed the prekindergarten campaign for Pew, commented to me, "The genius of the Pew campaign was reframing early education twice – from parents working to education – and then later to economic development, once Art Rolnick and James Heckman came along."[97]

Divorcing prekindergarten from child care also resulted in divorcing birth-to-three care and education from prekindergarten, even though there were important connections between publicly supported early education programs for infants/toddlers (think Early Head Start) and older children (Head Start). Before the campaign, of course, children from birth to age five were considered collectively in the context of child care policy. This strategic decision to distinguish prekindergarten from child care was important, and it has meant that for the past twenty years, the advances in preschool and prekindergarten education advanced by Pew have not mobilized concurrent progress in efforts to improve child care quality for children of the same age. Child care has been left behind in the push for early education. Even today, the separation of child care from prekindergarten remains influential. Child care retains its longstanding identity as supporting adult workforce participation (reflected in the frequent concern of women's advocates for increasing the number of child care "slots"), while preschool and prekindergarten programs are regarded primarily as early education. But if early learning is important because of the developing brain, why is this not as important to child care as it is to preschool and prekindergarten? Is it not possible to support adult workforce participation and children's cognitive development at the same time?

Two advocacy arms of the Pew campaign were most prominent in advancing the prekindergarten agenda. The National Institute for Early Education Research (NIEER), under the direction of Steven Barnett, was described earlier in this chapter. To complement NIEER's research and dissemination mission, Pew also created PreK Now in early 2005 as a successor to the Trust for Early Education, which had been established in 2002 at the beginning of the campaign. The mission of the two agencies was to advance the advocacy agenda of the campaign by providing support and technical assistance to state organizations as they built public enthusiasm for prekindergarten education. Under the leadership of its executive director, Libby Doggett, PreK Now also helped to build coalitions among the often-disparate local organizations with interests in preschool education, and PreK Now also coordinated sharing lessons learned across the states. Although PreK Now's strategies varied from state to state, they often included working directly with legislators and executive branch officials who were sympathetic to early childhood education, placing news stories (sometimes taken from NIEER) and opinion pieces in local media, convening conferences, creating websites and other digital media resources, enlisting the assistance of public relations agencies, responding to critics, and related activities. PreK Now's involvement was essential to the success of many state PreK advocacy efforts, especially in light of how disorganized and under-resourced were many state-level organizations concerned with early childhood education.

Although Pew's campaign was central to advancing prekindergarten as a public interest, Pew was not alone in funding this effort. A variety of other philanthropies were also part of the picture, including the David and Lucile Packard Foundation, the McCormick Tribune Foundation, and the Foundation for Child Development. Nevertheless, Pew's role was central. According to Pew's internal evaluation, PreK Now consulted in more than thirty states and the District of Columbia and counted eight states (plus DC) as having committed to universal prekindergarten as a result of its efforts by 2010. By the end of the campaign, enrollment in prekindergarten programs had nearly doubled, from 700,000 children in 2001 to more than

1.3 million in 2010, and state funding of prekindergarten more than doubled from $2.4 billion in FY 2002 to $5.3 billion in FY 2010.[98] Since the close of the campaign in 2011, there has continued to be improvement in funding and enrollment figures for prekindergarten – with the exception of 2020–2021 when the COVID-19 pandemic accounted for a sharp drop in prekindergarten enrollment across the country.[99] As the result of Pew's concerted ten-year campaign, it is fair to say that prekindergarten has become an increasingly important element of the early childhood education landscape. In 2021, a proposal for universal prekindergarten was included in President Biden's American Families Plan to provide two years of educational funding for all three- and four-year-olds.[100]

Pew's prekindergarten campaign consolidated the connection between early brain development and early education and established early learning as a significant public concern, in part because of its implications for school achievement and economic productivity. But for a campaign focused on early education, the campaign for prekindergarten education had remarkably little to say about the details: what kind of learning is important to school readiness, how three- to five-year-olds should be educated, the benefits of half-day versus full-day programs, the preparation of prekindergarten teachers, the involvement of families in prekindergarten learning, and other issues that have roiled the field of early childhood education over the years.[101] It is not difficult to perceive this as another strategic decision by Pew to maintain focus on early education as a general public interest rather than getting into the weeds of how it should be done, except for promoting high-quality programs (however they would be defined). As research findings on the variability in quality of prekindergarten programs across different states and their comparably variable benefits for children has accrued,[102] the wisdom of Pew's broad but nonspecific campaign agenda might be questioned. The failure to identify more specific implications of brain research for early childhood education underscores further that developmental brain science did not have the portentous implications for educational practice that early advocates had hoped for. Nor did it have an influence on child care policy, despite the fact that these programs provided environments of care for young children of the same age as those in prekindergarten programs.

Building the Business Case

With increasing attention to early brain development as an investment in young children, especially with the goal of promoting economic development in communities, it was easy to see a business argument emerging for early childhood in the years following 1997. From this perspective, local businesses as well as philanthropies and community organizations should be very interested in promoting the preparation of young children for school with the goal of improving reading, math, and noncognitive skills, high school graduation rates, postsecondary education attendance, and the development of a well-educated and economically productive workforce. Just as building human capital is a wise investment for public policy, it is also a wise investment for local businesses to strengthen the community workforce and build a consumer base.

Early in the Pew prekindergarten campaign, the Committee for Economic Development (CED) was enlisted as a partner. The CED is a nonprofit public policy think tank with a long and distinguished history of supporting important business concerns in the national interest. The CED generated support among the business community, for example, for the Marshall Plan after World War II, and contributed to the Bretton Woods Agreement that established the postwar Western economic order.[103] The CED issued a "call to action" for the expansion of preschool programs early in the Pew campaign, extending its own longstanding advocacy for early childhood education as an economic investment strategy.[104] The CED has continued to be a significant advocate for early childhood education since then, urging partnerships between businesses and national, state, and local policymakers, the dissemination of innovative practices, and other efforts to increase quality of and access to early education.

Pew also funded a new organization in 2006 called the Partnership for America's Economic Success (PAES) under the direction of Robert Dugger, a venture capital investor and managing director of the Tudor Investment Corporation. PAES is an organization of business leaders supporting efforts to help children become productive, successful adults in a global competitive environment. Consistent with the Pew campaign goals, PAES focused on prekindergarten education, disseminating information among its membership and to business and government leaders through speakers, meetings, and publications.

In 2012, after the prekindergarten campaign concluded, PAES became ReadyNation, and in 2014, following a brief affiliation with America's Promise (a large, national alliance of nonprofits, businesses, and community organizations focused on children and youth), ReadyNation became part of the Council for a Strong America, an organization of business leaders focused on children, youth, and their families.[105] Both the Council and ReadyNation enlist their membership in support of early childhood education, voluntary parental coaching, improved K-12 education and increased access to higher education through the publication of opinion pieces, a speaker's bureau, engagement with government leaders, conferences, and related activities. Their purpose is primarily hortatory, that is, to exert influence with opinion leaders, public officials, and other business leaders to collectively move the needle on the broad range of children's issues, especially in state ieglsiatures and Congress.

This is a fine and necessary goal. But consider the source. These are business leaders. The organizations they lead are in an ideal position in their communities to make the changes they advocate in support of young children and their families. Employers are also in an ideal position to improve workplace conditions for their employees. The changes required to support young children and their families are the changes in workplace practices and employee policies that have been long promoted by family advocates to create supportive child-family conditions for working parents.[106] They include on-site high-quality child care, paid family leave following the birth of a child or the illness of a family member, workplace schedules that can accommodate family members' needs and emergencies, appropriate job security to enable parents to plan their lives around their families, and other elements of constructive work-life fit. In the community, business leaders can combine corporate funding with community resources to support targeted goals for improving the availability of high-quality child care and early education for young children. They can fund an endowment to create financial support – such as scholarships – for low-income young children to attend high-quality preschool programs. They can directly invest in one or more local elementary schools so the cognitive skills acquired in strong early childhood programs are not lost. They can mobilize funding for community centers to build family-oriented resources in neighborhoods that lack them, and then contribute from their businesses as the first step. Business leaders can do these things.

There is considerable value, of course, when the business community adds its voice to others in support of the needs of young children and their families. Among the "wins" profiled in the ReadyNation quarterly newsletter[107] are meetings of members with legislative and executive leaders and presentations at local conferences that enable them to convey the importance of early childhood. But among these successes, there are few accounts of the actions taken by business leaders to directly improve conditions for their employees or their communities through their investment of corporate funds. Remarkably, this has remained true even during the current era when (at the time of this writing) many business leaders recognized that their employees were stressed by the very limited availability of satisfactory care for their children and that local providers were exhausted from coping with the effects of the pandemic. It is unfortunate that the quarterly newsletter does not include more frequent accounts of the actions that members have directly taken to change their workplace policies or address children's needs in the community. Even better would be if ReadyNation and the Council for a Strong America challenged its members to excel each other in their own business-related investments for young children in their workplaces.[108]

One of the reasons that business leaders fail to make the investments they urge on public officials is that the return on investment their businesses require is different from what they believe the public requires. Businesses require investments that promise more immediate benefits for the company; they can't wait for a well-educated preschool child to take a place in the community workforce before they benefit from the investment they made in the child's education years earlier.[109] But public officials are also reticent to make investments of public funds whose benefits to the public are unlikely to appear until long after their reelection. This is one of the enduring challenges of early childhood advocacy when investments in children require a long gestation before they provide rewards. I could find nowhere on the websites of the business organizations I've described here the recognition that their members' advocacy for children might be more convincing to policymakers or potential donors if they had already made the same investments in their businesses that they were urging on others – if they had "put their money where their mouth is," so to speak. At the least, their arguments for children may seem a little empty if child-friendly and family-supportive practices have not already been incorporated into their own business policies.

From Science to Policy

There were other initiatives like these emerging from the brain development revolution. The stories of this chapter illustrate the expansion of the movement from science to policy that accompanied and followed the events of 1997, and lead to several observations about how this occurred.

Wins and Losses

There were striking wins and glaring losses for the children's cause in the years following the *I Am Your Child* campaign. Contrary to the hopeful expectation of child advocates that public interest in developmental brain science would provide the final push necessary for real advances in long-standing child and family issues, what emerged in the past quarter century is a more mixed picture.

There have been significant advances in education, although not in revolutionary reforms to teaching practice or curricular content but rather in public acceptance of prekindergarten as a desirable and perhaps necessary prelude to primary school. As I documented in Chapter 1, some believe that prekindergarten is turning kindergarten into the new first grade with unknown long-term consequences for children's learning and development, but whatever the consequences, viewing early childhood as a formative educative period is here to stay. This is a real departure from traditional beliefs that early childhood has little to do with formal education, which should begin in middle childhood when children's minds are sufficiently rational and self-regulated. Developmental neuroscience informed a growing awareness that readiness to learn exists very early and that learning opportunities can be provided at much younger ages if they are designed in developmentally appropriate ways.

On the other hand, there have not been the advances in child care quality, access, and affordability that were an early part of the agenda of the brain development revolution, and which have become an even more serious concern as the result of the social disruptions of the 2020 pandemic. The win for children of prekindergarten and the loss for children of failure to improve child care are, as it turns out, related. Each derives from the strategic effort of the Pew campaign to divorce prekindergarten from child care and wed it to public education in order to advance the standing of prekindergarten in public awareness. This contributed to the success of Pew's prekindergarten campaign, but left child care out of the mobilization of public interest in providing young children with educationally enriching experiences before they entered school. In the United States, concern about the quality, affordability, and access to child care has persisted for more than fifty years without significant policy change, and it is difficult to foresee what can move the needle toward more affordable high-quality care for America's children in the future.

Another win of the brain development revolution was renewed attention to the early origins of the achievement gap and the learning opportunities that most benefit young children in poverty. This concern was apparent in initiatives ranging from Minnesota's Early Learning Scholarship program (and the St. Paul Early Childhood Scholarship pilot that preceded it) to multiple initiatives of California's First 5 county commissions to Heckman's widely cited argument that investing in disadvantaged young children promotes social justice as well as economic benefits. A common denominator to these efforts were the results emerging from several model early childhood programs such as Perry Preschool showing that the greatest benefits – and the greatest return on investment – derived from high-quality programs targeting the most economically needy children. These findings address a continuing debate in the early intervention field between supporting targeted or universal programs for young children. The different early education initiatives discussed in this chapter – universal prekindergarten on one hand, targeted early educational scholarships on the other – reflect this difficult debate. Attention to the learning needs of young children in poverty, whether in the context of targeted or universal programs, is one of the important wins of the brain development revolution.

On the other hand, the brain development revolution did not contribute to progress in attention to the broader needs of children in poverty. Despite considerable research described in Chapter 3 documenting the early and profound effects on brain development of children growing up in economic adversity, the failure of the *I Am Your Child* campaign to extend its concern to children in poverty probably contributed to neglect of this issue in its public policy applications. No major advocacy or philanthropic group took up the cause of poverty and children's brain development in a way that might have pushed this concern to national attention as Pew did with prekindergarten education. As I noted in Chapter 4, the result was a failure to attend to a range of public policy issues that might have been foregrounded in a brain-based campaign for children in poverty. These issues include attention to early nutritional inadequacy (especially for families living in food deserts), environmental toxins (especially in areas where young children live and play), early vision and hearing screening in the context of regular pediatric care, early and regular immunizations, and the internationalization of concern for childhood poverty in the context of periodic famine and world hunger.

This loss of attention to child poverty is especially infuriating because the years following 1997 witnessed two great successes in reducing child poverty. The first was in Great Britain through multiple initiatives of the Blair administration beginning in 1999. The second, and more recent, was in the United States through an expanded child tax credit as part of the American Rescue Plan in 2021. Both programs significantly reduced rates of child poverty and put each country on a trajectory to further reduce child poverty to historically low levels. But both programs were temporary, and child poverty rates rose significantly in each country in the years following their end. Each program shows that child poverty can be meaningfully reduced through concerted public will. The brain development revolution had the potential to mobilize public will in this manner.

There were other wins. The movement for universal child health care coverage in California had roots in First 5 and contributed political momentum to passage of the Affordable Care Act and its extension of coverage to children throughout the country, building on earlier achievements from passage of the Child Health Insurance Program. Obamacare also expanded coverage of prenatal care. But unfortunately, the brain development revolution did not inform public understanding of how important are critical elements of the mother's prenatal condition to fetal brain development, including the effects of the mother's stress, nutritional quality, substance exposure, disease risk, and other factors. This, too, may have derived from the little attention devoted to prenatal brain development in the messaging of the *I Am Your Child* campaign.

There were other benefits to public policy derived from growing public awareness of early brain development. Some of these are more difficult to document because they resulted from local initiatives (as in many of the First 5 county commission efforts) or were influential in diverse other emergent programs and policies. It is not difficult, for example, to view the 1997 campaign as establishing a receptive public for initiatives such as the Bush administration's No Child Left Behind Act of 2001 or the state-by-state implementation of quality rating and improvement standards for child care programs beginning in 2005. The brain development revolution had expansive impact, even though more could have been done.

The Perils of Overpromising

Some of the policy wins for children came at the cost of overpromising the expected benefits that would be derived from new initiatives. This tendency could already be observed in the *I Am Your Child* campaign, but the campaign's principal focus on what parents should do when children are young diminished attention to the later-life benefits that might result from their actions. When the brain development message was mobilized to motivate public investments in educational initiatives like preschool or prekindergarten, however, expectations for the long-term benefits of those investments began to ramp up excessively.

There are many problems with overpromising results based on science. With respect to developmental brain science, a fundamental problem is that promising gains to later educational attainment, adult earnings, and criminal desistance were based on some of the more misleading elements of the public messaging of developmental neuroscience. Especially misleading, as I discussed in Chapter 4, was the generalization of the simple neurodeterminism of developmental brain science to the complex, multicausal influences guiding the growth of adult workforce skills or criminality. "Use it or lose it" and "skill begets skill" are inadequate explanations for the probabilistic, contingent pathways from early experience to adult competencies. And although the findings from well-publicized early education programs like Perry Preschool initially supported some of these promises, the realization that later programs could not necessarily replicate these results underscored the weakness of the implicit logic models on which such predictions were based. Such overpromising also built on and reinforced some of the enduring American beliefs about young children and their development that I discussed in Chapter 4, such as that early experiences determine future development, that science can optimize or accelerate children's developmental accomplishments, and that there is untapped potential in the human brain – none of which is really true. The overpromising of developmental outcomes from early intervention supports an appealing portrayal of how early experiences lead directly to adult competency through the developing brain, but neither developmental neuroscience nor developmental science really supports this messaging.

This overpromising has all happened before, several times. One of the most relevant precedents is the momentum behind creating Head Start, a program to provide education and support for low-income children and their families, as part of the War on Poverty of the 1960s. Head Start was overpromised as an early childhood education program that would end poverty, enabling young children in economic difficulty to advance educationally and avoid welfare dependency and crime. Since its creation in 1965, Head Start has labored under these expectations even as evaluation studies have documented benefits for children and families. But evaluation results have failed to fulfill the unduly ambitious promises made at its founding, leading to periodic calls for its defunding.

Ed Zigler, a developmental psychologist at Yale University who helped design Head Start, defended the program as a member of the Nixon administration, and later assumed a prominent and highly respected role in the developing science and politics of early childhood education before his death in 2019. In a 2011 article titled "A Warning against Exaggerating the Benefits of Preschool Education Programs," Zigler cautioned against repeating the mistakes of Head Start in current efforts to advance early childhood education and prekindergarten. He had particularly critical words for economists:

> Today's most vocal preschool education advocates are economists, and they strike me as a mixed blessing.... Their cost-benefit analyses support their argument that early childhood programs are a good investment for taxpayers and will eventually raise the quality of the American work force and ensure the nation's productivity and competitiveness in global markets.... It seems to me the economists have brought the field full circle to Head Start's beginnings when the program was hurt by promises that this little preschool gesture would end poverty in America. If the savings to society that the economists are promising do not materialize or cannot be precisely quantified, the concept of preschool education will likewise disappoint. [110]

His arguments have contemporary resonance, but I think Zigler is a little tough on the economists and a little easy on his colleagues in developmental psychology. Many of us were complicit in the overpromising of results from early education programs, family support initiatives, and other efforts. Just as the national media attention to children's development in April 1997 cast a welcome spotlight on the science to which we were all committed, the national advocacy for early childhood education, prekindergarten, improved child care quality and access, paid parental leave, home visitation programs, and other initiatives provided a welcome opportunity to promote what we believed were worthwhile efforts to advance children's interests. To many psychologists this was a once-in-a-career chance to make a difference that made the exaggeration of research findings and their implications seem excusable.

The risk of overpromising, however, is that the credibility of scientists and (more importantly) the credibility of the science is at risk if the public eventually believes that they were sold a false bill of goods. The most attention-eliciting promises of what would result from early childhood interventions have generally failed to come to pass. Greater candor about the more modest but predictable developmental outcomes that could reasonably be expected from proposed programs – and the multidetermination of those outcomes – not only is scientifically more accurate but is also likely to be consistent with what many people already believe. If public officials discount confident reports of long-term benefits derived from early childhood programs as uncertain, in other words, this may be consistent with what the public also believes. By acknowledging the limitations of the evidence and the challenges of predicting developmental outcomes, research scientists, economists, and other experts likely accrue greater credibility as they advocate on behalf of children.

An Evolving Message

The public messaging of developmental brain science evolved as the public advocacy progressed. The *I Am Your Child* campaign was shaped by Reiner's view that the first three years are crucially important to human development. Consequently, the messaging of developmental brain science and its public policy applications was principally focused on the first three years, urging parents to be loving, warm, and responsive, encouraging the child's exploration and play, and talking to the child, with broader applications focused on expanding parental leave after a child's birth, providing home visitation, strengthening child care quality, and enhancing perinatal child health care, all to support early nurturant relationships. To the extent that these messages anticipated the later benefits of these practices for the child's development, these predictions were based on psychological theory and the benefits of early secure relationships for developing self-confidence, self-regulation, and healthy personality growth. The core of the messaging was embedded in progressive values concerning the need of young children for emotional support and the responsibility of parents and society to provide it.

The messaging expanded as the story of brain development was enlisted further into public policy advocacy. The goal was not just the growth of emotional security and self-confidence but also skill development and the growth of cognitive and noncognitive skills. These developing capacities were the result of investments not just by parents in the home but also by teachers and other adults in preschools and prekindergarten programs. The focus was not just the first three years but the duration of early childhood until school entry. The legacy of these investments was the creation of economically productive children who became adults who were capable of contributing to the local economy and benefiting the community in other ways. Psychological theory provided for Reiner the emphasis on early emotional security, but psychological theory does not typically portray children as economically productive contributors. Economics theory provided the basis for viewing young children's developing skills as human capital and how these skills became developmentally compounded through early experience to provide a return on investment. The first years last forever, but in the growth of economically productive skillsets rather than emotional security alone, consistent with neoliberal values.

This view was extended with the Pew Charitable Trusts' national campaign for prekindergarten, which portrayed young children as ready and eager learners if given the right environment to do so. By enlisting and expanding concern that young children might lack the readiness to succeed in the primary grades, the campaign's solution was prekindergarten education (without specifying what this should look like) supported by advocacy groups representing business leaders, law enforcement, and even K-12 educators. Whereas the *I Am Your Child* campaign looked to parental nurturance as the avenue for supporting the developing brain, the campaign for prekindergarten looked to well-prepared early childhood educators to do so. In the midst of all this, nobody asked about the large majority of children in child care.

The evolution of the public messaging of developmental brain science in the years following 1997 reflects how science communication changes as messages are adapted to different audiences, and as communicators have different goals and values in their messaging. It means that "follow the science" must adapt to a changing message as the science advances, advocacy expands, and its framing evolves.

In Chapter 4, I discussed the story of the *I Am Your Child* campaign and its aftermath to describe some of the challenges in the public communication of science, especially in the context of campaign journalism. The selectivity that is inevitably incorporated into public messaging, the recognition that what communicates well is not necessarily most important or accurate, and the influence of cultural values on what is heard together illustrate how difficult it is to convey complex scientific conclusions clearly and accurately.

This chapter continued that inquiry with the scope widened to include advocacy efforts of various kinds in the years following the brain development campaign. But similar themes apply. As the story of brain development found applications to different areas of public policy, the science continued to be difficult to communicate well as new voices entered the scene and because of the incentives of overpromising results. An evolving message attracted new audiences and issues to a brain development message that was sometimes misunderstood in its implications for changing children's lives. And in the end, the wins of the brain development revolution were substantive, even though far less than child advocates had hoped.

How the story of brain development has been oriented and framed has been a continuing theme throughout Chapter 4 and this chapter.

In Chapter 6, which follows, I examine the framing of the brain development message in greater detail. When messaging is for public understanding and policy advocacy, how do frames and metaphors advance these
goals while maintaining the accuracy of the science? By what criteria can
one judge the effectiveness of framing? And because frameworks are
necessarily selective in how the science is presented and heard, the familiar
question of selectivity presents itself: Who chooses what should be heard,
and why?

CHAPTER 6

Framing Developmental Science

In his book, *Outliers,* Malcolm Gladwell describes how the modern public education system took shape in America in the early nineteenth century.[1] At the time, rural schools closed in the spring and fall so that children could help during planting and harvesting seasons, and classes resumed in the summer and winter. Urban schools had a completely different calendar based on the schedules of working-class families. Schools in other parts of the country had their own calendars. To establish uniformity and ensure that children learned what they needed, the reformers of that era were guided by a way of thinking about the cultivation of the mind. The mind, in their view, requires work alternating with periods of rest and recovery, just as fields need to lie dormant after harvest to renew the soil. Too much studying could be harmful in a similar manner to how fields could be exhausted by overplanting. Thus the modern school calendar of shortened school days and a long summer vacation was established.

Gladwell contrasts this with what we find in Asian countries such as Japan and South Korea. In these countries, the school year is significantly longer – 243 days annually for Japanese children, compared with 180 for Americans – with longer school days. This calendar also relates to beliefs about the cultivation of the mind, but rice cultivation in Asian countries is a year-round activity. A rice farmer plants two or three crops annually because the nutrients carried by the irrigation water rejuvenate the fields – the more the land is cultivated, the more fertile it becomes. Thinking of children's minds as cultivations has created in both regions a metaphorical frame of understanding that led in very different directions: an emphasis on the requirements of rest and renewal in one, and a view that work leads to its own renewal in the other.

We will consider this account again, but for now it illustrates the influence of metaphors[2] and frames on how people think and communicate. We know that the mind is not a field, but it can be helpful to think about its cultivation and development in similar ways. We know that time is not really a flowing river, but thinking of it in this way carries meaning about the passage of time that is different from thinking of time as money – or, for that matter, that we are on borrowed time. In politics, people speak appreciatively of a grassroots campaign that emerges from constituents (even though it has nothing to do with lawns), and malign as "astroturf-ing" campaigns that falsely seek to create the same impression. Often the power of metaphors is in the evaluations and emotions they imply. Anticipating a rough road ahead is certainly much worse than expecting smooth sailing (even if we're not traveling anywhere), just as getting the cold shoulder is less desirable than being warmed by a friend's message. Metaphors can have layers of connotation that help to explain their deeper implicit meaning. To "fall" in love suggests being propelled unexpectedly and without self-control toward an unknown and perhaps unfortunate destination – which is, in fact, what some people experience (but fortu-nately not everybody).

Metaphors and frames have received special attention in recent years because of their influence on public communication and persuasion.[3] A classic example is the metaphor of the greenhouse effect that was used to mobilize public concern in the 1980s about the accumulation of carbon dioxide and other gases that trap heat in the atmosphere, because the effects of greenhouses on atmospheric warming could be easily understood. The "war" on drugs was popularized in the 1970s to characterize the government's aggressive approach to eradicating drug sources, incarcerat-ing drug dealers, and prosecuting drug users. The Obama administration explicitly abandoned this metaphor after 2009 because it favored preven-tive and therapeutic approaches to drug abuse over martial solutions.[4] Other frames used in political communications are "partial-birth" abortion enlisted by right-to-life organizations, the "death tax" used by opponents of estate taxes, and "carbon footprint" to encourage individuals to account for their own greenhouse gas emissions.

Frames are cognitive models by which people interpret the world and understand new information. Metaphors (and analogies and similes) are figures of speech in which one thing becomes understood as similar to or contrasting with something else, and they are an important part of how frames are evoked. Cognitive frames exist as one of many sophisticated mental shortcuts by which people efficiently respond to experience by relying on cues to connect new experience with existing knowledge. The study of frames and related mental shortcuts builds on decades of research in cognitive psychology, but it has also been taken up by scholars in communications, anthropology, political science, and linguistics because of how framing connects with cultural belief systems and the linguistic structuring of knowledge. Not surprisingly, this work also has applications to public communication enlisted for political persuasion and other pursuits.

Frames and the metaphors enlisted into frames are relevant to the themes of this book. The preceding chapters highlighted several examples of the framing of the story of brain development in public communication and advocacy. Describing brain development as the "wiring" of neural "circuits" to establish "connections" that become "activated" by experience evokes a mechanistic frame for understanding the developing brain that is consistent with neuroessentialism, as described in Chapter 2.[5] The economic assumptions of investment and capital appreciation ("skill begets skill") profiled in Chapter 5 are also framing elements of the brain development story, especially as it is applied to early education. Another framing element is early determinism – "the early years last forever" – built on American beliefs about young children leading to the expectation that influences on the developing brain will have enduring consequences, as described in Chapter 4. In each case, these framing elements become integrated into the public's growing knowledge of the science of early brain development in ways that fundamentally shape understanding and application of the science. It is easy to imagine that people could think about early brain development independently of these frames, but it is difficult to find examples of public communication that do not enlist them.

Frames and metaphors are important for understanding how existing frames can lead public understanding in specific directions. George Lakoff and Joseph Grady, for example, argue that because parents of young children are often most concerned with the safety and protection of their children while they are at work, the term "child care" lends itself to a portrayal as a protective container for the child while parents are away (as in "dropping off my kid at child care").[6] What follows from this "child storage" frame is a view of child care providers as package handlers, not highly skilled educators, whose major responsibilities are the safety of the environment, not its nurturant or cognitively stimulating qualities. They are "workers," not "teachers," who provide care, not education. Lakoff and Grady urge that the term "early education" should be substituted for "child care" or "day care" as part of reframing the child in these settings as more like a plant, not a package, that requires daily stimulation and nurturance in the company of adults who are skilled at providing education in a developmentally appropriate manner. This reframing is consistent, of course, with the strategic decision of the Pew Charitable Trusts to connect prekindergarten with education in the public mind and to distinguish it from child care, as described in Chapter 5.

The FrameWorks Institute, a Washington, DC, nonprofit, has significantly advanced understanding of the metaphors and frames that guide public thinking about children and has applied this knowledge to the development of sophisticated strategies for moving public response on a range of public policy concerns. The National Scientific Council on the Developing Child has allied the strategic frame analysis of FrameWorks with cutting-edge developmental science to create a comparably sophisticated communications strategy for enhancing public understanding of early brain development and its policy applications. Both groups were briefly profiled in Chapter 1, and I discuss their work in greater depth in this chapter.

FrameWorks Institute

The FrameWorks Institute[7] was founded in 1999 by Susan Nall Bales with a grant from the William T. Grant Foundation. Bales created FrameWorks after more than twenty years of working on women's and children's issues, most recently for six years as the director of strategic communications and children's issues at the Benton Foundation. The effort to improve the effectiveness of the communications strategies of progressive advocates led Bales, along with Franklin D. Gilliam, Jr., of UCLA, to develop *strategic frame analysis* and to implement it at FrameWorks.

The ideas of strategic frame analysis go back to the work of Gregory Bateson[8] and Erving Goffman[9] in the 1970s, both of whom wrote about the network of preconceptions by which people process information and interpret events. Influenced also by the thinking of communications theorist Shanto Iyengar[10] on how the frames provided by the media shape public debate about issues, Bales and Gilliam recognized that how information is communicated evokes interpretive frames in the minds of an audience that significantly influence their understanding and how they respond to the information. Frames are easily evoked by the language, examples, and metaphors that are used in narrative, and they tend to be strengthened whenever they are elicited. They constitute interpretive filters on the reception of information: ideas that are consistent with an individual's preexisting frame tend to be readily understood and accepted, while ideas that are inconsistent with a preexisting frame tend to be ignored or reinterpreted in a frame-consistent manner. American cultural frames about the risk-taking and impulsivity of adolescents create a lens, for example, by which the public internalizes news reports about teenage pathology and brain immaturity. In Chapter 2, I discussed American cultural beliefs concerning children and their development that likewise frame thinking about children.

From the perspective of frame analysis, it is not easy to change minds through direct persuasion, especially if the persuasive message contradicts preexisting views. Instead, persuasion must occur indirectly by introducing new frames and reframing existing understanding where possible while avoiding evoking frames that are inconsistent with the messaging. Conveying new information or a new argument is thus secondary to how FrameWorks engages in changing minds. Rather, it works within the public's existing knowledge to change the orientation they adopt to what they know or learn about a topic. The work of FrameWorks has shown how effective this approach can be to public messaging, in ways that are described below, because it encourages people to adopt new ways of thinking that are memorable, or "sticky"[11] in mind.

Cultural frames are widely shared, but groups and individuals also vary in the interpretive frames they apply to new information. Consequently, a skilled communicator must first understand how an intended audience is likely to respond to the information – or, more specifically, the interpretive frames the audience is likely to enlist to make sense of that information. Are those frames helpful to the audience internalizing the speaker's message, and, if not, is it possible through communication to alter which frames are elicited by altering how the information is presented or its content? Can the communication incorporate new framing elements in a manner that leads an audience toward the conclusions and applications that the speaker intends? This is the underlying approach behind strategic frame analysis. In developing this approach to public communication, Bales and Gilliam enlisted the work of George Lakoff, whose ideas about how progressives and conservatives frame public issues differently were already well known, as well as ideas from psychological anthropology, cognitive linguistics, and social psychology.[12]

Strategic frame analysis is formally based on an iterative, multimethod process involving several steps:[13]

- *Assessing communication goals* through interviews with key informants and sponsoring agencies to identify the central concepts and their implications (which FrameWorks calls the "untranslated core story") that a communications strategy should advance about a focus issue.

A review of relevant research literatures may also be part of this step. The core story involves not just the knowledge to be imparted but also the individual and collective action that should result – what people should know, and what they should do.

- *Cognitive interviewing*, or conducting "cultural models interviews," to identify the prior understandings and frames that the target audience uses in thinking about the issue. This is based on detailed one-on-one recorded conversations about the issue with twenty to fifty representative audience members with the goal of analyzing the reasoning underlying their judgments and the frameworks of understanding, or implicit ideas, that enter into their thinking. These are extracted in a qualitative analysis of the transcribed interview responses.

- *Media content analysis* is used to identify how visible or prominent is the issue in media coverage, and also how news media frame the issue, through a qualitative analysis of targeted media content.

- At this point in strategic frame analysis, researchers can begin to identify conceptual gaps between the expert informants' core story and how the media and target audience represent central issues. Furthermore, by identifying the framing elements associated with how the target audience thinks, it becomes possible to identify public frames that might be obstacles to accepting the core story and its implications. On this basis, a new draft messaging strategy can be designed to avoid unhelpful framing of the issue and engage reframing that can lead to new understanding.

- *Reframe development* identifies potential alternative frames and their elements (such as new explanatory metaphors, different examples, a new narrative "plot" or story line, a values orientation, or the use of alternative messengers) that might be more successful in shifting audience views in a different direction.

- *On-the-street interviews* are, as the name implies, brief interviews with representative members of the public in which candidate reframes are tested to explore their impact on how people reason about the issue and the implications they derive from it. The reframe can be presented orally, for example, in the context of a paragraph-length profile of a hypothetical news item that incorporates the new framing, followed by a series of questions to elicit the person's response and determine if the reframing was influential.

- *Survey experiments*, often administered in an online platform, are used to determine how candidate reframes affect the knowledge, attitudes, and policy preferences of a larger segment of the audience. These can take an experimental group design in which randomly selected groups of respondents are presented with an issue that is framed in different ways (along with a control group with no prior framing), followed by questions to evaluate the impact of the framing on how the respondent thinks about the issue and evaluates prospective public policy solutions.

- *Peer discourse sessions* are held in which the reframed issue is presented to small groups that are then asked to discuss the issue and its implications. Particular attention is devoted to whether the discussion enlists the new frame and moves in directions congenial to the communication goals.
- *Usability trials* are conducted in which participants who have heard the new message are asked to communicate the issue to a new, uninitiated respondent in order to see how much of the framing is enlisted and communicated to the new person.

A specific communications strategy may enlist some but not all of these steps, and the steps may not necessarily occur in this order. The method is iterative because the process can be backtracked if researchers discover that a potential reframing is unsuccessful in orienting audience members in the desired direction or produces added conceptual baggage that is problematic. The methods described here, consistent with FrameWorks's interdisciplinary origins, combine statistical analyses of large-sample survey data with qualitative conclusions drawn from interviews and small group sessions. This mixed-method approach seeks to document that reframing "works" through patterns of survey responses or inferences from interviews, typically illustrated by quotes from individual respondents in evaluation reports. The combination of quantitative and qualitative methods can be a strength for enabling a deep dive into respondents' thinking as well as testing alternative approaches with a large sample, although it is sometimes difficult to evaluate the specific data sources on which conclusions guiding framing choices are made.

The FrameWorks Institute website has an extensive library of reports, articles, and "toolkits" that provide examples of how these methods have been used and document FrameWorks's enlistment of strategic frame analysis to strengthen public communication on many specific issues.[14] The following is an example of this approach.[15]

Framing Child Mental Health

In an era of increased awareness of the impact of child stress and adverse childhood experiences, how should communication about child mental health be designed to improve public understanding? Can such efforts also motivate support for policies and programs that assist children? These questions are important because the public appears to have somewhat confused views about child mental health. Based on detailed, open-ended interviews with twenty people in Dallas and Cleveland, FrameWorks researchers concluded that people have difficulty understanding what mental health means for a child (because they believe that children's minds work differently from adults) or believe that child mental health is just a simpler version of adult mental health (because they think children have less to worry about). When people tried defining it, child mental health was considered to be emotional health (being happy), a product of parenting quality, or an equilibrium of brain chemicals. FrameWorks researchers analyzed a year of newspaper coverage of child mental health and found that the stories tended to focus on the difficulties for parents of managing a child's mental illness and the unpredictability of its changing severity.

Expert views of child mental health are more complex, of course, as revealed in interviews with seven child development experts. Experts emphasized the interaction between genes and environments (within and outside the home), the importance of the brain and the effects of chronic and severe stressors on brain functioning, the inseparability of child mental health and physical health, the potential of early mental health problems to have lifelong consequences, and thus the need for early intervention to improve child and family functioning. Interestingly, while experts tended to blur the line between mental health and mental illness, the public regarded them as separate and fairly distinct.[16]

It is easy to see how the public's limited conception of child mental health would blunt efforts to generate support for programs and policies to strengthen children's well-being. It is not just that the public has a less detailed and sophisticated model of child mental health compared with that of experts (that would be expected), but the uncertainty over whether child mental health exists and how to conceptualize it makes it difficult to consider potential prevention and treatment alternatives. Consideration is further impaired by the public's narrow understanding of the range of potential causes of mental illness in children (e.g., bad parenting, a chemical imbalance in the brain) compared with experts' view (genes, home environment, experiences outside the home, stress effects on brain functioning), and this may be exacerbated by media portrayals of child mental health crises as unpredictable and uncontrollable. If child mental illness is unpredictable, how can prevention and treatment be effective?

To reframe child mental health in a manner that would contribute to greater understanding and greater support for targeted policies, FrameWorks tested several message components. One component was to frame the issue along broad value principles. An online experimental survey of more than 4,000 respondents identified two values that, as frames, elicited the strongest support for child mental health policy.[17] They were *collective prosperity* (we all will prosper by promoting child mental health) and *ingenuity* (we can tackle difficult problems like child mental health with innovative solutions). The prosperity frame reads thus:

> Lately there has been a lot of talk about the role of society in supporting children. In particular, people have offered various explanations of why it is important to devote societal resources to children at the very earliest stages of life. For example, some people believe that early childhood development is important for community development and economic development. According to this view, skills and capacities that begin developing in early childhood become the basis of a prosperous and sustainable society – from positive school achievement to workforce skills to cooperative and lawful behavior. Have you heard of this explanation of why we should allocate societal assets to young children, because they predict our society's prosperity?[18]

Readers probably recognize that the collective prosperity frame is very similar to the economists' frame of investment and capital appreciation that was described in Chapter 5.

After reading this framing prompt, respondents were more supportive of statements promoting mental health policy compared with those reading alternative prompts embedded in the same general narrative. They endorsed the views, for example, that mental health services should be available and affordable to all, that professional training in child mental health should be prioritized, that early care and education professionals should receive required training in mental health screening and early detection, that victims of child abuse should be prioritized in mental health funding allocations to end the cycle of abuse, and similar statements. An important purpose of each value frame was to characterize child mental health as a societal responsibility rather than solely the responsibility of the child or the parents, and in this manner to broaden thinking about the policies by which society's interest in promoting child mental health might be advanced. The prosperity and ingenuity value frames did so in different ways, of course, with the former underscoring a transactional relation between child and societal benefits and the latter emphasizing the creative problem-solving by which a society can address an important need.

The FrameWorks researchers also investigated whether explanatory metaphors could contribute to increasing support for child mental health initiatives. As earlier described, metaphors (such as the carbon footprint) can be effective mental shortcuts to advance the frame and contribute to achieving the communication goal. Whereas a value frame is at a high level of abstraction, explanatory metaphors are typically more concrete and provide multiple levels of meaning and inference about the core concept. On the basis of on-the-street interviews with forty-nine respondents at three locations in Arizona, and subsequently from the results of an online survey of approximately 2,000 respondents, an explanatory metaphor called "levelness" was identified as most effective in communicating concepts about child mental health that were consistent with experts' views and that increased support for programs and policies supporting child mental health.[19] The levelness prompt reads:

> Scientists say that children's mental health affects how they socialize, how they learn, and how well they meet their potential. One way to think about child mental health is that it's like the levelness of a piece of furniture, say, a table. The levelness of a table is what makes it usable and able to function, just like the mental health of a child is what enables him or her to function and do many things. Some children's brains develop on floors that are level. This is like saying that the children have healthy supportive relationships, access to things like good nutrition and health care. For other children, their brains develop on more sloped or slanted floors. This means they're exposed to abuse or violence, have unreliable or unsupportive relationships, and don't have access to key programs and resources. Remember that tables can't make themselves level – they need attention from experts who understand levelness and stability and who can work on the table, the floor, or even both. We know that it's important to work on the floors and the tables early, because little wobbles early on tend to become big wobbles later. So, in general, a child's mental health is like the stability and levelness of a table.[20]

This metaphor proved useful in several ways. It implicitly portrayed mental health as something that all children have in greater or lesser amounts, and which directly affects their functioning. With respect to causation, the metaphor indicated that there can be multiple reasons for variability in mental health, and that preventive or remedial avenues exist to support child mental health. The metaphor also explicitly indicated that "tables can't make themselves level" to underscore the need for experts and practices to help children achieve well-being.

The framing elements of prosperity and ingenuity values combined with the levelness metaphor provided a scaffold for the development of a messaging narrative building on these ideas to communicate about child mental health. In the construction of the messaging, these framing elements were supplemented by background information (e.g., the prevalence of mental health problems in children) and context (e.g., examples of mental health disorders that are found in children), a problem statement, illustrative stories, considerations of tone and visual contributions to the framing (e.g., photographs, graphics, illustrations), the selection of a compelling messenger(s), and identification of policy avenues for addressing the problem. Consistent with communications science, the goal underlying the construction of messaging narratives such as this is to provide a consistent frame, avoid evoking alternative frames that would be unconstructive (e.g., parents are to blame; it's all in the genes), and lead audiences to the policy options that are part of the communication goal.

A Frame of Mind for This Work

The FrameWorks approach to public communications through strategic frame analysis is an evidence-based, systematic orientation to mobilizing public support behind progressive issues. The integration of concepts and methods from several academic fields concerned with the psychology and culture of communications provides FrameWorks with excellent tools for unpacking latent and manifest themes in public messaging and reconstructing more effective messaging by enlisting alternative frameworks of understanding. Moreover, its rigorously empirical approach helps to ensure fidelity between its rich theoretical foundations and the on-the-ground views of the public audience. Since its founding in 1999, FrameWorks has grown significantly, and in 2021 a FrameWorks UK branch was opened. In 2015 FrameWorks received a MacArthur Award for Creative and Effective Institutions.

From the perspective of understanding the messaging of early brain development, strategic frame analysis offers a theoretical structure and empirical orientation to the elements of effective messaging about the developing brain. I will explore its specific applications to the communication of developmental brain science in the next section. Before turning to the messaging of brain development, however, we should pause to consider how strategic frame analysis is conducted and what more we might want to know about its effects. As innovative methods do, this approach invites some questions about the application of strategic frame analysis by FrameWorks and its potential uses in other applications.

First, how should the audience(s) for messaging about early brain development be identified? In its qualitative research, FrameWorks typically seeks "engaged citizens" for its in-person evaluations whom it identifies as people registered to vote, who are attentive to the news, volunteer in their communities, and vary by gender, education, and other characteristics relevant to the topic. These respondents are not intended to be representative of the general population because these criteria exclude important subgroups, but are nevertheless expected to be somewhat diverse. FrameWorks's analyses of their responses are not usually broken down according to gender, education, political affiliation, and other characteristics because samples are usually too small for this to be useful. When researchers do this in large sample survey research, however, they report that responses to some framings differ by gender, political orientation, the extent of the respondent's "news attentiveness," and other characteristics. Those with "more strident" political viewpoints, for example, were more likely to endorse child mental health policies compared with those who were politically more moderate.[21]

As we might expect, different intended audiences for targeted messaging can differ in ways relevant to how a compellingly framed message should be created for them. Research by FrameWorks has shown that business leaders, for example, are biased in relation to children in ways that present messaging challenges. Their default model of development is maturational rather than complexly causal; they downplay environments in favor of a developmental explanation of self-causation (i.e., the self-made person); they have difficulty conceptualizing younger children and tended to reorient toward youth issues; their approach is results oriented ("skill begets skill"); and a model of sequence, structure, and recursive feedback in skill development is very attractive to them. A different framing might thus be necessary for business audiences compared with other audiences.[22] Likewise, legislators (especially at the state and local levels) are especially sensitive to the cost implications of alternative policy directions, favor targeted over universal approaches, and perceive children's issues in the context of the competing needs of other advocacies and constituents and less exclusively in terms of compelling children's needs. Different framing strategies or narratives might also be required for them.

In an increasingly polarized society, furthermore, it may not be wise to assume that responses from "engaged citizens" are necessarily representative of the frames of reference of members of the groups targeted for public communication. This is especially likely if targeted audiences are conservative rather than progressive and extremist rather than moderate in their political and cultural views. Although designing different communications strategies for different subgroups within the public is likely to be more difficult and (perhaps prohibitively) costly, it is unwise to fail to consider this diversity of perspective and orientation and to assume that one size of messaging fits all. At the least, the design of a communications strategy must have a well-defined target audience in mind, since communicating the need for child mental health policies to kindred progressives is a different task, for example, than communicating to committed conservatives. Yet it may be minds of the latter group that one most needs to change. FrameWorks's approach is to identify a framing approach that works with its test samples, and then adapt it as necessary to different targeted groups.

Second, and relatedly, what are the media that influence public attitudes? There was a time in the past when media influences could be summarized by an appraisal of coverage in the major newspaper dailies and the major television networks. No longer. The polarized news media today mirrors a polarized electorate, with progressives and conservatives favoring different news sources and rarely consulting the alternatives. At the same time, the news is increasingly derived from social media feeds that are complexly curated for individual users, and the same is true of tweets and posts that are managed according to sophisticated algorithms. The task of conducting a media content analysis is thus more complicated than it was a generation ago, especially if due consideration is devoted to capturing the different media sources used by different groups within the target audience. In 2021 when FrameWorks published the report "How Are Children's Issues Portrayed in the News? A Media Content Analysis,"[23] the news sources surveyed were all the conventional ones, such as the *New York Times, Wall Street Journal, Washington Post, Los Angeles Times*, and *Chicago Tribune*. The justification was that traditional news outlets tend to drive the narrative in other outlets, including social media, although no evidence for this was presented. The growing diversity of news sources, their alignment with distinct sociopolitical audiences, and the increasing influence of social media in an era when the business model of traditional news media is breaking down presents a growing challenge to efforts to characterize the influence of news media on how the public frames important issues, or the use of the media to advance alternative frames.

Third, what is the communication goal? This question is crucial because how the communication goal is defined drives the evaluation of messaging efficacy when respondents are asked how much they endorse statements reflecting elements of the goal. A frame, explanatory metaphor, or any other element of the messaging is determined to be more successful if it leads respondents to endorse the intended viewpoints. In the FrameWorks research, the communications goal is usually a combination of two things: a more accurate understanding of the science (defined as concordance with experts' views) and endorsement of the intended policy implications. Sometimes the policy endorsement is the sole communications goal, since FrameWorks was created to advance advocacy on progressive policy issues.[24] As Susan Bales wrote to me, "Policies, for FW, are dependent variables."[25]

The dual communication goals – science and policy – in most of FrameWorks's research are important. In many instances, perhaps most, science and policy lead in consistent messaging directions because the policy goal follows naturally from the scientific messaging (at least this is what child advocates believed in the wake of the *I Am Your Child* campaign, as described in Chapter 4). The view that mental health services should be available and affordable (without specifying who should pay) and the view that there should be increased professional training in child mental health each seems to be a natural derivative from understanding better the prevalence and seriousness of child mental health problems. On other policy matters, however, the science may not lead naturally in one direction. I suspect that most child mental health experts would hesitate to prioritize victims of child abuse in the allocation of mental health funds in light of the seriousness and prevalence of other kinds of child mental health problems. If a priority on child abuse victims is an important policy objective of the messaging campaign, it is possible that framing elements that lead respondents to this endorsement might compete with framing elements related to other policy objectives or communicating the science well.

In other instances, the scientific core story may be presented incompletely if elements of this story are incompatible with or irrelevant to the intended policy applications. Consider again the levelness metaphor. It is an excellent means of messaging expert knowledge of child mental health: that all children have it, that it affects how children are able to function, that many influences affect it, and so forth. It is also an excellent avenue for messaging certain policy implications: that it cannot be remedied by the child alone, but requires the assistance of others; that early interventions are important; that preventive as well as remedial interventions can be effective; and so forth. But the levelness metaphor does not communicate well certain other elements of the expert model, such as the interaction of internal qualities with environmental influences (genes and environment), and the inseparability of child mental health with physical health. The levelness metaphor also does not convey at all the emotional anguish that is central to mental illness: few things are as *un*emotional as a table.

To be sure, this observation is nothing more than acknowledging the limitations of *any* metaphor for communicating complex knowledge: metaphors are powerful but imperfect communication tools with unique strengths and weaknesses that require thinking carefully (as FrameWorks does) about the relative benefits and limitations of each. Metaphors are, in other words, selective in what they can communicate. In any messaging effort, in fact, several metaphors are incorporated such that each conveys a different side of the central issue, as we shall see in the next section. Conceptual and messaging dexterity is required to ensure that different metaphors and other framing elements lead consistently to the same story, and that the story is a good representation of the scientific core story and the policy goals. This is the challenge of the selectivity in the public communication of a scientific issue that has been discussed in previous chapters, and will be taken up again in the next.

Fourth, how enduring are the effects of well-designed messaging on the beliefs and attitudes of respondents? Best practices in psychological studies of intervention effects require follow-up studies to determine whether intervention outcomes were immediate but episodic or more sustained and perhaps enduring. The evidence for intervention efficacy is far stronger, of course, when it can be demonstrated that its effects are long-lasting. This is why, for example, the evidence from the Perry Preschool Project, described in Chapter 5, and some other well-known longitudinal studies of early education programs have been so influential. The same might be said of the effects of public communication: there is greater confidence in messaging when it can be demonstrated that its effects endure. Indeed, if the purpose of strategic frame analysis is to change how people think about an issue, evidence of enduring effects is proof of concept.

To my knowledge, there has been no follow-up research by FrameWorks of the long-term effects of its messaging on audience attitudes. As anyone who pursues longitudinal research is aware, doing so is labor- as well as time-intensive and significantly increases research costs, which are significant disincentives. But long-term studies of messaging influences can answer important questions about the effects of strategic frame analysis. And, of course, unless there is a long-term impact of a messaging strategy, there can be little expectation that it will create the changes in behavior concerning children that is the central purpose of the messaging.

These questions highlight the complexity of developing thoughtful messaging for public communication, even within the context of the innovative approach of strategic frame analysis. They also underscore how costly is the generation of a well-designed communications campaign if it takes these challenges seriously. FrameWorks's research is typically sponsored by agencies on limited budgets seeking assistance in creating more effective public messaging for advocacy purposes. If FrameWorks were required to consider the characteristics of different target audiences, the different media (and social media) influences on them, and the enduring impact of messaging, and to differentiate the science and policy elements of the communication goal, the effort would quickly become cost prohibitive. But these considerations are important to placing the work of strategic frame analysis within a broader context so that its strengths and weaknesses can be more thoughtfully appraised.

What are the implications of strategic frame analysis for the messaging of developmental brain science? For perspective on this question, I turn now to the work of the National Scientific Council on the Developing Child and its partnership with the FrameWorks Institute.

National Scientific Council on the Developing Child

The National Scientific Council on the Developing Child was created in 2003 and subsequently became part of the Center on the Developing Child at Harvard University in 2006.[26] Despite the official-sounding name, it is not a government agency but rather comprised of a dozen self-appointed research scientists who are prominent in their fields and with interests relevant to children's development, especially the developing brain. The work of the Council focuses on development in the early years rather than the full scope of childhood, although many of the materials produced by the Council are relevant to children of many ages.[27] Its mission, according to the Council's website, is "closing the gap between what we know and what we do to promote successful learning, adaptive behavior, and sound physical and mental health for all young children [and] . . . to build public will that transcends political partisanship and recognizes the complementary responsibilities of family, community, workplace, and government to promote child well-being."[28] The Council's goal is to be a credible, nonpartisan knowledge broker with impact.

The Council combined members of two groups that had been active in the years following 1997.[29] One was the MacArthur Research Network on

Early Experience and Brain Development, a group of a dozen scientists funded by the MacArthur Foundation in 1998 to study how the developing brain is altered by experience throughout the lifespan. Another was the Committee on Integrating the Science of Early Childhood Development, appointed in 1998, which wrote the *From Neurons to Neighborhoods* report that was profiled in Chapter 4. Jack Shonkoff, a pediatrician who was dean of the Heller School for Social Policy and Management at Brandeis University, was a member of each group. As the work of each group began to wind down, he perceived the opportunity to integrate them to further a shared goal of communicating the findings of developmental brain science to external audiences in a clear and compelling manner, with particular attention initially to influencing policymakers. Members of each group were also interested in correcting some of the misconceptions about the science that had emerged from the 1997 campaign. At an inaugural gathering in Alexandria, Virginia, in 2001, individuals selected from each group were invited to brainstorm about the best way of going forward. The Council was formed from this group two years later after receiving funding from the MacArthur Foundation.

Also participating in the 2001 meeting was Susan Bales of the FrameWorks Institute, beginning a longstanding association with the Council that fully integrated strategic frame analysis into its work.[30] Based on that meeting, Bales worked with her colleagues to develop a profile of public beliefs about young children's development. Based on cognitive interviews with fifty "civically active" adults and business leaders, twelve focus groups, and other sources, Bales and her colleagues concluded that the predominant public orientation to early childhood development was impoverished: people did not have a working model of child development.[31] To many, development is natural and automatic, a product of genes, luck, and good or bad parenting, but little else outside the "family bubble." Beyond describing children as sponges, blank slates, clay to be molded, or little adults there was meager understanding of what goes on within the "black box" of children's development. Most people also had limited understanding of how brain development fits into this picture.

As with child mental health, furthermore, the public's impoverished understanding of child development undermined its appreciation of the potential role of public policy in supporting healthy early growth.[32] Respondents strongly endorsed parental autonomy, for example, and resisted arguments for government influence or intervention into the family except in extreme circumstances. Viewing young children's development in terms of the family bubble of parenting and family, there was little conceptual space for understanding the influence of other relation-ships – with child care providers, educators, neighbors, even peers – and the role of school quality, community support, housing, health care, and parents' employment on the growth of young children. There was also little room for considering the impact of broader societal forces, such as poverty and discrimination. Viewing young children's growth as a narrow, closed system of genes, parenting, and luck also undermined the ability to consider how social conditions affect different elements of children's growth – social, emotional, cognitive, motivational – within the black box of early development. Taken together, these prevalent public frames isolated children within the domain of parental responsibility and made it difficult to justify any government responsibility. Simply stated, the public believed it doesn't take a village. Consequently, Bales and her colleagues showed the Council that there was a need to communicate developmental science more clearly and convincingly, and also to connect scientific themes with policies concerning children that were currently difficult for the public to perceive as important or necessary.

In light of this, the Council embarked on several steps. One was to engage in individual and group sessions of communications training directed by the FrameWorks staff. This was not an easy task. Some Council members, especially those who were on the committee that produced the *From Neurons to Neighborhoods* report, were already giving formal presentations about the report to state commissions, professional groups, philanthropic organizations, nonprofits, and other audiences. As academics, we were accustomed to straightforwardly presenting relevant information to interested (or mildly interested student) audiences with little regard for the interpretive frames of reference that audience members were bringing to what they heard. The claims of science are themselves sufficiently compelling to warrant attention and interest, right? There was little in the academic orientation of Council members to encourage them to refashion a presentation in light of those audience frames, to devise reframes that avoid the conceptual pitfalls of preexisting ways of thinking, and to use metaphors to convey scientific knowledge in a manner that was influential and memorable. The Committee had to learn to see the central goal of a public presentation as creating a framework of public under-standing rather than just conveying a body of new information.[33] Consequently, several training sessions were required, during which FrameWorks staff coached Council members on what was working and what was not working in their efforts to explain the science of early brain development to the public.

The Council also began producing several publications that incorporated this approach to public communication and sought to correct some of the misconceptions about early childhood development, especially brain development, that Bales and her group had identified. A series of "working papers"[34] was initiated in 2004, with three products in the first two years. The first, *Young Children Develop in an Environment of Relationships,*[35] addressed the diversity of relationships within and outside the home on which young children depend, and introduced the "brain architecture" metaphor (and later, in a 2009 revision, the "serve and return" metaphor) to illustrate the construction of brains over time and the importance of close relationships. The second working paper (also published in 2004), *Children's Emotional Development is Built into the Architecture of Their Brains,*[36] described early emotional development as comparably important to the better-recognized achievements of early cognitive and social growth. This paper also used the "brain architecture" metaphor to illustrate how emotional processes enlist and influence developing neurobiology. The third, published initially in 2005, *Excessive Stress Disrupts the Architecture of the Developing Brain,*[37] established early stressful experiences as significant challenges to healthy brain and behavioral development. This paper introduced the "toxic stress" metaphor to illustrate the adverse effects of stress and the buffering effects of supportive relationships for coping. Subsequent working papers on topics ranging from environmental toxins to early mental health to maternal depression to developing self-regulation appeared annually until 2012. Only three more papers have been published in the decade since then.

These initial working papers established the format and style that would characterize the series. Their focus was predominantly on early childhood, although some topics extended to later ages, and most devoted significant attention to biological processes in the brain or genome, often following the research interests of specific Council members. The working papers had a fairly standard format. A statement of "The Issue" profiled the topic of the paper, followed by a longer section, "What Science Tells Us" with major conclusions highlighted in boldfaced statements and subheadings. The next section, "Popular Misrepresentations of Science," explicitly called out errors in public understanding and explained what the science showed instead. The first two working papers were specifically chosen to address problems in public understanding, such as an impoverished appreciation of the importance of relationships outside the family bubble, and the need to expand the black box of development to encompass the influences of emotions and stress.

Each working paper concluded with two sections describing the connections between science and public policy: "The Science-Policy Gap" and "Implications for Policy and Programs." For the first working paper on relationships, for example, these concerned the influence of teacher-child relationships in early education programs, the need to extend the length and coverage of family and medical leave, and criticisms of mandated work requirements in welfare reform, especially for mothers with young children. For the working paper on stress, the policy implications included the need for paid parental leave following a baby's birth, high-quality child care, and greater access to early childhood mental health services. These policy applications were intended to derive directly from the scientific findings presented in the working paper, although most also mirrored the policy recommendations of *From Neurons to Neighborhoods*, which several Council members had helped to write. The policy recommendations also reflected the progressive policy views of most of the Council. The working paper on relationships, for example, had nothing to say about strengthening economic supports for parents to care for their children at home, such as through an expanded child tax credit, even though this would have been consistent with the themes of the report. The failure to include this more conservative policy option may have occurred because supporting parents to care for children at home would have evoked the family bubble frame that was inconsistent with the policy goals of the paper.[38]

Because of generous funding support, copies of the working papers have been available free of charge to interested readers, and all can be downloaded from the Center on the Developing Child website.[39] In light of the general goal of improving the public's and policymakers' understanding of early development, however, it is remarkable how technical these papers are. Each paper is heavily footnoted with scientific references, and the writing is at a fairly high level, implying the expectation of a well-educated audience (perhaps like the "civically active" adults FrameWorks interviewed) but not necessarily a general audience. The working papers have become, if anything, longer and more conceptually complex over time; for example, the statement of the issue for working paper 15 reads: "Health and Learning Are Interrelated in the Body but Separated in Policy." This academic tone is understandable because the writers of these reports were, after all, scientists at major research universities, and perhaps for this reason each paper carefully documented the research evidence supporting major conclusions about relationships, stress, and other topics at the time they were written.[40] The Council seems to have recognized the limited accessibility of the style and format of the working paper series, however, because there are now on the website a wide variety of more engaging and accessible materials based on the working papers: short videos, TED talk–style presentations by Council members and other researchers, InBrief capsules of take-home points, podcasts (some in the series called "The Brain Architects"), infographics, FAQs, and even materials from other organizations.

Creating the Core Story of Early Childhood Development

In addition to the working papers, the most important task of the Council in its early years was the development of what FrameWorks calls the "core story" of early childhood development. As earlier described, the core story represents a translation of expert understanding and thus constitutes a conceptual road map of communication goals, or the destination toward which the framing strategy should lead public understanding. If the public lacks a working model of child development, the core story is meant to communicate the working model of experts. The creation of a core story is thus crucial, but it can be challenging to create because of the difficulty of deciding the most important elements of expert knowledge meriting communication, as well as creating a coherent narrative for the public. This is especially so for a topic as broad as early childhood development.

The creation of the Council's core story took shape, in part, through the development of the working papers, and was formalized in 2007 in a series of eight propositions:[41]

- Child development is a foundation for community development and economic development, as capable children become the foundation of a prosperous and sustainable society.
- Brain architecture is constructed through an ongoing process that begins before birth and continues into adulthood. As it emerges, the quality of that architecture establishes either a sturdy or a fragile foundation for all the capabilities and behavior that follow.
- Skill begets skill as brains are built in a hierarchical fashion, from the bottom up. Increasingly complex circuits and skills build on simpler circuits and skills over time.
- The interaction of genes and experience shapes the circuitry of the developing brain. Young children serve up frequent invitations to engage with adults, who are either responsive or unresponsive to their needs. This "serve and return" process (what developmental researchers call contingent reciprocity) is fundamental to the wiring of the brain, especially in the early years.

- Cognitive, emotional, and social capacities are inextricably intertwined, and learning, behavior, and both physical and mental health are highly interrelated over the life course. You cannot address one domain without affecting the others (you can't have one without the other).
- Although manageable levels of stress are normative and promote growth, toxic stress in the early years (e.g., from severe poverty, severe parental mental health impairment such as maternal depression, child maltreatment, and/or family violence) can damage developing brain architecture and lead to problems in learning and behavior, as well as increased susceptibility to physical and mental illness.
- Brain plasticity and the ability to change behavior decrease over time. Consequently, getting it right early leads to better outcomes and is less costly, to society and to individuals, than trying to fix it later. We can pay now or we will pay more later for society's failure to promote healthy development in the earliest years of life.
- Effectiveness factors make the difference between early childhood intervention programs that work and those that do not work to support children's healthy development. These factors can be measured and can inform wise investments in effective policies and programs.

I have underlined the explanatory metaphors that help carry these messages, and they will be discussed later.

If the working papers are too complex for broad messaging, one strength of the eight propositions of the core story is that they are simply stated and are easily comprehended. They do not require extended elaboration for an audience to catch their meaning, and the use of memorable simplifying aphorisms and metaphors – such as "you can't have one without the other" and "we can pay now or we can pay more later" – support their intended understanding. These propositions are strongly focused on brain development, even though the supporting evidence (such as for "serve and return") is often drawn from broader research literatures in developmental science. Bales and her colleagues recognized (as did the creators of the *I Am Your Child* campaign years earlier) that the materialism of developmental brain science communicates well because it implies that physical changes (wiring and connections) in the brain result from early experiences through mechanistic causal processes. This contrasts with the more complex, multifaceted influences leading to mentalistic outcomes, such as feelings and thoughts, that also depend on context.[42] The materialism in this story is reflected in terms like brain architecture, wiring, circuitry, and sturdy or fragile foundation, each implying that predictable physical changes in the brain are determined by early experiences, and those physical changes determine behavior and development. This orientation also strengthens other elements of the core story messaging. The concept of toxic stress comes across as more tangible and compelling, for example, when it is described as leading to biological effects (disrupting brain architecture) rather than mentalistic outcomes (such as distress).

These eight propositions also present the science in a manner that supports policy from the first ("Child development is a foundation for community development and economic development") to the last ("[Effectiveness] factors can be measured and can inform wise investments in effective policies and programs"). In between is language urging early intervention to avoid costly later remediation; a description of toxic stress using examples of severe poverty, parental mental health impairment, family violence, and child maltreatment; and a portrayal of the hierarchical construction of early learning represented as skill begets skill. The latter expression should be familiar. James Heckman and Art Rolnick began collaborating with the Council in 2004, and the influence of their ideas, discussed in Chapter 5, are apparent in the core story. To the extent that in strategic frame analysis the scientific messaging is shaped both by the science and by its policy applications, these propositions reflect the influence of each in equal measure.

As a summary of developmental science and developmental neuroscience, of course, it would be difficult for eight propositions to suffice. Certainly, there could have been no expectation of telling the whole story of early development in this manner. The core story was intended instead to convey the most important elements of the science for advancing public understanding and policy mobilization about the importance of early development. It was also expected to correct misunderstandings in the public's view of early development that had been revealed in the research of Bales and her associates. Understood in this light, is there anything important missing from the core story?

One missing element is that there is nothing in the core story about the environment of relationships and its importance to brain and behavioral development. There is nothing to support broadening public understanding of the importance of children's relationships outside the family with educators, child care providers, peers, and others. This is surprising because the Council's first working paper was devoted to the environment of relationships beyond the family bubble. There is also nothing about the effects of broader societal forces on early brain and behavioral development such as culture and community (this is now a familiar story to readers).

Another missing element in the core story is the importance of the brain's plasticity to its continuing development throughout life. In the core story, plasticity is boiled down to a statement that brain plasticity decreases over time. But the brain's capacity to adapt to new experiences throughout life is really the "ongoing process" described in the second proposition by which brain architecture is constructed throughout life. Plasticity helps explain *why* the brain continues to develop throughout life. It deserves more attention because plasticity is also crucial to developmental remediation. In other words, the brain's lifelong plasticity is what permits neurobiological recovery and healing.

Finally, very little in the core story describes the child's active participation in the process of development with the exception of the "serve and return" metaphor. Developmental science underscores how much children bring about many of their own developmental achievements, such as studies revealing infants as experimental investigators of how objects move and collide, and the "use it or lose it" principle of developmental neuroscience likewise affirms the active role of young children in their developing brains. The failure to acknowledge children as active participants in their development was a lost opportunity to significantly open the black box of development to help people better understand *how* development occurs. Instead, it renders the developing person a passive element of their own developmental story.

It is important to repeat: there is no way that everything important about early development could be captured in a core story consisting of eight propositions. And many of these statements admirably (and succinctly) capture other central conclusions. Its description of the interaction of genes and experience calls to mind the strong statement in *From Neurons to Neighborhoods* that viewing nature and nurture as independent is "scientifically obsolete." The Council's introduction of the concept of "toxic stress" is one of its most important contributions to public understanding and has contributed to the growing recognition of adverse childhood experiences (ACEs) as threats to physical and mental health.[43] The interaction of cognitive, emotional, and social development was an important contribution to debates about school readiness when the core story was written, and this proposition remains important today as educators find a place for social-emotional learning in education. And even though some elements of these propositions are underspecified,[44] incorporating greater detail into the core story was probably not feasible for such a succinct expression of developmental science. The missing elements I have identified are important shortcomings, especially in light of the purposes of the core story, but the core story nevertheless captures many essential features of early childhood development.

When my graduate students read the core story,[45] they find this representation of child development compelling and are fascinated by the potential value of framing scientific communications in this manner. It takes further reflection (and seminar discussion) for them to realize just how difficult it is to distill the central conclusions of a vast scientific literature on development into a few propositions, especially if these propositions are meant to define a conceptual road map for communicating with the public. It cannot be surprising, therefore, that the Council's core story includes statements that are better representations of the science than others and that some elements of the core story are becoming dated in light of the advancing science.

The Council has never revisited the core story in subsequent years to update it in light of advances in research on early childhood development or developmental neuroscience. It remains substantially the same account that was written in 2007. However, in 2022 Shonkoff posted a brief on the website of the Center on the Developing Child that outlines what such an updating of the core story might include.[46] It expands the Council's focus on brain development to the growth of immune, metabolic, and other biological systems; broadens the Council's attention to early learning and skill development to include physical and mental health; and enlarges the Council's concern with maternal depression and child maltreatment, with attention to systemic racism. It offers a potential preview, therefore, for the elements that might be part of a new core story that has not yet been written.

Thinking Metaphorically

The expert's core story is central to framing a message. Other framing elements consist of explanatory metaphors, value principles (such as prosperity and ingenuity), and other narrative devices for advancing the overall orientation of the frame. In some respects, metaphors are even more important than other elements because good metaphors convey information at various levels of meaning and become memorable for this reason. *Toxic stress* is a good metaphor for conveying the potentially damaging physical and mental effects of chronic stress, leading most people to equate toxic stress with stress severity. Although the concept of toxic stress, as described in the Council's third working paper, also incorporates the role of social support as a stress buffer (so it makes certain experiences less toxic), it would have been difficult to find a conceptual metaphor to encompass both stress severity and its buffering influences. Toxic stress remains, despite this limitation, an influential and informative metaphor.

Another influential explanatory metaphor is *serve and return.* As Shonkoff and Bales noted in 2011, the Council struggled with the best metaphor to represent the give-and-take quality of responsive interaction in early social development. When the FrameWorks staff proposed the concept of "mirroring" that had tested well in public trials, I objected that the scientific research indicated that more than mirroring occurs between infants and adults as each is *modifying* their behavior in response to what the partner is doing. Consequently, FrameWorks developed "serve and return," which is a much better representation of this interactive process, drawing on the image of the volleying between tennis, volleyball, or soccer players during a match.[47]

The most important explanatory metaphor in the core story is brain architecture. The metaphor appears many times in the core story, working papers, and other Council communications. Brain architecture conveys important elements of both the science and the policy agendas of the core story. Concerning the science, it portrays early experience as, quite literally, foundational to all later development, and it contributes to the mechanistic portrayal of the wiring and circuitry of the developing brain. The metaphor conveys how architectural integrity can be threatened by experiences such as toxic stress, and therefore immediate efforts are needed to restore the structure's integrity. The concept of brain architecture also conveys the hierarchical nature of development that leads from simpler skills and circuits (or structural beams and columns) to more complex ones in progressive fashion. Later structures rely on earlier ones.

Concerning policy, the brain architecture metaphor implies that establishing a strong early foundation is of outsized importance to brain development compared with building on that foundation in later years. Attention to young children is warranted by the opportunity, as the foundation is established, to incorporate capacities that will become important as development proceeds. As the Champlain Towers collapse[48] in Miami in 2021 evocatively showed, remedying problems early and getting the foundation well established is crucial because later efforts to correct these problems may be more difficult, more costly, and perhaps impossible – with potentially disastrous consequences.

But like all metaphors, there are limitations to brain architecture. There is no indication of the adaptability, flexibility, or plasticity to changing conditions in the brain's continuing development (after all, architecture does not have much adaptability after the foundation has been established), even though these are hallmarks of the developing brain. There is no role for children as participants in their own development. Buildings do not design themselves, even a little. And buildings are isolated structures. They do not interact with other buildings or derive strength from them. No environment of relationships here. Taken together, the brain architecture metaphor, even when it is viewed in the context of the core story, captures important elements of development in the first five years but misses other important elements, and has little to say about what follows after early childhood.

Brains are not physical constructions, of course. Nor are they computers. Brains are not even magpies.[49] Each metaphor is helpful, within limits, for understanding and messaging the brain and its development. But developing brains *are* organic, so perhaps it is no accident that throughout this book researchers have used living things as metaphors for the developing brain. In the opening paragraphs of this chapter, Malcolm Gladwell described how the cultivation of fields in the United States and Asia provided metaphors for the cultivation of the young mind. In their efforts to describe the developing brain to educators (Chapter 5), Blakemore and Frith[50] evocatively wrote about the developing brain as a garden tended by astute, experienced, sensitive gardeners who can "do wonders with what is already there." In one contemporary effort to boost academic achievement called *Brainology*, primary grade students are encouraged to think of their brains as muscles that become stronger as they are exercised, but which also need adequate sleep and nutrition to function well.[51] Even Angelo, the father who was interviewed in Chapter 1, described young children as like "baby trees."

In a charming book titled *The Gardener and the Carpenter*, Alison Gopnik examines alternative metaphors for children and parenting. When parents are like carpenters, she writes, they are shaping the child as a developing construction into a final product that fits the parent's initial plan, or blueprint, for how the child should turn out (perhaps this extends to architects also). But when parents are like gardeners, they create a protected and nurturant space for plants to flourish in their own directions, accepting that plants may not turn out as the gardener expected because of the complexity and messiness of the growth process. Neither metaphor precisely fits how parenting actually occurs,[52] but the point is describing what the developing child is like. To Gopnik, children and their developing brains are less like buildings to be constructed from the ground up based on an established foundation, and more like plants that grow in predictable but sometimes unexpected ways based on the how they respond to the resources provided along the way.

Each metaphor has strengths and weaknesses, and appreciating its strengths requires also recognizing its weaknesses. An explanatory metaphor of the brain as a plant or tree highlights certain features of brain development that are different from those illuminated by brain architecture. While cultivation (such as good soil, adequate water, and sunlight) is important at the beginning to enable the plant to take root and become established, growing things do not continue to develop if soil, water, or sunlight become insufficient. Not just early but continuing care is needed. In this manner, growing things adapt to experiences throughout life that can strengthen or weaken its health. This adaptability often results from the plant's own activity, as witnessed by anyone who has seen branches and leaves grow selectively in the direction of available sunlight. Sometimes growing conditions enable the development of new capacities that did not exist earlier (such as the appearance of blossoms and fruit to seed the next generation) or result in developmental losses (as when leaves turn brown to preserve the plant's limited resources). In extremity, the plant might be stressed by frostbite or heat, but it can recover if the adverse conditions are not toxic, especially if stress abates. As development proceeds, the plant begins to look differently from how it did in immaturity, always identifiable (as an oak, a cactus, an orchid) but also capable of more than was true at the beginning. And many plants thrive in community, with root structures that are densely intermingled or foliage that intersects to create biological networks.

Brain architecture and the organic brain are two metaphors for brain development, each with distinct portrayals of how development unfolds (FrameWorks explored even more than these in its research for the Council). In the earlier discussion of strategic frame analysis, I noted that the selection of a metaphor depends on the communication goals to be accomplished: metaphors are strong or weak only in relation to their purpose in messaging. In the discussion thus far, I have emphasized the different strengths and weaknesses of alternative metaphors for communicating developmental science. But what about the second goal, that is, the strengths and weaknesses of these metaphors for promoting support for early childhood investments and other policies? On this question, the advantages of the brain architecture metaphor used by the Council are unparalleled. With its emphasis on establishing a strong, secure early foundation uncompromised by stress and capable of strengthening the emergence of new circuits and skills, the crucial importance of supporting early childhood development is unmistakable. By highlighting the importance of remedying early deficiencies promptly so they do not create more costly, enduring problems, especially in a context of diminishing plasticity over time, the brain architecture metaphor underscores the significance of early foundations. It is difficult to see other metaphors, including organic metaphors of brain development, as conveying such a strong message of early determinism and early investment. This might help to explain its place in the Council's communications because its power in conveying the importance of early investments in children's development outweighed its weaknesses in communicating developmental science. Other aspects of the brain development story, those not as easily communicated by the brain architecture frame, would have to wait for another day.

Framing Developmental Science

Strategic frame analysis is an innovative, empirical approach to science communication that has promise for messaging science clearly and accurately and for conveying its practical and policy implications. As applied by the FrameWorks Institute, its adaptability to a range of messaging goals and targets is apparent, and even though evidence for long-lasting effects of its messaging is lacking, its immediate effects on how people think about important issues can be significant. As it has been implemented by the National Scientific Council on the Developing Child, it has provided scholars and child advocates with a toolkit of metaphors, values, core propositions, and other narrative elements that can contribute sophistication to the messaging of developmental science and its implications. The work of the Council has helped to further advance the messaging of developmental brain science and its understanding by the public. This is impressive work.

Most who would seek to enlist strategic frame analysis into their communications work are not capable of funding the kind of original research on which FrameWorks builds its tools. But they can benefit from the unusual generosity of FrameWorks, which has created an extensive online library filled with reports of the results of their research, detailed descriptions of the methods and strategies used in their work, and specific suggestions for those who wish to communicate on the topics they have studied. It is unusual and commendable to find a private research organization conducting proprietary research making so many of their materials available for others to use.

Those who wish to enlist strategic frame analysis into their work might also benefit, however, from consideration of some of the questions and cautions that have been raised in this chapter. To create the best messaging strategy, for example, it is important to clearly identify the target audience to understand the frames of understanding this audience is likely to bring to a message and the consistency of those frames with others held by other audiences. As FrameWorks research has shown, it makes a difference whether the audience consists of business leaders, legislators, men or women, conservatives or progressives. One messaging strategy does not necessarily fit all audiences because different audiences bring different frames to the messaging, and further research is required to know how to adapt a messaging frame developed for one audience for a different one. It is also important to be clear about the communication goal(s) to be achieved by the messaging strategy, and especially the consistency between goals related to scientific communication and goals related to its policy applications. Do policy and practice applications necessarily follow seamlessly from the science, or is further reflection required about what goals the messaging strategy should seek to prioritize? Finally, *how* should the messaging be communicated? In light of the diversity of media avenues that exist and the expectation that targeted audiences are likely to favor certain avenues over others, careful consideration of how to reach the audience is obviously important. It is easy to communicate with those who share your values and goals, but those who do not may be the more important targets of persuasive communication.

The implementation of strategic frame analysis in the communication of developmental brain science by FrameWorks and the National Scientific Council raises other questions and cautions. Because developmental science is complex, selectivity in the communication of science is necessary, which has been a through line for this book. But also thematic are questions about how decisions should be made of what to include and what not. This is an especially challenging determination when the messaging goals include both accurate science and a policy agenda. What happens when these goals lead in inconsistent directions? Although the alliance of FrameWorks and the National Scientific Council has been a fruitful collaboration, it is also apparent that both the messaging of developmental science and its policy applications have been oriented toward a progressive approach to children's issues, involving enhanced public funding of programs for children and their families. But the children's cause is not just a progressive concern, and this may cause certain potential audiences to be lost to the messaging. This is especially likely when audiences consider the policy proposals following from the science, which may not be consistent with their values or the only alternatives for following the science.

Likewise, when do metaphors create an oversimplified and potentially misleading portrayal of development? "Skill begets skill" is an intuitively sensible and memorable aphorism. The problem is that research shows that the young children who benefit the most from early education programs are those who are *farthest behind* (does this mean "less skill begets more skill"?),[53] which means that this aphorism could be an obstacle to advocating targeted interventions for children who would benefit the most. Similar questions can be asked with respect to policy applications. Urging people to support early development, to intervene early because "we can pay now or we will pay more later," or to support policies that recognize the intersection of different developmental domains because "you cannot address one domain without affecting the others" all sound good in the abstract. But their significance for specific public policy initiatives is less clear.

An important general question concerning strategic frame analysis is the role of values in science communication. Values are framing elements that are often placed at the beginning of a messaging narrative because they establish a general, somewhat abstract, reason why people should be interested in an issue. Earlier I described the role of value frames in the messaging narrative for child mental health, using the example of the prosperity value frame to underscore the importance of supporting mental health in children. Values are crucial to advocacy because they can establish a shared orientation or common ground for supporting certain policies. Values are also important to developmental science because values concerning children and their welfare are often what motivate research scientists.

But values are not the same as science. Empirical evidence assumes a crucial role in establishing scientific conclusions but not in establishing values. Developmental scientists have, at times, been criticized for allowing their values to unduly influence the design of their research, such as in their selection of research participants, the use of measures that may be biased toward or against certain respondents, or even the way a research question is conceptualized, each of which can sway research results. The values of scientists can (and often do) influence their interpretation of research findings. It is not that values should – or even can – be absent in science.[54] Rather, it is that the influence of values should be transparent and not infiltrated into the scientific account. People should be able to distinguish between scientific conclusions and the values that scientists bring to their work.

With this in mind, look again at the Council's core story. The first proposition is not really a summary of the science of child development but rather a statement of values. More specifically, it is a statement of the prosperity value frame ("early childhood development is important for community development and economic development") that was enlisted in framing child mental health. The belief that early childhood investments yield greater economic prosperity in the community was discussed in Chapter 5 as a core feature of the economists' arguments for supporting young children. But the research evidence for this view is weak: as described in more detail in the preceding chapter, longitudinal studies of the long-term effects of early education programs do not reliably document long-term benefits for development (despite the early findings of programs like Perry Preschool) and there is even less support for the view that early education establishes a foundation for the economic development of communities. The prosperity frame also portrays early childhood investments transactionally, with investments in young children's development eventually benefiting adults in return. By 2021, however, even FrameWorks was beginning to reconsider this frame, with one report arguing that it can "end up instrumentalizing children, reducing them to a means of achieving cost efficiency. This framing can undermine concern about children as an end in themselves."[55]

The proposition that child development is a foundation for community and economic development is not a research conclusion.[56] It is rather a statement of values that supports investing in children's development. By including it in the core story, this value frame is disguised as science.[57] As Bruer commented in an interview, "we have to be careful in our attempts to use biology to justify our values"[58] because the authority of science does not vindicate value preferences.

It is important to distinguish values from science because while scientific debates can usually be resolved with evidence, the same is not true of value disagreements. Thus when values are presented as scientific claims they imply that they are supported by evidence and, for people who do not share those values, they communicate that something is amiss. This is important because science communicators often seek to appear nonpartisan in their presentation of the evidence for their arguments. Their implicit appeal is that the science compels certain public policy directions. But when values infiltrate the presentation of science, this argument loses credibility, and, by implication, so does the science.[59]

Science, Values, and Advocacy

The National Scientific Council strives to be a nonpartisan communicator of science. Because of its interest in becoming the go-to source of information about child development to policymakers, the Council early established a partnership with the National Conference of State Legislators. One of their joint activities was creating a Legislative Working Group consisting of five Council members and nine legislators from states throughout the country.[60] The legislative subgroup was bipartisan and varied in their prior interest in children's issues. This working group met on four occasions from 2005 to 2007 to discuss developmental science and its relevance to the policy issues the legislators were working on, as well as how to improve the communication of the Council's work. The meetings were interesting exchanges in which Council members learned how their work was perceived and what would be useful to policymakers, but they also learned other things, such as the following. Child advocates are not the only ones presenting benefit-cost figures and the promised future cost savings of their programs. Developmental science can be more influential when it is oriented to specific public issues of current concern rather than broad propositions about children's needs. Proposals for new investments are considered more seriously when advocates can show how they work budgetarily. Legislators have to consider the needs of children and families in relation to the other pressing demands on their funding priorities.

Above all, the legislators urged the Council not to use the science as advocacy. At one moment in the second meeting, Senator Bernest Cain of Oklahoma rejected the Council's nonpartisan label, arguing that we looked like advocates to him in our promotion of children's interests and in the kinds of programs we were proposing. To this conservative legislator from the Plains, our fidelity to an agenda that he did not share was apparent from the beginning in the Council's documents and presentations. To be sure, it probably would have been difficult for our group of academic researchers *not* to appear partisan in his eyes, but it didn't help that the policy proposals in the Council's working papers were all readily identifiable progressive priorities: high-quality child care, paid parental leave, greater child mental health services, and so forth. There was hardly anything that a conservative legislator would like, or could even recognize as consistent with conservative family values, such as a proposal to provide financial support to parents who wish to care for their young children full time at home.[61] Furthermore, in partnering with FrameWorks, a public communications organization created to advance progressive issues, the Council had committed itself to progressive advocacy involving public funding of large-scale programs that was, after all, the natural orientation of most of its members (several were coauthors of *From Neurons to*

Neighborhoods). But children's issues are not just a progressive cause, so this orientation to policy may contribute to the loss of important audiences for the brain development message.

Although the work with state legislators did not continue after the Legislative Working Group ended, the Council has continued its messaging activities in the years since and it has maintained a continuing association with the National Conference of State Legislatures.[62] The Center for the Developing Child at Harvard has developed a number of new initiatives in the years following. The National Scientific Council, together with the Frameworks Institute, remain models of innovative scientific communication for a generation of scientists committed to bridging science and policy to benefit young children. But its work illustrates the challenges, as well as the potential, of enlisting strategic frame analysis for messaging developmental brain science.

CHAPTER 7

Who Speaks for Developmental Science?

Before the beginning of the twentieth century, social reformers had relied mainly on moral admonition, but Progressive reformers believed that scientifically validated facts were an essential preliminary to effective social action. Adherents of the child development movement hoped, through scientific research, to discover optimum child-rearing methods and, through parent education, to foster their application. Philanthropic sponsors of the child development research institutes believed that scientific child rearing would produce a new kind of child who would grow into a new kind of adult, free of most of the afflictions and deficiencies of their progenitors.[1]

The currents of twentieth-century thought that led to the contemporary sciences of child development have their origins in an understanding of science in service of children's well-being. As documented by Alice Smuts in *Science in the Service of Children, 1893–1935*, this was also true of the public and private funders of this work, as well as the advocacy groups promoting greater attention to the needs of children. Developmental scientists and neuroscientists and their various sponsors are today, motivated by an effort to enlist their research to improve not just parenting but also education, health care, children's mental health, and the variety of public policies that can support children of all ages. They are motivated, in other words, by the view of the progressive reformers of the importance of science to effective social action, although the moral obligations in how society responds to the needs of the young are never far behind in their thinking. The story of the brain development revolution is an illustration of the effort to enlist developmental science to support children's welfare through its effective communication to parents, practitioners, and policymakers.

The brain development revolution took most developmental researchers by surprise in 1997 by how suddenly public attention became preoccupied by early childhood and the practices supporting early brain development.

Another surprise was that this attention was sustained in the years that followed as the science of early brain development became the touchstone for parenting guidance, early education initiatives, support for improvements in pediatric health care, commercial marketing of products for children, attention to the effects of stress on children's mental health, and a wealth of other issues that were framed by the developing brain. Although the revolution is over – replaced in public attention by wars, recessions, and a pandemic – it has had enduring impact on how people think about children and their development.

What was less recognized at the time, however, was how much the brain development revolution foreshadowed new ways of thinking about the communication of developmental science and its public policy implications in the context of a changing media environment. The communication of developmental science enlisted multiple messengers and communication avenues, finely crafted media, consideration of diverse audience concerns and expectations, and policy advocacy in ways that extended far beyond the conventional science journalism of the time, taking its cues from political campaigns (hence "campaign journalism"). It also involved efforts to frame the message in a manner that would be engaging and memorable and would motivate support for early childhood initiatives. In these and other ways, the messaging of early brain development anticipated science communication in the increasingly complex, diversified, and polarized media environment of the twenty-first century.

In this conclusion, I reweave some of the themes of the preceding chapters to address the questions that initially framed this inquiry. Then I turn to the three elements of the subtitle of this book – science, the media, and public policy – to explore how the brain development revolution provides lessons relevant to each that are important to current thinking about developmental science in the service of children.

Why Brain Development?

A primary question guiding this inquiry was: Why has brain development become the dominant lens through which we view young children's development today? The preceding chapters have identified several reasons:

- Deterministic, mechanistic explanations of human behavior and development have always attracted attention in the Western world, and neuroscience is the latest and most sophisticated of those explanations.

As described in Chapter 2, the biomedical technology of neuroimaging and experts' authoritative interpretation of the brain areas highlighted in a scan together support the belief that neuroimaging offers "visual proof" of the psychological processes underlying behavior and development. When combined with the neuroessentialist belief that these neurobiological processes are the fundamental causal agents of psychological functioning, it is easy to see how explanations of child development framed in terms of the developing brain would be compelling to the public. The uncomplicated neurodeterministic models by which people became acquainted with developmental neuroscience did not offer much attention to the multifold influences on psychological development nor the powerful influence of context and culture on children's brain and behavioral growth. These and other missing elements of the scientific story added to the straightforward connection between the experiential "wiring" of the developing brain and the development of psychological capacities.

- A uniquely influential three-year media campaign launched in April 1997 thrust early brain development to the forefront of national attention for a concentrated period, and provided the foundation for continuing messaging through follow-on media events designed to promote media momentum and further public engagement. In Chapter 4, I called this *campaign journalism*, and the *I Am Your Child* campaign is important because it enlisted a broad range of messengers and messages, bypassing typical forms of science journalism to reach a broad audience through multiple media forums. It thus foreshadowed emerging elements of the complex media environment in which current science communication takes place. Equally importantly, the *I Am Your Child* campaign established the central themes of the story of early brain development that would endure in public understanding and shape subsequent messaging, including early childhood as a unique period of rapid and formative growth of the brain and mind, an emphasis on the enduring effects of early experience, the significance of parental practices (such as nurturant care and enriching experiences) for brain development, and the dangers posed by early stress and deprivation.
- The brain development messaging subsequently expanded as advocates connected brain development to early education, children's health care, toxic stress and adverse experiences, parent support programs like home visitation, and even the economic prosperity of communities and society. As I describe in Chapter 5, the campaign for California's

Proposition 10 was the first to build from the momentum of the *I Am Your Child* campaign, and it stimulated voter approval of funding for First 5 California and created a model for several other states to create their own dedicated funding streams for early childhood programs. National attention to policy and practice concerning early brain development was furthered by Pew's state-level campaign for prekindergarten education and through the work of its advocacy agencies, PreK Now and the National Institute for Early Education Research (NIEER). In these advocacy campaigns, as well as in the work of economists, business leaders, and government officials, the brain development messaging expanded to incorporate broader claims about the effects of early investments in children on educational attainment, criminality, and employment in their later years, as well as the economic benefits to states and communities. Although these promises were not entirely justified by the neurodevelopmental research at the time, overpromising further stimulated public interest and support that might not have otherwise existed.

- The public policy implications of developmental neuroscience that were promoted by philanthropic and advocacy efforts were important not only to maintaining public interest in early brain development but also to focusing interest on specific implications of the science.
  A central reason that the promotion of prekindergarten education succeeded while little progress was achieved in improving child care, for example, is that the former was the focus of a ten-year campaign linking early brain development to prekindergarten, but there was no comparable campaign linking brain development to high-quality care for children of the same ages. In addition to prekindergarten, brain-based advocacy also contributed to substantial improvements in children's health care coverage, new approaches to addressing the early achievement gap, increasing attention to early childhood mental health, and, for parents, a new way of understanding their children's development. But one of the reasons there was never meaningful public engagement with the impact of poverty on brain development or other important issues (such as nutrition, environmental toxins, and prenatal development) is that there were no advocacy champions to create significant, sustained public messaging connecting these issues to developmental brain science, even though there was abundant scientific evidence to draw on.

- The importance of early brain development has been maintained in public awareness through the emergence of innovative and sophisticated messaging efforts, such as the work of the National Scientific Council on the Developing Child in collaboration with the FrameWorks Institute. Strategic frame analysis is a creative and potentially effective approach to science communication that has established concepts like toxic stress, brain architecture, and serve and return as compelling metaphors for understanding the developing brain, but it is not without its problems, as discussed in Chapter 6. The models and metaphors emerging from the work of the Council maintained close continuity with the earlier messaging of the *I Am Your Child* campaign and the *From Neurons to Neighborhoods* report, as well as with the cultural beliefs of Americans about children and the importance of early experiences. It seems likely that this continuity in messaging is one reason the brain development revolution has had such enduring impact. But it also meant that important dimensions of developmental brain science, such as the opportunities presented by early and continuing brain plasticity, remained under the radar, and the public policy implications of the science continued to be identified as progressive concerns.

The continuing influence of the brain development revolution is reflected in how important the story of developmental neuroscience has become to communicating about child development today, especially about children in the early years. Child advocates have known for many years that justifying new proposals, policies, or initiatives with reference to brain development enhances the chances of reaching an attentive audience. Journalists, columnists, bloggers, and others who write about children are aware of the value of interlacing references to brain development into their narratives, regardless of the significance or relevance of developmental neuroscience to the story. Academic researchers are also aware of the benefits of discussing their research with reference to brain development, even when their studies do not include neuroimaging of any kind.[2] The story of brain development, especially in the early years, has become part of the cultural currency of American (and, to a lesser extent, Western) understanding of child development.

Impact?

But beyond its influence as a rhetorical avenue, what difference has the brain development revolution really made? Some of its most important messages – such as the significance of early experiences, the importance of parental nurturance, the harmful effects of stress, the need for high-quality child care and other forms of family support – long preceded the 1997 campaign. Indeed, some of these messages are iconic to contemporary developmental science, which has portrayed early experiences as formative and parental care as fundamental for more than a century and from multiple theoretical viewpoints. Although the brain development revolution strengthened these messages with reference to their effects on the brain's wiring and functioning, developmental scientists and child advocates have been communicating these themes for a long time. Stated differently, if central messages of the brain development revolution repackaged longstanding messages about the needs of children, what new contributions did it provide?

I think the brain development revolution has provided, despite its limitations, several fundamentally important contributions to public understanding of child development.

First, it has really made a difference in thinking about children, especially in the early years. Before 1997, for example, most people thought little about the mental lives of babies, believing (as did developmental scientists two or three decades earlier) that cognitive growth became interesting and important later in childhood when, with the decline of egocentrism and the advent of logical reasoning, children could think more logically and benefit from formal instruction. Developmental scientists began to appreciate the surprising capacities of "the competent infant" in the 1970s, but the public's discovery of the infant's active, inquiring, inductive mind came much later, when the newborn's hunger for visual stimulation seemed to parallel the brain's exuberant synaptic proliferation, and behavioral research on early language acquisition paralleled neurobiological findings of brain's heightened responsiveness to language (as discussed in Chapter 3). Suddenly, early mental life became important, especially as the formative growth of mind and brain in the early years became understood as constituting a foundation for the reasoning abilities of the school-age child.

Before 1997, most people believed that the brain's developing structure and functioning were genetically fixed. The messaging of early brain development showed, through evocative research descriptions of environmental enrichment and deprivation, that the developing brain is far more pliable to environmental influences, and earlier in life, than people realized. Before 1997, the interconnected development of brain and mind made intuitive sense (at least in older children) although it was little understood. The messaging of early brain development showed how brain growth is significantly connected to developing emotions, self-regulation, social abilities, and other noncognitive skills from an early age, as well as providing a foundation for developing cognitive capacities. Before 1997, brain damage was believed to lead inevitably to irreversible impairments in behavior, but the messaging of brain development moderated this view along with new studies of the continuing plasticity of the human brain, and the hope this offers for remediation and recovery.[3] After 1997, moreover, it was increasingly possible to regard the plasticity of the brain as a lifelong characteristic of typically developing brains, and although plasticity diminishes with increasing age, it provides a basis for adaptive learning throughout. Together with the discovery that neurogenesis can occur during the adult years, these advances contributed to increasing attention by researchers (and by consumer marketers) to programs for stimulating neural flexibility and cognitive functioning in older adults. Each of these, and other messages, has contributed to valuable advances in public understanding of brain development.

Second, the brain development revolution has extended understanding of the practical implications of the science of child development – that is, how the science can be enlisted in the service of children. Although there is some disagreement among child advocates and policymakers owing, in part, to different priorities and value orientations, these disagreements have not deterred significant advances in programs and policies serving children that are at least partly attributable to public awareness of developmental neuroscience.

One of these concerns the effects of stress on developing brains, minds, and bodies. When developmental and clinical scientists of my generation were trained, many of us were told that young children are less susceptible to the harmful effects of stress because of the psychological immaturity that buffers their reactions to adversity. But the messaging about the harms of toxic stress from many communicators, including the National Scientific Council, reversed this view entirely and focused attention on the heightened vulnerability of young children to the toxic effects of adverse experiences, especially if young children lack adequate parental support. This led, in turn, to increased attention to research from the 1990s on the impact of adverse child experiences (ACEs) early in life and studies documenting their connection to adult physical and mental health problems. The realization that many ACEs are sources of toxic stress, especially for young children in social or economic adversity, led to broader concern about the early experiences contributing to mental health problems. This realization also stimulated increased attention to trauma-informed care and teaching practices to support traumatized children from early childhood through adolescence. Concern about the developmental effects of chronic stress also grew as parents considered the effects of the COVID-19 pandemic on their own children, and increased realization that even young children could experience mental health difficulties like depression or anxiety, a view that would have been dismissed years earlier. Although there are many currents feeding into today's awareness of children's susceptibility to stress and the supportive practices that can help to eliminate or reduce its effects, the messaging of developmental neuroscience has been an influential contributor by underscoring the neuro biological as well as behavioral dimensions of early stress.

Another advance in thinking concerns early education. As the Pew Board learned in 2001, growing public awareness of early brain development created a new opportunity to promote early learning through prekindergarten education. The portrayal of a rapidly developing brain and mind stimulated by formative experiences was a natural bridge to the promotion of early education, the board realized, but not of child care, which was encumbered by partisan debates about family and public responsibility for the care of young children. Consequently, the Pew campaign divorced its promotion of prekindergarten from the child care agenda, and succeeded by mobilizing public interest in promoting school readiness, closing the achievement gap, and improving K-12 educational achievement by supporting a year of prekindergarten education for four- and five-year-olds.[4] By the conclusion of Pew's ten-year campaign, prekindergarten was increasingly perceived as a desirable, if not essential, contributor to children's school achievement, so uncontroversial that it was a core component of President Biden's American Families Plan proposal in 2021. In a country in which nursery school or preschool experience was primarily for the children of parents who could afford it before 1997, preschool education has increasingly become perceived as a public good meriting public investment. Again, many currents have fed into this change in thinking about early education, and the brain development revolution has been an important one.

The brain development revolution also afforded practical guidance to parents, even as it raised their anxieties, at least for a while, about whether they were doing the right things to stimulate their baby's developing brain. It has given substance, for example, to the vague concept of "nurturing" a young child by embodying it in specific practices, such as mutually responsive sociability ("serve and return"), language stimulation even to preverbal infants ("talking, reading, and singing to your baby"), and

buffering stress. All of these practical admonitions assume greater significance because of the importance to the baby of the identity of the adult
doing these things. As the research in Chapter 3 describes, for example,
talking, reading, and singing is more influential coming from an animated
human partner (especially one the baby knows) than a video or recording,
and parents to whom a child is securely attached are excellent stress
buffers.[5] Guidance like this has given young parents the conceptual and
practical tools for feeling capable of supporting their young child's development, especially in the early months of infancy when parents can be
most insecure about their influence and efficacy as caregivers.

More broadly, the brain development revolution has provided parents
with a way of thinking about their child. Understanding that even a young
infant is a perceptive, mentally active, responsive young being takes parents
a long way toward becoming motivated to discern the mental states
underlying their baby's behavior. Mentally inquiring of the baby "what
are you trying to tell me?" or "what do you need now?" is the first step
toward what developmental scientists call "mind-mindedness," a habit of
mind that consist of becoming attuned to a young child's ongoing mental
states.[6] A mind-minded orientation to a baby or young child, stimulated
by the awareness from developmental science of the young mind's ongoing
inquiring, feeling, and thinking, is a stronger catalyst to sensitive responding than orienting to the baby as an erratic, unpredictable, delicate entity
requiring formulaic practices to pacify. Mind-mindedness continues to be
an important ingredient to sensitive parenting, incidentally, as children
gets older. In a sense, the brain development revolution has provided
parents with conceptual tools for establishing enduring habits of attunement to their developing child.

There is another contribution of the brain development revolution to
practice and policy concerning young children. It is the view – or, perhaps
more correctly, value – that the healthy development of young children is a
public responsibility yielding a public good. As a value, it is impossible to
point to specific findings from developmental science proving this claim.
But it is difficult to survey the changing landscape of public initiatives for
young children and their families without perceiving a growing consensus
that children's well-being is a shared responsibility rather than the family's
responsibility alone. In initiatives ranging from child health care to early
education to home visitation (and other family support programs) to the
evaluation of child care quality, the view prior to 1997 that these are
worthwhile concerns but not the responsibility of communities has shifted
toward greater public commitment to supporting families with young

children in these ways. Moreover, this is not only a progressive value today. Republican senators offered proposals in 2021 and 2022 for a child tax credit, paid family leave, and other initiatives that, while differing from those offered by Democrats, recognized the value of profamily policy proposals and the changing climate of opinion concerning government support of families with young children.[7]

On this issue, as with the others, many currents of thought have been influential besides developmental neuroscience. An important contributor has been the economists' arguments that investments in children yield meaningful and quantifiable benefits for communities because of their long-term benefits to children. I questioned in Chapter 5 the strength of the evidence that states and communities derive a significant long-term return from early childhood investments, arguing that these are highly contingent and uncertain contributions to benefit-cost calculations. But the evidence that near-term benefits to children are a significant return on investment is well supported, as described in Chapter 5.[8] There is evidence, for example, that children in early childhood education programs achieve more in the early primary grades, especially if they are from disadvantaged conditions, and especially if the quality of the K-12 school is strong. Depending on the form of public investment in children, furthermore, communities may also benefit in other ways, such as through income support policies that strengthen families, improved access to child health care that serves preventive purposes, and increased mental health screening for children and their family members.[9] The argument that establishing a public commitment to children's well-being yields quantifiable public goods has assumed greater force with these economics arguments and, even without the expectation of long-term returns, contributes to the view that children's well-being should be a shared responsibility because it yields a public good.

Finally, the brain development revolution has had impact by bringing new audiences to the table. As illustrated in the preceding paragraphs (indeed, throughout the book), men have become engaged contributors to a topic that was formerly considered to be a woman's issue, and men and women have come from fields not ordinarily associated with early childhood development: public policy, economics, and business, to name several. The messaging of developmental neuroscience has been communicated by celebrities, military leaders, philanthropists, and commercial retailers, as well as by journalists, communications firms, commentators, and (more recently) bloggers and social influencers. They have joined and sometimes overwhelmed the longstanding efforts of developmental researchers, child advocates, and policy wonks in promoting attention to the children's cause, and they have broadened the base of an interested and informed constituency.

The brain development revolution has had meaningful impact on public understanding and public policy. At the same time, there are important lessons it offers about science communication. These lessons concern the nature of the science itself that formed the core knowledge base for public messaging, the evolving media environment that constituted the forums for the messaging, and the impacts on public policy that derived from the messaging. I turn now to exploring these lessons further.

Science

Viewed as an example of science communication, it is striking how easily the brain development message was accepted by public audiences. Compared with past public communications concerning global warming, the disposal of nuclear waste, ending smoking, immunizing adolescents against the HPV virus, GMOs in the diet, and other controversial topics, the communication of developmental brain science was uncontroversial. The brain development revolution did not have to contend with polarized public opinion, public reactance to unfamiliar and unsettling ideas, a mobilized, vigorous opposition, or misinformation campaigns and conspiracy theories concerning scientists and advocates. There were no competing narratives about the meaning of the science, no opposition from public or private stakeholders or other interest groups, and no resistance from major political figures or public influencers. The brain development revolution had significant impact in part because its messages were uncontroversial, readily understood, and easily accepted.

One reason the campaign was uncontested is that its central messages concerned young children and embraced values and goals built on Americans' enduring beliefs about the importance of early experiences to a child's future. The framing of the messaging was congenial with what people already believed about young children, so who would disagree? Another reason the campaign was readily accepted is that it did not ask much of its audiences. They were not asked to use fewer fossil fuels, immunize their children, quit smoking, or avoid chlorofluorocarbons in their products. In fact, there could be no easier call to action than to nurture a child!

Even when the campaign pivoted to advocacy, audiences were not asked for much – neither a sustained commitment of time and energy, nor money (this came from a tobacco tax, a lottery, or public treasuries), nor even a pledge. Instead, audiences were asked to put pressure on policy-makers to enact or expand public programs for early education, child health insurance, family support, child care, and other concerns. When these advocacy efforts faltered, it was not because of vigorous opposition (child care funding the exception) or public resistance, but rather because these issues did not rise in public concern sufficiently to become a funding priority of policymakers (think child mental health services). The failure to ask more of audiences may, in fact, be one reason why the brain develop-ment revolution did not create a strong, sustained advocacy movement for young children with continued influence over the long term.[10] There have been significant achievements, but no continuing Children's Movement arising from new understanding of the developing brain.

As an example of science communication, therefore, the brain develop-ment revolution stands out as a success in public messaging. But as I noted in Chapter 4, what communicates well is not necessarily most important or accurate. Although most of the messaging about early brain development was consistent with the science, there are three problems that I have identified in the preceding chapters. The first concerns blending two different sciences of child development into one message with some misleading implications. Another was inattention to contextual influences on the development of brain and mind, despite the prominence of context in the science of child development. Both of these problems are somewhat unique to the brain development revolution. The third is a more general issue in science communication concerning selectivity in messaging the science.

Blending Developmental Neuroscience with Developmental Science

Beginning with Ron Kotulak's Pulitzer Prize–winning series for the *Chicago Tribune* in 1993, reporting about the developing brain has seam-lessly integrated findings from developmental neuroscience with the deeper knowledge base of developmental science. This integration has character-ized messaging about brain development ever since. The blending of these research fields makes sense. First, and most obviously, the science of behavioral development and that of developmental neuroscience address a common topic: the development of children. Although they use different methods and levels of analysis, they *should* yield consistent conclusions about the same developmental processes, as I argued in Chapter 3, and when they do so, it strengthens confidence in the findings of each field.[11]

Second, discoveries of each field can provoke questions relevant to the other, such as studying the neuroscience of statistical reasoning in infants or how social understanding is affected by mirror neurons. This stimulus is good for each field. Third, blending findings from each field can help researchers answer questions from the public about the meaning and significance of research discoveries. That is good for the public.

Blending the findings of developmental science and developmental neuroscience was particularly important as public understanding of the developing brain increased and interest in its practical applications grew. If early experiences are formatively important, people were quick to ask, what specific experiences are formative and how should parents ensure that these occur? If the timing of these experiences is important, what is the timetable for these windows of opportunity? The messaging of developmental brain science offered limited answers to these broad questions but more substantively addressed a range of more practical concerns, such as why nurturant care is important, how to help young children learn, the timing and significance of language exposure, the biological and psychological effects of stress, and other practical parenting concerns. Later, as the messaging of the brain development revolution expanded, the practical guidance also expanded to include the value of early childhood education, what should be included in early health care, and the characteristics of high-quality child care.

Nearly all of this practical guidance derived from studies of children's psychological development, sometimes from the cumulative discoveries of years of research before the emergence of brain development science. This is why some of these recommendations were not really very new. But when this guidance was presented in the context of brain development, it assumed greater salience and significance. This owes, in part, to the mechanistic determinism of neuroscience ("use it or lose it") that compelled attention but also raised parents' anxieties about providing just the right early experiences to support healthy brain growth. These anxieties were not unfounded in light of the studies of rats living in enriched environments, showing capabilities absent in those living in deprived environments, and startling neuroimages of the shrunken brains of three-year-olds growing up in "extreme neglect." The neurodeterminism of the messaging was also a foundation for (over)promising the enduring benefits of nurturant care and early education. After all, if these early experiences provide the right support to the developing brain, why wouldn't the resulting neural architecture scaffold constructive competencies in later years as skill begets skill?

By contrast, children's psychological development is much more multi-determined and probabilistic, based more on the cumulative effects of many influences over time than on the presence or absence of single critical experiences. It is also profoundly affected by the contexts that shape the experiences of children and the cultures that give them meaning. This is one reason why certainty about how individual children will be affected by specific early experiences is uncommon in developmental science.[12] As a consequence, parents, the public, and many policymakers were misled concerning how significantly early experiences determine later outcomes through the developing brain, especially because this messaging built on the intuitive neuroessentialism that most people brought to their hearing of the brain development story. Typical psychological development is not like rats growing up in cages or young children in profoundly deprived orphanages.

The first messaging problem of the brain development revolution, therefore, was failing to distinguish for audiences the straightforward causal mechanisms by which neural networks are formed from the vastly more complex and contingent processes influencing psychological development. Distinguishing these causal models would be challenging, especially because the brain development lead is what captured public attention and constituted a through line for the story of early child development. Consequently, this mechanistic causal story remained foregrounded, and constituted a continuing narrative frame that shaped understanding of all the messaging that followed. As the brain development story turned to policy and practice implications, furthermore, child advocates had few incentives to depart from this compelling neuroscience lead, especially because the messaging often motivated parents, policymakers, and practitioners to do the right things for young children, albeit for the wrong reasons. Parental nurturance and talking to the baby are benefits to early development for the security and language stimulation they provide, for example, even if they do not ensure later academic achievement; high-quality preschool education has immediate benefits for young children's cognitive skills, even if it does not ensure high school graduation or workforce skills. The brain development revolution accomplished many genuine wins of this kind for young children, even though the risk was that in needlessly arousing parental anxiety about stimulating brain development and overpromising some of the long-term benefits of early investments in children, trust in the messaging of developmental science could have become eroded.

It requires finesse in messaging science to describe to audiences the different causal mechanisms involved in different scientific fields, especially when those fields converge in explaining the complexities of child development. Such finesse might have required communicating to an interested public the *limits* of knowledge and its applications: that scientists are discovering the basic building blocks of the developing brain but its translation to children's thinking and reasoning remain uncertain, that studies show how parental nurturance makes young children emotionally secure but its impact on brain development is unknown, and that high-quality early education can increase the chances of better achievement in first grade, but continuing support is needed to promote high school graduation. Such a demeanor of scientific balance and modesty would have communicated better the state of the science and might also have strengthened public trust in what was messaged. The brain development revolution was unequal to this task.

Inattention to the Influence of Context

A second messaging problem was the failure to account for context. Children develop in an environment of relationships with adults within and outside the family, and their lived experience is shaped by culture, their economic conditions, the quality of their schools and neighborhoods, and, for some, experiences of exclusion and discrimination. But one would not know this from the messaging about brain development, which focused narrowly on the individual child in the family. Inattention to context characterized the *I Am Your Child* campaign, which did not bring into the messaging the effects of poverty, nutritional inadequacy, exposure to environmental toxins, inadequate health care, and other contextual influences on early brain development, despite considerable scientific research on these topics. Inattention to context led Proposition 10 advocates and economists to directly connect early investments in children to adult success, often without taking into account intervening influences – such culture, race, and language, as well as K-12 school quality, socioeconomic opportunity, and externalities in the economy – that mediate those outcomes. Inattention to context led education writers to apply brain development research to children's learning with little regard to the conditions of schools, neighborhoods, and families that have been so prominent in research on educational achievement during the past twenty-five years.[13]

Throughout these chapters, I have considered several explanations for why the messaging of developmental neuroscience was so decontextualized. Developmental neuroscience naturally draws attention to neurobiological processes within the child and less to the contextual influences surrounding the child. In a sense, going "under the skin" made it more difficult to go "over the skin" to the conditions of children's lives.[14] The "I am your child" theme personalized the messaging of brain development to establish its relevance to the audience, few of whom were likely to be living in economic distress or to be members of underrepresented communities. The effort to avoid crisis-oriented messaging steered the campaign further away from contextual topics like the effects of poverty, malnutrition, or environmental toxins on brain development.[15] Finally, I have speculated that perhaps the brain development messaging was influenced by the prominence of neoliberal thinking in the 1980s and its focus on the individual and the enhancement of human resources (such as the brain) to maximize economic productivity.[16]

Acknowledging the influence of context on brain development would have required recognizing that, for many children, healthy brain development is less a consequence of parental talking and reading than it is a product of food insufficiency, persistent family poverty, or environmental pollutants in drinking water or the playground.[17] This information would have increased the applications of developmental brain science to public policy, even though it would have required recognizing that to many in the target audience, these are influences on *other people's* children that warrant public concern. Harmonizing messages about "your child" and "other people's children" might have been possible, however, by noting that all families desire the healthy environments and nurturant relationships that young children need, but they differ in the obstacles to be overcome in providing these to their children, and this is where science-informed public policies can be helpful to everyone. Diversity in the practical applications of the brain development story by attending to context might have contributed to its relevance to diverse families.

Science Communication Is Selective

Science communication is necessarily selective. Coherent, comprehensible messages cannot be created if communicators do not foreground the most important themes. Indeed, effective science communication is based at least as much on thoughtful decisions about what to leave out as on decisions about what to include in the messaging. The important question is what is the basis for these decisions. The decision to reduce or eliminate certain elements of a scientific story is injudicious if it contributes to a significantly less accurate message or if it skews public understanding toward conclusions (including policy and practice applications) that are inconsistent with the science. A selective scientific message needs to be strategic in the selectivity.

The campaign's inattention to context is one of several examples of how the story of brain development incorporated important decisions about what to communicate. Throughout these chapters there have been other examples. There was the decision of the *I Am Your Child* campaign to emphasize influences in the first three years, despite the arguments of scientific advisors that the research did not support the focus on such a narrow developmental window. The campaign also created messaging that was congenial to audience beliefs and values, such as, optimistic American cultural beliefs about improving the human condition through children ("as the twig is bent …"). With the enlistment of brain development messaging into child advocacy, the story increasingly emphasized the long-term benefits of early investments in children's brain development, captured in return on investment calculations. Pew's campaign for prekindergarten linked early brain development to school readiness by arguing that both would be strengthened by a year of prekindergarten education (but not high-quality child care). The core story of the National Scientific Council on the Developing Child drew many of these messaging themes together in describing how the construction of brain architecture during the early years creates a strong or weak foundation for all that follows.

The selectivity in the messaging across these efforts reflected multiple goals:

- leading with a message – developmental neuroscience – that attracted attention and interest
- enlisting a frame (in the case of American cultural beliefs about children) or creating a frame (in the case of brain architecture) to facilitate acceptance of core messages about the formative importance of the early years, the long-term benefits of early childhood interventions, and the importance of parenting to healthy brain growth
- a call to action centered primarily on compelling public policies to support young children and their families[18]
- an economic/business/legislative case for early childhood investments justified by the benefits for the economy and programs paying for themselves
- a campaign for prekindergarten education centered on connecting early brain development to early learning and school readiness.

Taken together, these elements of the messaging led to a very effective public communications campaign for public and private investments in early childhood development. But viewed independently of this goal, the messaging risked creating misunderstanding or misapplication of the science as it related to other populations or public issues. The focus of the campaign on birth to age three diverted attention from the significant advances in brain development prenatally, attention which could have enhanced the guidance and support provided expectant mothers (and fathers) and stimulated public recognition that babies' brains are different at birth because of intrauterine experience. The recognition that brain development continues significantly after early childhood might have changed thinking about promoting healthy brain growth exclusively in the early years and instead promoted greater appreciation of the catalysts to neurocognitive growth that emerge at different ages. The implied developmental model of the brain development campaign was too limited because (in the words of *From Neurons to Neighborhoods*) it "begins too late and ends too soon."

The brain development messaging was also misapplied to certain populations of young children, especially those for whom the risks to healthy brain growth extended beyond the campaign's messaging. Jerome Kagan, a major figure in developmental science until his death in 2021, stated this problem evocatively:

> It is considerably more expensive to improve the quality of housing, education, and health of the approximately one million children living in poverty in America today than to urge their mothers to kiss, talk to, and play with them more consistently. Although a change in maternal behavior in this direction will have benevolent effects, those effects will be slim compared with the effect of changing current social policies.

Kagan went further:

> [I]t is a bit dishonest to suggest to poor parents that playing with and talking to their infant will protect the child from future academic failure and guarantee life success. The quality of the school, the motivation of the teachers, the values of peers, the mores of the neighborhood, and the child's identification with his socioeconomic class will exert important influence during the childhood years. Yes, of course, parents should be affectionate, playful, and conversational with their infants, but there are no guarantees.[19]

Kagan's last sentence applies, of course, to all parents: there are no guarantees. But as Malcolm Gladwell has noted, these messages are also "an unwitting act of reproach" to parents in economic adversity because it implies that if their children do not turn out as the children of privilege do, it might be their fault for having failed to do the right things to stimulate their child's brain early on.[20] At the same time, the incentives to create real improvements in housing, school quality, nutrition, and child care for impoverished families were weakened by the campaign's focus on parental nurturance rather than on these ecological and economic influences on the developing brain.

The story of early brain development, beginning with the *I Am Your Child* campaign and continuing through the Pew campaign for prekindergarten education to the present, was easily accepted by an interested public because it was uncontroversial, intuitively appealing, and readily understood. Incorporating the developmental experience of children living in economic adversity might have made the account more controversial and crisis-oriented. But just as effective framing elements can be adapted for different target audiences, one hopes that the framing can also be adapted for different sides of the scientific story. Perhaps a new metaphor to capture the effects of external conditions on the developing brain could be added to the publicly communicated story so this element of the science would not be overlooked. Or perhaps the use of contrastives (e.g., here is what children need for their brains to thrive … and some developing children need more) together with recognizing that economically advantaged and disadvantaged parents share in common their devotion to the healthy development of their young children, would help create a broader but comparably engaging message about early brain development.[21]

The lesson here is that scientific messaging must be selective, but it must also be strategic. It is crucial to create frameworks of public understanding that not only support the current messaging campaign, but can also accommodate future messaging about other aspects of the scientific story (i.e., aspects not currently part of the messaging). At the least, communicators should not enlist metaphors or frames that are inconsistent with the full account of developmental brain science. A campaign communicating that stress can be toxic to the developing brain can readily accommodate future messaging about the kinds of stresses that have this effect, such as the multisystemic stresses associated with family poverty. A campaign communicating that early experiences are important to the developing brain can probably accommodate future messaging about the fetal programming of brain growth, depending on the kinds of early experiences that are foregrounded in the campaign. By contrast, a campaign emphasizing that the early years establish the blueprint for lifelong brain functioning does not provide much room to accommodate an understanding of brain plasticity, either in adolescence or later in life. Such a frame might be useful for advocating support for early childhood programs, but it will run into problems if public interest turns to the nature of the developing brain in youth or adulthood. Stated simply, the lesson is to take the long view in the selectivity of messaging.

Have You Ever Argued with a Scientist?

One of the reasons the messaging of developmental brain science evolved over time was the participation of new communicators creating messages for new audiences. From the celebrity spokespersons of the *I Am Your Child* campaign to the economists who documented return on investment, the promotion of prekindergarten programs by the business leaders of ReadyNation, and the diverse interests on the California First 5 commissions, new voices brought different perspectives to the interpretation and applications of developmental brain research. This was, in fact, one of the reasons for the longevity and vitality of the messaging, and this meant that the brain development story had relevance to new and influential audiences.

Developmental scientists and developmental neuroscientists supported these new messaging initiatives as consultants and advisors, as well as through the work of the National Research Council's Committee on Integrating the Science of Early Childhood Development and Harvard's National Scientific Council on the Developing Child. Their work with the leaders of nonprofit organizations and philanthropies, communications specialists in advertising, the media, and organizations like FrameWorks, and political consultants, child advocates in local communities, and academics in other fields like economics and human ecology contributed to refining the messaging and grounding it in the practical concerns of parents and communities. These collaborations were valuable and necessary – especially if, as Shonkoff and Bales argued in "Science Does Not Speak for Itself," research scientists are not especially skilled (and many are not particularly interested) in translating developmental science to the public, practitioners, and policymakers.[22]

This brings us back to the question that opened this book: Who speaks for science? I close this section by arguing for a stronger leadership role for scientists themselves in the communication and application of research findings from their field. My reasons are based in the following question: Have you ever argued with a scientist? As a scientist myself who has occasionally done so, I can say that it is a challenging experience. It is challenging because a scientific argument often hinges on the data that each party can cite as supportive evidence. More than logical cogency or a compelling argumentative thread or references to other authorities, the evidence of scientific studies is the armament of a scientific argument. Listen to two scientists disagree about a matter of importance to each, and when one asks, "But have you read this recent study?" of which the other is unaware, you know the debate is nearing a conclusion. New research findings, especially if they are strong and relevant, usually carry the day.

Scientists respect the data they devote their professional work to creating, and to which they devote close attention when reading the work of their colleagues. It is from the compounding of data from new studies that general conclusions are derived that shape the future course of the science. Furthermore, the misuse of data – such as through its falsification, fabrication, or plagiarism – is a serious offense that can scar a scientific career or a field of study. Even more benign problems in scientific conduct, such as regularly ignoring conflicts of interest, using misleading methods or statistical procedures, or significantly overinterpreting results, can have reputational consequences. In these ways, science communication differs from other forms, such as political communication, in which the selective use of evidence, deliberate ambiguity, or claims that are misleading or factually incorrect are well recognized rhetorical strategies.[23] Indeed, the recent direction of science dissemination has been toward "open science" in which procedures of scientific inquiry are becoming more transparent and accessible to broad audiences. These are some of the reasons for the high and continuing public respect for the work of scientists. In a national survey in 2021 by the Pew Research Center, more than three-quarters (77%) of Americans reported having a confidence in scientists to act in the best interests of the public (29% reporting "a great deal" and an additional 48% reporting "a fair amount" of confidence), a proportion that is higher than in 2016.[24] In general, there is a shared belief that scientists strive to be truth-tellers to the world.

It is this respect for evidence that compels the leadership of developmental scientists and neuroscientists in the teams of communicators that create and refine future messaging about children's development. The work of public communication can often best occur in these collaborative partnerships, as the engagement of the FrameWorks Institute with the National Scientific Council on the Developing Child has demonstrated.[25] Scientists usually do not have the background and expertise to alone create and bring to scale a public communications effort. But with multiple voices involved in the scientific messaging, scientists are likely to be the most sensitive to the distinction between scientific veracity and communicative impact, which can easily become obscured, and to emphasize the former. And this is important. When they are clear and ethical communicators, scientists can also be trusted and compelling messengers of the science.

A similar conclusion was reached by a team of journalists, neuroscientists, representatives of scientific organizations, bioethicists, and several others in a report titled *Neurotalk: Improving the Communication of Neuroscience Research.*[26] Noting that the public communication of neuroscience is particularly prone to misinformation and inaccurate reporting, they argued that scientists, as "recipients of public funds and beneficiaries of scientific advances," have a special responsibility for public outreach. To support such outreach efforts in the future, they recommend three steps.

The first is a cultural change within the research world to substantively reward public communication activities, not just in response to invitations (such as public lectures, media interviews, and the like) but also in the initiation of efforts to inform public audiences about new discoveries and their implications, as well as to correct misinformation. At most research-intensive universities, these activities collectively fall under the "service" component of academic responsibilities that are rewarded much less than teaching and research. The authors argue that a cultural change is necessary within academic and nonacademic research institutions to esteem public engagement efforts. One part of this cultural change would be professional training in science communication for researchers at all career levels, from graduate students to senior scientists.

The second and third recommendations follow from the first. The authors recommend the development of a cadre of communication specialists in the scientific community with more specialized knowledge and skills in the public dissemination of neuroscience and the delegated time to actively monitor and contribute to emerging reporting of reports relevant to neuroscience. These efforts would require developing familiarity with new media, and might include organizing workshops and meetings with the goal of communicating science to broader audiences, and contributing to ongoing collaborations to further these goals. These are time-consuming activities that are beyond the capabilities of many scientists. In some respects, the role of these communication specialists on academic faculties would be comparable to those of teaching faculty who carry a larger instructional load while also conducting their own research programs, and who are professionally rewarded in relation to these responsibilities.

The third recommendation is for the development and funding of systematic research into the communication of and public engagement in neuroscience. With the support of academic institutions and research funders, such a research program would be devoted to expanding empirical knowledge of the public's understanding of neuroscience, the efficacy of alternative communication strategies, and the impact of specific messaging initiatives. It is not difficult to imagine such a research program, which might involve specialists from a variety of academic fields, building on and expanding beyond the work conducted by organizations like FrameWorks.

The *Neurotalk* recommendations are one proposal among many that can be envisioned for promoting deeper leadership by developmental scientists and neuroscientists in the public communication of science. There are other proposals, but there are also many obstacles to the success of proposals like these. Many scientists themselves would be among the first to point out that the significant public and personal investment in their research training should discourage the diversion of their efforts to activities for which they have not been trained and which have the potential for meaningfully reducing their research productivity.[27] Stated simply, scientists do science, not public communication. Likewise, academic institutions (especially private research institutions) have well-earned reputations for research excellence that build on the highly esteemed work of their faculty in laboratories, not in the Twitterverse. The professional reward structure of academic institutions exists for a reason, therefore, and it would be very difficult to change. And although public research universities must respond more than private institutions to the concerns of the public, reputational incentives based on research productivity still loom large in public perceptions of the strength of their university systems.

But there are also countervailing incentives. One of the strongest is that as the recipients of public funding for their research through grants and contracts, scientists have a reciprocal obligation to provide a return of that investment to the public. This can occur in many ways, such as through new product development, biomedical breakthroughs, and technological innovations, manifested in new patents. But when the primary public good generated by research investments is new knowledge, the public deserves to benefit from that knowledge. Unfortunately, the current incentives for this obligation to be actively fulfilled are very weak. The National Science Foundation, for example, lists one of the two merit criteria guiding the review of research proposals to be "broader impacts," but these impacts are often addressed in vague promises of possible societal benefits of the proposed research application. It would take a greater culture change in federal and private funding institutions to make the communication of scientific discoveries a professional obligation better recognized by academic researchers and their universities.

There are other incentives for greater engagement of scientists in public understanding. One is scientists' interest in maintaining the public's positive regard for science itself. Social and behavioral psychologists were stung in the 2010s by the dual revelations that some fundamental discoveries of the field could not be replicated, and that some researchers engaged in dubious practices to enhance the publication-worthiness of nonsignificant results. Since those revelations, the field has engaged in substantive efforts to increase the transparency of published research, including the practice of "preregistering" the research design and analysis plan before the research is conducted in order to require fidelity to the research plan and reduce post-hoc manipulations to create stronger findings. Behind these efforts is, I believe, professional concern for maintaining the integrity of behavioral science to maintain public respect and, as a result, policymakers' support for research funding. Scientific commitment to the clear and accurate communication of research discoveries to the public serves the same goal. In an era when well-established and emergent scientific discoveries can be readily questioned by audiences simply because they disagree with the findings or their implications, scientists have an interest in maintaining the respect of public audiences for the work they do. One way of doing so is by contributing to the accurate communication of scientific discoveries and the correction of misinformation when it emerges.

Another potential incentive for scientific leadership in the communication of developmental science comes from the public and private funders of research. As the excerpt from *Science in the Service of Children* that opens this chapter documents, the funders of research have long shared a commitment to supporting research and its public dissemination so that research discoveries would become practically beneficial to the care and development of children. Some private funders of developmental science have programs that support opportunities for researchers to apply their work to the practical concerns of programs and policy, and as noted, public agencies such as the National Science Foundation require attention to the broader impacts of proposed research in grant applications. It may be time to strengthen these enabling incentives with stronger requirements that make the provision of future funding contingent on a documented record of contributions to public understanding of science. Public and private funding agencies could do this, and in the past they have demonstrated their commitment to science in the service of children by actions such as these.

Engaging scientists in the leadership of public communication about developmental science faces other obstacles, but there are also some promising indications on the horizon that they may become more interested in this work than has been true in the past. I consider this further in the next section.

The Media

The media environment of science communication today is very different from what it was at the time of the *I Am Your Child* campaign. In the late 1990s, most people obtained their news from television and newspapers, and journalists were in a gatekeeping role for advancing public knowledge.[28] As I describe in Chapter 1, the "uneasy partnership"[29] between social scientists and journalists derived from the importance of journalists to the public dissemination of research and from the different cultures of the university and the newsroom. Because scientists were neither skilled nor particularly interested in devoting significant time and effort to translating their work for the public, science journalists did so, and in their reporting they also interpreted that work in relation to other discoveries (including discrepant findings) and current issues, and explained its limitations and broader implications. Science journalists thus served as gatekeepers but also as knowledgeable interpreters of the science both for the public and for policymakers, who trusted the reporting of science journalists for this reason.

The *I Am Your Child* campaign was, in this context, an entirely new way of communicating science that I have described as an example of campaign journalism. Campaign journalism bypasses traditional avenues of science journalism to carry a coherent and singular science message directly to the public during a concentrated period of time. The campaign mobilizes public interest through entertainment media, the creation of newsworthy political events, the release of digital media, state and local activities, and follow-up events to create a cascade of public attention that is designed to create media momentum. Its name derives, in part, from its resemblance to the strategies and goals of a political campaign. Campaign journalism is also distinctive for combining an uncritical scientific message (by contrast with the more critical reporting of science journalists) and wedding it to an advocacy agenda. As I describe in Chapter 5, the media momentum of campaign journalism is an asset to informing the public quickly and effectively, even though it is weaker in carrying a compelling advocacy agenda. There have been other examples of campaign journalism over the years, but the 1997 campaign is distinctive for its scope and impact, as well as its focus on young children.

The 1997 campaign also foreshadowed the environment of public communication that would become increasingly influential in the decades that followed as the business model of traditional journalism began to erode and new media emerged on the internet and other digital technologies.[30] People today receive news more frequently through online news sites and interactive digital media like Facebook, Twitter, and YouTube that curate the news and offer opportunities to comment on content and read the comments of others. News is also obtained through user-generated media content like blogposts or videos that incorporate commentary directly into the news report. The news reporting environment has also become increasingly polarized, as many of these alternative news sources connect users with others who have similar views so that users rarely encounter views that are divergent from their own. Many adults view cable news programs on networks like Fox or MSNBC that present news content with a political slant, and for many users, the news is curated by digital media algorithms based on their existing preferences. A report by the Pew Research Center of a 2022 national survey of how adults get their news noted that 82% report that they often or sometimes get news from a smartphone, computer, or tablet, which was higher than those who reported getting their news from television, radio, or print publications. Furthermore, 53% of respondents indicated that they preferred getting news on digital devices, such as news websites or apps or social media, compared with 33% preferring television and less than 10% each preferring radio or print.[31] Those who get their news from digital sources like these are most likely to be under age thirty.[32]

The opportunities today to bypass traditional science journalism are therefore abundant, and even more so as advertising dollars have increasingly shifted away from traditional news outlets and toward alternative media sources and many newsrooms can no longer afford to keep skilled science reporters on staff. The *I Am Your Child* campaign anticipated the current era when it is possible to carry a science message directly to the public through a variety of nontraditional media with the hope that the message will achieve media momentum (in other words, go viral). But even though messages may go viral, audiences are still not equipped with the analytic tools offered by a science journalist to evaluate the research critically and in the context of other research discoveries. This is one reason why the authors of *Neurotalk* are not alone in arguing that the lack of a critical lens in the messaging of science through alternative media is another reason for scientists themselves to take greater leadership in the communication of science.

The good news is that younger scientists appear to be much more willing to engage in public communication than their scientific forebears. This should not be surprising because young adults are frequent and experienced consumers and contributors to social media. In tweets, blogposts, podcasts, op-eds, and a growing number of social media channels and websites, a new generation of scholars has discovered that investing time and effort in reporting their work in nonacademic forums is not a professional liability. Instead, it can promote recognition within the academy as well as outside, a phenomenon that has been called the "medialization" of science.[33] Social media posts inform other scientists working in allied areas about research discoveries through collegial networks on Twitter or curated websites long before these discoveries have made their way through the time-consuming process of peer review and academic publication. A researcher may, in fact, achieve considerable professional as well as public attention from an op-ed published in a prominent forum long before the study is published in a research journal (and *much* greater impact if the research does not survive peer review).[34] Through these avenues, the review committees for job selection, promotion, and tenure may have already become familiar with a candidate's accomplishments long before reading a formal academic dossier. Professional visibility can be indexed in the number of views, hits, or retweets these posts have achieved as much as from an academic's h-index or i10-index.[35]

Young scientists have thus become more motivated and adept at communicating their work clearly and directly to audiences through nontraditional media. The concerns of earlier academic generations about when the science would be ready for dissemination or about being accused of pandering to the public are much less compelling in an era when academic networks are informal (via social media) as well as formal (via academic publishing), when the lines are blurred between public impact and professional impact, and when the new media environment of rapid information transmission does not wait for evidence of enduring, generalizable knowledge from peer reviewed papers. Viewed in this light, science does indeed speak for itself, at least by many young scientists who have grown up in the world of social media.

There are, to be sure, some problems with these new forms of science communication. One problem is how the brevity and style of alternative media can skew the content of science communication. If it is true that, as Marshall McLuhan claimed, "the medium is the message,"[36] then science communication is shaped by the media through which the science is conveyed. The problem of brevity is self-evident in the communication of complex research discoveries with nuanced implications. Less obvious is how the compelling need to attract likes, retweets, and other manifestations of attention to a post orients communicators toward messaging that is most eye-catching, arresting, compelling, controversial, and/or unexpected – hardly the forum for conveying a balanced, contextualized scientific discovery. There is also the problem of the confrontational, argumentative style of much of the discourse on social media, especially if the message needs to be defended against contrary misinformation, "what-if" counterarguments, and aggressive opposition.

An even broader concern is how the media environment shapes the determinations of what is news- or attention-worthy. If the medium puts a premium on information that is novel, is this consistent with the scientific premium on information that is reliable? There are media contexts in which audiences recognize the distinction between the novelty and reliability of the science reporting. When the pandemic was generating worldwide attention and concern, for example, scientists began posting preprints of their preliminary coronavirus research reports on delegated websites to quickly disseminate potentially important discoveries to the scientific community. This proved to be a valuable means of quickly advancing necessary news, even though researchers recognized that there was heightened risk of misinformation because these reports had received little or no peer review.[37] Indeed there were a number of reports of preliminary findings that were misleading and had to be retracted. But users recognized this risk. In the everyday reporting of science in tweets, posts, and other forums, however, the distinction between novelty and trustworthiness is not so clear, and this is a problem inherent to the new media environment of science communication.

Another problem with these new forms of science messaging is how the media orient toward self-promotion, which aligns with the professional orientation of researchers themselves. Whereas a science journalist usually has no particular interest in making a scientist's work look good and can therefore be more objective in assessing its contribution, researchers must regularly foreground their accomplishments in their applications for grant funding, the published reports of their research, their tenure and promotion dossiers, and even in their casual conversations with colleagues. Such a professional orientation is baked into the increasingly competitive world of academic research. In light of this, the brevity of alternative media can be a problem because it often permits room only for an announcement of achievement (a new lab finding, a new publication, a new idea) and little more. Even in longer forums, such as blog posts and op-eds, scientists often act not like science journalists but as self-promoters in presenting their research discoveries decontextualized from the allied findings of other researchers, contrary results from other labs, or alternative interpretations.

The lessons of the new media world that have emerged since the beginning of the brain development revolution, therefore, are that there are greater opportunities for transforming science communication, but also many challenges that must be taken seriously. When new media have emerged in the past (e.g., the printing press, telegraph, film and video technology, most recently digital media), its practitioners did not initially recognize how much the medium itself was affecting how they communicated with it.[38] And because most scientists who use digital media for scientific messaging already have considerable experience with its personal uses, it requires considerable perspective and practice to develop skill in using these media in ways that advance the broader goal of educating the public about science.

These challenges notwithstanding, the emergence of alternative media and the growing interest of a younger generation of scientists in communicating their work through these avenues holds considerable promise for the future messaging of developmental science. It means that scientists can build audiences for the science, correct misinformation, and spell out the implications of new discoveries in their own messaging. And if we are witnessing a generational shift in researchers' familiarity, ease, and dexterity in the use of alternative media for communicating science, this may contribute to a generational shift in the expectations of scientists as communicators to nonacademic as well as academic audiences.

Indeed, there are some indications that this is occurring in the frequency with which professional organizations like the American Psychological Association, the Association for Psychological Science, and the American Association for the Advancement of Science are sponsoring webinars and tutorials to encourage researchers' use of social media. The Alan Alda Center for Communicating Science[39] claims to have worked with over 15,000 scientists since its founding in 2009, and provides excellent guidance in styles as well as formats of public communication that can help scientists develop the skills necessary for broader outreach. Many universities sponsor faculty tutorials in the strategic use of social media, curated websites, blogposts, and other media for the public communication of research. The rapid growth of these programs and instructionals attests to the growing recognition by scientists, and their institutional and professional organizations, of the opportunities provided by new media for the communication of science.

What seems to be missing from these tutorials, however, is guidance concerning *what* to communicate, perhaps because of an assumption that researchers will be motivated to use these skills in the promotion of their own work. This is a reasonable assumption, and messaging of this kind serves the researcher's goals and those of their academic and professional partners. But is there more to the broader messaging of science to the public than the promotion of one's own work? Can digital media also be used to advance the public understanding of science more generally, such as by drawing attention to the work of another researcher that deserves prominence, or a body of important research that has received little notice? What if messaging highlighted limitations in current understanding that have implications for its applications, or profiled a scientific debate with significant practical implications? What if a blogpost or op-ed was devoted to the process by which new ideas are emerging in a field and the intellectual streams contributing to it? How digital media could be enlisted to advance public understanding of science is a question worth pondering as scientists master the tools of digital communication because it could contribute to a fuller understanding of the context of scientific discoveries while also educating the public about the nature of scientific inquiry.[40] In the new environment of alternative media, this is a hopeful possibility.

Policy

There can be various motivations to communicating science. One is to increase the storehouse of the background knowledge of public and policy-making audiences, which I called the "knowledge creep" in Chapter 5. Another is to correct misinformation, especially when it has arisen to advance the special interests of consumer marketers, parochial political groups, science skeptics, or simply those who misunderstand. A third reason is to influence policy in the service of children and their families. To their credit, virtually all those messaging about developmental science in the brain development revolution did so to advance children's interests along with the other purposes. Their goal was not just the communication of developmental science or the correction of misconceptions about the developing brain, but also to improve public policy and programs for children.

Their efforts have resulted in some impressive achievements for the children's cause as well as some lost opportunities, as I summarize in Chapter 5. Some of the disappointments were on issues that were long-standing goals of child advocates, such as improving child care quality, implementing paid parental leave, and strengthening family support policies. Some of the greatest wins have been on issues in which new advocates were recruited to the children's cause, such as the Pew Charitable Trusts, which conducted a savvy, strategic ten-year campaign for prekindergarten education.[41] Meaningful improvements in prenatal and pediatric health care were achieved through passage of the Affordable Care Act, a longstanding Democratic party priority. These efforts were led by individuals and groups who were not typically identified as child advocates.

From the beginning of the brain development revolution, advocacy on children's issues followed closely the messaging about brain development. The writers of the *Starting Points* report and the organizers of *I Am Your Child* campaign had clear policy objectives that they believed followed naturally from greater public understanding of early brain development, and they incorporated these policy objectives into their messaging about the developing brain. These included improvements in child care, paid parental leave, child health coverage, and family support. The integration of scientific messaging with policy advocacy continued through subsequent initiatives, such as the work of the Committee on Integrating the Science of Early Childhood Development, the arguments of the economists concerning early childhood investments, the Pew campaign for prekindergarten education, and the National Scientific Council on the Developing Child.

I have suggested that child advocates' belief that these policy objectives followed directly from the brain development story may have caused them to overlook the difficult political work that was required in order to advance these proposals with the public and policymakers. Careful, persistent attention to advocacy was essential because few of these policy goals were simple or noncontroversial. Claiming that early brain development mandated improvements in child care quality or paid parental leave or improved family support was fine as far as these claims went, but they often failed to answer the more challenging questions. Is the mandate for affordable, high-quality child care a public responsibility (if so, how: through market incentives? family subsidies? direct regulations?), a business responsibility (if so, what incentives would cause businesses to provide employee child care?), or a private responsibility (if so, how to strengthen the market in which parents seek services?). How should paid parental leave be funded: from businesses, a public subsidy to parents, redirected retirement or Social Security earnings, or something else? Who is responsible for scaling up the training infrastructure to significantly improve early childhood mental health services?

In each of these policy areas and others, the nature of campaign journalism was inadequate for clarifying these issues and creating a concerted policy advocacy agenda. Campaign journalism was excellent for generating media momentum behind the news of developmental brain science and its implications, but it was insufficient for the sustained public support needed to change policies concerning children, especially for complex and controversial issues like these. And there was no alternative platform for messaging a more persuasive policy argument that considered the value choices, financial considerations, implementation complexities, downstream consequences, or other policy dimensions of these proposals. Consequently, after engaging an interested public in the story of early brain development, it proved more difficult than expected to confer that engagement to the public policy implications that were, to child advocates, self-evident in developmental neuroscience.

The challenging questions entailed in the policy proposals emerging from the brain development revolution were challenging because they were matters not just of developmental science but also of social values. Values figure prominently in our thinking about children, of course, so it is unsurprising that values figure prominently in these issues as well. There are some bedrock values about children that are widely shared: that children deserve protection and care, that adults are responsible for providing them, and that special support is required for the children in greatest difficulty. Beyond these, however, are other values that orient policy choices addressing children's needs about which there is greater disagreement. What is the capacity of government action to improve families or support children? Where does private responsibility for children's welfare end and public responsibility begin? When should government agencies step in to fulfill responsibilities for children's well-being that private incentives (such as through parental or business incentives) have failed to achieve? Who bears the costs for assisting children with developmental or mental health problems? Does this have implications for the responsibility for prevention? The answers to questions like these are often implicit in the policy proposals of child advocates, and the argument that these proposals are "based on the science" obscures the inability of science to determine value choices like these. That is not what science does; instead, it is what the political process does. The political process was required in the initial planning and subsequent decisions of the California First 5 county commissions, for example, as commissioners from blue and red regions had to compromise to decide on values underlying funding priorities (e.g., are funds best used for broadening access, strengthening quality, or addressing unmet need?). But for other issues and contexts, it is difficult to perceive much evidence of a broad political discussion about how to best achieve the worthwhile goals for children that had been highlighted by the brain development messaging. Assumptions about the best means for achieving these goals were instead often implicit in the policy proposals of child advocates.

By distinguishing more clearly the scientific claims about early brain development from specific policy proposals, child advocates might have opened the door to creating broader coalitions of support for children's initiatives by recognizing that there are alternative avenues for following the science involving different value preferences.[42] Families with young children need greater financial resources to support the care of their young children, for example, and there are various proposals for doing so (e.g., an expanded child tax credit, an advance on future tax credits or other earnings[43]) whether families devote the funds to child care or to supporting a parent remaining at home to care for a young child. Even when the science is clear and unmistakable, there can be diverse policy implications that reflect the diverse value preferences of a pluralistic society. Distinguishing the conclusions of developmental brain science from how those conclusions should be acted on might also have prompted child advocates to prepare better for the hard political work involved in advancing the policies needed to support young children. In an increasingly polarized political environment, establishing common ground around basic conclusions from science and respecting the alternative policy directions to which they can lead might be the start to creating biipartisan coalitions of support around children.

In addition, distinguishing the developmental science from its policy implications might have softened the overpromising that was also a consistent characteristic of the brain development campaign. Having to better justify the expectation that early interventions would lead to improvements in high school graduation rates, teenage pregnancy prevention, adult workforce productivity, and other long-term outcomes might have caused child advocates to focus instead on the nearer-term results of these interventions that were better supported by research and were more realistic. In the end, the children's cause may not have been helped much by such overpromising. Legislators hear these promises of long-term benefits, often framed in benefit-cost estimates, from many other advocates, and there is evidence that they tend to discount these claims because of the inherent indeterminacy of estimating benefits years in the future (not to mention their need for benefits to appear before their next reelection campaign). Not even the business leaders of ReadyNation seemed to believe these claims enough to incorporate support for early education programs or on-site child care or paid parental leave into their own business practices (even though they advocated for public support of these proposals with government leaders). Rather than strengthening their policy arguments, overpromising may simply have caused child advocates to be perceived as making unrealistic claims based on the brain science.

The developmental story that is warranted by developmental science and the intervention studies is not that the right early experiences will necessarily have lifelong benefits. It is rather that high-quality, evidence-based interventions can make a difference, but that children's healthy development requires support throughout childhood in developmentally appropriate programs and practices supported by a society that makes healthy children a high priority. Such an argument is not as compelling as the view that early childhood investments will alone lead children to graduation and good jobs. It is just true.

Throughout this book, I have described the wins (and losses) of the brain development revolution for children's policy, but I should not close without considering the long view. Just as I described earlier in this chapter how the revolution led to enduring changes in how people think about early childhood, it has also contributed to changes in the policymaking world.

- A serious discussion of educational achievement cannot occur without consideration of young children's learning experiences prior to school entry and how those experiences prepare the child for school achievement. Prekindergarten preparation is increasingly regarded as desirable, even necessary, and it is now impossible to consider the children who are most at risk of academic underachievement without identifying the early childhood programs that might benefit them.
- The work of economists like Heckman, Rolnick, Grunewald, and Barnett has ushered in a systematic quantitative argument for early childhood programs that did not previously exist in psychology or

economics. They brought data to the table on return of investment in support of early childhood programs and challenged the advocates for other public investments (sports stadiums, anyone?) to provide comparable evidence. The field of labor economics has supplemented older models of human capital development to put new and unprecedented emphasis on early childhood development, and this paradigm shift has spurred new thinking within economics about the early origins of workforce development.[44]

• Meanwhile, the brain development revolution was a forerunner of a growing movement in the federal government to use data to document the efficacy of social programs and argue for their funding. This movement in domestic policy gathered steam during the George W. Bush presidency and flourished during Barak Obama's presidential terms, and it was manifested in the use of evidence-based evaluations to establish funding priorities for home visitation programs, adolescent pregnancy prevention programs, and many other domestic initiatives.[45]

• Finally, it is becoming increasingly ordinary to view early childhood investments as a significant avenue to improving children's lives, whether through the child care subsidies, universal prekindergarten, paid family leave, or an expanded child tax credit, all of which have been included in major domestic policy initiatives of the Biden administration.

In these and other ways, young children have a place in the fabric of American social policy that did not exist before public attention was focused on early brain development. The policy achievements that the brain development revolution helped to advance are likely to continue to reverberate in American domestic policy for quite some time.

But in the spirit of the social reformers at the turn of the twentieth century, I do not believe this is enough. We have embraced the Progressives' conviction that scientifically validated facts are an essential prerequisite to effective social action, and it has contributed to the construction of an edifice of evidence from the study of young children's developing minds and brains and its applications to programs and policies. This is a significant empirical foundation for informed public policy concerning young children.

But the social reformers of a century ago were also motivated by a moral imperative concerning the care of children. In our embrace of science, the moral imperative should not be overlooked because it underlies the values that motivate social action for children. What is our obligation to children? There are extensive literatures in philosophy, political science, and law and a UN Convention on the Rights of the Child to provide perspective on this question,[46] but they converge on the view that children have fundamental rights to care from adults that are not contingent on long-term benefits to society, return on investment, or even improving developmental outcomes. Simply stated, children's well-being is an end in itself.[47] It was this regard for children that motivated the social reformers of the nineteenth century like Charles Dickens to urge taking children from economically productive activity and putting them in schools.[48] Children rely on the solicitude of the adults who brought them into the world not just for their future but for their present welfare. We, in turn, are obligated to provide the best that we can give them. The science of developing brains, minds, and behavior serves that end.

Notes

Chapter 1

[1] Eliot 2009.

[2] H. Pellissier, "Your child's brain on technology: Television," GreatSchools, December 5, 2019. www.greatschools.org/gk/articles/child-brain-development-and-television/, retrieved May 10, 2021.

[3] T. Jablonski, "Infant probiotic: What to look for," Nestle Baby & Me, May 24, 2018. www.nestlebaby.ca/en/probiotics/what-to-look-for-in-infant-probiotic-products, retrieved May 10, 2021.

[4] Skolnick 2005.

[5] Zero to Three 2017.

[6] Watson 2011.

[7] Parker et al. 2018.

[8] Bohlander et al. 2017. I provided editorial assistance with this project.

[9] www.lumosity.com/en/, retrieved May 10, 2021.

[10] Bassok et al. 2016; see also M. Dahl 2016.

[11] Dmitrieva et al. 2007 .

[12] United States Census 2022.

[13] Sims 2017.

[14] Interview excerpt from the report of a national survey conducted by Zero to Three and the Bezos Family Foundation, National Parent Survey Report, June 6, 2016, www.zerotothree.org/resources/1425-national-parent-survey-report, retrieved October 11, 2020.

[15] This overview derives from contributions to Hwang et al. 1996.

[16] Aristotle 350 BCE.

[17] Locke 1693.

[18] Rousseau 1762.

[19] Dickens 1848.

[20] Freud 1899.

[21] Watson 1928b.

[22] Interestingly, the Industrial Revolution also set the stage for the recognition of adolescence as a distinct period of development as large numbers of youth migrated to the cities for labor, freed from family ties and constraints. See Fasick 1994.

[23] I am grateful to Carol Tavris for this insight: Tavris 1999.

[24] This early twentieth-century image from Piaget was recently reinvoked in the widely popular *The Scientist in the Crib: Minds, Brains, and How Children Learn*; Gopnik et al. 1999.

[25] Watson 1928a.

[26] A discovery resulting in large measure from John Flavell's influential *The Developmental Psychology of Jean Piaget*; Flavell 1963.

[27] Kennedy et al. 2022.

[28] Funk 2020.

[29] In references to "the science of human development," I have in mind contributions from multidisciplinary fields of inquiry into human development including developmental psychology, developmental neuroscience, developmental psychopathology, developmental behavioral genetics, molecular genetics, evolutionary biology, family sociology, and related academic disciplines.

[30] Wordsworth, "My Heart Leaps Up When I Behold."

[31] Shonkoff & Bales 2011.

[32] Shonkoff & Bales 2011.

[33] This expression was first attributed to President Harry Truman, but other politicians have also invoked this phrase; see I. Flatow, "Truth, deception, and the myth of the one-handed scientist," Humanist.com, October 18, 2012, https://thehumanist.com/magazine/november-december-2012/features/truth-deception-and-the-myth-of-the-one-handed-scientist/, retrieved May 26, 2021.

[34] Weiss & Singer 1988.

[35] Weiss and Singer did a content analysis and interviewed the journalists and social scientists who contributed to stories appearing in the *New York Times*, *Washington Post*, *Wall Street Journal*, *Newsweek*, *Time*, *U.S. News & World Report*, and on ABC, NBS, and CBS nightly news broadcasts.

[36] Caplan 1976.

[37] Thompson 1993.

[38] Weiss & Singer 1988.

[39] This term is borrowed from a 1979 study by Lindblom and Cohen that analyzed the reasons for dissatisfaction with social science as a contributor to social problem-solving, and offered several avenues by which social scientists could make their work more pertinent to the public forum; it remains an interesting and valuable read. Lindblom & Cohen 1979.

[40] This is the major finding of a national poll by the Kaiser Family Foundation conducted August 28–September 3, 2020. A. Keown, "Poll: Trust in Fauci and the CDC is declining ahead of the November election," Biospace, September 11, 2020, www.biospace.com/article/poll-finds-trust-in-fauci-and-the-cdc-is-declining-ahead-of-the-november-election/, retrieved October 28, 2020.

[41] Including different formal and informal avenues for the communication of science to relevant audiences, the influence of business and industry groups, and many other factors; for an illustration, consult Gough 2003.

Chapter 2

[1] *Atkins v. Virginia*, 536 U.S. 302 (2002).

[2] *Roper v. Simmons*, 543 U.S. 551 (2005).

[3] *Stanford v. Kentucky*, 492 U.S. 361 (1989).

[4] *Roper v. Simmons*, 543 U.S. 551 (2005), at 19.

[5] American Psychological Association 2004.

[6] Oral arguments for *Roper v. Simmons*, 543 U.S. 552 (2005). www.oyez.org/cases/2004/03-633, retrieved November 11, 2021. One has to feel a bit sympathetic with the unpolished discourse revealed in these court transcripts, recognizing that at any moment the attorney might be interrupted by a penetrating question from one of the Justices, and must therefore get as much said as quickly as possible.

[7] *Hodgson v. Minnesota*, 497 U.S. 417 (1990).

[8] American Psychological Association 1989.

[9] Steinberg et al. 2009.

[10] In their analysis of the literatures prevalent during different historical periods, Enright and his colleagues concluded that during economic downturns, teenagers are typically portrayed as immature, psychologically unstable, and in need of further education, but during wartime, the psychological competence of youth who are heading into service is emphasized instead. Enright et al. 1987.

[11] Wolfe & Mash 2006.

[12] Maroney 2013.

[13] Steinberg 2011.

[14] Racine et al. 2005.

[15] McCabe & Castel 2008.

[16] Weisberg et al. 2008.

[17] Michael et al. 2013.

[18] Steinberg 2011, p. 17.

[19] This statement is attributed to Marvin Minsky (1927–2016), an American cognitive and computer scientist who was one of the pioneers of artificial intelligence, a recipient of the 1969 Turing Award, and an advisor on Stanley Kubrick's movie *2001: A Space Odyssey*.

[20] There are various definitions of neuroessentialism in the literature, and they are not always in harmony. This is my best distillation, with reliance on Reiner 2011.

[21] Leong et al. 2020.

[22] Leong et al. 2020, p. 27731.

[23] Schachter & Addis 2007.

[24] Do et al. 2020.

[25] Mulders et al. 2018.

[26] For an excellent recent review of this research, see Heyes & Catmur 2022.

[27] See, e.g., Schmidt et al. 2021.

[28] See Blakemore 2012 and Mills et al. 2014.

29 They include the medial prefrontal cortex (medial Broadmann Area 10), temporoparietal junction, posterior superior temporal sulvus, and anterior temporal cortex, although the precuneus is sometimes also included in this network.

30 Mentalizing is associated with the growth of theory of mind discussed in Chapter 3.

31 Becht et al. 2021.

32 Lindquist et al. 2012.

33 See Barrett 2009 for a thoughtful, provocative expression of this view.

34 For a thought-provoking early study of emotion and culture, see Lutz 1988.

35 Lewin 1943.

36 Hilary Rose and Steven Rose make a similar point in their 2016 book. But for an alternative view, see Johnson 2013. Johnson does not disagree with my claim that neuroscience is atheoretical, but rather argues that research in this field is guided by a set of broader frameworks of assumptions that lack the systematic quality of a formal theory. I wouldn't disagree.

37 It is worth noting that neuroscience is not alone in its atheoreticality. Indeed, much of contemporary psychological science is less driven by theory than by cumulative empirical findings as researchers today are interested in allowing the dataset to speak for itself independently of a theoretical lens. There are strengths as well as weaknesses to this current orientation, discussion of which is left for another day.

38 This was the study described earlier in this chapter on adolescent brain maturation and developing friendship.

39 Alexander & Brown 2011.

40 Smith et al. 2018.

41 Euston et al. 2012.

42 Jobson et al. 2021.

43 I invite readers to do their own web search of different brain structures of interest to see how diverse are the descriptions of the functions in different empirical studies.

44 Poldrack 2011.

45 Poldrack 2011 has additional proposals for managing problems of reverse inference.

46 One way it does so is through epigenetics, an important and rapidly growing field of science describing the impact of experience on gene expression. A discussion of epigenetics is beyond the scope of this chapter, or this book, but it will increasingly shape our understanding of the intersection of heredity and environment in the years to come.

47 Childhood poverty is one of the most well-documented harms for brain development. For a paper that is representative of a vast research literature, consult Evans et al. 2012.

48 Among the more interesting examples of this are studies of London cab drivers, whose memorization of intricate street routes has been found to be associated with enhanced hippocampal development, and who are now being studied to

determine whether this can contribute to developing diagnostics for Alzheimer's disease, which is characterized by diminishing hippocampus size and function as well as memory impairments. Taxi Brains Project, Spiers Lab, https://spierslab.com/taxi-brains-project/, retrieved January 6, 2021.

49 Hines 2020. But also see Eliot et al. 2021.
50 Mulders et al. 2018.
51 Ironically, dualism is inconsistent with neuroessentialism (in case you were wondering). Rather, neuroessentialist thinking is more consistent with materialism, which I described earlier as the view that physical matter (in this case, the brain) is the fundamental reality to all things. The irony is that neuroessentialist thinking tends to fundamentally divide brain (biological) and mind (psychological) in a manner that accords with dualistic ideas. Despite the fact that most scientists are materialists, dualistic thinking tends to endure, especially in psychology, and this will be apparent in Chapter 3.
52 Monterosso et al. 2005.
53 Aono 2019.
54 Monterosso & Schwartz 2012.
55 Schwartz & Beyette 1996.
56 Lesher 1997.
57 Chen & Chen 2017.
58 Buchanan & Hughes 2009.
59 Qu et al. 2020.
60 Qu et al. 2018.
61 Qu et al. 2018, p. 774.
62 Telzer et al. 2013.
63 Qu et al. 2020.
64 Casey et al. 2011; Steinberg 2010.
65 For a review of the model and a review of research, consult Shulman et al. 2016.
66 Shulman et al. 2016.
67 Shulman et al. 2016, p. 113.
68 Jessor et al. 2003; Lansford et al. 2020.
69 Qu et al. 2020.
70 See, e.g., Luciana 2013.
71 American Psychological Association 2004.
72 Romer 2010.
73 Bjork & Pardini 2015.
74 Moffitt 2006.
75 Steinberg 2020, pp. 365–366. This conclusion is shared by other authorities on adolescent development; see, e.g., Coleman 2011.
76 Committee on the Science of Adolescence, Board on Children, Youth, and Families 2011.
77 This is perhaps why some adults experience a midlife crisis when they divorce, make career changes, lose friends and familiar social networks, take a new lover, or relocate during a life transition.

[78] For an important critique of the dual-systems model and the proposal of an alternative experience-driven model of the growth of adolescent decision-making, see Romer et al. 2017.

[79] Examples from relevant studies include a modified version of the Iowa Gambling Task (four decks of cards appear on a screen, with the ability to draw cards from each deck yielding game money rewards or losses, with reward orientation measured by the frequency of drawing from decks providing rewards), the Stoplight game (a simulated driving game with the goal of reaching a destination as quickly as possible, passing through intersections marked with traffic signals, with risk behavior indexed by the number of intersections passed without stopping), and the familiar Stroop task (identifying as quickly as possible the color of the text of words appearing on a screen, when some of the words name colors that are different from the color of the text, with self-regulation indexed by the number of correct responses). These examples are drawn from Steinberg et al. 2018 and Steinberg et al. 2008.

[80] Christopher Lee Simmons, Murderpedia, https://murderpedia.org/male.S/s/simmons-christopher.htm, retrieved January 16, 2022.

[81] Choudhury et al. 2012.

[82] Collins 1990.

[83] Monterosso et al. 2005.

[84] However, biological causes also led to perceptions that the person's behavior was less susceptible to deterrence or treatment.

[85] Johnson et al. 2009.

[86] *Graham v. Florida*, 560 U.S. 48 (2010).

[87] *Miller v. Alabama*, 567 U.S. 460 (2012).

[88] *Montgomery v. Louisiana*, 577 U.S. __ (2016).

[89] *Jones v. Mississippi*, 593 U.S. __ (2021).

[90] Bonnie & Scott 2013; Maroney 2013; Shen 2013.

[91] Geldhof et al. 2015.

[92] I should add that this is not a chapter about whether adolescent defendants should be treated more protectively than adults, a topic that involves more than the developmental status of the adolescent brain. My own view is that while courts should undertake the kinds of individualized determinations of culpability that the *Roper* court avoided, the orientation toward justice should always be allayed with mercy.

[93] Furthermore, there are some (such as Bruner 1986) who argue that developmental science is itself a value-laden enterprise that takes cues from the culture about the developmental outcomes that are normative and valued.

Chapter 3

[1] This highly condensed, brief overview of the neurobiology of brain development cannot substitute for a more detailed and systematic presentation of the research in this area, which is beyond the scope of this book. For that,

I recommend Stiles 2008, and, for more focused coverage, Johnson & De Haan 2015 and Nelson et al. 2006. For a thought-provoking, condensed summary, consult Grigorenko 2017.

[2] Dekaban & Sadowsky 1978.

[3] Cowan 1979.

[4] Eriksson et al. 1998.

[5] Gould et al. 1999.

[6] Erickson 2011.

[7] Schoenfeld & Gould 2012.

[8] Baptista & Andrade 2018.

[9] Huttenlocher & Dabholkar 1997.

[10] It is a densely packed organ also because the young brain produces significantly more neurons (as well as synapses) than it will retain at maturity, so pro-grammed neuronal cell death (apoptosis) during the same period eliminates excess neurons from the brain.

[11] Patoine 2005.

[12] Kolb 1989 analogizes this aspect of early brain development to how a sculptor creates a statue. The sculptor might assemble the statue by attaching small pieces of marble together, which would be analogous to the brain's growth if the brain progressively built up synaptic networks from the ground up. Instead, the sculptor might chisel a block of marble down to the appropriate configuration. This is a better analogy to how the brain initially overproduces synapses (i.e., the large block of marble) and subsequently refines it down (or sculpts it) through experience.

[13] Huttenlocher & Dabholkar 1997.

[14] Johnson & de Haan 2015.

[15] Grigorenko 2017.

[16] An important and continuing task for developmental neuroscience is further specifying the kinds of experiences on which the genetic program of brain development relies. Beyond basic sensory experiences, for example, how important are the social experiences that come from nurturant care, such as stress buffering, opportunities to explore in safe environments, or trust in other people that contribute to the growth of essential cognitive skills?

[17] A pseudonym bestowed by those who worked with her.

[18] For an evocative account of Genie's story, see Rymer 1994.

[19] Johnson & de Haan 2015 provide an excellent and more detailed discussion of research concerning each of these topics, and more.

[20] Nelson & Webb 2003.

[21] In these tasks, infants are repeatedly shown a sequence of lights on a screen; implicit learning is demonstrated when they spontaneously anticipate the next location where a light will appear without any evidence of having a conscious memory of the sequence.

[22] Rivera-Gaxiola et al. 2005.

[23] Mills et al. 1993.

[24] In behavioral studies, these and other aspects of self-regulation are called executive functions. They will be discussed later in this chapter.

[25] This is known as the classic "A not B" task created by Piaget to study the infant's understanding of object permanence. An object is hidden several times at one location (A) and the infant is allowed to retrieve it each time. Next, the object is hidden in an adjacent location (B) while the infant watches. Now the infant is allowed to retrieve the object. Piaget discovered, and later researchers have confirmed, that younger infants persist in searching for the object at A, and it is not until around eight months of age that they search at B if they are allowed to do so immediately. With increasing age, infants manage to search correctly over longer delays.

[26] Casey, Trainor, Orendi, et al. 1997.

[27] Casey, Trainor, Giedd, et al. 1997.

[28] This is, like the overview of developmental neuroscience, brief and highly condensed. For those who are interested in more extended coverage, I recommend a good, current textbook in developmental psychology – which tend to come in child/adolescence and lifespan versions. The texts by John Santrock are excellent, such as Santrock 2021.

[29] Representative of the yield of this reexamination of early thinking in the 1970s was the influential volume entitled, ironically, "the competent infant"; Stone et al. 1974.

[30] Gibson & Walker 1984

[31] For a good review, see Spelke 1990.

[32] Wood & Spelke 2005; Wynn 1992.

[33] Kim & Spelke 1992, 1999.

[34] Cohen & Oakes 1993.

[35] Spelke & Kinzler 2007.

[36] Chomsky 1968.

[37] Werker & Polka 1993.

[38] De Boysson-Bardies 1989.

[39] Saffran & Kirkham 2018.

[40] Carey 1978.

[41] Poulin-Dubois et al. 1996.

[42] Wellman & Gelman 1992.

[43] Gelman 2009.

[44] Gelman 2005.

[45] For an example of these clever studies, see Gelman & Wellman 1991.

[46] As an illustration (and with one of the cleverest titles of a research report): Taylor et al. 2009 (titled "Boys will be boys; cows will be cows: Children's essentialist reasoning about gender categories and animal species").

[47] *Men Are from Mars, Women Are from Venus*, the early 2000s best-seller, reflects the same kind of essentialist mindset observed in children.

[48] Gelman 2009.

[49] Bauer 2013.

[50] Aguiar & Baillargeon 1998.

51 Xu & Garcia 2008.
52 Stahl & Feigenson 2015.
53 Munakata et al. 2012.
54 Müller & Kerns 2015.
55 Lieberman et al. 2017.
56 This same-race discrimination is weaker when infants are living in multiracial contexts.
57 An important exception to orienting toward people who share the same characteristics with the infant is gender: male and female infants both look longer at women over men.
58 Rhodes & Baron 2019.
59 It is not apparent, at least in early childhood, that they have a negative bias against outgroup members. Rather, they simply prefer members of their own group.
60 Wellman 2015.
61 Repacholi & Gopnik 1997.
62 As Alison Gopnik has noted, even in Berkeley (where the research was conducted), toddlers prefer goldfish crackers to broccoli.
63 Wellman 2015.
64 Brink et al. 2015; Hughes & Leekham 2004.
65 This is called "mental state language," and it can be observed when the adult talks about how another person thinks, feels, or is motivated, or about the adult's or child's own feelings or desires, such as in the context of storybook reading.
66 Skinner et al. 2020.
67 Meins 2013.
68 Kuhl et al. 2003.
69 Hirsh-Pasek et al. 2015.
70 Wang et al. 2015.
71 Kopp & Lindenberger 2011.
72 Gelman et al. 2014.
73 Moriguchi 2014.
74 Tomasello 2016.
75 Meltzoff 1995.
76 Butler & Markman 2012.
77 Butler & Walton 2013.
78 Gaskins et al. 2017.
79 Thompson 2014b.
80 Bachleda & Thompson 2018; Thompson 2001a.
81 Alison Gopnik argues that infants are thus "more conscious" than are adults; see Gopnik 2009.
82 This is important to the applications of developmental neuroscience to public policy, as illustrated in Chapter 2; see Thompson 2012.
83 Gweon & Saxe 2013.
84 Lany & Saffran 2013.

85 Ghetti & Fandakova 2020.
86 Buss 2015; Fodor 1983; Marcus 2004.
87 I should acknowledge that neuroscientists use the term "brain modules" in describing neurocircuitry, but this term has a different meaning from the concept of mental modules used in developmental psychology (and, for that matter, philosophy).
88 This view of development is classically expressed in Heinz Werner's famous orthogenetic principle: "whenever development occurs it proceeds from a state of relative globality and lack of differentiation to a state of increasing differentiation, articulation, and hierarchic integration," which was initially described in Werner 1940.
89 Elman et al. 1996; see also Hernandez et al. 2019.
90 Postle 2006.
91 Sterck 2010.
92 In psychology, consciousness is also seen as an emergent function derived from (but not reducible to) a variety of mental constituents.
93 To be fair, developmental scientists also find it challenging to study children's conceptual change through mental disequilibrium in real time.
94 Wagmiller & Adelman 2009.
95 Duncan et al. 2010.
96 Data from Current Population Reports of the US Census Bureau, www .census.gov/data/tables/time-series/demo/income-poverty/cps-pov/pov-01 .html, retrieved April 7, 2022.
97 Brooks-Gunn & Duncan 1997.
98 This is a good place to acknowledge that not all families experience the multisystemic stressors associated with economic adversity, and not all children living in such families experience the physical and mental health outcomes described here. Like all psychological research, these descriptions are generalizations based on research studies that also document the variability of outcomes for these children. The findings described in this section indicate, however, that the conditions associated with poverty have significant consequences for a large proportion of the children who experience them.
99 Conger et al. 2012.
100 Brito & Noble 2014.
101 Hair et al. 2015.
102 Evans & Kim 2013.
103 Hanson et al. 2013.
104 In Chapter 2, I briefly discussed the biological embedding of experience in the developing brain and other biological systems, and indicated (in note 46) that epigenetic processes may be partly responsible. Epigenetics describes how environmental influences can alter gene expression without changing underlying DNA, and it is significantly changing scientific understanding of the interaction of heredity and environment. There is growing evidence that the effects of poverty on children's development may arise, in part, through

epigenetic effects on gene expression, which is another illustration of the biological embedding of experience (in this case, poverty).

[105] Thompson & Haskins 2014.
[106] Troller-Renfree et al. 2022.
[107] Steiner 2020.
[108] Cusick & Georgieff 2016.
[109] Seifer & Parade 2020.
[110] Lumey et al. 2007.
[111] Schulz 2010.
[112] Gluckman & Hanson 2005.
[113] Dunkel Schetter & Tanner 2012.
[114] Monk et al. 2019.
[115] Posner et al. 2016.
[116] Davis & Thompson 2014.
[117] O'Donnell et al., 2014.
[118] Thompson 2014b.
[119] Olds et al. 2007.
[120] Sisk 2017. This author reminds us that traditionally, adolescent impulsivity and poor responsibility were attributed to "raging hormones." Now developmental neuroscience "marries raging hormones with the haywire prefrontal cortex" in these explanations.
[121] Larsen & Luna 2018.
[122] Byrne et al. 2017.
[123] Goddings et al. 2019; Vijayakumar et al. 2018.
[124] Blakemore & Mills 2014.
[125] Dai & Scherb 2019.
[126] Dahl et al. 2018.
[127] Morimoto et al. 2019.
[128] Wang et al. 2018.
[129] Duti et al. 2018.

Chapter 4

[1] Thompson 2001b; Thompson & Nelson 2001.
[2] Rose & Rose 2016.
[3] The series was subsequently reprinted in Kotulak 1996.
[4] To his credit, Kotulak's series devotes attention to the influence of neurotransmitters, genes, and alcohol on violent conduct; considers brain plasticity and repair; and even has some words about brain aging.
[5] Carnegie Task Force on Meeting the Needs of Young Children 1994.
[6] Mann 1994.
[7] There is an interesting irony in Reiner's treatment by a Kleinian psychotherapist. Kleinian therapy is noteworthy for its emphasis on the child's unconscious fantasy life as the primary influence on psychological development,

much more influential than the child's genuine experiences with other people. The founder of attachment theory, John Bowlby, had been trained and mentored by Melanie Klein, but he made a dramatic break with her over this issue because he felt that the security that young children actually experience, not fantasize, is most important. The irony is that attachment theory is a significant contributor both to Reiner's views of the importance of the first three years and to the encouragement of the *I Am Your Child* campaign that parents nurture and provide emotional support to their young children. Reiner's sister, Annie Reiner, is a well-known Kleinian psychotherapist who also encouraged his reflections on his early childhood experiences. Reiner appears to have combined a focus on early childhood from Kleinian theory with an emphasis on parental nurturance from attachment theory in his thinking about the needs of young children.

[8] This account of the development of the *I Am Your Child* campaign draws from original interviews I conducted with some of the principals in the years immediately following the campaign's launch, including Michael Levine, Ellen Galinsky, Meg Bostrom, and Nina Sazer O'Donnell, along with conversations with Sharon Begley. I also drew on a 1997 report to funders of the *I Am Your Child* campaign, and a written 2001 report by Michael Levine (then executive director of the I Am Your Child Foundation) to the Ewing Marion Kauffman Foundation. My initial account of the development of the campaign was published as Thompson 1998 (which is no longer available). The most helpful reporting I have found of the campaign is from the *Los Angeles Times*, in particular, Smith 1998 and Adato 2002. See also Bruer 1999 and Tabor 1997.

[9] The campaign appropriated a 1970s Barry Manilow song of the same name as its theme music.

[10] These included the Irving Harris Foundation, the Charles A. Dana Foundation, and the Robert R. McCormick Tribune Foundation.

[11] Shore 1997.

[12] L. Jacobson, "What did California's novel approach to funding early-childhood programs achieve?," K-12 Dive, October 9, 2018, www.k12dive .com/news/what-did-californias-novel-approach-to-funding-early-childhood-programs-ac/532191/, retrieved May 26, 2022.

[13] Clinton 1996.

[14] Klein 1997.

[15] White House Conference on Early Childhood Development, https://clinton .presidentiallibraries.us/items/show/2812, retrieved April 29, 2022.

[16] One speaker talked about child care concerns, bypassing both the "tough question" raised in *Rethinking the Brain* about whether mothers should remain at home and the equally tough question of how a concern with child care quality squared with the administration's recently passed welfare reform law that capped benefits and required recipients to return to work.

[17] The broadcast was repeated by ABC on August 17.

[18] On a mock *Jeopardy* show, for example, Alex Trebek posed the answer prompt to Rosie O'Donnell: "In the first three years of a baby's brain development, trillions of these connections form the physical maps that govern, among other things, emotional stability and human attachment but, if not made, will severely restrict that child's capacity to successfully integrate into society," to which she replied to this clearly non-*Jeopardy* type of question with the answer: "What are synapses?"

[19] Zero to Three 1997. Also see Parents unsure on emotional upbringing, UPI, April 17, 1997, www.upi.com/Archives/1997/04/17/Parents-unsure-on-emotional-upbringing/2037861249600/, retrieved April 29, 2022.

[20] Quoted in Bruer 1997, p. 52.

[21] Bower 1997.

[22] Epstein 1997.

[23] Duerksen 1997.

[24] Beck 1997.

[25] Parker 1997.

[26] Nash 1997, pp. 48–56 ("the day-care dilemma" appears on pp. 58–62).

[27] Begley 1996.

[28] Greenough 1997.

[29] Thompson & Nelson 2001.

[30] Bruer 1997.

[31] Bruer 1999.

[32] Boldt 1999.

[33] Charen 1999.

[34] White House Conference on Early Childhood Development (see n. 15).

[35] Interestingly, while Bruer cites my research as showing that early attachments do not have lifelong consequences (contra "the first years last forever"), this is a different argument from my own conclusion that early attachments, while not determinative, nevertheless predispose the child to important social and personality outcomes, a conclusion I wrote in 1996 and which remains true today.

[36] See, e.g., Nachmias et al. 1996.

[37] Gopnik et al. 1999.

[38] *The Scientist in the Crib* also illustrated how difficult it is for developmental neuroscientists to model the effects of children's own thinking on their cognitive growth, which I described in Chapter 3, because of the limits of neuroimaging to capture this self-organizing feature of cognitive development.

[39] Readers will recognize that this view of the child's active role in their own development was also discussed in Chapter 3 as one of the orientations of developmental scientists that is not easily conceptualized and measured in developmental neuroscience.

[40] White House Conference on Early Childhood Development (see n. 15).

[41] The most relevant research report from this project published at the time of the White House Conference is NICHD Early Child Care Research Network 1997.

42 The NICHD study described here was originally designed to follow the sample for three years, which would provide enough time to address questions of the immediate developmental impact of child care experience. It was subsequently extended for three additional longitudinal phases to address an expanding series of questions, and, through additional sources of funding, the sample has now been studied through early adulthood. Because of its long-term scope and diversity of measures, it has become a scientific treasure for developmental researchers.

43 Harris 1998.

44 Begley 1998; the cover asked, "Do Parents Matter?"

45 Gladwell 1998.

46 I was a member of the committee, and much of this account is drawn from my notes and recollections of the committee's work.

47 My thanks to Brian Riley, a graduate student in one of my seminars at UC Davis, for contacting Hyman and confirming my recollection of this remark.

48 National Research Council and Institute of Medicine 2000.

49 All quoted material is taken from the Executive Summary of the report.

50 This quote comes from early in chapter 8, "The Developing Brain."

51 This is from the Executive Summary of *From Neurons to Neighborhoods*.

52 National Research Council 2012.

53 Lindblom & Cohen 1979.

54 In human children, sadly, developmental dysfunction can arise from gross deprivation or abuse (think of Genie in the preceding chapter, who was denied human warmth and language for her first thirteen years). Moreover, many of the developmental outcomes that people care most about – cognitive achievement, self-regulatory skills, positive social skills, good physical and mental health – are profoundly affected by the multifaceted challenges of poverty and its enduring effects on children in their families, neighborhoods, and schools, as discussed in Chapter 3. Even in these difficult conditions, however, negative developmental outcomes are more probable but still uncertain in light of the variety of sources of developmental resilience within and surrounding the child. This is part of what makes the study of behavioral development so interesting but its prediction to developmental outcomes so contingent and indeterminate.

55 Giffin & Mitchell 1978. See also Bruer 1999.

56 Recall also the discussion of developmental cultural neuroscience in Chapter 3, which indicates that culture plays a role in the developing brain as well as in thinking and behavior.

57 Teaching at a public research university on the West Coast with substantial numbers of students from other cultures, I have learned that sometimes I have to painstakingly explain the meaning of this and other American folk aphorisms that contain elements of human wisdom, since they are not necessarily familiar to students growing up in other cultures (who have their own sayings about children's development).

58 Kagan 1998.

59 As discussed in Chapter 2, cultural beliefs about adolescence likewise condition acceptance of messages about the behavior and development of teenagers, as illustrated by the ready acceptance by Americans of narratives of troubled, impulsive, sensation-seeking youth, consistent with Americans' beliefs about adolescence. Narratives of competent, self-regulated youth preparing for the future would be more accepted among the Chinese, whose stereotypes of adolescence are more positive and constructive. As discussed in Chapter 3, the developmental science may be more consistent with the Chinese portrayal than the American one.

60 Bruner 1986.

61 Importantly, media coverage of the Columbine High shootings in April 1999 turned to the brain development research in adolescence as one avenue to explaining the violent tendencies observed in its perpetrators. But this coverage occurred two years after the *I Am Your Child* campaign.

62 Perhaps to counter this tendency, when speakers like Donald Cohen and Barry Brazelton at the White House Conference on Early Childhood Development and Learning spoke about young children in troubled families, the parents in these examples were consistently presented as well meaning but lacking necessary support and resources. The same was true of the profiles of programs to assist parents presented in the ABC special produced by Reiner.

63 See Rose & Rose 2016 for insightful arguments on this matter.

Chapter 5

1 Speech of Governor Zell Miller of Georgia to the General Assembly on January 13, 1998, with his message detailing his 1999 budget recommendations. It was sent to me on April 31 of that year by Scott Frederking, Coordinator of Human Development.

2 Because the "Mozart effect" has assumed the status of a "scientific legend" (Bangerter & Heath 2004) and I still encounter people who believe in it, I should point out that it was based on a small 1993 study of the effects of listening to Mozart on the short-term reasoning skills of college students, not the brain development of young children. The conclusion of an authoritative review of nearly forty well-controlled studies of the Mozart effect is summarized in its title: "Mozart Effect – Schmozart Effect" (Pietschnig et al. 2010). The evidence has simply not confirmed that such an effect exists. Nevertheless, at the time of the *I Am Your Child* campaign, the idea that the rhythms of classical music and the counting in notational structure could stimulate brain growth related to the processing of logical patterns and spatial-temporal reasoning was one of the themes of Katie Couric's *Today* show series in April 1997 and other discussions of the early experiences provocative of brain development – including Governor Miller's innovative proposal to the Georgia legislature.

3 State of Florida Senate Bill 660, May 21, 1998.

4 Karoly et al. 1998.
5 Knitzer & Adely 2001.
6 Levine & Smith 2001.
7 Hearing before the Subcommittee on Human Resources of the Committee on Government Reform and Oversight, House of Representatives, 105th Congress (second session), *Early Childhood Interventions: Public-Private Partnerships*, July 16, 1998, Serial No. 105-170, Washington, DC: US Government Printing Office. www.govinfo.gov/content/pkg/CHRG-105hhrg51012/pdf/CHRG-105hhrg51012.pdf, retrieved May 24, 2020.
8 National Research Council and Institute of Medicine 2000, p. 385.
9 Due to the reluctance of the Georgia legislature, the weak science underlying the Mozart effect did not have significant financial implications for the state budget. But the Walt Disney Company was not so fortunate, in 2009 having to refund consumers who purchased their Baby Einstein videos (which consisted of entertaining images and animations against a background of classical music) in response to a lawsuit that claimed that there was no scientific evidence behind Disney's claim that the videos had educational value. Lewin 2009.
10 Bruer 1997.
11 Caplan 1979; Caplan & Nelson 1973; Weiss 1978, 1980, 1987.
12 This term refers to the gradual infiltration of knowledge into people's baseline understanding, *not* the know-it-all who offends everybody by always having the right answer.
13 Lindblom & Cohen 1979; Weiss 1980.
14 I was a speaker at one of the early planning events with PBS in which PBS celebrities, such as Jim Lehrer, pledged their enthusiastic support for the brain development message.
15 Adato 2002.
16 I recognize, of course, that county commissions were also subject to political interests, horse-trading among competing priorities, pressure from county officials, and other elements of local politics – but these might have had the effect of speeding up the process of disbursing funds rather than slowing it down.
17 In situations where it appears that research provides straightforward answers to difficult choices like these, it is often because the research itself incorporates values congenial to the answers it provides.
18 A doctoral dissertation by Stephanie Reed Drake offers an insightful ethnography of the development of both First 5 California and First 5 Santa Barbara, highlighting the formal and informal influences that guided decisions concerning the strategic plan and the funding priorities adopted at the county level. Drake 2008 .
19 Rivera 2002.
20 Pyle 1999.
21 L. Jacobson, "One California county epitomizes positive impact of home visiting amid national trend," K-12Dive, October 20, 2018. www.k12dive.com/news/one-california-county-epitomizes-positive-impact-of-home-visiting-amid-nati/539055/, retrieved June 1, 2022.

22   Bodenhorn & Kelch 2001.

23   Drake 2008.

24   Emerson 2019.

25   L. Jacobson, "What did California's novel approach to funding early-childhood programs achieve?," K-12Dive, October 9, 2018. www.k12dive .com/news/what-did-californias-novel-approach-to-funding-early-childhood-programs-ac/532191/, retrieved June 1, 2022.

26   The county commissions created the First 5 Association of California soon after they began their work. The First 5 Association is a nonnprofit to provide support, information sharing, and other resources to the fifty-eight county commissions; https://first5association.org.

27   Friedman 2000.

28   Stephanie Drake's first-person interviews with the First 5 Santa Barbara county commissioners illustrates this poignantly; see Drake 2008.

29   Lest readers interpret this last comment as unfairly critical of program planners, I should point out how often program evaluations are enlisted for premature appraisals of program outcomes before the program has been fully implemented, or holding program outcomes against unduly high expectations. Both occur with distressing frequency in the outcomes- and evidence-based evaluation of promising program initiatives, leaving a sad legacy of promising interventions that have been prematurely discarded and defunded. This is especially true of human services initiatives, in which program outcomes are often difficult to measure appropriately and are affected by many influences besides those affected by the intervention. They also require time to emerge after the program begins. All of these risks applied to the kinds of programs supported by the First 5 commissions, even though some attention to program evaluation at the outset might have enabled commissioners to have more to say about the effects of Proposition 10 today.

30   Alvarez et al. 2018.

31   First 5 San Joaquin 2013.

32   I am grateful to Linda Jacobson for drawing my attention to these outcomes; Jacobson, "One California county" (see note 21).

33   Adato 2002.

34   These figures are from www.macrotrends.net/states/california/property-crime-rate-statistics, retrieved June 12, 2022, with data from *Crime in the U.S.,* Federal Bureau of Investigation, https://ucr.fbi.gov/crime-in-the-u.s.

35   Data are taken from the NAEP Data Explorer: www.nationsreportcard.gov/ndecore/xplore/nde, retrieved June 13, 2022.

36   First 5 Center for Children's Policy 2020.

37   See, e.g., Bernzweig et al. 2021 and S. Alonso, "School readiness assessment finds only 40% of children surveyed are ready for kindergarten," press release, Sonoma County Department of Health Services, April 24, 2017, www.ccfc.ca .gov/pdf/commission/meetings/handouts/Commission-Handouts_2018-04-SP/School%20Readiness%20Article.pdf, retrieved June 13, 2022.

[38] Other states include Arkansas (3% sales tax on beer for state prekindergarten programs passed in 2001) and North Carolina (North Carolina Education Lottery established in 2005 to fund early education programs among other purposes). See National Conference of State Legislatures, Early Care and Education (n.d.), *Dedicated Funding for Early Care and Education Voter Approved & Enacted Local and State Measures*, www.ncsl.org/documents/cyf/ FundingHandout_32019.pdf, retrieved September 5, 2022.

[39] Quoted in Jacobson, "What did California's novel approach" (see note 25).

[40] When some public health officials, who had been urging social distancing and other preventive measures in the wake of the COVID-19 pandemic, reversed course and justified the collective protests that erupted in the wake of the George Floyd murder – claiming that the advance in social justice warranted collective action – it constituted a significant breach in the willingness of many people to further trust the recommendations of these authorities concerning COVID.

[41] Heckman 2000.

[42] As this list of skills suggests, these capabilities are anything but "noncognitive." Social skills, self-discipline, even risk aversion require careful assessment of the predicted effects of one's actions in time. In his effort to distinguish a suite of alternative skills from those conventionally deemed "cognitive" (and often measured by intelligence or achievement testing), Heckman unfortunately chose a contrastive but very misleading term, and one that regrettably inclined toward a devaluation of these skills because they are, well, noncognitive.

[43] Heckman identified social skills and self-discipline in the 2000 paper, later adding other noncognitive skills in subsequent writing, such as Heckman 2007.

[44] Heckman 2000, p. 5

[45] See, e.g., Heckman 2008.

[46] Heckman, 2000, p. 17.

[47] Heckman 2000, p. 22.

[48] Heckman 2000, p. 20.

[49] Heckman 2000, pp. 50–51.

[50] The earliest appearance of this figure is in Carneiro & Heckman 2003, and it was subsequently published in Heckman 2004 and, in a slightly elaborated version, in Heckman 2008.

[51] In addition, further evidence may be starting to change the shape of the curve. One recent study comparing benefit to cost ratios of 248 programs for recipients ranging in age from early childhood to adulthood failed to replicate the Heckman curve (see Rea & Burton 2020). Instead, benefit-cost ratios tended to be more consistent across ages for recipients in different programs.

[52] There is also the Heckman equation: "Invest + Develop + Sustain = Gain," https://heckmanequation.org/the-heckman-equation/, retrieved June 20, 2022. Not quite as impressive as the Heckman curve, but fully consistent with the views of early childhood advocates nonetheless.

[53] Sims 2017.

[54] Allen 2011.

[55] Speaking at a conference in Anchorage about early brain development in March 2002, I heard the Alaska director of corrections, Margaret Pugh, explain why she chaired the Children's Cabinet of Governor Tony Knowles. "Basically, it is to put myself out of a job," she said.

[56] Child advocates frequently comment that this is a substantially better rate of return than investing in the stock market.

[57] Schweinhart et al. 2005.

[58] Barnett & Masse 2007; Reynolds et al. 2011.

[59] Cannon et al. 2017; Dalziel et al. 2015.

[60] Duncan & Magnuson 2013; McCoy et al. 2017.

[61] Duncan & Magnuson 2013, pp. 109–110.

[62] See Bartik 2011, however, for an unusually detailed (and thoughtful) analysis of the potential economic benefits that may accrue at the local level.

[63] Heckman 2006.

[64] They provide the greatest contribution to benefit-cost calculations; Phillips et al. 2017.

[65] Rolnick & Grunewald 2003.

[66] For a complete presentation of Rolnick and Grunewald's proposal, see www .minneapolisfed.org/article/2005/early-childhood-development-on-a-large-scale.

[67] There was also an infant program focused on parental mentoring alone.

[68] Gaylor et al. 2011.

[69] Minnesota Department of Education, *Early Learning Scholarships Program*, 2022, https://education.mn.gov/MDE/fam/elsprog/elschol/index .htm retrieved July 5, 2022.

[70] The 2021 edition of the *State of Preschool Yearbook* can be found at https:// nieer.org/wp-content/uploads/2022/04/YB2021_Full_Report.pdf.

[71] Other quality indicators include specialized training for teachers in early childhood education or child development, at least fifteen hours of annual in-service training for staff, and vision, hearing, and health screenings of children, together with referrals when warranted.

[72] Friedman-Kraus et al. 2022, p. 27.

[73] See note 2.

[74] As I pointed out in note 9, in 2009 Disney had to acknowledge the lack of scientific evidence for the Mozart effect in the failure of their products to improve cognitive and language skills, and it provided refunds to consumers who had purchased Baby Einstein products. Lewin 2009.

[75] See Byrnes 2007 for a critique of these and other wayward early applications of developmental neuroscience to education. For an expanded but somewhat earlier treatment, see Byrnes 2001.

[76] See, e.g., Temple et al. 2003.

[77] Blakemore & Frith 2005a. For a summary of their primary arguments, see Blakemore & Frith 2005b.

[78] Royal Society 2011.

[79] I am grateful to Rose & Rose 2016 for noting this.

[80] Suskind & Denworth 2022.

[81] An important exception, as noted earlier, are the implications of developmental neuroscience for therapeutic intervention, especially in the case of speech and language disorders, where there have been innovative and creative brain-based therapies developed.

[82] Bruer 1997.

[83] www.SantiagoDeclaration.org.

[84] Beginning with the National Commission on Excellence in Education 1983.

[85] Thompson 2014b.

[86] Cusick & Georgieff 2016.

[87] Hackman & Farah 2009.

[88] Luby et al. 2013.

[89] The same is true, incidentally, of research on adolescent brain development discussed in Chapter 2.

[90] With the exception of the *From Neurons to Neighborhoods* report.

[91] Rose & Rose 2016.

[92] Pew consistently referred to prekindergarten as its goal, even though the terms "preschool" and "prekindergarten" are often used interchangeably in the field. To the extent that a distinction can be made between them, preschool typically serves children in a broader age range, often beginning as early as two and a half or three years, while prekindergarten programs have a greater focus on the year just preceding kindergarten entry. In addition, prekindergarten programs have a stronger and more explicit focus on school readiness compared with preschool programs, for which early education is a more general theme.

[93] The account that follows draws on Bushouse's (2009) excellent analysis of the influence of Pew in advancing the prekindergarten agenda, as well as documents from the Pew Charitable Trusts: Watson 2011; Baxter (n.d.); Urahn & Watson 2007. I also benefited from a number of email exchanges with Sara Watson.

[94] According to Sara Watson, who directed Pew's prekindergarten campaign, Steve Barnett was a significant catalyst to the prekindergarten focus of the Pew initiative.

[95] Bushouse, 2009, p. 2.

[96] Bushouse 2009, pp. 155–156.

[97] Email exchanges with Sara Watson, August 3, 2022.

[98] Watson 2011; Baxter (n.d.).

[99] Friedman-Kraus et al 2022.

[100] The proposal was not funded.

[101] National Research Council and Institute of Medicine 2015.

[102] Phillips et al. 2017.

[103] www.ced.org, retrieved July 12, 2022.

[104] Research and Policy Committee, Committee for Economic Development 2002.

[105] www.strongnation.org/readynation.

[106] Those advocates include Ellen Galinsky (an early contributor to the *I Am Your Child* campaign) and the Families and Work Institute, www.familiesandwork.org.

[107] www.strongnation.org/readynation/about-us/special-bulletins-newsletters.

[108] From the ReadyNation website: "ReadyNation membership involves no costs, meetings, or obligations. You choose if, when, and how to respond to our occasional invitations to take action (just a few times each year)." www.strongnation.org/readynation/join-us, retrieved July 12, 1222.

[109] Although this is true, I am reminded of a conversation with an Alaska oil company executive after I spoke at the Alaska Governor's Summit on Early Education in 2007 just before Governor Sarah Palin. He spoke of the need in his industry for "patient capital" that could not promise a one-year or even a five-year return on investment, but rather required a longer expected return in light of how long it takes to develop promising oil fields. This is, of course, not an uncommon point of view in contemporary American industry, where long-term product development is often necessary, and as well suited to investments in children as oil fields.

[110] Zigler 2011, p. 198.

Chapter 6

[1] Gladwell 2008.

[2] We can also include analogies, similes, and the like.

[3] The work of George Lakoff has been influential on this topic; see Lakoff 2002.

[4] Fields 2009.

[5] Chapter 2 also included a discussion of the prevalent frame through which the public – and many social scientists – perceive adolescence, and the mistakenly negative view of youth that has influenced the design and interpretation of studies of adolescent brain development as well as Supreme Court decisions.

[6] Lakoff and Grady 1998.

[7] www.frameworksinstitute.org.

[8] Bateson 1972.

[9] Goffman 1974.

[10] Iyengar 1991; Iyengar and Kinder 1987.

[11] Bales 2014.

[12] As a reflection of this interdisciplinary approach, FrameWorks's early years enlisted the knowledge and methods of anthropologist Axel Aubrun and linguist Joseph Grady of the firm Cultural Logic, as well as public opinion analysis by Meg Bostrom of Public Knowledge. All three currently work with Topos Partnership, a consulting firm they cofounded in 2007, and which uses similar methods to those of Frameworks. www.topospartnership.com

[13] These steps are based on: www.frameworksinstitute.org/about/how-we-do-it/. For greater depth on each of these steps, see Davey 2009.

[14] www.frameworksinstitute.org/library/.

[15] The following account is based on Bales 2014 and Kendall-Taylor & Stevens 2017. Additional technical reports from this project can also be found in the FrameWorks Institute library: www.frameworksinstitute.org/library/.

[16] Kendall-Taylor 2009.

[17] The other values tested included future (children are our future), responsible management (it is important to incorporate new findings about child development into health and education systems), health (investments in better children's health result in economic and health benefits for society), and vulnerable children (society should invest in programs that help the most vulnerable children).

[18] Manuel & Gilliam 2009.

[19] Other simplifying models tested included brain architecture, brain health, roots, cornerstone, and game plan; Erard et al. (2010) identified these without elaboration in their report.

[20] Erard et al. 2010.

[21] Manuel & Gilliam 2009.

[22] Frameworks Institute 2009.

[23] Hestres 2021.

[24] See, e.g., Manuel 2009.

[25] Bales, personal email communication, October 3, 2022.

[26] I was a member of the National Scientific Council on the Developing Child from its founding until my departure in 2010, and the discussion that follows draws on my experiences during those years as well as the published documents and other materials of the Council.

[27] In 2016, a group of developmental scientists specializing in adolescence created the Center for the Developing Adolescent, which became affiliated with UCLA in 2021. In its size, mission, and funding it closely resembles the Center on the Developing Child, particularly the National Scientific Council on the Developing Child.

[28] https://developingchild.harvard.edu/science/national-scientific-council-on-the-developing-child/.

[29] The account that follows draws from Center on the Developing Child 2014.

[30] Also present were Cathy Trost of the Casey Journalism Center for Children and Families, David Lawrence, Jr., of the Early Childhood Initiative Foundation, and Janice Genevro of the Center for the Advancement of Health.

[31] FrameWorks Institute 2005.

[32] Interestingly, when a somewhat similar battery of cognitive elicitations was tested in a nationally representative survey of over 1,000 adults nearly twenty years later, FrameWorks researchers concluded that although there were indicators of improvement in public understanding, some of the less constructive framing of child development that had been earlier documented remained. L'Hôte & Volmert 2021.

[33] It is interesting to consider how differently an undergraduate class might seem if an instructor were to incorporate some of these approaches to

communication with the students. It is equally interesting to think of how different the student experience would be in such a class.

34 The term "working paper" was initially chosen with the expectation that the papers would be revised as scientific advances warranted doing so. As it turns out, since 2004 only two of the working papers (on toxic stress and mental health) have been updated for this reason. Others have been lightly revised to incorporate new framing research, and, to my knowledge, none has been revised to bring the policy applications into greater currency.

35 National Scientific Council on the Developing Child 2004a.

36 National Scientific Council on the Developing Child 2004b.

37 National Scientific Council on the Developing Child 2005.

38 Although the policy directions of the working paper series were underdeveloped, the National Scientific Council collaborated with a second group of academics formed at the Center on the Developing Child called the National Forum on Early Childhood Program Evaluation to produce a monograph titled "A Science-Based Framework for Early Childhood Policy." The policy proposals in this document, based on the Council's core story, are much more detailed, including attention to income supports for families in economic adversity, two-generation programs to provide multigenerational assistance, prenatal medical care and postnatal health care for young children, and environmental policies to eradicate neurotoxins in air, water, and foods. Center on the Developing Child 2007.

39 The entire series of working papers can be found at https://developingchild .harvard.edu/resourcecategory/reports-and-working-papers/.

40 This is why they were considered "working papers" with the expectation that the rapidly advancing research literature would compel updating them.

41 It is surprisingly difficult to identify the Council's core story because it varies in different publications; compare National Scientific Council on the Developing Child 2007; National Scientific Council on the Developing Child 2014; Shonkoff & Bales 2011. I use the version presented by Shonkoff and Bales because it is the most sophisticated presentation of the core story.

42 FrameWorks Institute 2005.

43 The Council emphasized in the third working paper that toxic stress is a function of not just stress severity but also the availability of supportive relationships to buffer the effects of stress on the child. This nuance is left out of the statement about toxic stress in the core story, but fortunately is emphasized in other Council materials.

44 For example, the "ongoing process" by which brain architecture is constructed, the nature of the interaction between genes and experience, and the kinds of effectiveness factors that make policies and programs effective

45 I have assigned Shonkofff & Bales 2011 annually in my classes for the last several years.

46 Shonkoff 2022.

47 Even this improved metaphor is a less than ideal representation of research on early face-to-face interaction, however, because developmental scientists have

long known that infants and adults are out of sync about a third of the time when they are interacting together (see Tronick & Gianino 1986). This occurs because the baby or the adult can become distracted by the variety of interruptions that intrude from older siblings, the phone, or the baby's physiological needs. Eventually, of course, adult and baby get back on track. One way that the "serve and return" metaphor could be helpfully extended (and reduce the likelihood that adults will feel like interactive failures) is to incorporate the recognition that each tennis or volleying game lasts a short while before someone (quite literally) drops the ball. Likewise, infants and parents serve and return until one partner gets distracted ... and then they get back to it again.

48 "Surfside Condominium Collapse," Wikipedia, https://en.wikipedia.org/wiki/Surfside_condominium_collapse, retrieved August 17, 2022.

49 I owe Annie Murphy Paul (2021) for this provocative metaphor, with her comment on the magpie's uncommon intelligence and its ability to make complex nests out of whatever the environment offers. And (I would add) its attraction to bright shiny objects.

50 Blakemore & Frith 2005b.

51 Porter et al. 2022.

52 Or parenting in all contexts. Gopnik seems to have economically advantaged parents in mind: she seems to be primarily concerned about the helicopter parents who constantly monitor and guide the child's development. But parents raising children in more economically difficult conditions may need to be more like carpenters to help ensure that their children develop the skills necessary to survive and thrive in their neighborhoods and schools.

53 Phillips et al. 2017.

54 Bruner 1986 argues that values are, in fact, fundamental to developmental science in how developmental outcomes are valued and even regarded as normative. His argument, like mine, is that these values should be as explicit as possible to be clear about why research data lead to certain conclusions about children's growth. When the influence of values is implicit, developmental theories tend to be an echo of the values of the broader culture in how researchers think about children's development.

55 L'Hote & Volmert 2021, p. 22.

56 To be sure, one could argue that improving child development "shifts the odds" in favor of achieving a more prosperous and sustainable society. But for this statement to have any meaning, it is necessary to clarify: How much?

57 FrameWorks distinguishes values as a narrative device, included at the beginning of the message to engage the public, from values as foundational beliefs. But I suspect that the values that engage audiences in a message are engaging because they are foundational, and this is certainly true of the values discussed here. One alternative is to find another way of opening the narrative that captures audience attention. Another alternative is to distinguish the opening value proposition from the description of the science that follows.

58 Quoted in Adato 2002, p. 16.

[59] To be clear, there are many reasons that people might disagree with policy proposals based on developmental science. Research scientists are in a stronger position to make their case if their proposals derive from the conclusions of their research in clear and direct ways.

[60] I was a member of the Legislative Working Group during my years with the Council, and this account is based on my notes from our meetings and summaries produced by Council staff.

[61] In recent years, conservative proposals to accomplish this have included an expanded child tax credit; Zeballos-Roig, 2022. Katharine Stevens and Matt Weidinger from the American Enterprise Institute have proposed doing so by allowing families to advance future payments of the Child Tax Credit to finance care options for families when children are young up to a maximum of $15,000 annually per child; see Stevens & Weidinger 2021.

[62] For the Council's own account of its history, consult Center on the Developing Child 2014.

Chapter 7

[1] Smuts 2006, p. 7.

[2] An acquisitions editor of a major publisher who was considering the proposal for this book told me that if he offered me a contract, I had to guarantee *not* to insist on a picture of the brain on the cover of the book. "Everybody wants to put the brain on the dust jacket, regardless of whether it has any relevance to what they have written about," he explained. Perhaps this is an illustration, at least for one person, of "neurofatigue."

[3] Stories of the brain's surprising recovery from injury or disease appear from time to time in the popular media as they do in the research literature. One of my favorite stories is of Amber Ramirez, who underwent a surgical cortical hemispherectomy at age fifteen to control repeated seizure activity. Her profound impairment shortly after the removal of the left half of her brain was expected, but several follow-up accounts documented astonishing improvement. In the latest account twenty-three years later, Amber was reported having completed high school and working and living independently, which was a consequence of the neural "rewiring" that enabled many of the functions of the diseased left hemisphere to be assumed by the right. Some motor limitations and language difficulties were among the few remaining indications of the effects of the surgery, but she no longer is impaired by seizures. The neurobiological plasticity reflected in this account is especially impressive given that Amber was an adolescent at the time of her surgery, far beyond the early windows of opportunity emphasized in the *I Am Your Child* campaign. Lange-Kubick 2022.

[4] As Brenda Bushouse (2009) has noted, the Pew campaign contributed to publicizing and, to some extent, creating the "problem" of school readiness that could be solved by a year of prekindergarten.

5 Gunnar & Donzella 2002.
6 Meins 2013 (see also Chapter 3).
7 Zeballos-Roig 2022.
8 Duncan & Magnuson 2013; Phillips et al. 2017.
9 There is growing evidence that social safety net and cash transfer programs may also have lifelong benefits for children by promoting healthy early childhood development. National Academies of Science, Engineering, and Medicine 2019.
10 Another reason may be that except for those who are professionally enlisted into the children's cause, the major constituency for such a movement are parents of young children. The problem is that they experience these issues as salient concerns for a few years until their children move on to school, at which time they also move on to other concerns.
11 And when they do *not* yield consistent conclusions, it elicits further examination of whether differences are based in different methods or different ways of conceptualizing developmental processes, or whether explanations in one field can readily be modeled in the other. Chapter 3 provided examples of each kind of desynchrony between developmental science and developmental neuroscience.
12 The dual concepts developmental scientists use to describe this difficulty in developmental prediction are *multifinality* (individuals can begin with similar experiences and influences but reach very different outcomes) and *equifinality* (individuals can begin with very different experiences and influences but follow different pathways to reach similar outcomes). Both multifinality and equifinality are typical in psychological development.
13 Inattention to context also caused the American Psychological Association to argue to the Supreme Court that characteristics of adolescent brain development alone predispose to impulsivity and sensation seeking, rather than acknowledging that the incentives and protections of an adolescent's environment are better predictors of the potential for risk taking than the developing brain alone, as documented in Chapter 2.
14 This is a more general problem of neuroscience, not just as it concerns children; see Choudhury & Slaby 2012.
15 To its credit, the *I Am Your Child* campaign and subsequent messaging drew consistent attention to some important contextual issues, most notably the importance of child care quality and child health care, and contributed to significant progress for children on the latter.
16 Rose and Rose 2016 argue that a neoliberal orientation is a general characteristic of the public policy applications of neuroscience.
17 Even though developmental cultural neuroscience was still years away, recognition of how the nurturance of infants and education of young children occurs differently in different cultural communities would have also broadened the messaging; see Chapter 2.
18 The progressive tenor of the brain development revolution is reflected in the call for action focused on expanding public programs and policies; a more

conservative approach would have emphasized parental and family responsibility and enablement.

[19] Both passages are from Kagan 1998, p. 91.

[20] Gladwell 2000, p. 87.

[21] Not surprisingly, FrameWorks has devoted thought to this issue; see Miller et al. 2021.

[22] Shonkoff & Bales 2011.

[23] Jamieson 2017.

[24] Kennedy et al. 2022.

[25] I recognize and appreciate the work of special colleagues, sometimes known as "science celebrities," who seem to do this all on their own: they are excellent public communicators of their science who are sought by reporters, policymakers, and others for their views. But science celebrities have usually reached this status because of their longstanding cultivation of relationships with journalists as well as their own active use of social media and the devotion of a not insignificant proportion of their professional time to these efforts. This is not necessarily a good model for the typical bench scientist who should also contribute to the public communication of science in their own ways.

[26] Illes et al. 2010.

[27] Similar arguments can be made (and often implicitly are offered) for reducing the responsibilities of frontline scientists to undergraduate teaching, ordinary service contributions, and administrative (and committee) duties.

[28] Akin 2017.

[29] Weiss & Singer 1988.

[30] Schäfer 2017.

[31] See also Mitchell et al. 2020.

[32] Forman-Katz & Matsa 2022.

[33] Weingart 2012.

[34] There remains the risk that a researcher's visibility is too great a result of social media hits rather than academic cites, which one researcher has quantified as "the Kardashian index": a measure of the discrepancy between a scientist's social media profile and publication record; see Hall 2014. Hall's choice of name for the index reflects the high visibility of Kim Kardashian on social media without having achieved anything of consequence in science, politics, or the arts.

[35] h-index and i10-index are both well-known measures of a scholar's impact through the number of their publications and the number of citations to their publications.

[36] McLuhan 1964.

[37] Yan 2020.

[38] Gershberg & Illing 2022.

[39] www.aldacenter.org.

[40] In an amazing and strange illustration of this, the social media manager of the meat product Steak-umm, Nathan Allebach, began tweeting messages in 2020 that constituted a primer on scientific literacy, critical thinking,

debunking misinformation, and other skills in response to the pandemic and growing political polarization, but having nothing to do with the meat product. A typical post: "friendly reminder in times of uncertainty and misinformation: anecdotes are not data. (good) data is carefully measured and collected information based on a range of subject-dependent factors, including, but not limited to, controlled variables, meta-analysis, and randomization." The posts can be found here: https://twitter.com/steak_umm/status/1336348473713680385

[41] Pew's commitment of more than $100 million to this campaign was also a significant ingredient to its success.

[42] I recognize that child advocates during this era had difficulty enlisting conservative allies to their effort. It is difficult to estimate how much success might have derived from accommodating conservative ideas about child- and family-friendly policies into the proposals deriving from the brain development campaign, but even if the effort did not result in success, it might have communicated the recognition that children's well-being is an issue on which people of diverse political positions can find initial common ground.

[43] This proposal is described by Stevens & Weidinger 2021.

[44] I am grateful to Rob Grunewald for alerting me to this.

[45] Haskins & Margolis 2014.

[46] Consult Thompson & Baumrind 2019 for an overview of these issues.

[47] In claiming that children's well-being is an end in itself, not a means to an end (such as enhanced future outcomes or economic productivity), I am simply extending an argument to children that most adults would claim to be true of themselves.

[48] See Chapter 1.

Works Cited

Adato, A. (2002). The education of Meathead. *Los Angeles Times Magazine*, January 20, pp. 14–33. www.latimes.com/archives/la-xpm-2002-jan-20-tm-24150-story.html, retrieved January 14, 2023.

Aguiar, A., & Baillargeon, R. (1998). Eight-and-a-half-month-old infants' reasoning about containment events. *Child Development, 69*, 636–653.

Akin, H. (2017). Overview of the science of science communication. In K. H. Jamieson, D. M. Kahan, & D. A. Scheufele (Eds.), *The Oxford handbook of the science of science communication* (pp. 25–34). New York: Oxford University Press.

Alexander, W. T., & Brown, J. W. (2011). Medial prefrontal cortex as an action-outcome predictor. *Nature Neuroscience, 14*, 1338–1344.

Allen, G. (2011). *Early intervention: Smart investment, massive savings.* Second independent report to Her Majesty's Government. https://core.ac.uk/reader/4153920, retrieved June 29, 2022.

Alvarez, M., Golden-Testa, K., Navarro, A., & Nolledo, R. (2018). *A golden opportunity: Lessons from California on advancing coverage for all children.* Los Angeles, CA: Children's Partnership. https://health4allkids.org/wp-content/uploads/2018/01/Golden-Opportunity-Lessons-From-Californias-Journey-to-Advancing-Coverage-for-All-Children-Report.pdf, retrieved June 3, 2022.

American Psychological Association (1989). Amicus curiae brief filed in U.S. Supreme Court in *Hodgson v. Minnesota*, 497 U.S. 417 (1990). www.apa.org/about/offices/ogc/amicus/index-chron, retrieved November 15, 2021.

(2004). Amicus curiae brief filed in U.S. Supreme Court in *Roper v. Simmons*, 543 U.S. 551 (2005). www.apa.org/about/offices/ogc/amicus/roper.pdf, retrieved November 11, 2021.

Aono, D., Yaffe, G., & Kober, H. (2019). Neuroscientific evidence in the courtroom: A review. *Cognitive Research: Principles and Implications, 4*, 40.

Aristotle (350 BCE). *The History of Animals*, Book VIII, Part 1, translated by D. W. Thompson (Oxford: Clarendon, 1910).

Atkins v. Virginia, 536 U.S. 302 (2002).

Bachleda, A. R., & Thompson, R. A. (2018). How babies think. *Zero to Three Journal, 38*(3), 4–10.

Bales, S. N. (2014). Haruv Award Lecture: Stickiness is an empirical pursuit: The case for reframing child mental health. *American Journal of Orthopsychiatry, 84*, 12–18.

Bangerter, A., & Heath, C. (2004). The Mozart effect: Tracking the evolution of a scientific legend. *British Journal of Social Psychology, 43*, 605–623.

Baptista, P., & Andrade, J. P. (2018). Adult hippocampal neurogenesis: Regulation and possible functional and clinical correlates. *Frontiers in Neuroanatomy, 12*, article 44.

Barnett, W. S., & Masse, L. N. (2007). Comparative benefit-cost analysis of the Abecedarian program and its policy implications. *Economics of Education Review, 26*, 113–125.

Barrett, L. F. (2009). The future of psychology: Connecting mind to brain. *Perspectives on Psychological Science, 4*, 326–339.

Bartik, T. J. (2011). *Investing in kids: Early childhood programs and local economic development.* Kalamazoo, MI: Upjohn Institute.

Bassok, D., Latham, S., & Rorem, A. (2016). Is kindergarten the new first grade? *AERA Open, 1*, 1–31.

Bateson, G. (1972). *Steps to an ecology of mind.* Novato, CA: Chandler Publishing.

Bauer, P. J. (2013). Memory development. In J. L. R. Rubenstein & P. Rakic (Eds.), *Neural circuit development and function in the brain* (pp. 297–314). New York: Academic Press.

Baxter, L. (n.d.). *An evaluation of Pew's pre-kindergarten initiative.* Washington, DC: Pew Charitable Trusts. www.pewtrusts.org/en/about/how-we-work/lessons-learned/expanding-prek-education, retrieved July 9, 2022.

Becht, A. I., Wierenga, L. M., Mills, K. L., Meuwese, R., van Duijvendoorde, A., Blakemore, S.-J., Güroglu, B., & Crone, E. A. (2021). Beyond the average brain: Individual differences in social brain development are associated with friendship quality. *Social and Affective Neuroscience, 16*, 292–301.

Beck, J. (1997). For kids, learning doesn't start in school. *Chicago Tribune*, May 4.

Begley, S. (1996). Your child's brain. *Newsweek*, February 19, pp. 54–62. (1998). The parent trap. *Newsweek*, September 7, pp. 50–59.

Bernzweig, J., Branom, C., & Wellenkamp, J. (2021). New directions in kindergarten readiness. *Zero to Three Journal, 41*(Suppl.). www.zerotothree.org/resources/3857-perspectives-new-directions-in-kindergarten-readiness, retrieved June 13, 2022.

Best, J. R., & Miller, P. H. (2010). A developmental perspective on executive function. *Child Development, 81*, 1641–1660.

Bjork, J. M., & Pardini, D. A. (2015). Who are those "risk-taking adolescents"? Individual differences in developmental neuroimaging research. *Developmental Cognitive Neuroscience, 11*, 56–64.

Blakemore, S.-J. (2012). Development of the social brain in adolescence. *Journal of the Royal Society of Medicine, 105*, 111–116.

Blakemore, S.-J., & Frith, U. (2005a). *The learning brain: Lessons for education.* Oxford: Blackwell.

(2005b). The learning brain: Lessons for education: A precis. *Developmental Science, 8*, 459–471.

Blakemore, S.-J., & Mills, K. L. (2014). Is adolescence a sensitive period for sociocultural processing? *Annual Review of Psychology, 65*, 187–207.

Bodenhorn, K. A., & Kelch, D. R. (2001). Implementation of California's Children and Families First Act of 1998. *The Future of Children, 11*, 150–157.

Bohlander, A., Lerner, C., & Thompson, R. (Eds.). (2017). *The growing brain: From birth to 5 years old. A curriculum for early childhood providers.* Washington, DC: Zero to Three.

Boldt, D. (1999). Drilling holes in myth about first three years. *Baltimore Sun*, August 30, p. 20.

Bonnie, R. J., & Scott, E. S. (2013). The teenage brain: Adolescent brain research and the law. *Current Directions in Psychological Science, 22*, 158–161.

Bower, C. (1997). Study hear examines babies' brain growth. *St. Louis Post-Dispatch*, August 5, p. 1A.

Brink, K. A., Lane, J. D., & Wellman, H. M. (2015). Developmental pathways for social understanding: Linking social cognition to social contexts. *Frontiers in Psychology, 6*, article 719.

Brito, N. H., & Noble, K. G. (2014). Socioeconomic status and structural brain development. *Frontiers in Neuroscience, 8*, article 217.

Brooks-Gunn, J., & Duncan, G. J. (1997). The effects of poverty on children. *The Future of Children, 7*, 55–71.

Bruer, J. T. (1997). Education and the brain: A bridge too far. *Educational Researcher, 26*, 4–16.

(1999). *The myth of the first three years.* New York: Free Press.

Bruner, J. (1986). Value presuppositions of developmental theory. In L. Cirillo & S. Wapner (Eds.), *Value presuppositions in theories of human development* (pp. 19–28). Hillsdale, NJ: Erlbaum.

Buchanan, C. M., & Hughes, J. L. (2009). Construction of social reality during early adolescence: Can expecting storm and stress increase real or perceived storm and stress? *Journal of Research on Adolescence, 19*, 261–285.

Bushouse, B. K. (2009). *Universal preschool: Policy change, stability, and the Pew Charitable Trusts.* Albany: State University of New York Press.

Buss, D. (2015). *Evolutionary psychology: The new science of the mind* (6th Ed.). London: Routledge.

Butler, L. P., & Markman, E. M. (2012). Preschoolers use intentional and pedagogical cues to guide inductive inferences and exploration. *Child Development, 83*, 1416–1428.

Butler, L. P., & Walton, G. M. (2013). The opportunity to collaborate increases preschoolers' motivation for challenging tasks. *Journal of Experimental Child Psychology, 116*, 953–961.

Byrne, M. L., Whittle, S., Vijayakumar, N., Dennison, M., Simmons, J. G., & Allen, N. B. (2017). A systematic review of adrenarche as a sensitive period in neurobiological development and mental health. *Developmental Cognitive Neuroscience, 25*, 12–28.

Byrnes, J. P. (2001). *Minds, brains, and learning: Understanding the psychological and educational relevance of neuroscientific research.* New York: Guilford.

(2007). Some ways in which neuroscientific research can be relevant to education. In D. Coch, K. W. Fischer, & G. Dawson (Eds.), *Human behavior, learning, and the developing brain: Typical development* (pp. 30–49). New York: Guilford.

Cannon, J. S., Kilburn, M. R., Karoly, L. A., Mattox, T., Muchow, A. N., & Burnaventura, M. (2017). *Investing early: Taking stock of outcomes and economic returns from early childhood programs.* Santa Monica, CA: RAND Corporation. www.rand.org/pubs/research_reports/RR1993.html, retrieved January 5, 2023.

Caplan, N. (1976). Social research and national policy: What gets used, by whom, for what purposes, and with what effects? *International Social Science Journal, 28,* 187–194.

(1979). The two-communities theory and knowledge utilization. *American Behavioral Scientist, 22,* 459–470.

Caplan, N., & Nelson, S. D. (1973). On being useful: The nature and consequences of psychological research on social problems. *American Psychologist, 28,* 199–211.

Carey, S. (1978). The child as word learner. In J. Bresnan, G. Miller, & M. Halle (Eds.), *Linguistic theory and psychological reality* (pp. 264–293). Cambridge, MA: MIT Press.

Carnegie Task Force on Meeting the Needs of Young Children (1994). *Starting points: Meeting the needs of our youngest children.* Waldorf, MD: Carnegie Corporation of New York.

Carneiro, P., & Heckman, J. (2003). *Human capital policy.* National Bureau of Economic Research Working Paper 9495, February. www.nber.org/papers/w9495, retrieved June 16, 2022.

Casey, B. J., Jones, R. M., & Somerville, L. H. (2011). Braking and accelerating of the adolescent brain. *Journal of Research on Adolescence, 21,* 21–33.

Casey, B. J., Trainor, R., Giedd, J., Vauss, Y. Vaituzis, C. K., Hamburger, S., Kozuch, P., & Rapoport, J. L. (1997). The role of the anterior cingulate in automatic and controlled processes: A developmental neuroanatomical study. *Developmental Psychobiology, 30,* 61–69.

Casey, B. J., Trainor, R. J., Orendi, J. L., Schubert, A. B., Nystrom, L. E., et al. (1997). A developmental functional MRI study of prefrontal activation during performance of a go-no-go task. *Journal of Cognitive Neuroscience, 9,* 835–847.

Center on the Developing Child (2007). *A science-based framework for early childhood policy: Using evidence to improve outcomes in learning, behavior, and health for vulnerable children.* https://harvardcenter.wpenginepowered.com/wp-content/uploads/2016/02/Policy_Framework.pdf, retrieved January 8, 2023.

(2014). *A decade of science informing policy: The story of the National Scientific Council on the Developing Child.* https://developingchild.harvard.edu/

resources/decade-science-informing-policy-story-national-scientific-council-developing-child/, retrieved July 29, 2022.

Chabot, M. J., Kwan, K., Guenzburger, G. V., Lavezzo, M., & Pressfield, L. (2021). *Adolescent births in California, 2000–2018*. Sacramento: California Dept. of Public Health. www.cdph.ca.gov/Programs/CFH/DMCAH/surveillance/CDPH%20Document%20Library/Adolescents/Adolescent-Births-in-CA-2018.pdf, retrieved June 3, 2022.

Charen, M. (1999). Child's first three years not as critical. *Omaha World-Herald*, September 22, p. 24.

Chen, B.-B., Li, X., & Chen, N. (2017). Positive youth development in China. In R. Dimitrova (Ed.), *Well-being of youth and emerging adults across cultures* (pp. 35–48). New York: Springer.

Chomsky, N. (1968). *Language and mind*. New York: Harcourt, Brace.

Choudhury, S., McKinney, K. A., & Merten, M. (2012). Rebelling against the brain: Public engagement with the "neurological adolescent." *Social Science & Medicine, 74*, 565–573.

Choudhury, S., & Slaby, J. (2012). Introduction: Critical neuroscience – between lifeworld and laboratory. In S. Choudhury & J. Slaby (Eds.), *Critical neuroscience: A handbook of the social and cultural contexts of neuroscience* (pp. 1–26). London: Blackwell.

Clinton, H. R. (1996). *It takes a village, and other lessons children teach us*. New York: Simon & Schuster.

Cohen, L. B., & Oakes, L. M. (1993). How infants perceive a simple causal event. *Developmental Psychology, 29*, 421–433.

Coleman, J. C., (2011). *The nature of adolescence* (4th Ed.). New York: Routledge.

Collins, W. A. (1990). Parent-child relationships in the transition to adolescence: Continuity and change in interaction, affect, and cognition. In R. Montemayor, G. R. Adams, & T. P. Gullota (Eds.), *Advances in adolescent development, Vol. 2: From childhood to adolescence: A transitional period?* (pp. 85–106). Newbury Park, CA: Sage.

Committee on the Science of Adolescence, Board on Children, Youth, and Families (2011). *The science of adolescent risk-taking: Workshop report*. Washington, DC: National Academies Press.

Conger, K. J., Martin, M. J., Reeb, B. T., Little, W. M., Craine, J. L., Shebloski, B., & Conger, R. D. (2012). Economic hardship and its consequences across generations. In V. Maholmes & R. B. King (Eds.), *The Oxford handbook of poverty and child development* (pp. 37–53). New York: Oxford University Press.

Cowan, W. M. (1979). The development of the brain. *Scientific American, 241*, 112–133.

Cusick, S. E., & Georgieff, M. K. (2016). The role of nutrition in brain development: The golden opportunity of the "first 1000 days." *Journal of Pediatrics, 175*, 16–21.

Dahl, M. (2016). 5 big ways kindergarten has changed since the 1990s. The Cut, June 21. www.thecut.com/2016/06/5-big-ways-kindergarten-has-changed-since-the-1990s.html, retrieved May 10, 2021.

Dahl, R. E., Allen, N. B., Wilbrecht, L., & Suleiman, A. B. (2018). Importance of investing in adolescence from a developmental science perspective. *Nature, 554*, 441–450.

Dai, J., & Scherb, K. S. (2019). Puberty and functional brain development in humans: Convergence of findings? *Developmental Cognitive Neuroscience, 39*, 100690.

Dalziel, K. M., Halliday, D., & Segal, L. (2015). Assessment of the cost-benefit literature on early childhood education for vulnerable children: What the findings mean for policy. *SAGE Open, 5*, 1–14.

Davey, L. (Ed.) (2009). Special issue: Framing youth development for public support. *New Directions for Youth Development*, no. 124.

Davis, E. P., & Thompson, R. A. (2014). Prenatal foundations: Fetal programming of health and development. *Zero to Three Journal, 34*, 6–11.

de Boysson-Bardies, B., Halle, P., Sagart, L., & Durand, C. (1989). A crosslinguistic investigation of vowel formants in babbling. *Journal of Child Language, 16*, 1–17.

Dekaban, A. S., & Sadowsky, D. (1978). Changes in brain weights during the span of human life: Relation of brain weights to body heights and body weights. *Annals of Neurology*, 4, 345–356.

Dickens, C. (1848). *Dombey and son*. London: Bradbury & Evans.

Dmitrieva, J., Steinberg, L., & Belsky, J. (2007). Child-care history, classroom composition, and children's functioning in kindergarten. *Psychological Science, 18*, 1032–1039.

Do, K. T., McCormick, E. M., & Telzer, E. H. (2020). Neural sensitivity to conflicting attitudes supports greater conformity toward positive over negative influence in early adolescence. *Developmental Cognitive Neuroscience, 45*, 100837.

Drake, S. R. (2008). *It's all about the children: An ethnographic study of the First 5 Children and Families Commission of California*, unpublished doctoral dissertation, University of California, Santa Barbara. Available at www.proquest.com/dissertations-theses/all-about-children-ethnographic-study-first-5/docview/304663954/se-2?accountid=14505, retrieved June 1, 2022.

Duerksen, S. (1997). Researchers unsure about link between music and IQ. *San Diego Union-Tribune*, June 11, p. E-1.

Duncan, G. J., & Hoynes, H. (2021). Reducing child poverty can promote children's development and productivity in adulthood. *SRCD Child Evidence Brief*, no. 11, October. www.srcd.org/sites/default/files/resources/CEB-Child%20Tax%20Credits_final.pdf, retrieved September 21, 2022.

Duncan, G. J., & Magnuson, K. (2013). Investing in preschool programs. *Journal of Economic Perspectives, 27*, 109–132.

Duncan, G. J., Ziol-Guest, K. M., & Kalil, A. (2010). Early-childhood poverty and adult attainment, behavior, and health. *Child Development, 81*, 306–325.

Dunkel Schetter, C., & Tanner, L. (2012). Anxiety, depression and stress in pregnancy: Implications for mothers, children, research, and practice. *Current Opinion Psychiatry, 25*, 141–148.

Dutil, C., Walsh, J. J., Featherstone, R. B., Gunnell, K. E., Tremblay, M. S., Gruber, R., Weiss, S. K., Cote, K. A., Sampson, M., & Chaput, J.-P. (2018). Influence of sleep on developing brain functions and structures in children and adolescents: A systematic review. *Sleep Medicine Reviews, 42,* 184–201.

Eliot, K. (2009). *Pink brain, blue brain: How small differences grow into troublesome gaps – And what we can do about it.* New York: Houghton Mifflin Harcourt.

Eliot, L., Ahmed, A., Khan, H., & Patel, J. (2021). Dump the "dimorphism": Comprehensive synthesis of human brain studies reveals few male-female differences beyond size. *Neuroscience and Biobehavioral Reviews, 125,* 667–697.

Elman, J., Bates, E., Johnson, M., Karmiloff-Smith, A., Parisi, D., & Plunkett, K. (1996). *Rethinking innateness: A connectionist perspective on development.* Cambridge, MA: MIT Press.

Emerson, S. (2019). California's First 5 programs evolve as smoking declines and tobacco taxes go away. Daily Democrat (Woodland, CA), January 3. www.dailydemocrat.com/2019/01/03/californias-first-5-programs-evolve-as-smoking-declines-and-tobacco-taxes-go-away/, retrieved June 1, 2022.

Enright, R. D., Levy, V. M., Jr., Harris, D., & Lapsley, D. K. (1987). Do economic conditions influence how theorists view adolescents? *Journal of Youth and Adolescence, 16,* 541–559.

Epstein, B. (1997). Stimulation in child's early years crucial to development. *Tampa Bay Times,* July 16, p. 3D.

Erard, M., Kendall-Taylor, N., Davey, L., & Simon, A. (2010). *The power of levleness: Making child mental health visible and concrete through a simplifying model: A FrameWorks research report.* Washington, DC: FrameWorks Institute. www.frameworksinstitute.org/publication/the-power-of-levleness-making-child-mental-health-visible-and-concrete-through-a-simplifying-model/, retrieved July 25, 2022.

Erickson, K. I., Voss, M. W., Prakash, R. S., et al. (2011). Exercise training increases size of hippocampus and improves memory. *PNAS, 108,* 3017–3022.

Eriksson, P. S., Perfilieva, E., Bjork-Eriksson, T., Alborn, A.-M., Nordborg, C., Peterson, D. A., & Gage, F. H. (1998). Neurogenesis in the adult human hippocampus. *Nature Medicine, 4,* 1313–1317.

Euston, D. R., Gruber, A. J., & McNaughton, B. L. (2012). The role of medial prefrontal cortex in memory and decision making. *Neuron, 76,* 1057–1070.

Evans, G. W., Chen, E., Miller, G. E., & Seeman, T. (2012). How poverty gets under the skin: A life course perspective. In R. King & V. Mahalmes (Eds.), *The Oxford Handbook of Poverty and Child Development* (pp. 13–36). New York: Oxford University Press.

Evans, G. W., & Kim, P. (2013). Childhood poverty, chronic stress, self-regulation, and coping. *Child Development Perspectives, 7,* 43–48.

Fasick, F. A. (1994), On the "invention of adolescence." *Journal of Early Adolescence, 14,* 6–23.

Fields, G. (2009). White House czar calls for end to "war on drugs." *Wall Street Journal*, May 14. www.wsj.com/articles/SB124225891527617397, retrieved August 17, 2022.

First 5 Center for Children's Policy (2020). *Reading our state: How kindergarten readiness inventories can benefit California*. https://first5center.org/assets/files/kri-paper-v6-WEB.pdf, retrieved June 13, 2022.

First 5 San Joaquin (2013). *Building blocks for school success: Findings from a 5-year longitudinal study. Executive summary*. https://harderco.com/wp-content/uploads/2016/08/First5_SJ_Building-Blocks-For-School-Success_Feb_2013.pdf, retrieved June 3, 2022.

Flavell, J. H. (1963). *The developmental psychology of Jean Piaget*. Princeton, NJ: D. Van Nostrand.

Fodor, J. A. (1983). *The modularity of mind*. Cambridge, MA: MIT Press.

Forman-Katz, N., & Matsa, K. E. (2022). *News platform fact sheet*. Washington, DC: Pew Research Center. www.pewresearch.org/journalism/fact-sheet/news-platform-fact-sheet/, retrieved January 15, 2023.

FrameWorks Institute (2005). *Talking early child development and exploring the consequences of frame choices: A FrameWorks message memo*. Washington, DC: FrameWorks Institute. www.frameworksinstitute.org/publication/talking-early-child-development-and-exploring-the-consequences-of-frame-choices/, retrieved July 31, 2022.

(2009). *Talking to business leaders about early childhood development: A FrameWorks message brief*. Washington, DC: FrameWorks Institute. www.frameworksinstitute.org/wp-content/uploads/2020/03/ecd_business_leaders_brief.pdf, retrieved July 25, 2022.

Freud, S. (1899). *The interpretation of dreams (Die Traumdeutung)*. Translated by James Strachey. London: Hogarth, 1953.

Friedman, M. (2000). *Results accountability for Prop 10 commissions: A planning guide for improving the well-being of young children and their families*. Unpublished paper prepared for the Center for Healthier Children, Families and Communities, University of California, Los Angeles. www.impactstrategist.com/wp-content/uploads/2015/12/Prop10GuideV4.pdf, retrieved January 14, 2023.

Friedman-Kraus, A. H., Barnett, W. S., Garver, K. A., Hodges, K. S., Weisenfeld, G. G., Gardiner, B. A., & Jost, T. M. (2022). *The state of preschool 2021*. New Brunswick, NJ: National Institute for Early Education Research. https://nieer.org/wp-content/uploads/2022/04/YB2021_Full_Report.pdf, retrieved July 3, 2022.

Funk, C. (2020). *Key findings about Americans' confidence in society and their views on scientists' role in society*. Washington, DC: Pew Research Center. www.pewresearch.org/fact-tank/2020/02/12/key-findings-about-americans-confidence-in-science-and-their-views-on-scientists-role-in-society/, retrieved May 25, 2020.

Gaskins, S., Beeghly, M., Bard, K. A., Gernhardt, A., Liu, C. H., Teti, D. M., Thompson, R. A., Weisner, T. S., & Yovsi, R. D. (2017). Meaning and methods in the study and assessment of attachment. In H. Keller & K. A. Bard (Eds.), *The cultural nature of attachment* (pp. 195–229). Cambridge, MA: MIT Press.

Gaylor, E., Spiker, D., Williamson, C., & Ferguson, K. (2011). *Saint Paul Early Childhood Scholarship evaluation: Final Evaluation Report – 2008–2011*. Menlo Park, CA: SRI International. https://hubert.hhh.umn.edu/ECEpdf/ Scholarships2008-2011FinalFullReport.pdf, retrieved July 5, 2022.

Geldhof, G. J., Bowers, E. P., Mueller, M. K., Napolitano, C. M., Callina, K. S., Walsh, K. J., Lerner, J. V., & Lerner, R. M. (2015). The five Cs model of positive youth development. In E. P. Bowers, G. J. Geldhof, S. K. Johnson, L. J. Hilliard, R. M. Hershberg, J. V. Lerner, & R. M. Lerner (Eds.), *Promoting positive youth development* (pp. 161–186). New York: Springer.

Gelman, S. A. (2005). *The essential child: Origins of essentialism in everyday thought*. Oxford: Oxford University Press.

(2009). Learning from others: Children's construction of concepts. *Annual Review of Psychology, 60*, 115–140.

Gelman, S. A., Ware, E. A., Kleinberg, F., Manczak, E. M., & Stilwell, S. M. (2014). Individual differences in children's and parents' generic language. *Child Development, 85*, 924–940.

Gelman, S. A. & Wellman, H. M. (1991). Insides and essences: Early understandings of the non-obvious. *Cognition, 38*, 213–244.

Gershberg, Z., & Illing, S. (2022). *The paradox of democracy: Free speech, open media, and perilous persuasion*. Chicago: University of Chicago Press.

Ghetti, S., & Fandakova, Y. (2020). Neural development of memory and metamemory in childhood and adolescence: Toward an integrative model of the development of episodic recollection. *Annual Review of Developmental Psychology, 2*, 365–388.

Gibson, E. T., & Walker, A. S. (1984). Development of knowledge of visual-tactual affordances of substance. *Child Development, 55*, 453–460.

Giffin, F., & Mitchell, D. E. (1978). The rate of recovery of vision after early monocular deprivation in kittens. *Journal of Physiology, 274*, 511–537.

Gladwell, M. (1998). Do parents matter? *The New Yorker*, August 17, pp. 52–64.

(2000). Baby steps: Do our first three years of life determine how we'll turn out? *New Yorker*, January 10, pp. 80–87.

(2008). *Outliers: The story of success*. New York: Little, Brown.

Gluckman, P., & Hanson, M. (2005). *The fetal matrix*. Cambridge: Cambridge University Press.

Goddings, A.-L., Beltz, A., Peper, J. S., Crone, E. A., & Braams, B. R. (2019). Understanding the role of puberty in structural and functional development of the adolescent brain. *Journal of Research on Adolescence, 29*, 32–53.

Goffman, E. (1974). *Frame analysis*. Cambridge, MA: Harvard University Press.

Gopnik, A. (2009). *The philosophical baby*. New York: Farrar, Straus and Giroux.

(2016). *The gardener and the carpenter*. New York: Farrar, Straus and Giroux.

Gopnik, A., Meltzoff, A. N., & Kuhl, P. K. (1999). *The scientist in the crib: Minds, brains, and how children learn*. New York: Morrow.

Gough, M. (Ed.) (2003). *Politicizing science.* Stanford, CA: Hoover Institution Press.

Gould, E., Beylin, A., Tanapat, P., Reeves, A., & Shors, T. J. (1999). Learning enhances adult neurogenesis in the hippocampal formation. *Nature Neuroscience, 2,* 260–265.

Graham v. Florida, 560 U.S. 48 (2010).

Greenough, W. T. (1997). We can't focus just on ages 0 to 3. *American Psychological Association Monitor,* November, p. 19.

Grigorenko, E. (2017). Brain development: The effect of interventions on children and adolescents. In D. Bundy, N. de Silva, S. Horton, D. T. Jamison, & G. Patton (Eds.), *Disease control priorities, Vol. 8: Child and adolescent health and development* (pp. 119–131). Washington, DC: World Bank.

Gunnar, M. R., & Donzella, B. (2002). Social regulation of the cortisol levels in early human development. *Psychoneuroendocrinology, 27,* 199–220.

Gweon, H., & R. Saxe (2013). Developmental cognitive neuroscience of theory of mind. In J. L. R. Rubenstein & P. Rakic (Eds.), *Comprehensive developmental neuroscience: Neural circuit development and function in the healthy and diseased brain* (pp. 367–377). Amsterdam: Elsevier and Academic Press.

Hackman, D. A., & Farah, M. J. (2009). Socioeconomic status and the developing brain. *Trends in Cognitive Sciences, 13,* 65–73.

Hair, N. L., Hanson, J. L., Wolfe, B. L., & Pollak, S. D. (2015). Association of child poverty, brain development, and academic achievement. *JAMA Pediatrics, 169,* 822–829.

Hall, N. (2014). The Kardashian index: A measure of discrepant social media profile for scientists. *Genome Biology, 15,* 424.

Hanson, J. L., Hair, N., Shen, D. G., Shi, F., Gilmore, J. H., Wolfe, B. L., & Pollak, S. D. (2013). Family poverty affects the rate of human infant brain growth. *PLoS ONE, 8,* e80954.

Harris, J. R. (1998). *The nurture assumption: Why children turn out the way they do.* New York: Free Press.

Haskins, R., & Margolis, G. (2014). *Show me the evidence: Obama's fight for rigor and results in social policy.* Washington, DC: Brookings Institution Press.

Heckman, J. J. (2000). Policies to foster human capital. *Research in Economics, 54,* 3–56.

(2004). Lessons from the technology of skill formation. *Annals of the New York Academy of Sciences, 1038,* 179–200.

(2006). Skill formation and the economics of investing in disadvantaged children. *Science, 312,* 1900–1902.

(2007). The economics, technology, and neuroscience of human capability formation. *PNAS, 104,* 13250–13255.

(2008). Schools, skills, and synapses. *Economic Inquiry, 36,* 289–324.

Hernandez, A. E., Claussenius-Kalman, H. L., Ronderos, J., Castilla-Earls, A. P., Sun, L., Weiss, S. D., & Young, D. R. (2019). Neuroemergentism: A framework for studying cognition and brain. *Journal of Neurolinguistics, 49,* 214–223.

Hestres, L. E., Rochman, A., Busso, D., & Volmert, A. (2021). *How are children's issues portrayed in the news? A media content analysis.* Washington, DC: FrameWorks Institute. www.frameworksinstitute.org/publication/how-are-childrens-issues-portrayed-in-the-news/, retrieved July 25, 2022.

Heyes, C., & Catmur, C. (2022). What happened to mirror neurons? *Perspectives in Psychological Science, 17,* 153–168.

Hines, M. (2020). Neuroscience and sex/gender: Looking back and forward. *Journal of Neuroscience, 40,* 37–43.

Hirsh-Pasek, K., Adamson, L. B., Bakeman, R., Owen, M. T., Golinkoff, R. M., Pace, A., Yust, P. K. S., & Suma, K. (2015). The contribution of early communication quality to low-income children's language success. *Psychological Science, 26,* 1071–1083.

Hodgson v. Minnesota, 497 U.S. 417 (1990).

Hughes, C., & Leekam, S. (2004). What are the links between theory of mind and social relations? Review, reflections and new directions for studies of typical and atypical development. *Social Development, 13,* 590–619.

Huttenlocher, P. R., & Dabholkar, A. S. (1997). Regional differences in synaptogenesis in human cerebral cortex. *Journal of Comparative Neurology, 387,* 167–178.

Hwang, C. P., Lamb, M. E., & Siegel, I. E. (Eds.) (1996). *Images of childhood.* Mahwah, NJ: Erlbaum.

Illes, J., Moser, M. A., McCormick, J. B., Racine, E., Blakeslee, S., Caplan, A., Hayden, E. C., Ingram, J., Lohwater, T., McKnight, P., Nicholson, C., Phillips, A., Sauvé, K. D., Snell, E., & Weiss, S. (2010). Neurotalk: Improving the communication of neuroscience research. *Nature Reviews Neuroscience, 11,* 61–69.

Iyengar, S. (1991). *Is anyone responsible? How television frames political issues.* Chicago: University of Chicago Press.

Iyengar, S., & Kinder, D. R. (1987). *News That matters: Television and American opinion.* Chicago: University of Chicago Press.

Jamieson, K. H. (2017). The need for a science of science communication: Communicating science's values and norms. In K. H. Jamieson, D. M. Kahan, & D. A. Scheufele (Eds.), *The Oxford handbook of the science of science communication* (pp. 15–24). New York: Oxford University Press.

Jessor, R., Turbin, M. S., Costa, F. M., Dong, Q., Zhang, H., & Wang, C. (2003). Adolescent problem behavior in China and the United States: A cross-national study of psychosocial protective factors. *Journal of Research on Adolescence, 13,* 329–360.

Jobson, D. D., Hase, Y., Clarkson, A. N., & Kalaria, R. H. (2021). The role of the medial prefrontal cortex in cognition, ageing and dementia. *Brain Communications, 3,* article fcab125.

Johnson, M. H. (2013). Theories in developmental neuroscience. In J. L. R. Rubenstein & P. Rakic (Eds.), *Neural circuit development and function in the brain* (pp. 191–205). New York: Academic Press.

Johnson, M. H., & de Haan, M. (2015). *Developmental cognitive neuroscience: An introduction* (4th Ed.). New York: Wiley-Blackwell.

Johnson, S. B., Blum, R. W., & Giedd, J. N. (2009). Adolescent maturity and the brain: The promise and pitfalls of neuroscience research in adolescent health policy. *Journal of Adolescent Health*, *45*, 216–221.

Jones v. Mississippi, 593 U.S. __ (2021).

Kagan, J. (1998). *Three seductive ideas*. Cambridge, MA: Harvard University Press.

Karoly, L. A., Greenwood, P. W., Everingham, S. S., Houbé, J., Kilburn, M. R., Rydell, C. P., Sanders, M., & Chiesa, J. (1998). *Investing in our children: What we know and don't know about the costs and benefits of early childhood interventions*. Santa Monica, CA: RAND.

Kendall-Taylor, N. (2009). *Conflicting models of mind in mind: Mapping the gaps between the expert and public understandings of child mental health as part of strategic frame analysis: A FrameWorks research report*. Washington, DC: FrameWorks Institute. www.frameworksinstitute.org/wp-content/uploads/2020/03/childmentalhealthculturalmodels.pdf, retrieved January 14, 2023.

Kendall-Taylor, N., & Stevens, A. (2017). Can frames make change? Using communications science to translate the science of child mental health. In M. H. Maurer (Ed.), *Child and adolescent mental health* (pp. 59–71). London: Intech Open. www.intechopen.com/books/5470, retrieved July 25, 2022.

Kennedy, B., Tyson, A., & Funk, C. (2022). *Americans' trust in scientists, other groups declines*. Washington, DC: Pew Research Center. www.pewresearch.org/science/2022/02/15/americans-trust-in-scientists-other-groups-declines/, retrieved November 16, 2022.

Kim, I.-K., & Spelke, E. S. (1992). Infants' sensitivity to effects of gravity on visible object motion. *Journal of Experimental Psychology: Human Perception and Performance*, *18*, 3385–3393.

(1999). Perception and understanding of effects of gravity and inertia on object motion. *Developmental Science*, *2*, 339–362.

Klein, J. (1997). Clintons on the brain. *New Yorker*, March 17, pp. 59–63. www.newyorker.com/magazine/1997/03/17/clintons-on-the-brain, retrieved January 14, 2023.

Knitzer, J., & Adely, F. (2001). *Executive summary: Learning from Starting Points: Findings from the Starting Points Assessment Project*. New York: National Center for Children in Poverty, Columbia University. https://academiccommons.columbia.edu/doi/10.7916/D8QR55V9, retrieved May 23, 2022.

Kolb, B. (1989). Brain development, plasticity, and behavior. *American Psychologist*, *44*, 1203–1212.

Kopp, F., & Lindenberger, U. (2011). Effects of joint attention on long-term memory in 9-month-old infants: An event-related potentials study. *Developmental Science*, *14*, 660–672.

Kotulak, R. (1996), *Inside the brain: Revolutionary discoveries of how the mind works*. Kansas City, MO: Andrews and McMeel.

Kuhl, P. K., Tsao, F.-M., & Liu, H.-M. (2003). Foreign-language experience in infancy: Effects of short-term exposure and social interaction on phonetic learning. *PNAS*, *100*, 9096–9101.

Lakoff, G. (2002). *Moral politics: How liberals and conservatives think* (2nd Ed.). Chicago: University of Chicago Press.

Lakoff, G., & Grady, J. (1998). Why early ed benefits all of us. In S. N. Bales (Ed.), *Effective language for discussing early childhood education and policy* (pp. 7–19). Washington, DC: Benton Foundation.

Lange-Kubick, C. (2010). A new life for Amber. *Lincoln Journal-Star*, January 14, p. A1. https://journalstar.com/news/local/a-new-life-for-amber/article_78afdaea-06e9-11df-a7c6-001cc4c03286.html, retrieved September 7, 2022.

Lansford, J. E., Zietz, S., Bornstein, M. H., Deater-Deckard, K., et al. (2020). Opportunities and peer support for aggression and delinquency during adolescence in nine countries. *New Directions in Child and Adolescent Development*, *172*, 73–88.

Lany, J., & Saffran, J. R. (2013). Statistical learning mechanisms in infancy. In J. L. R. Rubenstein & P. Rakic (Eds.), *Comprehensive developmental neuroscience: Neural circuit development and function in the healthy and diseased brain* (pp. 231–248). Amsterdam: Elsevier and Academic Press.

Larsen, B., & Luna, B. (2018). Adolescence as a neurobiological critical period for the development of higher-order cognition. *Neuroscience and Biobehavioral Reviews*, *94*, 179–195.

Leong, Y. C., Chen, J., Willer, R., & Zaki, J. (2020). Conservative and liberal attitudes drive polarized neural responses to political content. *PNAS*, *117*, 27731–27739.

Lesher, A. I. (1997). Addiction is a brain disease, and it matters. *Science*, *278*, 45–47.

Levine, M. H. & Smith, S. V. (2001). Starting points: State and community partnerships for young children. *The Future of Children*, *11*, 142–149.

Levine, R., & LeVine, S. (2016). *Do parents matter?* New York: Public Affairs.

Lewin, K. (1943). Psychology and the process of group living. *Journal of Social Psychology*, *17*, 113–131.

Lewin, T. (2009). No Einstein in your crib? Get a refund. *New York Times*, October 23, section A, p. 1. www.nytimes.com/2009/10/24/education/24baby.html, retrieved January 6, 2023.

L'Hôte, E., & Volmert, A. (2021). *Why aren't kids a policy priority? The cultural mindsets and attitudes that keep kids off the public agenda: A FrameWorks strategic brief.* Washington, DC: FrameWorks Institute. www.frameworksinstitute.org/publication/why-arent-kids-a-policy-priority-the-cultural-mindsets-and-attitudes-that-keep-kids-off-the-public-agenda/, retrieved July 31, 2022.

Lieberman, Z., Woodward, A. L., & Kinzler, K. D. (2017). The origins of social categorization. *Trends in Cognitive Sciences*, *21*, 556–568.

Lindblom, C. E., & Cohen, D. K. (1979). *Usable knowledge: Social science and social problem-solving.* New Haven, CT: Yale University Press.

Lindquist, K. A., Wager, T. D., Koger, H., Bliss-Moreau, E., & Barrett, L. F. (2012). The brain basis of emotion: A meta-analytic review. *Behavioral and Brain Sciences*, *35*, 121–202.

Locke, J. (1693). *Some thoughts concerning education.* London: Churchill.

Luby, J., Belden, A., Botteron, K., Marrus, N., Harris, M. P., Babb, C., Nishino, T., & Barch, D. (2013). The effects of poverty on childhood brain development: The mediating effect of caregiving and stressful life events. *JAMA Pediatrics, 167,* 1135–1142.

Luciana, M. (2013). Adolescent brain development in normality and psychopathology. *Development and Psychopathology, 25,* 1325–1345.

Lumey, L. H., Stein, A. D., Kahn, H. S., van der Pal-de Bruin, K. M., Blauw, G. J., Zybert, P. A., & Susser, E. S.(2007). Cohort profile: The Dutch Hunger Winter Families Study. *International Journal of Epidemiology, 36,* 1197–1204.

Lutz, C. (1988). *Unnatural emotions: Everyday sentiments on a Micronesian atoll and their challenge to Western theory.* Chicago: University of Chicago Press.

Mann, J. (1994). Children in crisis. *Washington Post,* April 15, p. E3.

Manuel, T. (2009). *Refining the core story of early childhood development: The effects of science and health frames: A FrameWorks research report.* Washington, DC: FrameWorks Institute. www.frameworksinstitute.org/publication/refining-the-core-story-of-early-childhood-development-the-effects-of-science-and-health-frames/, retrieved August 19, 2022.

Manuel, T., & Gilliam, F. D., Jr. (2009). *Advancing support for child mental health policies: Early results from Strategic Frame Analysis experimental research: A FrameWorks research report.* Washington, DC: FrameWorks Institute. www.frameworksinstitute.org/publication/advancing-support-for-child-mental-health-policies-early-results-from-strategic-frame-analysis-experimental-research/, retrieved July 25, 2022.

Marcus, G. (2004). *The birth of the mind: How a tiny number of genes creates the complexities of human thought.* New York: Basic.

Maroney, T. A. (2013). Adolescent brain science after *Graham v. Florida. Notre Dame Law Review, 86,* 765–793.

McCabe, D. P., & Castel, A. D. (2008). Seeing is believing: The effect of brain images on judgments of scientific reasoning. *Cognition, 107,* 343–352.

McCoy, D. C., Yoshikawa, H., Ziol-Guest, K. M., Duncan, G. J., Schindler, H. S., Magnuson, K., Yang, R., Koepp, A., & Shonkoff, J. P. (2017). Impacts of early childhood education on medium- and long-term educational outcomes. *Educational Researcher, 46,* 474–487.

McLuhan, M (1964). *Understanding media: The extensions of man.* New York: McGraw-Hill.

Meins, E. (2013). Sensitive attunement to infants' internal states: Operationalizing the construct of mind-mindedness. *Attachment & Human Development, 15,* 524–544.

Meltzoff, A. N. (1995). Understanding the intentions of others: Re-enactment of intended acts by 18-month-old children. *Developmental Psychology, 31,* 838–850.

Michael, R. B., Newman, E. J., Vuorre, M., Cumming, G., & Gerry, M. (2013). On the (non)persuasive power of a brain image. *Psychonomic Bulletin & Review, 20,* 720–725.

Miller v. Alabama, 567 U.S. 460 (2012).

Miller, T. L., Volmert, A., Rochman, A., & Aassar, M. (2021). *Talking about poverty: Narratives, counter-narratives, and telling effective stories.* Washington, D.C.: FrameWorks Institute. www.frameworksinstitute.org/publication/talking-about-poverty-narratives-counter-narratives-and-telling-effective-stories/x, retrieved September 27, 2022.

Mills, D. L., Coffey-Corina, S. A., & Neville, H. J. (1993). Language acquisition and cerebral specialization in 20-month-old infants. *Journal of Cognitive Neuroscience, 5*, 317–334.

Mills, K. L., Lalonde, F., Clasen, L. S.,, Giedd, J. N., & Blakemore, S.-J. (2014). Developmental changes in the structure of the social brain in late childhood and adolescence. *Social Cognitive and Affective Neuroscience, 9*, 123–131.

Mitchell, A., Jurkowitz, M., Oliphant, J. B., & Shearer, E. (2020). *Americans who mainly get their news on social media are less engaged, less knowledgeable.* Washington, DC: Pew Research Center. www.pewresearch.org/journalism/2020/07/30/americans-who-mainly-get-their-news-on-social-media-are-less-engaged-less-knowledgeable/, retrieved September 28, 2022.

Moffitt, T. (2006). Life-course persistent versus adolescence-limited antisocial behavior. In D. Cicchetti & D. Cohen (Eds.), *Developmental psychopathology, Vol. 3: Risk, disorder, and adaptation* (2nd ed.) (pp. 570–598). New York: Wiley.

Monk, C., Lugo-Candelas, C., & Trumpff, C. (2019). Prenatal developmental origins of future psychopathology: Mechanisms and pathways. *Annual Review of Clinical Psychology, 15*, 16.1–16.28.

Monterosso, J., Royzman, E. B., & Schwartz, B. (2005). Explaining away responsibility: Effect of scientific explanation on perceived culpability. *Ethics & Behavior, 15*, 139–158.

Monterosso, J., & Schwartz, B. (2012). Did your brain make you do it? *New York Times*, July 29, section SR, p. 12. www.nytimes.com/2012/07/29/opinion/sunday/neuroscience-and-moral-responsibility.html, retrieved September 19, 2012.

Montgomery v. Louisiana, 577 U.S. __ (2016).

Moriguchi, Y. (2014). The early development of executive function and its relation to social interaction: A brief review. *Frontiers in Psychology, 5*, article 388.

Morimoto, K., & Nakajima, K. (2019). Role of the immune system in the development of the central nervous system. *Frontiers in Neuroscience, 13*, article 916.

Moshman, D. (2011). *Adolescent rationality and development* (3rd Ed.). New York: Psychology Press.

Mulders, P., Iera, A., Tendolkar, I., van Eijndhoven, P., & Beckmann, C. (2018). Personality profiles are associated with functional brain networks related to cognition and emotion. *Scientific Reports, 8*, 13874.

Müller, U., & Kerns, K. (2015). The development of executive function. In L. S. Liben & U. Müller (Eds.), *Handbook of child psychology and developmental science, Vol. 2: Cognitive processes* (7th Ed.) (pp. 1–53). New York: Wiley.

Munakata, Y., Snyder, H. R., & Chatham, C. H. (2012). Developing cognitive control: Three key transitions. *Current Directions in Psychological Science, 21*, 71–77.

Nachmias, M., Gunnar, M., Mangelsdorf, S., Parrit, R. H., & Buss, K. (1996). Behavioral inhibition and stress reactivity: The moderating role of attachment security. *Child Development, 67*, 508–522.

Nash, J. M. (1997). Fertile minds. *Time*, February 3, pp. 48–56.

National Academies of Sciences, Engineering, and Medicine, Committee on Building an Agenda to Reduce the Number of Children in Poverty by Half in 10 Years (2019). *A roadmap to reducing child poverty*. Washington, DC: National Academies Press. https://nap.nationalacademies.org/catalog/25246/a-roadmap-to-reducing-child-poverty, retrieved April 27, 2023.

National Commission on Excellence in Education (1983). *A nation at risk: The imperative for educational reform*. Washington, DC: US Government Printing Office. https://files.eric.ed.gov/fulltext/ED226006.pdf, retrieved July 15, 2022.

National Research Council (2012). *From neurons to neighborhoods: An update: Workshop summary*. Washington, DC: National Academies Press.

National Research Council and Institute of Medicine (2000). *From neurons to neighborhoods: The science of early childhood development*. Committee on Integrating the Science of Early Childhood Development. Washington, DC: National Academy Press.

(2015). *Transforming the workforce for children birth through age 8: A unifying foundation*. Committee on the Science of Children Birth to Age 8: Deepening and Broadening the Foundation for Success. Washington, DC: National Academies Press.

National Scientific Council on the Developing Child (2004a). *Young children develop in an environment of relationships*. Working Paper no. 1. https://developingchild.harvard.edu/resources/wp1/, retrieved August 2, 2022.

(2004b). *Children's emotional development is built into the architecture of their brains*. Working Paper no. 2, https://developingchild.harvard.edu/resources/childrens-emotional-development-is-built-into-the-architecture-of-their-brains/, retrieved August 2, 2022.

(2005). *Excessive stress disrupts the architecture of the developing brain*. Working Paper no. 3. https://developingchild.harvard.edu/resources/wp3/, retrieved August 2, 2022.

(2007). *The science of early childhood development: Closing the gap between what we know and what we do*. https://developingchild.harvard.edu/resources/the-science-of-early-childhood-development-closing-the-gap-between-what-we-know-and-what-we-do/, retrieved August 3, 2022.

(2014). *A decade of science informing policy: The story of the National Scientific Council on the Developing Child*. https://developingchild.harvard.edu/science/national-scientific-council-on-the-developing-child/, retrieved August 3, 2022.

Nelson, C. A., de Haan, M., & Thomas, K. M. (2006). *Neuroscience and cognitive development*. New York: Wiley.

Nelson, C. A., & Webb, S. J. (2003). A cognitive neuroscience perspective on early memory development. In M. de Haan & M. H. Johnson (Eds.), *The cognitive neuroscience of development* (pp. 99–126). Hove: Psychology Press.

NICHD Early Child Care Research Network (1997). The effects of infant child care on infant-mother attachment security: Results of the NICHD Study of Early Child Care. *Child Development, 68,* 860–879.

O'Donnell, K. J., Glover, V., Barker, E. D., & O'Connor, T. G. (2014). The persisting effect of maternal mood in pregnancy on child psychopathology. *Development & Psychopathology, 26,* 393–403.

Olds, D. L., Sadler, L., & Kitzman, H. (2007). Programs for parents of infants and toddlers: Recent evidence from randomized trials. *Child Psychology and Psychiatry, 48,* 355–391.

Parker, E., Diffey, L., & Atchison, B. (2018). *How states fund pre-K: A primer for policymakers.* Denver, CO: Education Commission of the States. www.ecs.org/wp-content/uploads/How-States-Fund-Pre-K_A-Primer-for-Policymakers.pdf, retrieved May 10, 2021.

Parker, K. (1997). Babies' brains and government schemes. *Orlando Sentinel,* April 27.

Patoine, B. (2005). Mental retardation: Struggle, stigma, science. *Cerebrum* (publication of the Dana Foundation). https://dana.org/article/mental-retardation-struggle-stigma-science/, retrieved February 16, 2002.

Paul, A. M. (2021). *The extended mind: The power of thinking outside the brain.* New York: Mariner Books.

Phillips, D. A., Lipsey, M. W., Dodge, K. A., Haskins, R., Bassok, D., Burchinal, M. R., Duncan, G. J., Dynarski, M., Magnuson, K. A., & Weiland, C. (2017). *Puzzling it out: The current state of scientific knowledge on pre-kindergarten effects: A consensus statement.* www.brookings.edu/wp-content/uploads/2017/04/consensus-statement_final.pdf, retrieved June 20, 2022.

Pietschnig, J., Voracek, M., & Formann, A. K. (2010). Mozart effect – Schmozart effect: A meta-analysis. *Intelligence, 38,* 314–323.

Poldrack, R. A. (2006). Can cognitive processes be inferred from neuroimaging data? *Trends in Cognitive Sciences, 10,* 59–63.

   (2011). Inferring mental states from neuroimaging data: From reverse inference to large-scale decoding. *Neuron, 72,* 692–697.

Porter, T., Molina, D. C., Cimpian, A., Roberts, S., Fredericks, A., Blackwell, L. S., & Trzesniewski, K. (2022). Growth-mindset intervention delivered by teachers boosts achievement in early adolescence. *Psychological Science, 33,* 1086–1096.

Posner, J., Cha, J., Roy, A. K., Peterson, B. S., Bansal, R., Gustafsson, H. C., Raffanello, E., Gingrich, J., & Monk, C. (2016). Alterations in amygdala-prefrontal circuits in infants exposed to prenatal maternal depression. *Translational Psychiatry, 6,* e395.

Postle, B. R. (2006). Working memory as an emergent property of the mind and brain. *Neuroscience, 139,* 23–38.

Poulin-Dubois, D., Lepage, A., & Ferland, D. (1996). Infants' concept of animacy. *Cognitive Development, 11,* 19–36.

Pyle, A. (1999). Setting the pace for windfall. *Los Angeles Times*, November 25, section A, pp. 46–48.

Qu, Y., Jorgensen, N. A., & Telzer, E. H. (2020). A call for greater attention to culture in the study of brain and development. *Perspectives on Psychological Science, 16*, 275–293.

Qu, Y., Pomerantz, E. M., McCormick, E., & Telzer, E. H. (2018). Youth's conceptions of adolescence predict longitudinal changes in prefrontal cortex activation and risk taking during adolescence. *Child Development, 89*, 773–783.

Qu, Y., Pomerantz, E. M., Wang, Q., & Ng, F.-Y. (2019). Early adolescents' stereotypes about teens in Hong Kong and Chongqing: Reciprocal pathways with problem behavior. *Developmental Psychology, 56*, 1092–1106.

Racine, E., Bar-Ilan, O., & Illes, J. (2005). fMRI in the public eye. *Nature Reviews Neuroscience, 6*, 159–164.

Rea, D., & Burton, T. (2020). New evidence on the Heckman curve. *Journal of Economic Surveys, 43*, 241–262.

Reiner, P. B. (2011). The rise of neuroessentialism. In J. Illes & B. J. Sahakian (Eds.), *The Oxford handbook of neuroethics* (pp. 161–175). Oxford: Oxford University Press.

Repacholi, B. M., & Gopnik, A. (1997). Early reasoning about desires: Evidence from 14- and 18-month-olds. *Developmental Psychology, 33*, 12–21.

Research and Policy Committee, Committee for Economic Development (2002). *Preschool for all: Investing in a productive and just society*. New York: Committee for Economic Development. www.ced.org/pdf/Preschool-for-All.pdf, retrieved July 12, 2022.

Reynolds, A. J., Temple, J. A., White, B. A., Ou, S.-R., & Robertson, D. L. (2011). Age-26 cost-benefit analysis of the Child-Parent Center Early Education Program. *Child Development, 82*, 379–404.

Rhodes, M., & Baron, A. (2019). The development of social categorization. *Annual Review of Developmental Psychology, 1*, 359–386.

Rivera, C. (2002). Veteran educator to head county's preschool effort. *Los Angeles Times*, November 15.

Rivera-Gaxiola, M., Silva-Pereyra, J., & Kuhl, P. K. (2005). Brain potentials to native and non-native speech contrasts in 7- and 11-month-old American infants. *Developmental Science, 8*, 162–172.

Rolnick, A., & Grunewald, R. (2003). *Early childhood development: Economic development with a high public return*. Minneapolis, MN: Federal Reserve Bank of Minneapolis. www.minneapolisfed.org/publications_papers/studies/earlychild/abc-part2.pdf, retrieved July 5, 2022.

Romer, D. (2010). Adolescent risk taking, impulsivity, and brain development: Implications for prevention. *Developmental Psychobiology, 52*, 263–276.

Romer, D., Duckworth, A. L., Sznitman, S., & Park, S. (2010). Can adolescents learn self-control? Delay of gratification in the development of control over risk taking. *Prevention Science, 11*, 319–330.

Romer, D., Reyna, V. F., & Satterthwaite, T. D. (2017). Beyond stereotypes of adolescent risk taking: Placing the adolescent brain in developmental context. *Developmental Cognitive Neuroscience*, *27*, 19–34.

Roper v. Simmons, 543 U.S. 551 (2005).

Rose, H., & Rose, S. (2016). *Can neuroscience change our minds?* Cambridge: Polity Press.

Rousseau, J. J. (1762). *Emile, or Treatise on education (Emile, ou De l'education)*, edited and translated by Alan Bloom. New York: Basic Books, 1979.

Royal Society (2011). *Neuroscience: Implications for education and lifelong learning*. London: Royal Society. https://royalsociety.org/~/media/Royal_Society_Content/policy/publications/2011/4294975733.pdf, retrieved July 6, 2022.

Rymer, R. (1994). *Genie: A scientific tragedy* (2nd Ed.). New York: Harper Perennial.

Saffran, J. R., & Kirkham, N. Z. (2018). Infant statistical learning. *Annual Review of Psychology*, *69*, 181–203.

Santrock, J. W. (2021). *Life-span development* (18th Ed.). New York: McGraw-Hill.

Schachter, D. L., & Addis, D. R. (2007). The optimistic brain. *Nature Neuroscience*, *10*, 1345–1347.

Schäfer, M. S. (2017). How changing media structures are affecting science news coverage. In K. H. Jamieson, D. M. Kahan, & D. A. Scheufele (Eds.), *The Oxford handbook of the science of science communication* (pp. 51–60). New York: Oxford University Press.

Schmidt, S. N. L., Hass, J., Kirsch, P., & Mier, D. (2021). The human mirror neuron system – A common neural basis for social cognition? *Psychophysiology*, *58*, e13781.

Schoenfeld, T., & Gould, E. (2012). Stress, stress hormones, and adult neurogenesis. *Experimental Neurology*, *233*, 12–21.

Schulz, L. C. (2010). The Dutch Hunger Winter and the developmental origins of health and disease. *PNAS*, *107*, 16757–16758.

Schwartz, J. M., & Beyette, B. (1996). *Brain lock*. New York: HarperCollins.

Schweinhart, L. J., Montie, J., Xiang, Z., Barnett, W. S., Belfield, C. R., & Nores, M. (2005). *Lifetime effects: The High/Scope Perry Preschool Study through age 40*. Ypsilanti, MI: High/Scope Press.

Seifer, R., & Parade, S. H. (2020). Teratology. In J. B. Benson & M. M. Haith (Eds.), *Encyclopedia of infant and early childhood development* (2nd Ed.), Vol. 3 (pp. 344–355). New York: Elsevier.

Shen, F. X. (2013). Legislating neuroscience: The case of juvenile justice. *Loyola of Los Angeles Law Review*, *46*, 985–1018.

Shonkoff, J. P. (2022). *Re-envisioning early childhood policy and practice in a world of striking inequality and uncertainty*. Center on the Developing Child, Harvard University. https://developingchild.harvard.edu/re-envisioning-ecd/ retrieved January 8, 2023.

Shonkoff, J. P., & Bales, S. N. (2011). Science does not speak for itself: Translating child development research for the public and its policymakers. *Child Development*, *82*, 17–32.

Shore, R. (1997). *Rethinking the brain: New insights into early development.* New York: Families and Work Institute.

Shulman, E. P., Smith, A. R., Silva, K., Icenogle, G., Duell, N., Chein, J., & Steinberg, L. (2016). The dual systems model: Review, reappraisal, and reaffirmation. *Developmental Cognitive Neuroscience, 17,* 103–117.

Sims, M. (2017). Neoliberalism and early childhood. *Cogent Education, 4,* 1–10.

Sisk, C. L. (2017). Development: Pubertal hormones meet the adolescent brain. *Current Biology, 27,* R706–R709.

Skinner, A. L., Olson, K. R., & Meltzoff, A. N. (2020). Acquiring group bias: Observing other people's nonverbal signals can create social group biases. *Journal of Personality and Social Psychology: Interpersonal Relations and Group Processes, 119,* 824–838.

Skolnick, D. (2005). The sweetest baby milestones. *Parents, 80,* 134–139.

Smith, L. (1998). Directing a crusade. *Los Angeles Times,* February 25, pp. E1–E6. www.latimes.com/archives/la-xpm-1998-feb-25-ls-22611-story.html, retrieved January 14, 2023.

Smith, R., Lane, R. D., Alkozei, A., Bao, J., Smith, C., Sanova, A., Nettles, M., & Killgore, W. D. S. (2018). The role of medial prefrontal cortex in the working memory maintenance of one's own emotional responses. *Scientific Reports, 8,* 3460.

Smuts, A. B. (2006). *Science in the service of children, 1893–1935.* New Haven, CT: Yale University Press.

Spelke, E. S. (1990). Principles of object perception. *Cognitive Science, 14,* 29–56.

Spelke, E. S., & Kinzler, K. D. (2007). Core knowledge. *Developmental Science, 10,* 89–96.

Stahl, A. E., & Feigenson, L. (2015). Observing the unexpected enhances infants' learning and exploration. *Science, 348,* 91–94.

Stanford v. Kentucky, 492 U.S. 361 (1989).

Steinberg, L. (2010). A dual systems model of adolescent risk-taking. *Developmental Psychobiology, 52,* 216–224.

Steinberg, L. (2011). *Should the science of adolescent brain development inform public policy?* Henry and Bryna David Lecture, National Academy of Sciences, Washington, DC.

Steinberg, L. (2020). *Adolescence* (12th Ed.). New York: McGraw-Hill.

Steinberg, L., Albert, D., Cauffman, E., & Banich, M. T. (2008). Age differences in sensation seeking and impulsivity as indexed by behavior and self-report: Evidence for a dual systems model. *Developmental Psychology, 44,* 1764–1778.

Steinberg, L., Cauffman, E., Woolard, J., Graham, S., & Banich, M. (2009). Are adolescents less mature than adults? Minors' access to abortion, the juvenile death penalty, and the alleged APA "flip-flop." *American Psychologist, 64,* 583–594.

Steinberg, L., Icenogle, G., Shulman, E. P., Chein, J., et al. (2018). Around the world, adolescence is a time of heightened sensation seeking and immature self-regulation. *Developmental Science, 21,* e12532.

Steiner, P. (2020). Brain fuel utilization in the developing brain. *Annals of Nutrition and Metabolism, 75*, 8–18.

Sterck, E. (2010). Theory of mind: Specialized capacity or emergent property? *European Journal of Developmental Psychology, 7*, 1–16.

Stevens, K. B., & Weidinger, M. (2021). *Improving early childhood development by allowing advanced child tax credits.* Washington, DC: American Enterprise Institute. www.aei.org/articles/improving-early-childhood-development-by-allowing-advanced-child-tax-credits/, retrieved September 10, 2022.

Stiles, J. (2008). *The fundamentals of brain development.* Cambridge, MA: Harvard University Press.

Stone, L. J., Smith, H. T., & Murphy, L. (1974). *The competent infant: Research and commentary.* New York: Basic.

Suskind, D., & Denworth, L. (2022). U.S. kids are falling behind global competition, but brain science shows how to catch up. *Scientific American, 326*, 48–53. www.scientificamerican.com/article/u-s-kids-are-falling-behind-global-competition-but-brain-science-shows-how-to-catch-up/, retrieved July 6, 2022.

Tabor, M. B. W. (1997). Actor-director focusing on children. *New York Times*, August 6, sec. B, p. 8. www.nytimes.com/1997/08/06/us/actor-director-focusing-on-children.html, retrieved January 14, 2023.

Tavris, C. (1999) The myth of the first three years. *New York Times Book Review*, October 17.

Taylor, M. G., Rhodes, M., & Gelman, S. A. (2009). Boys will be boys; cows will be cows: Children's essentialist reasoning about gender categories and animal species. *Child Development, 80*, 461–481.

Telzer, E. H., Fuligni, A. J., Lieberman, M. D., & Galvan, A. (2013). Meaningful family relationships: Neurocognitive buffers of adolescent risk taking. *Journal of Cognitive Neuroscience, 25*, 374–387.

Temple, E., Deutsch, G. K., Poldrack, R. A., Miller, S. L., Tallal, P., Merzenich, M. M., & Gabrieli, J. D. E. (2003). Neural deficits in children with dyslexia ameliorated by behavioral remediation: Evidence from functional MRI. *PNAS, 100*, 2860–2865.

Thompson, R. A. (1993). Developmental research and legal policy: Toward a two-way street. In D. Cicchetti & S. Toth (Eds.), *Child abuse, child development, and social policy* (pp. 75–115). Norwood, NJ: Ablex.

(1998). Making brain development headline news. *Family Futures, 2*, 32–36.

(2001a). Development in the first years of life. *The Future of Children, 11*, 20–33.

(2001b). Science vs. sound bites: Science and advocacy in public information campaigns for children. *The Children's Beat, 8*, 14–15.

(2012). Bridging developmental neuroscience and the law: Child-caregiver relationships. *Hastings Law Journal, 63*, 1443–1468.

(2014a). Stress and child development. *The Future of Children, 24*, 41–59.

(2014b). Why are relationships important to children's well-being? In A. Ben-Arieh, F. Casas, I. Frones, F. Cases, & J. E. Korbin (Eds.), *Handbook of child well-being: Theories, methods, and policies in global perspective*, Vol. 4 (pp. 1917–1954). Dordrecht: Springer.

Thompson, R. A., & Baumrind, D. (2019). Ethics of parenting. In M. H. Bornstein (Ed.), *Handbook of parenting, Vol. 5: The practice of parenting* (3rd Ed.) (pp. 3–33). New York: Taylor & Francis.

Thompson R. A., & Haskins R. (2014). Early stress gets under the skin: Promising initiatives to help children facing chronic adversity. *The Future of Children Policy Brief*, Spring, 1–7.

Thompson, R. A., & Nelson, C. A. (2001). Developmental science and the media: Early brain development. *American Psychologist*, *56*, 5–15.

Tomasello, M. (2016). Cultural learning redux. *Child Development*, *87*, 643–653.

Troller-Renfree, S. V., Costanzo, M. A., Duncan, G. J., Magnuson, K., Gennetian, L. A., Yoshikawa, H., Halpern-Meekin, S., Fox, N. A., & Noble, K. G. (2022). The impact of a poverty reduction intervention on infant brain activity. *PNAS*, *119*, e2115649119.

Tronick, E. Z., & Gianino, A. (1986). Interactive mismatch and repair: Challenges to the coping infant. *Zero to Three Journal*, 6, 1–6.

United States Census (2022). *CPS historical time series on school enrollment*. Washington, DC: US Census Bureau. www.census.gov/data/tables/time-series/demo/school-enrollment/cps-historical-time-series.html, retrieved January 14, 2023.

Urahn, S. K., & Watson, S. (2007). The Pew Charitable Trusts: Advancing quality Pre-K for all; Five years later. www.pewtrusts.org/~/media/legacy/uploadedfiles/wwwpewtrustsorg/reports/pre-k_education/prekarticle0207pdf.pdf, retrieved July 10, 2022.

Vijayakumar, N., Op de Macks, Z., Shirtcliff, E. A., & Pfeider, J. H. (2018). Puberty and the human brain: Insights into adolescent development. *Neuroscience and Biobehavioral Reviews*, *92*, 417–436.

Wagmiller, R. L., & Adelman, R. M. (2009). *Childhood and intergenerational poverty: The long-term consequences of growing up poor*. New York: National Center for Children in Poverty. www.nccp.org/wp-content/uploads/2020/05/text_909.pdf, retrieved April 7, 2021.

Wang, S., Harvey, L., Martin, R., van der Beek, E. M., Knol, J., Cryan, J. F., & Renes, I. B. (2018). Targeting the gut microbiota to influence brain development and function in early life. *Neuroscience and Biobehavioral Reviews*, *95*, 191–201.

Wang, Z., Williamson, R. A., & Meltzoff, A. N. (2015). Imitation as a mechanism in cognitive development: A cross-cultural investigation of 4-year-old children's rule learning. *Frontiers in Psychology*, 6, article 562.

Watson, J. B. (1928a). *Psychological care of infant and child*. New York: W. W. Norton.

(1928b). *The ways of behaviorism*. New York: Harper & Brothers.

Watson, S. D. (2011). The right policy at the right time: The Pew Prekindergarten Campaign. In E. Zigler, W. S. Gilliam, & W. S. Barnett (Eds.), *The Pre-K debates: Current controversies and issues* (pp. 9–20). Baltimore, MD: Paul H. Brookes.

Weingart, P. (2012). The lure of the mass media and its repercussions on science. In S. Rödder, M. Franzen, & P. Weingart (Eds.), *The sciences' media* connection: *Public communication and its repercussions* (pp. 17–31). Dordrecht: Springer.

Weisberg, D. S., Keil, F. C., Goodstein, J., Rawson, E., & Gray, J. R. (2008). The seductive allure of neuroscience explanations. *Journal of Cognitive Neuroscience, 20,* 470–477.

Weiss, C. H. (1978). Improving the linkage between social research and public policy. In L. E. Lynn (Ed.), *Knowledge and policy: The uncertain connection* (pp. 23–81). Washington, DC: National Academies Press.

   (1980). Knowledge creep and decision accretion. *Knowledge: Creation, Diffusion, Utilization, 1,* 381–404.

   (1987). The diffusion of social science research to policymakers: An overview. In G. B. Melton (Ed.), *Reforming the law: Impact of child development research* (pp. 63–85). New York: Guilford.

Weiss, C. H., & Singer, E. (1988). *Reporting of social science in the national media.* New York: Russell Sage Foundation.

Wellman, H. M. (2015). *Making minds: How theory of mind develops.* New York: Oxford University Press.

Wellman, H. M., & Gelman, S. A. (1992). Cognitive development: Foundational theories of core domains. *Annual Review of Psychology, 43,* 337–375.

Werker, J. F., & Polka, L. (1993). Developmental changes in speech perception: New challenges and new directions. *Journal of Phonetics, 21,* 83–101.

Werner, H. (1940). *Comparative psychology of mental development.* New York: International Universities Press.

Wolfe, D. A., & Mash, E. J. (Eds.) (2006). *Behavioral and emotional disorders in adolescents: Nature, assessment, and treatment.* New York: Guilford.

Wood, J. N., & Spelke, E. S. (2005). Chronometric studies of numerical cognition in five-month-old infants. *Cognition, 97,* 23–39.

Wynn, K. (1992). Addition and subtraction by human infants. *Nature, 358,* 749–750.

Xu, F., & Garcia, V. (2008). Intuitive statistics by 8-month-old infants. *PNAS, 105,* 5012–5015.

Yan, W. (2020). Coronavirus tests science's need for speed limits. *New York Times,* April 21, section D, p. 7. www.nytimes.com/2020/04/14/science/coronavirus-disinformation.html, retrieved October 16, 2020.

Yeo, S. K., & Brossard, D. (2017). The (changing) nature of scientist-media interactions: A cross-national analysis. In K. H. Jamieson, D. M. Kahan, & D. A. Scheufele (Eds.), *The Oxford handbook of the science of science communication* (pp. 261–272). New York: Oxford University Press.

Zeballos-Roig, J. (2022). Signs of a midterm backlash are mounting for the GOP after Roe was overturned. Here are 3 proposals put forward by Republicans to support families. *Business Insider.* www.businessinsider.com/gop-family-proposals-child-benefits-midterm-backlash-roe-overturned-2022-9, retrieved September 7, 2022.

Zero to Three (1997). *Key findings from a nationwide survey among parents of zero-to-three-year-olds.* Washington, DC: Zero to Three. www.upi.com/

Archives/1997/04/17/Parents-unsure-on-emotional-upbringing/
2037861249600/, retrieved April 29, 2022.
Public perceptions of baby brain development: A national survey of voters. Zero to
Three.   www.zerotothree.org/resources/2124-public-perceptions-of-baby-
brain-development-a-national-survey-of-voters, retrieved March 1, 2022.
Zigler, E. (2011). A warning against exaggerating the benefits of preschool
education programs. In E. Zigler, W. S. Gilliam, & W. S. Barnett (Eds.),
The pre-K debates: Current controversies and issues (pp. 197–200). Baltimore,
MD: Paul H. Brookes.

Index

About the Author

Ross A. Thompson is Distinguished Professor of Psychology at the University of California, Davis, where he directs the Social and Emotional Development Lab. Thompson studies the psychological development of young children, parent-child relationships, and the applications of developmental science to public policy problems such as early childhood mental health, child poverty, maltreatment prevention, and early education. His work integrates understanding of the developing brain with early experiences in both typical and at-risk children, and he consults extensively with legislative committees, public agencies, and private foundations.

Thompson was president of the Board of Directors of Zero to Three, a national nonprofit devoted to the healthy development of young children and their families, in 2015–2018. He currently serves on the boards of the Buffett Early Childhood Institute and the Stein Early Childhood Development Fund. He has served three terms as associate editor of *Child Development*, the flagship journal of the Society for Research in Child Development.

Thompson received the Urie Bronfenbrenner Award for Lifetime Contribution to Developmental Psychology in the Service of Science and Society from the American Psychological Association in 2018. He has also received the Ann L. Brown Award for Excellence in Developmental Research in 2007, the University of California, Davis, Distinguished Scholarly Public Service Award in 2011, and the Distinguished Undergraduate Teaching Award in 2019. He also received the Outstanding Research and Creative Activity Award from the University of Nebraska in 2000, where he was a lifetime member of the Academy of Distinguished Teachers.

Thompson has published six books, several best-selling textbooks, and over 300 papers related to his work. His most recent book is *Attachment: The Fundamental Questions* (Guilford, 2021). He has also written or coauthored *Toward a Child-Centered, Neighborhood-Based Child*

Protection System (Praeger, 2002); *The Postdivorce Family: Children, Families, and Society* (Sage, 1999); *Preventing Child Maltreatment through Social Support: A Critical Analysis* (Sage, 1995); *Socioemotional Development* (University of Nebraska Press, 1990); and *Infant-Mother Attachment* (Erlbaum, 1985).

Milton Keynes UK
Ingram Content Group UK Ltd.
UKHW 1536270923
420088UK00021B/137